Rethinking the World

Rethinking the World

Peter Pogany

Shenandoah Valley Research Press

iUniverse, Inc.
New York Lincoln Shanghai

Rethinking the World

iUniverse books may be ordered through booksellers or by contacting:

iUniverse
2021 Pine Lake Road, Suite 100
Lincoln, NE 68512
www.iuniverse.com
1-800-Authors (1-800-288-4677)

With gratitude to Blue Ridge Academic Life for its generous support and encouragement. The views expressed in this publication are exclusively those of the author.

ISBN-13: 978-0-595-41079-8 (pbk)
ISBN-13: 978-0-595-67868-6 (cloth)
ISBN-13: 978-0-595-85438-7 (ebk)
ISBN-10: 0-595-41079-0 (pbk)
ISBN-10: 0-595-67868-8 (cloth)
ISBN-10: 0-595-85438-9 (ebk)

Printed in the United States of America

This book is dedicated to those who valiantly struggle to save the planet from a global society that treats its economy as if it were a race car to be driven at maximum speed. They cannot succeed now because change in the typical mind set does not occur without a period of rupture during which mankind has no choice but to use itself as a guinea pig. They are still immensely valuable. Our admiration for the "idealism" they demonstrate in the streets and at a thousand symposia raises the hope that the genes needed for a more intelligent and noble future are in all of us.

Contents

Prologue

◆

The death of Schopenhauer...not what it seemed

When the great German philosopher, Arthur Schopenhauer, died in 1860, his young disciples kept a quiet vigil in his honor. Stunned by the smile that death had not erased from their idol's face, they were even more surprised when an eerie crackle broke the mournful silence in the dead of night. What was going on? Cadavers don't smile or make noises. Did the professor want to communicate from the Cimmerian empire of sunless shadows? After all, didn't he teach us that the end of life is not the end of existence; that life is a dream and death is an awakening? Did he find a way, even from beyond the bourne of the undiscovered country, to reassure us that man's fear of dissolution is a wrong-headed absurdity? He was a demiurge, after all! Others entered the room, which was soon completely illuminated. There on the floor were Schopenhauer's dentures, a mid-19th century wooden masterpiece that *rigor mortis* had jettisoned from the legendary thinker's mouth. More light had dispersed the supernatural and the mystical. The dead no longer smiled. What remained was empirically revealed secularized objectivity, the only orientation capable of stopping the noisy engine room of churning phantasmagoria.

But doesn't the world seem sadly bleak if we preclude metaphysical speculations and curb the audacities of the intellect? Besides, brutal "show me" materialism moves either toward incoherence or sterile rationalism. Seeing only with the mind, stretching its ability to balance ambiguities, and shutting out the "in-your-face" concrete, turns out to be just as significant in searching for the coveted certainty (the order behind the disorder) as is enlightenment through sensory experiences. We know by now that the fence once believed to have guarded the enclave of "positive knowledge" exists only part time. It is there and it is not. The human sense of divine pedigree, allied with the mind's irrepressible drive to apprehend the infinite and authenticate the capture, blurs demarcations between the non-mysterious and the mysterious on the frontiers of knowledge. To the mind's credit, the overreach has not escaped its critical faculty. It keeps exposing its connate incapacity to recognize such dividing lines and manages even to give implicit advice on how far the wise owl of fancy can fly forward in the lightless maze without losing our pragmatic selves.

A new mentality has emerged—one that finds it possible to live with the premise that all mental functions have physico-chemical groundings and with the conviction that the obscure voice whispering into our innermost hearts "there is something, there must be something" is not a mere hallucination. A polyphony to be cherished and cultivated.

Introduction

The engineer showing off a completely automatic assembly line turns off the lights. Taken aback, the visitors hear the clashing and groaning of electro-mechanical devices in the pitch dark. Spooky! The machines cease to have form and function yet they "know" precisely how to go on fitting, cutting, and uniting without "seeing." A single entity of organized matter is driven by some common will.

We can make a similar shift of perspective in analyzing human affairs. Let us turn off the bright lights that flood the stages on which the "histories, comedies and tragedies" of the world shape individual lives and the destinies of nations and consider cultural evolution nothing more or less than organized matter on the move. This approach frees us from doctrines that exhort, threaten, and reprimand in their quest to survive and garner support. It allows us to transcend canned academic authority and the political heat of the moment.

The "old" (Marxist) historical materialism cannot fill the need, not only because it flunked history (and economics and psychology), but also because its "materialism" became superannuated. Its "matter" vanished into warps of space-time; gutless assemblages of shuffling, trembling particles that behave like waves if they so please; probability clouds caught up in a cosmic sequel to the Big Bang. Nineteenth century science believed that matter was knowable through the accumulation of experimental knowledge. There was Darwin, organic chemistry, the never ceasing succession of miracles produced by the emerging technical civilization. "Poor Aristotle," the scientists of the era thought, with his intertwined form and substance; earth, air, water, and fire. (Excuse me?) And now there is "poor Marx" with his querulous and, in retrospect, pathetic berating of Hegel, who dared to consider "the life processes of the human brain, i.e., the process of thinking" the central issue of historical evolution, when it should have been clear to anyone with an iota of modern analytical common sense that thoughts were external to the objective reality of matter. Contemporary "brain science" could not disagree more. Thoughts and emotions, and hence, convictions, have become perceivable in terms of biology, chemistry, and physics.

Science also re-mystified matter and became more explicit about the human limitations involved in finding ultimate explanations. Lightness and darkness, silence and sound are meaningless outside the realm of sensory perception; space, time, and causality are part of an evolutionary heritage. The "real" world remains terminally occluded. The mind perceives it in a way that allows it to be alive. We are bound inseparably with what we observe in a medium of constantly transforming matter that escapes full comprehension. Accumulated knowledge suggests that humans are billions of highly evolved, overgrown super-molecules (or "intensely conscious mice"?) that swarm in ever larger numbers on a piece of rock that wobbles, spins, revolves, and soars into nothingness at break-neck speed with an agitated, burning furnace in its interior.

Counterpoised to its total irrelevance in nature's broader context, *homo sapiens* is infinitely relevant by its own valuation. A physical view of cultural evolution and history is scooping whatever can be scooped from the infinitely insignificant vantage point to examine it from the infinitely significant one.

What appears as history—the clash of nations, social conflicts, leading personages moving on the center stage of world events—is a material process. It is the complexifying self-organization of interconnected, brain-anchored codes on a global scale. The motions of this cerebral web provide a fitting interpretation ("hermeneutic") of the flow of recorded events during the past two centuries, marking the age of *global systems*. Mankind is part of an irreversible, "one-way" transformation. This basic physical unfolding is manifest in individual and group imperatives that mesh and compete and create *relative global steady states* separated by *chaotic transitions*.

By identifying the development of civilization as the observed phenomenon of an underlying thermodynamic process, the modern era becomes the tip of near eternities of a cave-dwelling prehistory that molded humans into what they are, with all their yet to be discovered, finality-rejecting potential. But because thermodynamic evolution is more general than biological evolution, we must see through the organism to analyze history as a material process. Therefore, we are not studying the evolved biological bases of behavior and psychology. This subject belongs to the domain of specialists in Darwinian anthropology. Rather, we are going to show what happened to biologically evolved behavior during the past two hundred years, what phases it had to traverse and why; remembering, of course, that human ingenuity and culture can never undo or put on hold the forces of biological evolution.

We shall demonstrate that the emerging conflict between the expanding human empire—a hyper-cyborg Leviathan—and the Earth's material limitations may yet lead to a new beginning on a higher plateau. The socioeconomic evolution of the past two centuries revealed steady direction and the ability to reorganize on the global-scale. The genes, the physical carriers of biological heredity, evidently have emergent properties. They have proven to be capable of going through stages of supra-individual, planet-wide arrangements, while preserving the germ of the next, more complex one. If the species' self-organization succeeds in renewing itself in a superior edition, the generations living in those times might look back at the currently expiring age of petroleum and self-hypnosis about the possibility of infinite growth in a closed space with dismayed comprehension.

The historical materialism of the present will also be outdated. By looking at past ways of understanding matter and history one can easily recognize that the materialist explanation of history itself is subject to evolution. Unlike the "new" in New (or "supply side") Economics–a product of the 1980s–which implied a definitive reform in economic thinking, our "new" is explicitly labeled "nonfinal." In *new historical materialism*, a theory that we shall introduce in the ensuing pages, only the *new* remains unchanged. Rethinking the world and its future is a recurring necessity, fraught as it may be with inadvertent subjectivity or manipulative bias.

Humanity's impending violent argument with itself is of momentous concern. If the race has further significant evolutionary potential, it will have to equip itself with a shared megaperspective on its past and future that is physically relevant and has a high moral content. For that, the global society will have to absorb the postmodern era's lessons on pluralism and equality, but will also have to abandon its epistemic defeatism and its craving for the acid bath of nihilistic disunity.

Admittedly, not even the contemplation of the world as a mere flux of substance can claim total objectivity. It is pointless to tell a piece of rock that "abstracting away from time, you are dust." But telling people that they are caught up in an inexorable physical process that will carry them through turmoil and grief in order to arrive at a better global organization cannot be done without some implicit expectation. Could the mind's keen awareness and huge information-processing capability–the individual's virtually unlimited reservoir of behavioral alternatives–make a difference? Could it reduce the extent and duration of the suffering? There is no clear answer. The observer is entangled with the observed, putting a limit on the externality and independence of the observation. This means some rancor or enthusiasm here and there, according to the context. Our solace for this unavoidable shortcoming is that these biases are neurophysiological entities. They are alive in many with the potential to survive and evolve into pro-active convictions.

1

Lessons from Studying the Past

[Studying history to identify fundamental patterns that may help foretell the future has not met with success. However, the passage of time sharpens perspectives and tells successive generations what analysis can and cannot do. Linking the advantage of a long perspective on modernity with advances in natural sciences, we discover that world history is the costume drama version of a material transformation in the *terrestrial sphere*. This view takes into account the physical constraints of human expansion and protects against ideologically motivated answers concerning the directionality of universal history.]

Communism and fascism both staked their legitimacy on interpretations of the past projected into the future. These two world history-shaping political movements ultimately failed, dragging down with their propaganda, flags, and stirring marches the credibility of discovering the direction of universal history. Can such a discovery be made at all? A glance at the charts that illustrate the ride of humanity through the ages as seen by 20 distinguished philosophers of history, including Adam Smith, Hegel, Marx, Spencer, Spengler, Toynbee, and Teilhard, would discourage all hope.[1] It might even cast some doubt on the sanity of the whole undertaking. There are straight lines, waves, loops, spirals, and terraced plateaus.[2] Individually, each classic of macrohistorical analysis looks brilliant, coherent, and even prophetic; however, taken together they could not be used as a proof that mankind understands its progression. The philosophy of history appears to be like a confused skein of threads. A casual indictment might sound like this: "One great thinker proves that things have never changed and never will; the other that they always did and always will. One recommends that you seek personal aggrandizement to improve the lot of the world; another that you start a revolution, and yet another that you pray."

---

1. See *Galtung and Inayatullah, 1997*.
2. Op. cit., Appendix B.

This is, of course, a false perception. Comprehension of the past increases as data, experience, and knowledge accumulate with time. Just like the ancestry of a family, the antecedents of the "current state of the world" never cease to grow. Contemporaries see things that people who lived even two decades ago could not because they lacked the necessary information to do so. Since history is a cumulative process of knowledge acquisition—movement along a "learning curve"—the work of every major macrohistorian is crucial in feeding analysis. They are all needed to turn history into a single, intelligible source of edification for those who ask "What have we learned?" and "Why is today's look at the past different from yesterday's?"

WHAT WE HAVE LEARNED

Beliefs come and go; "periodization" remains suspect; "historical necessity" is Janus-faced

The *philosophes* of mid-18th century *Enlightenment* were convinced that mankind could perfect itself and its institutions.[3] The scientific picture of the world centered on the discoveries of Isaac Newton (1642-1727) while retaining in the background the belief of Aristotle (cc. 384-322 BCE) that nothing in the universe can exist without a purpose, a specific end, a *telos*. The combination of rigid mechanical motions on the celestial highways and the universality of purpose implied harmonious *determinism* throughout nature, including society. The ideal

---

3.   The Age of Enlightenment (*Enlightenment*) began during the 1720s and ended with the outbreak of the French Revolution in 1789. Many authors consider it the last phase of the *Age of Reason*, a period that began in the 17th century as the newly embraced empiricism and rationalism turned with full force against the medieval world view.

The expression *philosophes* covered a broad category of professional interests, from philosophy proper to natural sciences, economics, medicine, and interdisciplinary, "polymath" pursuits. The following personalities are usually mentioned among the French luminaries who left behind evidence of enduringly valid observations about social and economic evolution: Charles-Louis de Secondat Montesquieu (1689-1755), François-Marie Arouet Voltaire (1694-1778), George-Louis Leclerc de Buffon (1707-1788), Julien Offray de LaMettrie (1709-1751), Jean-Jacques Rousseau (1712-1778), Denis Diderot (1713-1784), Claude-Adrien Helvétius (1715-1771), Jean Le Rond d'Alembert (1717-1783), Anne-Robert-Jacques Turgot (1727-1781), and Antoine Caritat de Condorcet (1743-1794).

final state may have seemed far away, but the direction was clear. *Reason*, manifest in the nascent industrial applications of science and a growing *harmony*, recognized in the spread of wealth and influence beyond the exclusive group of landed aristocracy, promised *progress*. The *Enlightenment* gave a sense of direction. The rights to life, liberty, and property ("the natural rights of man") will be embraced since they are "natural;" and from this embracement, social, economic, and political institutions announcing the dawn of a "New Jerusalem" here on Earth will be born. In the liberal traditions they helped create, the *philosophes* were strongly hopeful, but not fanatical or dogmatic, concerning the fulfillment of their credo.

Immanuel Kant (1724-1804) saw the world very much in the spirit of the *Enlightenment*. Although the "Sage of Königsberg" was drawn toward the profundities of natural sciences, metaphysics, and moral philosophy, thus remaining at arm's length from politics, he made some vital and abiding observations about society and history. He was, in his own way, a champion of individual freedom and corruption-free public life, and he strongly believed that mankind was moving on a path of accelerated progress toward general prosperity and "eternal peace." The tracts he left behind on universal history and international relations contained valuable pragmatic insights for later generations. They inspired Woodrow Wilson and provided specific advice that led to the establishment of the League of Nations, the predecessor of the United Nations.

The extent to which the intellectually well-founded hopefulness for mankind's future was comprehended and believed to be history's direction outside the salons of Paris, the coffee houses of London, some German universities, and Masonic lodges across the world, is buried in the past. Labeling the *Enlightenment* as the *Zeitgeist* of mid-18th century sounds correct, but it may be useful to reflect upon why. When translated into observable phenomena, the "spirit of the times" means the worldwide similarity of public opinion on certain crucial issues. But there was no "world public opinion" in the 18th century in the way we interpret the expression. Most of the human population was still in the yoke of uncontested feudal and colonial oppression. The 18th century's deficiency in mass alphabetization and the absence of idea diffusing media make it impossible two-and-a-half centuries later to state with absolute assurance that the *Enlightenment* dominated minds, even in Western Europe, where it first saw daylight and edged its way into social and political agendas.

Nevertheless, in retrospect, the *Enlightenment* appears as a historical necessity. It paved the way for the bourgeoisie to expand its ranks and influence, thereby facilitating the development of commerce and industry. In areas where industrial and commercial capital accumulated, the ideals of the *Enlightenment* had to become the beliefs of progressive elements and had to be embraced eagerly by those segments of society that directly benefited from their advancement. This was the case in Britain (including the rebellious American colonies), France, Germany, the Netherlands, and Northern Italy, where the energies for rapid industrialization were building up.

In the end, Western Europe's urban intellectuals and its growing middle class—limited segments of society in a relatively small portion of the planet—came to represent world public opinion by default. The secular, materialistically oriented ideals of the *Enlightenment* had no competition on the global cultural scene and they offered something for almost everyone. They could count on a "universal appeal" because they sent the message of "freedom" to those in poverty, ignorance, and isolation, even if the message did not get through; and by not threatening those who, because of their privileged social position or dogmatic persuasion, were hostile or remained in opposition, they could symbolize an open door and an extended hand.

With these qualifications, the *Enlightenment* may be considered the *Zeitgeist* of mid-18th century. *Ex post*, it was an inescapable stage of global development, not a whim or a *random* choice. Although it became the mindset of only a minority of the people living at the time, it was alone in representing the only direction in which the world could possibly move by a hypothetical consensus.

Not until after the Cold War did such an optimistic, world-federating belief with rational and moral appeal, hopeful about a peaceful attainment of general welfare, reappear. For a brief period in the 1990s, it seemed that the summit had been reached; that despite the many isolated armed conflicts around the world, history as a sequence of bloody confrontations among nations, social classes, and ideologies, with epoch-marking personalities leading the charge, was coming to an end. Finally, the world discovered itself as a community and was headed toward the prevalence of democratic political and market economic institutions. The future began to look like a linear evolutionary trajectory, a straight road to ever improving living standards. Finding civil and equitable solutions to the outstanding problems of underdevelopment, poverty, and pollution—leaning on market mechanisms to the extent possible—appeared more than just an option; it became the only rational way to march forward.

Throughout the period between the French Revolution and the 1990s, no secular ideology offered a vision of the future that (A) came complete with rationally provable, commonly graspable reasons for its inevitability; (B) had a global scope; (C) could count on approval across national borders and social classes; (D) was optimistic about mankind's end state, and (E) could conceivably be implemented through universal consent, i.e., without violence. The lack of these attributes appeared in different forms and combinations during the 19th century, at the turn of the century, during the turbulent period that stretched from 1914 to 1945, and during the Cold War.

The scientific view of a calculable and predictable, mechanically designed universe with a built-in purpose and final state continued to dominate 19th century thinking about society and history.[4] Preoccupation with history's directionality survived, but that was about all that remained common among the fragmented perceptions. Although it assured the world of a shiny future, the philosophy of Georg Wilhelm Friedrich Hegel (1770-1831) was too obscure and too removed from the natural sciences to be widely comprehended on rational grounds. It also considered tumultuous struggles and bedlam the only means by which the world could reach its promising terminal state. Thus, the Hegelian perception of history's unfolding showed only criteria (B) and (D). Although it never ceased to exert a considerable appeal, it had to share the stage with other convictions, even during its author's lifetime.

Political economy was much closer to empirical sciences than Hegel's dazzling symphony of "absolute knowledge" (*das absolute Wissen*). But it did not play a cheerful tune. Its canonical sound, strongly influenced by Thomas Robert Malthus (1766-1834) and David Ricardo (1772-1823), evoked a rather unappetizing final equilibrium. Returns on economic resources (e.g., land, labor, and capital) tend to decline over the long run. This would lead the world to an impoverished, overcrowded, dismal state. Orthodox political economy feared negative developments without offering a program to avoid them. Thus, it conformed only to criteria (A) and (B).

If the early socialist critics of *laissez faire*, e.g., Charles Fourier (1772-1837), Robert Owen (1771-1858), and Claude-Henri Saint-Simon (1760-1825), had doubts about this pessimistic view, revolutionary socialists, who based their convictions primarily on the publications of Karl Marx (1818-1883) and Friedrich Engels (1820-1895), rejected it with scathing hostility and painted a rosy future for humankind. The philosophers of socialism carried on Hegel's optimism of a coming ideal world. "Scientific socialism" could be turned into commonly understood, rational explanations for the masses (the task of "agitation and propa-

---

4.   Pierre-Simon Laplace (1749-1827), who further elaborated on Newtonian astronomy and is considered one of the classics of probability theory, propounded the exact predictability of the future based on accumulated information about the past. His name is tied to Newton's in references to classical *determinism* in physics and, more generally, in natural science-oriented philosophy.

ganda" or "agitprop" as it later came to be called in the communist movement).
Marxism carried attributes (A), (B), and (D), but it could not deliver on (C) and
(E). "Communism" never had a wide appeal, and the attainment of material
riches "for everybody according to his needs" required armed confrontations with
the protectors of the bourgeois system and whoever else stood in the way. If one
accepts a program that is theoretically inevitable, but meets resistance, then the
force involved in its realization must be large enough to make good on its inevitability. This formula ratchets up modest philosophical theorizing to fanatical
beliefs in historical necessity. The 20th century witnessed the horrors of its practical implementation.

Charles Darwin (1809-1882) finally uprooted the Aristotelian credo, according to which human existence has a direction in the same way a pile of building
materials is determined to become a house, while a blueprint is guiding the
expense of required energy. Then, at the turn of the century, belief in the
mechanical nature of the world along with common sense objectivity of scientific
explanations suffered a major blow. Relativity and quantum theory made it abundantly clear that human comprehension of nature (whether one moved toward
the infinitely large or the infinitely small) had not even scratched the surface. By
revealing the power of an uncontrolled subconscious mind and irrational drives,
the Viennese psychoanalyst Sigmund Freud (1856-1939) destroyed trust in the
easy understandability of personal motives and conduct.[5] Man was plucked from
the fairy-tale world of illusions about order outside and inside of himself. The
ratio of what was considered known to the unknown took a sudden turn downward and the secretive natural world no longer seemed all that easy to colonize.
As a result, science did not contribute a feeling of trust in convictions that human
society, as part of nature, was also moving on unchangeable tracks toward a specific future.

From the closing decades of the 19th century until the outbreak of World
War I in 1914, living standards increased significantly in Europe and America.
Global economic growth outpaced population growth, particularly in the developed world, which, by that time, included Japan. The swelling sinews of geographic interconnectedness, faster and longer railroads, ever bigger steamships
transporting increasing numbers of people and volumes of merchandise across
national frontiers; wire communications, photography and cinematography
spreading information and images across the planet, awakened the idea of "one

---

5.   Although Freud published some of his key works around the turn of the 20th century,
      his teaching penetrated popular thinking only after the Great War.

world." Despite its periodic crises and gross uncertainties, the prevailing global order (based on *laissez faire* economic principles and "metal money," i.e., gold and silver) began to look like the final destination of humanity's social and economic (socioeconomic) development. History's direction has been found. Concern about the subject declined.

Economists, mainly university professors, turned from disequilibrium analysis of the extreme long run to the equilibrium of the present; to the study of the market system's robust self-sustenance, holding out the prospect of indefinite balanced growth. Practitioners of the new profession began to rely on mathematics and statistical data. They proclaimed their wish to be useful for business in its day-to-day operations and offered public policy advice and social commentary. The calculus of decentralized decision-making (the Marginal School) and the analysis of *general equilibrium* appeared. Among the lasting achievements of many great talents of the epoch, the life works of Leon Walras (1834-1910) and Alfred Marshall (1842-1924) attest to the transformation of political economy into economics practiced by university trained professionals.

It might seem that during the pre-World War I decades, the attributes of the *Enlightenment* regarding the future almost came together. Economics took care of (A), the extant *global system*, *laissez faire/metal money* accounted for (B); the direction pointed toward an optimistic end state of general prosperity (D) that was achievable peacefully by everybody going about their daily business (E). However, universal appeal (C) was missing. Radical ideas to transform societies through revolution and the stiffening convictions in support of aggressive nationalism spread in the wake of the *global system*'s growing inability to accommodate the world's demographic and economic expansion.

Once Newtonian physics-inspired classical *determinism* abandoned historical directionality on the street corner, collective morality, with its many possible perspectives, was added to the molten experience of the lived moment. Rational, commonly understood arguments for mobilizing massive commitments to implement social agendas and political programs began to rely on pure persuasion, on the competitive *entrainment* of minds. With a world population of between one and two billion, and with the relentless growth in productivity, the activism to force world history on a man-made orbit could harness gargantuan doses of individual will and industrial prowess.

If the Marxist-Leninist direction of history did not conform to *Enlightenment* criteria, 20th century ideologies behind national efforts to radiate power beyond the frontiers and soak up economic resources made a mockery of them. Their inward-looking, chauvinistic credos drew from ethnic myths and fanatic tales of courage and boldness. "Blood and soil!" *Vita Periculosa*! They complied with criteria (A) and (B), but in brutally conflicting ways. One nation's belief that history's direction was favoring its expansion went straight against another nation's belief, "over my dead body." Obviously, no doctrine in support of imperialism could garner universal acclaim; (C) was out of the question. Each imperialist power monopolized the optimistic end state for itself, (D) also fell to the wayside. Since military conquest was its avowed mode of self-expression, aggressive nationalism naturally rejected (E). Fascism, which took control of millions of minds during the 1930s, degenerated the farthest from *Enlightenment* criteria in viewing the ages to come.

The period of 1914-1945, which, for reasons introduced later, will be labeled a *chaotic transition*, saw the clash of nations and aggressive political movements with invincible trust in the realization of their respective programs. It witnessed the first tentative steps of a new ideology in support of reformed capitalism. Visions of the future blurred into disorder. From the vantage point of the average individual, preoccupation with the constantly changing face of threat and impermanence gave way to uncertainty and withheld judgment about the world's destiny. The *Enlightenment* seemed like a distant period of cultural history. The very concept of "history's direction," whether attached to nationalistic programs of conquest or to the liberation of mankind through the dictatorship of the proletariat, became more a menace than a promise.

During the Cold War, both "capitalism" and "socialism" claimed global scope (B) and expressed, although in a split vision, optimism about the world's future (D). However, the rest of the criteria were missing. While communist propaganda could keep the worldwide jury out on the economic performance of a secretive and interminably orchestrating Soviet Union, it succeeded in preventing the non-communist world from proving that its own *mixed economy* cum liberal democratic political model was mankind's final institutional equilibrium: absence of (A). Although communism did not have "universal appeal," Soviet propaganda (most successful outside communist controlled areas) disallowed the appeal of the Western socioeconomic model from becoming universal: absence of (C). Finally, neither system could spread without a global cataclysm of unimaginable proportions: absence of (E).

The 1990s finally reunited (A), (B), (C), (D), and (E). (A) reappeared with its *Enlightenment* strength, based on mathematical economics and the rational expectation that the optimal choice would not be rejected. The *multilateral*, neoliberal approach to domestic and international economic organization had a global scope (B). Despite being subjected to severe intellectual and political criticism, it was the only coherent program that could count on "universal appeal," satisfying (C), because it foreshadowed progressive improvement for most. It envisaged an optimistic final equilibrium for the planet—presence of (D)—which, because of its liberal, relaxed, non-dogmatic disposition, was ostensibly reachable without war, revolution, or terror—conformity with (E). Communist states continued to exist in the post-Cold War era, but their obvious inability to fulfill the promise of material well-being and individual freedom (based on the original, Marxist-Leninist doctrine) made it clear to nearly everyone in the world: Communism is the temporary control of an area by a communist party. To the part of the global population that lived through the aftermath of the collapse of the East European Soviet Empire, the idea of communism did not simply disappear. It became totally unmasked, revealing its ridiculously vulgar core. Once conditions forced a communist party in the former Eastern Bloc to relinquish the society under its control, its members became the backbone of the new propertied class through the position of strategic superiority they occupied in the denationalization or privatization process. Once they had the chance to own capital, the enthusiastic enforcers of collective control over "the means of production" turned out to be latent lovers of capitalism.

When horse-drawn omnibuses appeared in the towns of the Hapsburg Empire in the late 1800s, ringing in the era of urban mass transportation, a dumfounded and distressed Austrian countess, perhaps nervously fanning herself, was heard to remark, "My God! What else can happen in this world?" Indeed. Since the dawn of modernity, mankind went through incredible episodes of self-deception, strife, and sacrifice, particularly during the first half of the 20th century, until the prospect of a general good, achievable through universally supported peaceful means, would reappear. During the heady days following the Cold War, the world resembled King Tantalus of Greek mythology. When he tried to quench his thirst with water near his lips or appease his appetite with fruit within his grasp, he saw the water recede and the tree branch edge away. Nature does not leave things on linear paths for long. "Just administer the success; the future has been taken care of" cannot be a global principle of long-lasting notoriety. The post-Cold War era ended on 9/11/2001.

◆   ◆   ◆

The history of beliefs is not restricted to mere changes in their contents. It also reveals a fluctuation in their intensity. If one considers world history an epiphenomenon that accompanied the growth of global population and the expansion of economic activities, then the crises in global self-organization over a large time span provide the most plausible explanation for varying levels of preoccupation with world affairs. Observing also the imperfect recurrence of previous states (such as the similarities of beliefs about the long-term perspective during the mid-18th century and at the end of the 20th century) one may also recognize that the process underlying world history must be unidirectional, hence irreversible. This must be the case, since the reproduction of identical anterior states is one of the hallmarks of reversible processes. In such processes, states are independent of the direction in which time flows. If you look at two peaks of a perfect wave (such as the *sine* curve from high-school trigonometry), you can determine arbitrarily which came first. The future and the past are interchangeable. The history of beliefs shows that this cannot be the case in cultural evolution. When the production of novelties is inevitable (as in unidirectional time evolutions), the reproduction of anterior states may occur according to certain finite criteria (such as our A,B,C,D, and E above), but similarities between any two subsequent states can always be disproved by the introduction of additional ones. If we establish further conditions such as "envisaged the complete emancipation of women" (F) and "raised the prospect of unlimited socioeconomic equalization across the globe" (G), the post-Cold War era is no longer comparable with the *Enlightenment*.

In our times, tentativeness came to signify philosophical objectivity and ideological neutrality. Putting subdivisions of the past (periods or phases), identified through historical and social analysis, "under erasure" voluntarily may be a good standard of impartiality; willingness to pick up a sledge hammer and join others in deconstructive critique may be the highest.

In the end, the reality of human interactions is what contemporaries hold about it. Seeing this reality "move" across time (regardless of the analytical vantage point) means that thinking about social and economic arrangements cannot remain stationary. Thinking about the ways of the world is part of an irreversible process; it must always renew itself. Consequently, the perception of history depends on where one is in the flow of time. Historiography, the principles and methodology involved in writing history, itself, is part of an evolutionary process. Philosophy, a seemingly impractical preoccupation in the mesmerizing progression of the moment, always agitated by innumerable forces and volitions that are never clearly understood, becomes significant in the long view backward. It has an important social function, at least because the valuation of the past is the evolving function of living *discourse*.[6]

---

6.   See the Glossary for a definition of *discourse*.

After observing two centuries of persistently enduring trends in the growth of human population and economy, some *deterministic* force, the uninterrupted operation of a hidden cause behind world history, can be supposed. Once a process is considered *deterministic* (even if only partially so), human analysis tends to deduce *necessity* from major developments that occurred on the path to present conditions, regardless of where *ex ante* expectations concerning their realization were on the scale from "thin chance" to "absolute inevitability." We shall find that the deceptiveness of "historical necessity" appears in different ways between *ex post*, backward looking, and *ex ante*, forward looking assessments.

Ideology scavenges on natural sciences

Discoveries in natural sciences, when applicable to ideological issues, are put to use immediately, both to protect the extant social-political order and to attack it.

To cite a flagrant example, neither the most committed admirers nor the most passionate haters of *laissez faire* wasted any time in pouncing upon and expropriating Darwin's fundamental idea that objective reality ("nature"), which passes judgment on individual adaptations to protect and continue existence, bears the primary responsibility for sculpting the human being. The British philosopher and publicist, Herbert Spencer (1820-1903), is emblematic of the first category. He coined the slogan "survival of the fittest" to justify the contrast between glittering wealth and industrial squalor and to present it as the price modern society must pay for progress.

There is indeed a strong analogy between natural selection's capacity to create a grand order by testing organismal ability to survive in a hostile, dangerous, and unforgiving environment and free competition-created social wealth through the individual firm's ability to endure in the treacherous and brutal marketplace. Conversance between Darwinism and unregulated capitalism was logical, since Darwin was inspired not only by Thomas Malthus, but also by Adam Smith. Of course, later history rejected the view that the conditions for biological survival could be equated with those that determine differential socioeconomic success. (Not to mention that biologists consider "survival of the fittest" an eminently flawed reading of Darwin.)

Marxists, on the other hand, who severely criticized Smith and had an unabashed contempt for the views of Malthus, saw a similarity between Darwin and Marx because both were scientific revolutionaries, both embraced historical analysis as the principal research method, and both aroused the ire of scholars, philosophers, and the pious bourgeois. In the words of Engels, spoken at Marx's funeral in 1883, "Just as Darwin discovered the law of development of organic nature, so Marx discovered the law of development of human history."[7] Of course, the spiritual grandfathers of communism completely overlooked the lack of support for revolution in Darwin's teachings. Darwinism was an argument for gradual social transformation, not an invitation to mount the barricades and run into government buildings with bayonets fixed.

Nascent jingoism in Central Europe also drew justification from Darwin. The stronger prevails. This is the fundamental law of nature. If our country was excluded from the rewards of territorial expansion into other continents when we were weak, aren't we justified to stake our claims now when we are strong? The "survival of the fittest" could be applied not only to individuals and social classes, but also to nations.

Between the two World Wars, biologists began to synthesize Mendelian genetics and Darwinian natural selection. This did not sit well with Soviet ideology, since it left out "revolution" as the critical process in nature, and hence, in society. The orientation toward cross-fertilizing experiments in pre-revolutionary Russian horticulture, which continued under the USSR, and politics came together in Soviet Academe to crystallize an alternative theory of heredity around the persona of agronomist and devout communist Trofim Denisovich Lysenko (1898-1976).

Lysenko argued that characteristics acquired under certain conditions can be inherited. Although the theory was poorly documented and risked ridicule from the start, it was fully embraced in Stalin's empire following World War II. Lysenko's ideas were taught in every high-school biology class. Those who disagreed in the West were considered quacks who betrayed the international proletariat by trying to use biology to justify reactionary bourgeois social conditions. "Shattering heredity," whether you talked about plants or individual conduct, had to be accepted. Lysenko began to fall from grace toward the end of Stalin's life and became a nonperson after the dictator's death.[8]

Breakthroughs in natural sciences continue to be used in attacking and defending monotheistic ontology (i.e., philosophical interpretation of "being"). Biological evolution discredits the notion that a bearded Divine Father kneaded man and woman into their contemporary forms. But it could not kill God cosmologically. The gap is too big between the simplicity of the elements and chem-

---

7.   *Marx and Engels, 1968*, p. 435.
8.   Modern molecular biology detected some "Lamarckian" phenomena of inheriting acquired characteristics. But these results in no way bring Lysenko's theory and experiments closer to *bona fide* science. See *Steele, Lindley, and Blanden, 1998*.

ical compounds found on Earth relative to the astonishing complexity of DNA. "God refuses to die." Concerning the creation of our universe, modern cosmogony bases its explanation on the Big Bang that occurred several billions years ago. And many physicists with a deistic bent agree!

Bringing natural sciences to the witness stand in support of a social ideology has been fraught with controversy. But if natural sciences cannot help the world link its past with its future, what can?

Doubts persist about the discoverability of universal history

Perhaps no other author is quoted more often when questioning the feasibility and usefulness of historical analysis-based predictions than Karl Raimund Popper (1902-1994).[9] The dedication of his 1957 book, *The Poverty of Historicism*, reflects the experience that conditioned his thinking. "In memory of the countless men and women of all creeds or nations or races who fell victims to the fascist and communist belief in Inexorable Laws of Historical Destiny." He wrote from the perspective of a contemporary observer of the two savage political movements that shook the world. He witnessed the worst of the 20th century and dealt mainly with convictions about "historical necessity," the extreme point on the intensity scale of beliefs. No wonder that he, and countless others, remained forever skeptical about the need and the ability of humans to interpret history and determine where it leads.

Among Popper's arguments on why history's direction is not for us to divine, the following appear to be the most consequential. *First*, the expansion of human knowledge, spearheaded by major scientific discoveries, shapes history. Uncertainty about the future expansion of knowledge is aligned with uncertainty about the insights the expanded knowledge will provide about human affairs. Consequently, history defies systematization that links past and future. *Second*, theories about history's general laws are metaphysical propositions that cannot be falsified (proven to be wrong) by empirical methods, such as laboratory experiments or statistics. Even worse, when a proposition for a chemical or physical law is tested, the scientists bending over their instruments can usually say something objective and meaningful about the world even if the test fails and the proposition must be

---

9.   Isaiah Berlin (1909-1997) is a close second. His lecture, entitled *Historical Inevitability*, delivered on May 12, 1953 at the London School of Economics and Political Science, remains a standard reference on the subject.

dropped. However, no such help is forthcoming when one deals with theories about historical laws, which are, *par excellence*, metaphysical in nature. The world has no objective information about what it would be like if the theory happened to be false, beyond of course, the word of the theory's proponents. When the ideology that forecasts the direction of history collapses under the weight of unforeseen circumstances, the fanatics who subscribed to it will land in a moral quagmire without a compass or perhaps even in the courtroom.

Third, a prediction, particularly a detailed one, tends to be false by having an impact on the event predicted. Popper evocatively called this the "Oedipus effect," after the Greek legend dramatized by Sophocles. Oedipus, trying to avert the tragedy foretold by the oracle, meets his sad fate exactly because he heeded the oracle. The evasive steps he took in response to the prophecy sealed his fate. If someone makes a widely heeded prediction, expectations and plans will change in response. Expectation is a factor in the contingency of unfolding scenarios.[10]

Fourth, there is contradiction between the wish of the "evolutionist" to discover the true law of history and everybody's best interest. Seeing into the future would lead to scientific control of human nature and curtailment of spontaneity, that is, the variety in thought and action from which an unhampered interaction among events and circumstances could identify the optimal by weeding out the useless and redundant.

These are insights of great depth and enduring significance. The problem is that a gap exists between logic and morality on the one hand and the dynamics of global-scale reorganization on the other. If we consider the evolution of the world a physical process, divergence in the beliefs of history's inexorable destiny appears to be inevitable itself.

Beware of meganarratives

The postmodern disposition of the mind that forcefully characterized the closing quarter of the 20th century has left an indelible mark on historiography. It is now hard to imagine anyone attempting to identify stages in an all-embracing reductive explanation of cultural evolution without thinking of "deconstruction,"

---

10. The "Oedipus effect" has a corresponding principle in quantum mechanics: Observation alters the outcome of certain processes. Since Popper's writings, the subject has also been studied by economists. Dynamic analysis has shown that "myopic" rationality-generated actions can change expectations and lead to market disequilibrium. Information, whether it is an augury of historical inevitability or an iron-clad stock market forecast, will perturb the multiplicity of simultaneous interactions.

"logocentricity," *discourse*, or the "text and context" linkage. The postmodern period resulted in some abiding observations about the pitfalls of verbalizing perspectives on the past. In general, the postmodern view on "mega" or "grand" or "master" narratives ranges from suspicion to complete dismissal.[11] The common ground of this sweeping negativity is disproved epistemic objectivity and the author's (conscious or subconscious) disinterest. Many aspects of the postmodernly inspired "rien ne vas plus" in historical analysis are here to stay. Proof is that even arguments against its skepticism must lean on concepts introduced by the "classics" of postmodern thought. In some ways this situation is reminiscent of early populist attacks against Freud a century ago, invoking his "subconscious" intentions to discredit Christian values.

New historical materialism maintains that cultural evolution necessitates *meganarratives*. Without Marx, wrong as "Marxism" as a *meganarrative par excellence* has proved to be, the world would not have found its way to modern capitalism, a compromise between primitive *laissez faire* and the specter of unending public disorder. If we consider cultural evolution a unidirectional physical process, then seeing in postmodernism an eternal mode of approaching history (dismissing even the possibility of its universal comprehension) leads to the acceptance of the species' extinction. Denying the existence of collective memory and commonly definable goals based on a voluntarily embraced structure of thought among equals under the condition of clearly recognized threat to the species' prosperity (survival in the extreme) adds (through *bricolage* in philosophy, linguistics, and literary criticism) to a very pessimistic *meganarrative*, heralding "the end of man."

◆   ◆   ◆

Despite the huge hits and misses of major ideologies and heaps of less significant, half-forgotten attempts to discover universal laws behind historical data, interest in the subject has risen from its ashes like the phoenix of ancient legends. The human has an unstoppable drive, at least to try, in the words of Goethe, to "…detect the inmost force, which binds the world, and guides its course."[12] But there is a good reason beyond mere intellectual curiosity why there have been and will always be *meganarratives*. Cultural evolution as a phyletic process in a period

---

11.   Much of postmodern literature labels universal explanations of history as "metanarratives." We do not use "meta" in this sense because the word will have a different, specific meaning in the remainder of the text.

12.   From Bayard Taylor's translation of *Faust*.

of global level self-organization demands comprehensive, necessarily history-based views when it is in a "relative steady state." It demands a clash of such views when it is in the process of self-searching dynamic transition.

Experience and analysis warn people to be wary of new discoveries regarding history's direction. They may be nothing but attempts to force the past to confess what one wants to hear about the future, to impose a doctrine on historical data through false analogies and skewed inferences. More lethally, visions of the future with far-reaching agendas, supported by state structures, can create monsters. These lessons cannot be repeated enough. One can only hope that the world has learned them. But one can never be sure. It seems that in some periods of history, conceptualizations of its direction *per force* become separated from the moral quality of the deeds they imply.

We now turn to answering the second question. "Why is today's look at the past different from yesterday's?"

NEW CONDITIONS FAVORING THE SEARCH FOR THE MACROPAST-MACROFUTURE LINK

The 200-year advantage

History never stops lecturing. If people do not revise their views about the past, they are not listening to the teacher. The sheer possibility of looking at a longer stretch of the past allows the current generation to recognize more comprehensive patterns in world history than was allowed to earlier generations. The past 200 years, taken as a unit of analysis, reveal the trend of closer public monitoring and guidance of aggregate economic activities. The *laissez faire* organizational principle gave way to the *mixed economy*. This evolution had a global dimension, which was expressed in the appearance of *multilateralism* after World War II. *Multilateralism* refers to the existence of an all-inclusive institutional framework for global cooperation and coordination among national governments. Glancing back over the past two centuries, as if looking downward from a higher point on the mountain, one can distinguish between two distinct, consecutive *global systems*: the *laissez faire/metal money*–implying *zero multilateralism*–(from the 1830s to 1914) and the *mixed economy/weak multilateralism* (1945 to present). A turbulent and irrational period (1914-1945) led from the first *global system* (GS1) to the second one (GS2). Significantly, identification of GS2 as *the global system* was not complete until the collapse of the Soviet Union in 1991, marking the end of the Cold War.

In this light, communism and fascism may be regarded as subprocesses in the *chaotic transition* that prevailed between 1914 and 1945 and did not subside until 1991. They were unique occurrences in the course of humanity's tentative, unconscious adaptive transformation. Considering the two violent crusades of the 20th century nothing but an eternal proof that the combination of naive masses and evil men can create monstrosities on a global scale is not making use of the extended perspective.

Globalization as a simplifying factor

Today, people preoccupied with world problems such as hunger, pollution, and the depletion of nonrenewable natural resources, are no longer considered the impractical, romantic dreamers they were thought to be half a century ago. Globalization, worldwide integration, or tightening global interconnectedness led to this point. From large numbers of disconnected hordes roaming the landscape to city states, nations, integrating regions of nations, and *multilateral* institutions, human self-organization progressed toward greater scope and complexity.

Looking 200 years into the future, it is not unrealistic to presume that humankind will become a self-conscious evolutionary actor by organizing itself into a "homogenous polity." Such a "fully" *hominized* world (expression of Teilhard) would be able to weigh alternatives, select from them, and explicitly articulate and implement the most appropriate one. This assumption makes macrohistoric analysis with an eye on the future more manageable.

Growth in the opportunity to apply natural sciences to historical analysis

Leading academic circles in the social sciences and the *humanities* never extended a warm invitation to the student of nature to help examine cultural evolution. By now, however, advances reported in physics and biology make the available help so abundant and relevant that it is hard to ignore.[13]

Modern science allows for the generalization of cultural evolution "below" the level of the organism, into the realm of mass and energy. In the end, humans and all the objects they produce are "organized matter," composed of molecules,

---

13. See *Wilson, 1999.*

atoms, and subatomic particles. Given the fixity of earthly matter that the expanding human system can incorporate, universal history may be considered a non-equilibrium thermodynamic process. It is the unidirectional, complexifying self-organization of a material system, a phenomenon studied in nonequilibrium thermodynamics.

Much of the world's scientific community came to view behavior as an equilibrium arrangement, a compromise, as it were, between genetically determined tendencies and the environment. Moreover, according to neurobiologists, all that is mental (e.g., memory, thought, and emotion) is tied to physico-chemically perceivable structures and functions in the brain. If the particulars of the socioeconomic environment, where adaptation for differential individual success takes place, the DNA molecules that guard biological heredity, and the behavior that balances environment and heredity can all be found in the brain, one must conclude that the nonequilibrium thermodynamic process of global evolution takes place in the *mind*, the brain's function space. This idea, expressed by Condorcet and tied to the Hegelian philosophy of history, is confirmed by contemporary scientific rationality, and it lies in the general direction of empiricist brain research.

Practical urgency and democratic experience

The planet is filling up to its brim with people and their artifacts. One no longer needs to be a prophet or a scientific genius to figure out that the human maelstrom flowing over the brim would have severe consequences. If humanity wants to live near the Earth's capacity to support life and avoid decline, it will have to learn to own the future and act as a single decision maker. At present, the world is an unconscious entity. Its current way of approaching the future has no meaningful form or content.

Popper abhorred the idea of long-term, collective planning. However, he would surely agree that new perspectives and opportunities in analyzing the timescape left behind could lead to the conclusion that these activities are imperative for the continued prosperity of the species. As the national political experience of post-World War II industrial democracies proved, belief in "historical necessity" can change from uncritical, monoideistic convictions of a minority to the faith of the majority in the fulfillment of worthy goals. The extension of this experience to world affairs should no longer be seen as absurd. The emergence of global consciousness and ethics in the environmental/conservation movements and the powerful drive toward unlimited pluralism proves that. After all, not every passionate belief about a future state of the world is imposture or error wait-ing to assume monstrous proportions.

◆   ◆   ◆

Global history is a "disequilibrium thermodynamic process" manifest through transformations in billions of physically interconnected cerebral cortices. This theory provides the most general physical context for analyzing the world's cur-rent movement toward conflict. By tying human progression to a materially interpreted evolution, its epistemic base is as solid as the inescapable use of lan-guage–with its centerless, collectively determined, always shifting significations–permits it to be. There is nothing ethnocentric about thermodynamics. Sociopo-litical and historical theories may characterize phases in physically-interpreted *cultural evolution* but they do not determine them.

The future suggests a new balance between "historicism" and "humanism," in favor of the first and in the interest of the second. "Historical necessity" now stands naked in the public square of philosophical opinion with a "Shame on me" tag around its neck. But this concept assumes new meaning if we recognize that the inexorable push for infinite growth in a limited space violates immanent laws of nature.

2

Culture, Cultural Evolution, and Socioeconomic Organization

[*Cultural evolution* is species-wide (phyletic) self-strengthening or self-propagation. Historically, it is measurable by the number of people alive, the per capita income or output, and progress registered in social and economic equality. *Cultural evolution* may be represented as a trajectory in a three-dimensional "phase space." This trajectory has been upward sloping for the past two centuries. *Culture* as a state of *cultural evolution*. The hierarchy of socioeconomic environments and systems. The over-arching presence of the *global system* through a nest of increasingly local adaptations. From the individual's vantage point, the layers of the hierarchy and the physical conditions of the environment fuse into a singular *arena*. The *global system* is a huge balancing act; the nature of its transformation. Why *cultural evolution* represents progress and why it cannot be an entirely *random* process.]

CULTURE AND CULTURAL EVOLUTION

The dictionary definition of culture is the "way of life" of a community or society. Of course, the "way of life" has a virtually endless number of aspects. It is at once dominant customs, social ethics, individual behavior, sexual mores; social, economic, legal organization, religion, artistic expressions and tastes, level of science and technology, endowments in material goods, conditions of life, and more. Each aspect lends itself to in-depth studies and comparisons across geographic areas and time. Connecting human history with the transformation of matter requires a precise definition. Since we shall consider *culture* a state of *cultural evolution*, let us begin with the latter.

Global cultural evolution (henceforth *cultural evolution*) is the self-strengthening or self-propagation of the species. Historically, growth in the "strength of the

26

species" could be characterized by the coincidental increase in the quantity and improvements in the quality of human life. Three *cultural evolutionary indices* may be used to evaluate this process: world population, per capita output (income), and a global "socioeconomic equality index," which measures progress in social and economic equalization, the result of the uninterrupted search for ways to adjust the delicate balance within and among communities. World population is considered a quantitative measure. The per capita output or income, although calculated from two quantities, characterizes the quality of life.[1] Progress registered toward social and economic equality or *socioeconomic equilibrium* is a qualitative indicator.

It may be agreed that socioeconomic equalization has been a recognizable component of human history. In Europe, for example, the Roman Republic represented advancement compared to Greek antiquity. Whereas the Hellenic world lived with deeply ingrained convictions about disparities (as illustrated by the belief in the separate lives of humanoid deities), the stoic Roman civilization inclined toward weakening the patrician-plebeian dividing line and moved close to recognizing "natural rights," the self-understood equality among men. During the centuries that followed, the spread of monotheistic religions served the cause of socioeconomic equalization by expanding and deepening the credo of "universal brotherhood," by developing the socio-psychological recognition of the weak, the poor, and the subjugated. The *Enlightenment* envisaged the unlimited application of institutionally secured political and legal rights and the equalization of economic opportunities.

Given the recorded secular trend of growing productivity in the modern capitalist era, one may recognize the inevitability of past progress in socioeconomic equalization, *ex post*. Mass production, which is the crucial threshold in the rise of productivity, demands mass consumption. Historically, this iron-clad condition required that personal incomes keep pace with the increase of productivity. The bulk of the purchasing power had to flow toward the middle of the income scale; extreme richness had to be sized down and the ranks of the poor had to be thinned out, increasing the importance of the middle class.

Higher productivity and incomes also meant (and still do) higher levels of education and greater consciousness of one's own value. While the growth in self-respect, rising expectations, and the inclination to be more exacting push individ-

---

1.   Per capita energy production/consumption would have been an alternative index. We chose per capita output which, by virtue of national accounting identities, equals per capita income, a term directly related to the everyday concept of living standard.

uals toward socioeconomic equality from the *interior*, commercial and political competition, which raise the overall degree of respect accorded to each person, pull them toward it from the *exterior*. Civil liberties and political rights expanded through legislation and the transformation of social customs. Facilitated by the increasing relative abundance of consumables and the decreasing demand for excruciatingly burdensome physical labor, a palpable tide of good will moved across social class boundaries.

To appreciate the historic movement of socioeconomic relations, some quantifiable aspects of this process must be identified. A *Socioeconomic Equality Index* (SEEI) may be built on the above described income redistributive and political/legal equality-promoting travel companions of socioeconomic progress. Accordingly, the suggested SEEI is composed of the combination of two variations: the middle class index (MCI) and a political/legal rights index (PLRI):

$$SEEI = MCI \times PLRI$$

MCI is the percentage of middle class in the total population defined in terms of mid-range income, e.g., the percentage of individuals living on income that excludes the bottom and top deciles. MCI $=1$ would mean complete income equality, a theoretical maximum for the relative size of the middle class, making the term itself meaningless.[2] Similarly, PLRI $= 1$ would signify complete equality for each (adult) individual in the political arena and before the law, by statute and social acceptance.

From 1800 to 2000, the value of SEEI increased,[3] at least in the *vanguard*, or the ensemble of industrialized countries with democratic political institutions.[4] The index had to tend upward because both its components (MCI and PLRI) did. Improvement in income distribution is a logical concomitant of industrialization, an observation confirmed by contemporary data: Developed countries have a larger middle class than underdeveloped ones. Equivalently, income differentials are harsher in poor developing countries than in the developed ones.[5] PLRI grew with the removal of restrictions to vote or hold office based on prop-

---

2.   MCI may be approximated by subtracting the "Gini coefficient" from 1. The "Gini" is a frequently used measure of income distribution. But in contrast to MCI, the more even the distribution (a proxy for the importance of the middle class in the population) the closer its value to zero.

3.   No attempt is made to estimate this index. Statements concerning its presumed increase during the past two centuries rely on well known historical data.

4.   The founding members of the Organization for Economic Cooperation and Development (OECD) may be a good approximation of the *vanguard*.

erty, education, and religion; the abolition of slavery, progress in the status of women, increased care and respect given to the weak and helpless; and with growing general sensitivity to civil rights. At the national level, it grew as a result of decolonization, the globalization of economic relations, and participation in international organizations. The diffusion and enhancement of democratic institutions accompanied the growth of SEEI. This growth has been inseparable from the increase in upward mobility and the decrease in downward mobility. Since the widening and strengthening system of social safety nets (the major means of curtailing downward mobility) is financed largely through progressive taxation, its extension redistributes income from higher to lower income earners. The rise in the index may also be seen as the "democratization of consumption" (measured, for example, by the ratio of goods and services available to the average person to the number of goods and services available only to the richest 10 percent).

Reduction in social and economic inequities strengthens polities by mobilizing initiatives and eliminating tensions and distortions that weaken the community. To take the simplest example from physics, the distribution of molecules in a closed system (such as a jar) is the most stable equilibrium. It is the one to which the system tends to return following *random* collisions among the molecules and the one that shows no new trends. The molecules may be compared to individuals who try to maximize their welfare, that is, to control as much as they can of the closed system's space, its single resource, and have varying capabilities and opportunities to do so. The elimination of disequilibrium in this hyper-simple analogy is movement toward an equal distribution of space among the "molecules."

Evolutionary psychology, game theory, and cultural anthropology confirm what appears logical in retrospect: The lack of willingness to tolerate social and political inequities and economic parasitism over the long haul coincides with the rational choice to exploit human resources in the service of improved average welfare.[6] The influential mid-20th century Jesuit biologist, Pierre Teilhard de Chardin, a distant relation of Voltaire's, was absolutely correct when he argued that the liberation of individual energies and the leveling of classes, the universalization of "liberty, equality, and fraternity," the democratic principles of the French Revolution, are biological necessities.[7]

---

5.   International comparisons on income distribution may be found, for example, in the *World Development Report*, published regularly by the International Bank for Reconstruction and Development (The World Bank).

6.   See for example, *Wright, 2001*, pp. 82-85.

7.   *Teilhard de Chardin, 1964*, p. 238.

The slow and painful process of social and economic equalization had to take place. It had been "programmed" into the expansion and complexification of socioeconomic relations over the macrohistoric time scale. Providing the individual with an increasing choice of consumables must accompany growing productivity, but so must the number and quality of opportunities for people to sustain themselves and seek differential socioeconomic success. Nevertheless, complete socioeconomic equalization could not have been an ideal or absolute goal under recorded *cultural evolution*. The possibility of becoming rich and opting out from working life altogether remained a major individual motivation. Moreover, relatively high income differences revealed themselves as more conducive to economic growth than egalitarian distributions. Economists even talk about an optimum level of income inequality whose violation through measures of leveling would harm overall per capita economic growth, another summary indicator of *cultural evolution*.

Cultural evolution means that despite the growing human biomass, the significance of the average person increases. The joint occurrence of these two enduring trends is crucial to labeling the past an "evolution." By the standards of *cultural evolutionary indices*, the species has strengthened itself during the past 10 to 12 thousand years, since the times when agriculture first appeared in the world's most advanced regions as the mainstay of economic activity.

Naturally, the process of self-propagation through *cultural evolution* has been far from even or balanced over time and space. Population growth often got ahead of output increases, and progress in the qualitative indices in one place may have coincided with stagnation and temporary retrogression in another. Socioeconomic equalization suffered many setbacks. The very concept lost its meaning amidst the moral and political disorder of "1914-1945." In recent times, a worldwide increase in income inequality among and within nations (even in the *vanguard*) has been noted. Nonetheless, in the long-term rear view and in the aggregate, *cultural evolution*, as measured by its three indices, appears to be a determined march.

The macrohistoric balance of the past two centuries shows that the three *cultural evolutionary indices* are tied together; none of them could move ahead indefinitely and leave the other two stationary; no pair of them could take off, leaving the third one behind. As productivity (per capita income) increased, so did the importance of the individual as a matter of necessity, even if history recounts this process as the result of inspired reforms led by outstanding personalities.

Levels of population have been estimated for even longer periods than the past two hundred years.[8] With regard to the period under consideration, DeLong presents data for every 25 years from 1800 to 2000, except for 1825. Using his data, and extrapolating for 1825, we obtain the following time series:

	Population (in billions)	Global GDP per capita (in 1990 international $s)
1800	.900	195
1825	1,039	242
1850	1,200	300
1875	1,325	429
1900	1,625	679
1925	1,898	1,108
1950	2,516	1,622
1975	4,079	3,714
2000	6,272	6,539

These numbers, venturesome as they may be with the extrapolation, leave no doubt about the validity of the trend they show.

Because SEEI also had to increase during 1800-2000, the three *cultural evolutionary indices* form a temporal bond. We can visualize *cultural evolution* for the period in a *phase space*, where every *cultural evolutionary index* occupies a coordinate.[9] By an imaginary scaling of the data to 1800, we obtain an upward sloping trajectory. It rises from 1800 = 0 and goes through each subsequent quarter century. Each data point after 1800 (i.e., 1825, 1850, 1875, 1900, 1925, 1950, 1975, and 2000) will be farther from the origin (1800) than the preceding one. This trajectory is the statistical symbol of *cultural evolution*.

If a team of sociologists, historians, economists, and statisticians calibrated a handy composite index of *cultural evolution* for each year beginning with 1800 = 100, an alternative pictorial representation could reduce *cultural evolution* to a

---

8. See J. Bradford DeLong (Department of Economics, U.C. Berkeley), *Estimating World GDP, One Million B.C.-Present*, found on March 23, 2004, at www.j-bradford.net.

9. If we actually wanted to plot the *cultural evolutionary indices* and show the trajectory, we would need to "normalize" their divergent scales. The population is in billions, the per capita income in hundreds or thousands of dollars, and the SEEI moves from near zero toward, but falling significantly short of, one.

two-dimensional graph. Using the horizontal axis to indicate the passage of time from 1800 to 2000, the constructed index would depict *cultural evolution* as an upward sloping curve.

Both economic data and historical experience demonstrate that success in *cultural evolution* at the national level depended crucially on which of the three indices led. Per capita income growth (implying technological progress and increases in physical and human capital) revealed itself to be much more conducive to the evolution of the other two indices than starting with a spurt in population or trying to foster personal welfare through enforced measures of egalitarianism.

From the definition of (*global*) *cultural evolution* follows the interpretation of *global culture*. *Global culture* (henceforth *culture*) is the status of *cultural evolution*, a general indicator of the species' strength. It is the "state of the world" according to *cultural evolutionary indices*. It is the overall condition of phyletic self-empowerment; *opus humanum*, as characterized by the number of people, material welfare, and progress achieved in interpersonal balance.

Culture compresses information about the most frequently considered aspects of culture in the dictionary (nonitalicized) meaning of the concept. For example, the size of the population relative to a given surface, such as the Earth, and the level of per capita output or income, imply a certain level of science and technology, the mode of social, economic, and legal organization.

SOCIOECONOMIC ORGANIZATION

A socioeconomic environment is embedded in each culture, regardless of the size and shape of the territory over which it extends. The distribution of property, collective response to internal and external shocks or gradual changes through the political process are its social aspects. Macroeconomic conditions (such as aggregate income, employment, and the price level) and microeconomic conditions (those that influence producer and consumer decisions, the mechanism of resource allocation) are its economic components. Each socioeconomic environment has a system of explicitly stated principles of coordination (e.g., laws, rules, and regulations). The culture, with its functioning social and economic organization, is integrated with the physical environment, made up of natural features (e.g., topography, climate, and mineral and energy resources) and man-made factors such as production facilities and the infrastructure. From the individual's point of view, the socioeconomic and physical aspects of the environment fuse into an integrated structure of externalities that must be taken into consideration in the course of satisfying the internal drive for differential success.[10]

Individual fitness is no longer measured merely by biological survival and reproductive success evidenced by the number of offspring. Instead, it is measured by relative income, psychic satisfaction, and biological self-propagation as seen in the level of care and education accorded to children and the potential wealth left to them.[11]

The socioeconomic environment is not only a venue for competition but also for cooperation, exemplified by agreements such as employer/employee, seller/buyer relations that specify respective roles and gains in interactions. The competitive/cooperative socioeconomic environment is effective to the extent that it is leveled; that is, when each participant's chances for differential success are limited only by talent, health, and ambition. Historically, the notion of "equal opportunity" has been applied only within, rather than across socioeconomic estates, classes, groups, or national boundaries. The fading of sharp dividing lines among stratified "playing fields" is a fairly recent development. Complete satisfaction with the extent to which a socioeconomic environment is objective and fair–"meritocratic"–does not exist. Broad acceptance of comparative opportunities remains the practical, although minimum, safe standard by which society can live in peace.

Unlike the harsh and unforgiving natural environment, the competitive/cooperative socioeconomic environment can be understanding and responsive. Failure under modern socioeconomic arrangements is censored not with physical demise, but with lower income, lack of social appreciation, and handicaps inflicted on the descendants in their quest for differential success. The welfare state tries to put people back on their feet. It provides public support to those who are anxious to

---

10.   The current text uses expressions that are directly applicable to the past two centuries, i.e., to *modern history*. They are not directly applicable to societies that preceded the global era of cultural evolution. For example, if we regress into the culture of the Pleistocene horde, the "law" becomes the word of the Big Man; the "price level" transmogrifies into exchange values in red salt or dried fish bone; the "infrastructure" into the Meeting Tent and the Warehouse for food supplies and weapons.

11.   Biologists refer to the maximization of offspring as the "r-strategy" (or r-selection) in distinction from "K-strategy" (or K-selection) that tends to improve the descendent generation's qualitative attributes. The so-called "demographic transition" from high to low population growth, which accompanied the rise of per capita income in the industrialized countries and is currently observable in the developing world, may be labeled as a society-wide shift from a predominantly "r" to a predominantly K-strategy. For details, see, for example, *Wilson, 2000*.

bequeath copies of their genes to posterity but lack the material means to do so at a level that would satisfy "basic human needs," however these may be interpreted according to time and place. This social response is logical since not all participants can show average performance, let alone win medals, in mass competitions. "Killing off the poor" would violate the species' most elemental instinct for survival. A reduced population, "rid of the poor," would have poor again relative to its redefined average income. Continued neglect of those who drift toward the bottom of the socioeconomic scale would tend to dissolve the human biomass.

Despite the widely recognized advantages of the welfare state, the individual did not become "spoiled." Even in countries known to be the most solicitous of human needs, people would not think otherwise. The socioeconomic environment has proved to be severe and rigorous enough to force the majority of individuals to tap into all their reserves of ingenuity and exert all their efforts to live up to expectations, to "make good" in the *arena*.

Socioeconomic environments and their hierarchy

A nest of communicative socioeconomic layers surrounds the individual. The immediate layer is the *personal socioeconomic sphere*. It includes areas and objects in the individual's possession or under its control. Its main possible (not necessarily actual) components are real estate, designated workplace, consumer goods, capital goods, land, natural resources, and any material object with or without market value. Although the items that compose the *sphere* are not located contiguously, they may be added in the abstract to form a more or less closed space that contains a more or less fixed amount of matter. "Personal" means "familial," i.e., every adult member of a kin-based household regards the entire *sphere* as its own. This *sphere* may be used to signal actual or sought socioeconomic status.

The classical indicators in the dominance hierarchy are *wealth, power,* and *influence.* Taken separately or together, they represent control over scarce (priced) possessions. Individual *wealth* is a fund of valuables. *Power* is access to goods and services through one's contacts or position, rather than through direct payment, e.g., the executive's use of the company jet. *Influence* is the capacity to affect someone else's success in accumulating *wealth* or acquiring *power* (e.g., through helping others obtain high-paying or perk-laden positions). Since it usually takes *wealth* and *power* to help someone become wealthier and more powerful, *influence* is obtained by directly accessing persons already endowed with *wealth* and *power,* by appealing to their sense of obligation or wish to extend their supporting network; perhaps making use of their susceptibility to charm and charisma.

The success of the *vanguard*, in comparison with the rest of the world, may be attributed to the relatively greater significance of *wealth* within the composite scale and the relatively more prominent role of entrepreneurship and other forms of creative accomplishments in acquiring *wealth*. In dictatorial states, *power* and *influence* are more dominant. In such states, a complicated scheme of uninterrupted reciprocation within the ruling elite is the dominant source of exceptional endowments in consumer goods and access to the enjoyment of social wealth.

Wealth-power-influence is the best understood socioeconomic scale, the *lingua franca* among status communications. Socrates, Plato, the Cynics, Jean Jacques Rousseau, and some songwriters may disagree. They are not representative of ground-level, proximal reality. Individual actions aimed at maximizing *wealth, power, and influence* remain the most adaptive. They correspond most directly to success in increasing the *personal socioeconomic sphere*. Other patterns of behavior, including extreme nonconformism, may be viewed as mere responses to this ancient and stubbornly undying, mammonish, canonical scale.

Limitations imposed by modern social organization notwithstanding, the individual in materialistically well-to-do countries retains "sufficient" discretion to communicate self-valuation through dressing, grooming, adorning the body, and decorating the exteriors and interiors of property and areas under personal control–"sufficient" to ensure the contentment and excitation needed to affirm life, for wanting to perpetuate it. Much of the economy in the industrialized world runs exactly on what Thorstein Veblen (1857-1929) called "conspicuous consumption." The rise of per capita income expanded opportunities for such "consumerism," increasing the size and contents of the *personal socioeconomic sphere*. This general tendency has been a critical factor in preserving social tranquility, despite the enormous and well-known differences among *spheres*.

Living out life's desires and subtle impulses is, of course, not restricted to preoccupation with the *personal socioeconomic sphere*. But the dividing line between "socioeconomic" and "other" behavior is uncertain and porous. Consider the well-known overlap between the so-called "sex drive" and the search for socioeconomic status. As car manufacturers and advertisers are acutely aware, they can increase sales by combining a powerfully dashing, sporty design with an elegant chassis that implies wealth.

The *personal sphere* is nested in the *surrounding socioeconomic milieu*, which is the individual's immediate socioeconomic context, its socioeconomic habitat. It comprises the persons who determine one's level of income–the classically interpreted status–and many others, some of whom are voluntarily chosen and others who are not. For the average individual, job-related human contacts, the neighborhood of the living quarters, the social network, and people met in short-lived contacts (e.g., sales personnel) or in even more fleeting and *random* encounters (e.g., complete strangers in a public conveyance or at some commercial venue) represent the *surrounding socioeconomic milieu*. The number of individuals filling it may be limited to hundreds and the space it occupies may be no larger than the interconnected enclosures of the workplace, home, and one's regular "stomping ground." This is the average, of course. Movie stars, extraordinary achievers in various domains, or "world leaders" are known by billions. Their "stomping ground" is the planet.

No two individuals have identical *surrounding socioeconomic milieus*, not even if each belongs to the innermost core of the other's *milieu*. Through the dynamic interplay among *personal socioeconomic spheres*, most socioeconomic interactions occur in *surrounding socioeconomic milieus*.

The local community, with its administrative borders and polity, has its own characteristic *local socioeconomic environment*. (A *surrounding socioeconomic milieu* may belong to two or more *local socioeconomic environments* if the individual works in an enfranchised city but lives in a neighboring county that has its own local government.) To continue along the administrative unit basis of nests, *local socioeconomic environments* combine to form larger ones; for example, states in the United States or provinces in Canada, to constitute the *national socioeconomic environment*.

The conglomeration of interdependent national socioeconomic environments is the *global socioeconomic environment*. It is a mosaic of overlapping, nationally compartmentalized *surrounding socioeconomic milieus*. It twists and turns as population grows and per capita output rises, as distributive struggles among individuals, communities, and countries continue. Events ranging from local significance (e.g., neighborhood-altering construction projects, the ebb and flow of employment opportunities) to international conflicts, revolutions, and civil wars with worldwide consequences ceaselessly agitate the *global socioeconomic environment*. Droughts, floods, earthquakes, epidemics, and the vagaries of weather mingle with human dynamics. But temporal fluctuations and spatial unevenness notwithstanding, *cultural evolution* (as measured by our three indices) continued during the past two centuries, increasing the number and size of *personal socioeconomic spheres* and overlapping *surrounding milieus*, altering their interactive shuffling all the time, and changing their fundamental framework of interactions twice: first, when GS0 (late feudalism/emergent capitalism) "switched" to GS1 and then, when GS1 "switched" to GS2.

Since socioeconomic environments may be determined according to different territorial criteria, such as geographic (e.g., the Pyrenees or the Yucatan Peninsula); administrative (e.g., village, county, district); ethnic, regional within a nation (e.g., the "South" in the United States), or among nations (e.g., the EU), they form an overlapping continuum. By selecting the administrative hierarchy of systems within socioeconomic environments (i.e., local, intermediary, national, regional, *multilateral*), we can simplify the task of recognizing the "vertical" coherence of socioeconomic organization.

Socioeconomic systems and their hierarchy

A "socioeconomic system" is the ensemble of the corresponding socioeconomic environment's fixed organizational principles. It remains unwritten at the individual level, where the *personal socioeconomic sphere* is managed. However, it is formally expressed through the institutional frameworks at all administratively identified levels. The system of the *surrounding socioeconomic milieu* is a hybrid. It unites informal and formal elements.

The *national system* reflects *mesoscopic* adaptation to the *macroscopic* force field exerted by the prevalent *global system*. All the subnational, administratively delineated systems conform to nationally mandated principles and templates. The independence of subnational systems is limited to the vacuum left by the national system, as well as by other, subnational systems that include it. The system of the *surrounding socioeconomic milieu* (as identified by a specific individual) is composed of the systems of the enveloping environments and those of the individuals who fill it. The limitation of local independence becomes apparent in the system of the *surrounding socioeconomic milieu*. For example, in the contemporary *vanguard*, as in many other countries, laws and regulations affecting working conditions and employer/employee relations originate at the national level.

Above the *surrounding socioeconomic milieu*, the socioeconomic system in force constrains and channels interactions not only among the members of the given community, but also with other communities of the same hierarchical level, e.g., relations among counties and states in the United States and among countries in international relations. The *global system* is an obvious exception regarding this second type of interaction, since it does not regulate relations with "extraterrestrials."

Moving down in the hierarchy of nested systems, each layer incorporates the influence of the systems from the layers above. Ultimately, although indirectly, through several instances of narrowing local applications, the *global system* shows up in the *personal socioeconomic sphere.* The relative size and importance of the *personal socioeconomic spheres* reflect the success of *microscopically* created, "individual systems" as adaptive responses to *surrounding socioeconomic milieus.* Each *personal socioeconomic sphere* may be regarded as a *microscopic* adaptation whose relative size and evolution over time reflects the *macroscopic* system via a *mesoscopic* adaptation. (In italics, *macroscopic* always refers to the global, *mesoscopic* to the national, and *microscopic* to the individual level.)

Socioeconomic ethics (rules of conduct in socioeconomic relations) belong to the environment, rather than to the system. This follows simply from definition, since we restrict "fixed organizational principles" to externally (nonsomatically) stored laws, rules, and regulations. The consequence of cutting ahead in the line at the bank or grocery store, in violation of the widely upheld ethical rule not to do so, may be the insistence of the waiting crowd that the offender wait his or her turn, or the behavior may be tolerated with censuring glances and contemptuous facial expressions. A businessman may renege on a verbal promise (violating socioeconomic ethics) without suffering apparent or immediate punishment. However, he is not allowed to get away with violating a signed contract. Contract law, with its enforcement mechanism, is part of the "system."

Examining the *global socioeconomic environment* "from the bottom up," it becomes apparent that ethical precepts are the most explicit in its smallest building blocks, at the personal level. Individual standards of behavior add up to social values that may be reflected in laws and institutions; however, they are not legislated. When we look at the personal system "from the top down," we recognize its dependence on the *global system,* even in the domain of ethics. This strange reciprocity hints at the complicated dynamics involved in the transformation of *global systems,* a process which, according to the thermodynamic perspective on history, is a physical necessity.

Individual vantage points

The complex mixture of opportunities, constraints, incentives, and prohibitions stashed into the *surrounding socioeconomic milieu* presents itself as a single reality to the individual. It is the *arena* in which competitive fitness is tested. Growing sovereignty in choosing it (i.e., "mobility") has been part of the socioeconomic equalization process. Microeconomic rationality suggests that *surrounding socioeconomic milieus* will be selected to maximize individual movements along the scale of *wealth-power-influence.* The *milieu* can be "refreshed" without geographic displacement (e.g., by changing employment; leaving out some persons and including others). One may even transform the way the *milieu* functions. Here again, socioeconomic equalization widened the margin of opportunity. The average person's chances to participate in local politics and the opportunities for individual voices to be heard increased over time.

The geographic selection of the *surrounding socioeconomic milieu* and the opportunity to transform it promise only limited possibilities for expanding the *personal socioeconomic sphere*. In well integrated countries, *local socioeconomic environments*, which impose themselves on the *surrounding milieus*, strongly resemble one another. Their attributes, derived from national and global sources, are omnipresent and firmly fixed. They define social and economic relations that are malleable neither to personal interventions nor to ingenious efforts by elected officials.

Understanding socioeconomic layers and the opportunity of influencing them decline precipitously as we leave the local level (i.e., the *personal sphere*, the *surrounding milieu*, and the *local environment*). The public at large may have some solid and realistic notions about the national environment and system and may feel empowered to influence them through the electoral process, dissent, and protest. However, the average individual has only spotty and diffused ideas about the *global socioeconomic environment* and the *global system* and feels no power to affect them. For most people, the world "as is" and the order in it, are fuzzy abstractions, dismissed with a wave of the hand. The characteristics of the *global system* have the smallest chance to be noticed. Even if they were identified, criticism would seem to be a pointless waste of energy from the vantage point of adaptive behavior.

When an entrepreneur comes to town to start a new business, he bases his calculations foremost on the competition in his line of commerce and on the area's income level; that is, he assesses the conditions of supply and demand. He also considers many other aspects of the socioeconomic environment without necessarily being conscious that they reflect the attributes of enveloping systems. For instance, he counts on a relative stability of the price level; is obligated to live by certain standards in labor-management relations; and considers the taxes to be paid in support of the national socioeconomic safety net among his unavoidable expenses. In an analytical mode, he may remember that he is living with the institutions of the post-World War II era. (Government responsibility for the stability of the price level, fixed standards in labor-management relations, and socioeconomic safety nets did not exist under GS1.) In a competitive mode, he wastes no time thinking about why "givens" are "givens." If he did, he would resemble a distracted matador, who, upon entering the arena, grumbles about the size of the ring and muses over the height of the railings instead of concentrating on the bull.

The fusion of the nested environments and systems from the individual's point of view does not mean that society at large does not distinguish among them. More than that, some specialize in analyzing the "environment" (e.g., sociologists), others in implementing the "system." Attorneys practicing business law locally, nationally, or internationally must "pass the bar" and keep up with new developments in their field. They are operating the *global system* indirectly and perhaps unconsciously. Employees at *multilateral* organizations (such as The World Bank, the International Monetary Fund, and the World Trade Organization) operate the prevailing *global system* (GS2) directly and consciously.

The *surrounding socioeconomic milieus* are homogenous and objective to the extent that they contain characteristics valid to all of them and apply to everyone. The similarities in *surrounding socioeconomic milieus*, at least within a nation, contain the characteristics of the *global system*. But they are also heterogeneous and subjective. Heterogeneous because, as stated earlier, no two individuals have identical *surrounding socioeconomic milieus.* They are subjective because the way the individual perceives the *surrounding socioeconomic milieu* is uniquely determined by biological heredity in combination with personal circumstances and history.

Each individual creates a mental image of its *surrounding socioeconomic milieu* without noticing the role broader societies play in the process. In fact, the individual is convinced that it is completely apart from the environment whose mental picture it creates and recreates. Given social education-dictated symbol/referent relations ("meanings") and patterns of general experiences in socioeconomic environments, the internalized *global system* suggests opportunities and obstacles as well as certain vital technical details for personal conduct. Satisfaction with one's own adaptive success means the implicit acceptance of the internalized *global system.*

Some philosophers claim that the existence of the self is the only reality one can know for certain. This school of thought is called *solipsism.* It is certainly correct inasmuch as all ideas about the world are produced in the same brain that stores information about it. As far as the material basis of mental activities is concerned, it is the only clearly proven source. However, *solipsism* is reduced to a misleading illusion if we recall that some of the knowledge about our *surrounding socioeconomic milieus* (specifically those derived from the *global system*) is alike in many selves, proving the existence of a supra-individual reality–the system of interactions.

Let us point out that intersubjective networking as an externality faced by the individual is not restricted to *global-system*-determined interactions. Some internalized information stands for trans-epochal principles of self-conduct (as succinctly expressed by the Ten Commandments); while others pertain to ephemeral whims that personal authority (e.g., a workplace supervisor) may impose on the *surrounding socioeconomic milieu.*

The privileged attention accorded to the quotidian renders the *global system* virtually unnoticed as long as personal adaptations are considered successful on a massive scale. The heterogeneity and relative malleability of the *surrounding socioeconomic milieus,* the subjectivity involved in perceiving them, and the remoteness of the influence of the *global system* upon them, all contribute to the stability of the nested hierarchy of localized systems. This hierarchic structure of the world order is collectively constructed. It is everybody's structure, but it is beyond anybody's ability to alter its norms.

People not only adapt to the *global system,* as it is incarnated in the multitude of *surrounding socioeconomic milieus,* but they also help maintain it indirectly or directly, unconsciously or consciously. They also oppose it in a large variety of ways, indirectly or directly, unconsciously or consciously. The protestors of globalization and *multilateral* organizations oppose GS2 consciously and directly. But anyone who identifies a local problem that is simply unsolvable under the institutional order brought into existence by the prevalent *global system* opposes the *system* indirectly and unconsciously. For example, recommendations to stop the spread of environmental decay qualify as indirect and unconscious protest against GS2 because the recommendations do not take into account that, given the prevailing world order's characteristic socioeconomic behavior and techno-economic decision space, global economic expansion is as inseparable from GS2 as growing worldwide environmental decay is from global economic expansion. Most opposition remains unknown to the opposers, who, like Moliere's *Would-Be Gentleman,* speak prose without even noticing it.

World order seems to be distant from and subordinate to daily life, when, in reality, it is always present and plays a defining role in it. We breathe GS2 and speak its language (see Chapter 6) even when we oppose it. The *global system* erects the invisible walls and passageways within which the *Hidden Hand* (as Adam Smith understood it) is allowed to operate.

Cultural evolution increased the number of competitors and cooperators while disconnecting them. The accountant who works for a car manufacturing company in Japan cooperates with the salesman at a dealership somewhere in North America. The same accountant in Japan competes with someone who cleans the windows in a European showroom where cars made by a competing manufacturer are sold. This increasing depersonalization of cooperative and competitive contacts, in combination with the increasing interconnectedness through globalization, is the "complexification of socioeconomic organization"–a faithful companion of *cultural evolution*.

More on the global system

The *global system* is the most comprehensive characterization of an epoch's social and economic organization, manifest in the institutions and legal framework of worldwide political and economic cooperation. World order has revealed its widely perceptible institutional basis since the first third of the 19th century. The penultimate, cohesive epoch before the emergence of *global systems* (GS0 in symbolic shorthand) lasted from 1500 to the outbreak of the French Revolution in 1789. What happened since the beginning of GS1 is *modern history*; what happened since 1500 is *history*; what happened before 1500 is *historia*.

Some time had to pass before the existence of *global systems* as phases in a unidirectional, sequential process could be recognized. But once the recognition occurs, the perspective on world history changes and phenomena formerly considered separate unite under a common framework. There is a thesis, according to which 19th century romanticism in art and literature gave rise to the socialist movement in Europe. Our theory suggests that the two were different manifestations of the same phenomenon, namely the erosion of GS1's ability to support *cultural evolution*. Romanticism expressed a passive, moralistic indignation over the excesses of *laissez faire* and the neglect of individuality, whereas the socialist movement advanced propositions to replace GS1 with a system whose primary utility for the world turned out to be assistance in identifying GS2 parameters. Artistic, literary expressions may have catalyzed the socialist movement, but certainly did not cause it.

A *global system* becomes global through its prevalence in the most advanced countries. These are the industrialized democracies–the *vanguard*. Despite its name, the *vanguard* does not only look forward; it also looks around and is the guard of the *global system*, or to use a modern analytical term, "the blocking coalition" that prevents any attempt to replace it. The *vanguard* is model and sentry at once.[12] Still, the positive role it has played and continues to play in world affairs makes it worthy of the flattering title. In *modern history*, the *vanguard* reached the highest levels of productivity and, relative to the rest of the world, succeeded the most in de-differentiating socioeconomic conditions.

Even countries in defiance of, or in opposition to, the reigning *global system* must define themselves in reference to it and must interact with the rest of the world on its terms. The institutions of the *global system* and its all-encompassing organizing principles prevail over dissenting, "out-of-line" subsystems. During the Cold War, the Eastern Bloc (The USSR and its East European satellites) lived in an alternative to the *mixed economy* and its leaders hoped to replace GS2 *multilateralism* with their own version of international cooperation. However, the exchange of goods within the bloc remained a fraction of world trade and its members had to conduct business with the rest of the world in the terms of GS2. Planned commodity swaps on a barter basis turned out to be an unsuccessful "invasion" of GS2. Currency-based trade and capitalist financial institutions and methods remained unharmed and dominant.

The *global system* may be recognized by interpreting historical data (i.e., by identifying GS0, GS1, and GS2) and by its negation through a society-wide examination and judgment of its incapacity to solve certain outstanding problems. The large variety of unbroken oppositions, protests, and expressions of dissatisfaction over problems it cannot possibly solve prevent us from considering the socioeconomic order a part of the natural world in the same way that we accept gravity or electromagnetism. This reflex-like society-wide phenomenon is not organized or cohesive. It comes from all strata of society and from all sectors and branches of economic organization. (For more on this subject, see Chapter 3.)

The *global system* reflects enduring aspects of socioeconomic relationships. It adheres strictly to its basic principles and fundamental characteristics (inspiring certain kinds of national institutions and socioeconomic environments), even if it adapts over time and lives through crises. Major national regulations revising the relationship between metal (gold and silver) and paper currency during GS1 left the metal-based monetary order the same, at least when one compares it with the post-1945 monetary system. During GS2, *multilateral* institutions may have gone through significant alterations (e.g., the "collapse" of the Bretton Wood system); and together they may have grown in importance since 1945, but, as a unified framework of international coexistence and cooperation, they remained essentially intact. Once GS2-typical individual and collective behavior no longer suffices to ensure a positive global perspective, the current world order will pass

---

12. Arnold J. Toynbee (1889-1975), historian and philosopher of history, assembled a great deal of evidence to demonstrate that mover-shaker minorities evolve from being "creative" to becoming "dominant," not excluding overlap between the two roles for a certain period.

too. Sandwiched between GS1 and (the hypothetically adopted) GS3, GS2 will reveal itself to be a macrohistoric phase, just as GS1 was.

As will be argued, the *global system* is written into the neocortex in the "language" of matter through linguistic symbolisms. Its presence is realized through signals that preserve their physico-chemical characteristics to ensure the continued identity of the *global system* despite the untold variety in individual conditions, major transformations in the world, and as the torch of life is passed from one generation to the next. Self-organization on a global scale is grounded in the *mind* (the brain's function space). Self-reorganization through the transformation of the *global system* or the alteration of shared consciousness about everyday conditions must take place there. From this perspective, world history is humanity's neuro-psychological biography.

A huge balancing act

A *global system* becomes a stationary resting interval only in retrospect, when it is identified as an inviolably closed epoch of history. Then a valid perspective on the epoch's macrohistory emerges. However, in any given moment during its existence, the *global system* is constantly buffeted by progression through its life cycle. It appears more like a tenuous balance of power, not only among the *vanguard* and the rest of the world, but also within the *vanguard*. The prevalence of the *global system* is a statistical phenomenon. Despite the great differences with which nations and the multitudes adapt to it, and despite the disorder and the unpredictability that characterize the world at any given moment, the *global system* remains definable and robust.

This phenomenon is well known in many sciences. In economics, the study of simultaneous equilibrium in all markets (resources and goods), in all nations, and in all economic relations became a specialized field of inquiry.[13] Theories of gen-

---

13.   General equilibrium theory in economics is the result of a monumental intellectual enterprise of several generations. An article by K.J. Arrow and G. Debreu, entitled "Existence of an Equilibrium for a Competitive Economy," published in *Econometrica* in July 1954, is regarded as the watershed in the development of today's applied (or computable) general equilibrium models used by international organizations, governments, and universities around the world to assess economic trends and to analyze policy alternatives. (Subsequently, both Arrow and Debreu earned the Nobel Prize in economics.) For a complete survey of the theoretical foundations of general equilibrium models, see V. Ginsburgh and M. Keyzer, "The Structure of Applied General Equilibrium Models," The MIT Press, 1997.

eral equilibrium are based on the observation that the market economy exists, prospers, and develops without a central authority telling firms what to produce and consumers what to buy. A sturdy tendency to restore equilibrium emerges from the decentralized decisions of sovereign producers and consumers, often causing havoc in particular markets, and pauses or reversals in economic growth. Through unremitting perturbations and occasionally significant shocks, levels of supply and demand search for one another in each market and in the aggregate. Thus, the competitive market economy is a "statistical system" or, equivalently, it shows "stochastic stability."

Institutions are not explicitly present in the equations and identities of general equilibrium models that describe the competitive economy; however, they are there implicitly. Market forces exert their balancing effects in a legally enforced institutional framework that provides, among many other things, a monetary and fiscal system. Therefore, the calibration of all-inclusive, cross-country, multisectoral general equilibrium models makes sense only during the established reign of a *global system.*

Whereas economic general equilibrium models approach the proof of order amidst the disorder of the world by relying on "average" or "typical" behavior,[14] the following example taken from the realm of statistical mechanics emphasizes the disorderly, varied compliance at the most detailed, microscopic level.

A simplified tenet of equilibrium statistical mechanics asserts that the macroscopic state will have an overbearing influence on microscopic states without being exacting and stern about the details.[15] An experiment with paramagnetism (the behavior of substances that have only a moderate susceptibility to magnetism) may help elucidate this phenomenon.[16] If we fill a tube with oxygen (liquid or gas) and place it in an external magnetic field, the oxygen molecules, tiny magnets in their own right, will align themselves with the poles of the magnetic field. The negative side of the molecule will turn toward the positive pole of the magnetic field and vice versa. Experiments have shown that, on a microscopic level involving individual molecules, compliance with the external magnetic force will not only be less than perfect but will also be half-hearted and capricious. The heat

---

14. In economic general equilibrium models, individuals are abstracted into a single utility-maximizing "representative consumer" and firms are abstracted into a profit-maximizing "representative producer."

15. See *Ruelle, 1991.* Historians of physics often cite the publications of Max Born (1882-1970) as the first milestone in statistical mechanics.

16. Erwin Schroedinger (1887-1961) used this example to illustrate the statistical nature of biological phenomena in his 1944 classic "What is Life?" (See *Schroedinger, 1967.*)

motion among molecules that causes them to agitate, shuffle, and interact without pause, will give the picture of a disorderly, if not chaotic, response to external magnetism. Nevertheless, the preponderance of rough and partial alignments on the molecular level will make the general principle of alignment precise and predictable at the level of the system. The large variety of partial compliances and the vagaries of *chaotic* interplay on the microscopic level translate into a strict order on the macroscopic level.

Probabilities (i.e., mathematically expressed likelihoods) are used to guess the level of alignment of individual oxygen molecules (or a group of them). This short cut is necessary because the observer has neither the means nor the interest to trace the movements of a single molecule to its *deterministic* core. Yet every event (the effect of one or more causes) that may seem *random* could be proven to be *deterministic* if we could just delve into it deeply enough and for a long enough period of time.

You stand in line in the Post Office and you would like to deal with one particular clerk among the three at the counter. Five persons are ahead of you. To establish with certitude whether or not your desire will be fulfilled, you would need perfect knowledge of what is going on at the counter now; what the people ahead of you have in mind, and how long it is going to take. Even so, you could not be one hundred percent sure. Someone could change his mind; some unforeseen event may intrude; spontaneous exchanges or unforeseen difficulties might throw the calculations off. Too much information, some of which is inaccessible, is needed to deal with too many unknowns. But do you really care that much? One falls back on simple probability. The *chances* of dealing with one particular clerk are one in three, i.e., one third. You will be helped; that is certain. Who will help you, and therefore, your trajectory to the counter remain *indeterminate*.

Similarly, conducting case studies on the behavior of particular molecules in the paramagnetic experiment goes beyond means and interest. It is sufficient to know that although a single molecule's behavior may vary beyond human ability to explain or predict, it will contain some level of conformity with the macroscopically imposed environment. The preponderance of "some conformity" will exclude configurations among the molecules that *en gros* contradict the system's unique characteristic of magnetic alignment.

The illustration of human relations with molecular behavior obviously requires some caveats and qualifications. In contrast to the paramagnetic experiment in which the benevolent science teacher observes the tube filled with oxygen from the outside, the *global system* (the external magnetic field) is developed by human organisms (the super-molecules) which are, of course, inside the tube.

Under these circumstances, as mentioned above, valid generalizations about what is going on in the tube and what happens to the external magnetic field require "hindsight." Further, the relationship between the *global system* and individuals around the world is much more complicated than the one between the external magnetic force and individual oxygen molecules. The connection among individuals (*microscopic* level) to form a *global system* (the *macroscopic* level) is not as direct as among molecules and takes place through an intermediate *mesoscopic* unit–the nation.

It is hard to see how the wildly disparate activities and behaviors of a barber in Houston, Texas and those of a Chinese peasant in Sichuan Province hang together under the current *global system.* However, each individual is connected to a nation (the United States and China), whose relations (composed of cooperative and competitive features) are an obviously recognizable component of the *global socioeconomic environment* that has a *system.* To see how the *macroscopic* order of the *global system* finds expression on an individual level, we must aggregate individuals into intermediary *mesoscopic* clusters–nations. The *macroscopically* imposed order, acting like an "external" magnetic field, compartmentalizes populations through this *mesoscopic* level. The *macroscopic* order prevails through various expressions of compliance with the *global system*'s principles on the *mesoscopic* level, which will appear as "the system" to its *microscopic* inhabitants. As much as national behavior may vary, it uniquely defines the *global system.* Personal behavior within a nation, with all its possible variations, shows sufficient compliance to be pervasive and dominant at the global level.

By labeling the prevalence of a *global system* "statistical," one combines well defined characterization at the global level with the probabilistic free play of *mesoscopic* aggregates, and within those, the free play of *microscopic* (individualistic) elements. Without the need to trace all the national or individual factors and decisions that affect the existence of a system, we know that *mesoscopic* and *microscopic* configurations must reflect *macroscopically* determined, enduring aspects of socioeconomic relations.

The crucible of global transformation

Difficulties in the process of changing any socioeconomic system increase as one moves farther away from the sovereign personal center and its kin-based extension–the family. Manifestly, the transformation of the *global system* (abbreviated as *global transformation*) is the most difficult because the number of people involved in it is at its maximum and because understanding of the system itself, let alone the process whereby it changes, is at its minimum, perhaps zero, *ex ante*.

The *global system* is temporary stasis manifest in national institutions and characteristic socioeconomic behavior. Given a rough constancy of ecological conditions, it endures as long as the compromise it represents between the socioeconomic environments it brought into existence and the human element lasts. Then it must change. But how? A *global system* is not hooked up to a diagnostic instrument that would monitor its progression through life. No central authority thinks up and evaluates alternatives for it. Consequently, its transformation must be the collective work of individuals. As Marx and Engels insisted, institutions shape thinking; however, institutions are "thinking" too. Thus, the collective transformation of global institutions means roughly that everybody's thinking must shape everybody's thinking under the particular condition that nobody's particular thinking is capable of shaping it. In practice, individual demands must always be pooled and translated into concerted actions to change any (multiperson) system. This process is particularly complex and drawn out in *global transformation*. Contradictory visions of the future must be sorted out through mankind's convulsive argument with itself–a period of blunders, discord, and delirious ordeals.

As the *global system* ages and becomes increasingly identified as the culprit behind the negative experiences and prospects in *surrounding socioeconomic milieus*, the disparate and unconnected streams of political sentiments and agendas begin to sort out affinities. Social and political groups form larger alliances whose mutual repulsion will disrupt the *global system*, plunging the world into disorder. Its onslaught presupposes a large-scale and contagious dissatisfaction. Many people must be convinced that the order under which they live is flawed beyond local dimensions and easy, practical remedies. But the subjectivity of *surrounding socioeconomic milieus* and the amalgamation of the external into internal reality make rebellion against the system slow to start.

To compete effectively, the individual must accept things as they are. It would lose self-esteem, weakening its will, and thereby the chances for successful differential performance, if it turned against the broader enveloping systems at the drop of a hat. Experience shows that the average adult goes a long way to blame itself or others in its immediate environment before it can be persuaded to confront the sanctioned and idealized institutions of the established order. Unwillingness to rebel is indefinitely bolstered by hope and belief that making adjustments in the *personal socioeconomic sphere* and finding a better *surrounding socioeconomic milieu* could provide satisfactory conditions for personal drives. The opposition of particular thinking to general thinking seems hopeless. In its prime, the *global system* is almighty. It appears to be "terminal" rather than "interim."

The reluctance to deviate from the rational, adaptive behavior known from analytical (as distinguished from evolutionary) game theory is so deeply ingrained in the individual that to "accomplish" the *global transformation* (i.e., to go through "1914-1945"), the potentially failed alternatives to GS1 (i.e., aggressive nationalism and international socialism) had to disguise themselves as legitimate, potentially enduring establishments with the power to reward *microscopic* adaptations.

◆   ◆   ◆

As Darwin said, each individual is engaged in a three-way struggle: with the physical environment, with organisms of other species, and with individuals of the same species. *Cultural evolution* may be considered progress because, through the associated accumulation of scientific-technological knowledge, humankind has advanced in controlling its physical environment, reduced its struggle with other species to medical battles against harmful viruses and bacteria, and moderated the fierceness of competition among its own ranks. Although "man against man" remains the most intense and dominant form among the three types of confrontation, *cultural evolution* tended to reduce social tensions. The growth of productivity allowed and demanded humane social policies, the creation of the "welfare state," which, for reasons of collectively judged interest (assuming the appearance of moral impulse or adherence to elevated social values), protects the genes of those who fall behind in the socioeconomic realm.

All the arguments in subsequent chapters are based on the conviction that *cultural evolution* has benefited mankind. It enhanced humanity's collective self-esteem, emancipating it *vis-à-vis* the physical environment. It increased the species' overall fitness in the struggle for existence and tended to make life longer and more fulfilling. *Cultural evolution* gave more in *freedom from want* than it took away in *freedom of action*. Higher productivity and more people forced stricter rules and greater pressure for conformity and compromise on the individual, but the balance is still positive. Personal freedom, the integrated and inseparable mix of *freedom from want* and *freedom of action*, is the greatest in the *vanguard*. Those who live outside of it, the majority of the planet's inhabitants, know it the best. (More on individual freedom in Chapter 10.)

One may object, and not without reason, that we use our own generation's opinion of *cultural evolution* as a backward applicable standard. Even an 18th century man, who considered himself progressive and subscribed to *Enlightenment* ideals, might see things differently. "Crowds, buildings on top of buildings, all these people with their gadgets, scurrying around in self-propelled, four-wheeled enclosures while talking into their palms; the beautiful landscape around my ancestral home is now a lot for parking the aforementioned enclosures; the air is foul, it is hard to breathe. And why are members of the laborious classes and colored people smiling at me as if they were my equals? And women judges? You call this progress?" There may be no truly objective transgenerational standards. Judgment is conditioned by the environment as the environment conditions judgment; and those alive always have the last word.

3

Macrohistory and Metahistory

[The generalization of Karl Polanyi's "double movement" is key to formulating *macrohistory* and *metahistory*. *Macrohistory* of the past 200 years through the evolution of *global systems*: GS1, *global transformation* (1914-1945), and GS2. *Metahistory* expands the concept of *global system* to *relatively steady socioeconomic conditions* and the concept of *global transformation* to *chaotic transition*. This allows the analysis of emerging capitalism in feudalistic framework (GS0) along with GS1 and GS2, and "1789-1834" along with "1914-1945." The *metahistory* of 1500-2000 shows a persistent rhythm of the world process, revealing its thermodynamic-evolutionary nature. Connection to Hegel and other philosophers.]

Macrohistory refers to developments that affected continents or the entire world over centuries. In this case, "meta" stands for the intention to transcend the concise facticity of macrohistory in search of general patterns. Macrohistorians are also metahistorians if they reassemble and characterize developments in order to demonstrate stages and identify regularities and consistencies in the progression of events. Metahistory pares down macrohistoric information and refocuses it. If macrohistory were a two-hour movie about what happened to the world during the past two centuries, metahistory would seek patterns in the fluctuation of light and sound and would record the acceleration or deceleration of movements.

Metahistory is the missing link between the biologically expressed thermodynamic process of *cultural evolution* and the socially focused macrohistory. It goes beyond macrohistory to faceless principles that explain how the growing magnitude of somatic and extrasomatic energy incorporated into *culture* retains direction while its self-organization complexifies. Because it reduces macrohistory to the operation of abstract rules, metahistory represents the *deterministic* component of *cultural evolution*.

Before we describe the proposed theory's *macrohistory* (henceforth in italics), a few words about Karl Polanyi's discovery, which is basic to it.

KARL POLANYI: A SOURCE OF EPIPHANY

The setting sun of the Austro-Hungarian Monarchy fermented a cosmopolitan, intellectual brilliance whose effects on global civilization are still being felt. Karl Polanyi (1886-1964), economic historian, anthropologist, sociologist, social philosopher, lawyer, and linguist, was a shining example of that last, influential generation that was nurtured under the moribund wings of the Hapsburg eagle. His father was a railroad engineer and his mother, Cecilia Wohl, kept a literary salon in Vienna and Budapest, Austria-Hungary's two capitals. Karl was born in Vienna, but he soon became Károly when the family settled in Budapest. He studied law and liberal arts there and became a practicing lawyer. Life was good for many, but was bad for even more. Poverty and ruthless oppression festered in the shadow of Franz Joseph's throne. Like many other intellectuals, Polanyi also leaned toward the political left.

The Great War found him in the Imperial and Royal ("K und K") cavalry. He was captured by the Russians, but returned to Hungary soon after the 1917 cease-fire. Hungary's 1919 communist coup d'etat awakened in him the hope of democratically-based social progress in the region. Of course, this did not happen. Hungary's Soviet Republic brought terror and came to a violent end in three months.

In 1920, he met his match—Ilona Duczynska, a diplomed engineer, writer, and political activist who played a prominent role in the 1919 "Commune." Ilona and Károly became companions in a life full of hard trials. They first settled in Vienna, since Ilona would have been prosecuted in Hungary for her role in the failed communist government. Károly became Karl again and made his living from journalism. His revolutionary anger against social injustice resurfaced in his writings and associations, but he remained well within the legal bounds of Vienna's liberal traditions. He soon recognized the deadly danger that was coming his way in the early 1930s as the Nazis moved toward power in Germany and found support in the newly created Alpine republic. The couple moved to Great Britain and became British subjects.

Polanyi's reputation as an excellent lecturer with original, non-Marxist anti-*laissez faire* views spread to America. He taught at Bennington College in Vermont from 1940 to 1943 and was Visiting Professor of Economics at Columbia

University in New York after the war. Karl and Ilona elected not to join the communist world of Eastern Europe following World War II. It was a wise decision. The Rakosi regime, which became the surrogate of Stalin's terror state in Hungary, executed numerous liberally disposed individuals who had participated in the socialist-communist movement.

Karl Polanyi's economic philosophy criticized the "consumer society." It could not have found a worse place and time than America of the early 1950s. Western governments, with the United States in the lead, backed by public opinion and the vast majority of economists and other social scientists, defended the importance of the market in the *mixed economy* and in international economic relations. The Western body politic reacted not only to the Marxist propaganda coming from the Eastern Bloc, but also against the "homegrown" political left that wanted to shift the "mix" in the *mixed economy*, which was still in its formative years, toward more "state" and less "market." Although he stopped teaching, Karl Polanyi received research grants in the United States and became a classic of political economy, with unique, independent views.

In *The Great Transformation* (1944), Polanyi demonstrated that *laissez faire capitalism* developed during the 19th century as the major economic powers saw to the creation of national markets for labor, land, and money, as well as to the unfettering of goods and services markets. Conditions for the establishment of the system may have been present, but it took active state intervention, the creation of new institutions, the introduction of some legislative and administrative measures, and the voiding of some others, to clear the ground for the free play of market forces. Polanyi argued that before the establishment of *laissez faire capitalism*, the economic functions of local and national communities were "embedded" in their social relations, i.e., institutions, laws, customs, and ethical values. The establishment of *laissez faire* overturned this relationship by subordinating society to the market or by "disembedding" society.

With carefully documented arguments, Polanyi showed that the *laissez faire* system provoked a widely-based, uncoordinated, and protracted backlash that, although for very different reasons, included practically every segment of society in the industrialized and industrializing countries. Workers and miners demanded that their wages, hours of work, and working conditions be regulated; capitalists wanted protection against monopolies and the crudest forms of market conduct, and broad society wanted product safety regulations and other public services. The *laissez faire* system (GS1 in our interpretation) unleashed a reflex-like, unrelenting, society-wide reaction against itself.

Polanyi's thoughts help disperse false impressions about history. It is neither a series of loosely connected events whose origins reside in the national psyche and in the subjective will of political leaders, nor a tale about the "market" and how its eternally and universally valid principles became institutions and how these institutions evolved. He reminded his readers and audiences that humans are cooperative beings with a penchant for sharing. Creativity, ingenuity, and entrepreneurship are motivated by ancient, deeply ingrained desires to serve communal objectives and earn social standing. Mere *mammonism* (rational compliance with the adaptive drive toward differential socioeconomic success along the canonical scale) cannot explain history. Humanity cannot be equated to tradesmen with insatiable appetites for pecuniary recompense. Polanyi considered the social Darwinist view that the *laissez faire* system is a jungle, where every man battles every other man for maximum gain, a phase, a time-dependent illusion that will pass.

At this point the reader might think that Polanyi was an effective and passionate critic of GS1, whose relevance had to decline as GS2 became encrusted in the *global socioeconomic environment*. But then came globalization and the reflex-like movement against it.

After the conclusion of the Uruguay Round, which established the World Trade Organization (WTO), governments tried to create a planetary *laissez faire* system–an action that provoked a worldwide protest to disable or eliminate it. The protest movement included as its target the whole economic-financial apparatus of *multilateral* cooperation, primarily the WTO, the International Monetary Fund, and The World Bank (i.e., GS2's international institutions). Economists of the neoliberal mold (practically the entire economics profession in the 1990s) used arguments in support of complete trade liberalization that were similar to the ones their predecessors used in support of the *laissez faire* system in England in the 19th century. And the reasoning behind the reflex-like enmity against economic liberalization was reminiscent of the polemic deployed against the "One Big Market" of yore: The global society had been subordinated to the global market. There it is again–the "Polanyian double-movement." But this time, the broad-based opposition to allowing the market to regain its role as the natural mode of social organization was aimed at the *multilateral* framework of international cooperation.

Legitimation, progressive as it may be, is a claim to permanence. It brings convention, dogmatic conformity, and indifference. While it opens new passageways, it also eliminates old ones and creates new obstructions. As soon as some doors close, the tapping on them begins. Heterodoxy shouts that the closures are abnormal and unnatural; orthodoxy replies that they are as normal as anything that springs from the very germ of nature, and it secures the bolts. Order and its defiance (from remonstrations to riots) are like a hyperdynamic, dialectical couple. They cannot live with or without one another. These confrontational tendencies are permanent in human organizations. They embody the *second law of thermodynamics*, the nemesis of structure and permanence (more on this subject in Chapters 5 and 10). The "Polanyian double-movement" only helps us see them on a global scale and in a longer historical context. Support of and opposition to a *global system* confirm its (provisional) existence through the continuous and reciprocal relationship between assertion and negation.

The generalization of Karl Polanyi's "double movement" provides the backbone of *macrohistory*. The introduction of a world system and immediate, society-wide opposition to it was not isolated to 19th century *laissez faire*.

MACROHISTORY THROUGH THE PRISM OF GLOBAL SYSTEMS

As the title suggests, *macrohistory* can be regarded as socioeconomic evolution. This makes *macrohistory* the synopsis of the human drama on the subject of how the species organized itself to facilitate *cultural evolution*. So far, the drama has had three acts: GS1, *global transformation,* and GS2.

GS1 did not spring onto history's stage fully armed like Pallas Athena from the head of Zeus. Its principles emerged from a causal chain of developments that fade into the murky, ante-primitive past, to surface in distinct half-formulations during early recorded history. They appeared in more and more complete forms until they gradually filled the air and became law and axiom—quasi-religious convictions fixed firmly in individual minds.

Names and historical episodes cited in connection with the development of the first *global system* serve only as color codes on trees along a nature trail. The spotty record still suffices to discover direction. Social, economic, religious, scientific, and cultural histories during the prelude to modern capitalism tell of an incessant pressure and catalysis, sometimes silent and low-key, sometimes noisy and violent, that moved Europe into the driver's seat of world history and toward the great transformation of its agricultural, feudalistic-aristocratic societies of the late Renaissance into industry-oriented, bourgeois-liberal national systems in the 19th century.

During 1500-1789 (GS0), the world underwent sweeping changes as preparations for the age of *global systems* accelerated. European explorations and colonization nearly completed geographic globalization. Modern scientific thinking emerged and vital discoveries were made in physics, chemistry, biology, medicine, and astronomy. The period is noted for recognizing individual liberty as a "natural law" and the nation as a form of sovereign territorial organization; for discovering social progress and prying the frozen fingers of dogmatic thinking from the human mind. Among many classics of intellectual history, Bacon (1561-1626), Galileo (1564-1642), Shakespeare (1564-1616), Hobbes (1588-1679), Moliere (1622-1673), Locke (1632-1704), Newton (1642-1727), Bach (1685-1750), Hume (1711-1776), and Adam Smith (1723-1790) graced GS0's timescape. The period also hosted the Wars of Religion, the English Civil War, the *philosophes,* the *Enlightenment,* and the development of the economic doctrine called *laissez faire.*

Although the philosophy of *laissez faire*[1] was born in 18th century France, it reached full maturity as a socioeconomic organizational principle and agenda in the British Isles. As is well known, David Hume, Adam Smith, Thomas Robert Malthus (1766-1834), Jean Baptiste Say (1767-1832), David Ricardo (1772-1823), and Jeremy Bentham (1748-1832) were among the historical apostles of *laissez faire.* John Stuart Mill (1806-1873) is recognized as the chronologically last major philosophical patriarch and first influential critic of the ideology.[2]

Entrepreneurial intelligence, allied with the drive for profit and led by supply and demand conditions on unhampered markets, will take care of economic progress, as if guided by a *Hidden Hand.* This is the basic principle of economic organization under *laissez faire.* Its more detailed elaborations demonstrate that

---

1. The expression itself was coined by the French Physiocrats. François Quesnay (1694-1774) was their most celebrated representative. Jacques C. M. Vincent de Gournay (1712-1759) is credited for introducing the slogan *laissez faire et laissez passer* to characterize and complete the meaning of *laissez faire.* It may be translated as "stand by and do nothing in the face of actions freely chosen by others."

2. The ethical and analytical roots of *laissez faire* capitalism may be traced back to antiquity, in particular to the Greek philosopher Aristotle (384-322 BCE) who separated a commodity's use value from its price, tackled the issue of "just price," and condemned "monopoly." His economic philosophy may be interpreted as the earliest implicit understanding of the importance of free competition. The scholastic philosophers of the 16th century, whose probing minds often strayed from dissecting the efficacy of God's grace, explicitly recognized the desirability and fairness of competitive market prices, thus also qualifying as evolutionary ancestors on the analytical side of *laissez faire* (see *Schumpeter, 1954,* p. 99).

the system maximizes both the efficient use of economic resources (land, labor, and capital) as well as social welfare (utility); and that occasional downturns in the "trade cycle" are self-correcting.

Laissez faire ensures efficiency through competition that leaves the allocation of resources in the hands of those who respond to the fullest extent, with the greatest alacrity, and through the application of the most productive technology to satisfy society's needs. Increases in the prices of commodities in short supply express social needs. Higher prices mean more income for those who provide the needed supplies; more income means a greater ability to hire labor and invest. Thus, competition guarantees that the goods desired by society will be delivered; that this will happen in the most efficient ways, and that participants in the economic process will earn their fair rewards. Those who are ahead in responding to society's material demands will earn more than those who fall behind in the race. This scheme of economic organization was completed with the social philosophy of freedom of enterprise, that is, to seek wealth with equal rights. All these ideas were in harmony with the natural order of the universe discovered during GS0.

David Hume's disquisition on the "price-specie flow" (part of his *Essays*, published in 1752) laid the groundwork for making *laissez faire* a global organizational principle. In his still widely read "gold standard manifesto," Hume presented the mechanism that could hold the world's nationally compartmentalized economies in harmony. He explained lucidly that if all national monetary systems were based on the gold standard (i.e., exchanged paper money for gold at a fixed rate, thereby also fixing exchange rates among national paper moneys) and if governments overcame their "jealous fear" of losing gold (i.e., if they just did not interfere) trade flows would steady themselves by tending to eliminate nationally recorded trade deficits and matching surpluses. (The two must *per force* equal since the world is a closed economy; all trade shipments remain on the planet.) Surplus countries (those registering more exports than imports over a given period) would attract gold from the deficit countries (the ones that imported more than exported). However, since the domestic "exchange rate" between gold and paper (called the "official parity") is fixed, as are the international exchange rates among the national currencies, prices must decline in the deficit countries and increase in the surplus countries, creating the force that would reverse the respective balance of payments positions. Goods would flow from the deficit to the surplus countries while gold would move in the opposite direction.

To secure the efficacy of this natural equilibration, banks had to gear their credit policies accordingly. Credit would have to be restricted in the deficit countries, contracting the money supply and reducing both imports and the prices of domestic products. In contrast, credit would have to be expanded in the surplus countries to raise domestic prices, thereby reducing exports and opening the door wider for low-priced goods from the deficit countries. Such accommodating monetary measures later became known as "the rules of the game," an expression attributed to John Maynard Keynes (1883-1946). Banks in the deficit country would be inclined to protect their gold by raising interest rates. Higher rates meant less loan activity, a contraction in the domestic money supply, lower prices, greater export potential, and the attraction of foreign deposits (since these would earn more). The opposite incentive would affect banks in the surplus countries where gold has accumulated. Gold might be good to have and pleasant to look at, but it earns no interest. Consequently, surplus country banks would be motivated to buy domestic, interest-bearing assets, thereby increasing the money supply and pushing down interest rates. Domestic funds in search of higher earnings would be attracted to the higher interest rates offered by banks in the deficit countries. Capital outflow meant gold outflow because the potential depositor in the surplus country would demand gold for his domestic currency to buy the deficit country's currency. Although a bank in the deficit country might accept the surplus country depositor's (foreign) currency, it would want to exchange it for the gold of the foreign-currency-issuing (surplus) country. The same principles would apply if governments extended the use of metal as a monetary base to include silver. Silver remained important through most of GS1, but gold gained the upper hand and eventually became dominant.

In reality, the adjustment prompted by imbalances was a much more complicated phenomenon than what was implied by the bare-bones model of the "price-specie flow" and the "rules of the game." Many experts now contend that prices were not as flexible as the model presumed, that gold movements among countries did not take place to the extent one would expect, and that the "rules of the game" were never followed to the letter. Willingness to inflate in the gold-accumulating country and deflate in the gold-losing country, thereby undergoing different kinds of economic pains to accomplish the common goal of adjustment, may have been weak from the start. However, these deviations from the ideal do not change the fact that international economic relations founded on metal money brought relative harmony, stability, and mutual gains to nations that shared the paradigm. One may even venture to say that nations did play by the "rules of the game," if we redefine the "game" as "engage in discrete, national banking practices to allow the evolution of the economy within your borders, but without stretching your gold or preventing its efflux to the point where public trust in paper/sovereign convertibility would be shaken."

Laissez-faire economic principles, in combination with the species-based monetary system, formed a comprehensive, inherently rational, universally applicable socioeconomic model upon which national institutions and individual situations could be built and maintained.

In the aftermath of the Napoleonic Wars, the menace of popular uprising disappeared in Europe. Tempers calmed down. Drastic measures to create large and freely accessible labor pools became socially and politically feasible. The opportunity arose to put the technological potential created by the (First) Industrial Revolution (cca. 1780-1830) to wealth-generating use. Nowhere was the coincidence between the green light for a major social restructuring and the roaring and puffing industrial takeoff more potent than in Britain. The 1821 activation of the "Resumption Act of 1819" made the convertibility of notes into gold effective. An intense flurry of legislation occurred between 1831 and 1841. Enactment of the "Poor Law Amendment" (the abolition of "Speenhemland") in 1834 was the critical moment, making the year the symbolic birth date of GS1. By voiding the obligation of feudal lords to take care of the poor and helpless living in their properties, and establishing workhouses for those who remained unemployed, the "poor legislation" created a reserve army of industrial workers that invited capital investment. 1834 also saw the legal elimination of slavery in the British Empire. Legislation concerning electoral franchise pushed to enhance the influence of urban centers and curb the power of landed aristocracy and the church.[3] Progressive as these laws were from the point of view of the bourgeoisie, they effectively deprived the newly created industrial proletariat of the vote. The spectrum of legal conditions set the SEEI at a low starting point, allowing it to struggle upward, satisfying for decades the *global system*'s inherent need to show socioeconomic progress. The period that began with the French Revolution in 1789 and ended with the British legislative process cited above, which reached its highwater mark in 1834, may be seen as a *chaotic transition* similar to "1914-1945." (The parallel between GS0—>GS1 and GS1—>GS2 will be important in delineating *metahistory*.)

The world's first national economy with capitalist commodity and resource markets stepped into the arena of universal history, and the rest of the economically, socially, and scientifically weightiest nations followed. Measures to create similar *laissez faire* arrangements spread across Europe (sometimes in the wake of

---

3.   For the legislative, social, and political background of GS1, see *Polanyi, 1957.*

political upheavals) and then to the rest of the world. The American Republic was born with the preconditions and a natural proclivity for *laissez faire*. International trade grew. Britain's repeal of the protectionist "Corn Laws" in 1846 is considered the key legislative event that led to worldwide trade liberalization. Despite the use of tariffs by governments to raise revenue and/or to protect their domestic industries, free trade reigned until the outbreak of World War I. That is, trade was free relative to what followed.

Great Britain occupied a unique position of power and leadership in the world. It enjoyed industrial superiority, acquired as a result of the Industrial Revolution, and it was an unequaled maritime power. The militarily invincible superpower with global reach became the staunchest supporter of free trade and the model of prudent public and private finance. Views uttered by a member of Her Majesty's Government or a leading banker in the City of London reverberated throughout the Continent and in the far corners of the world. This status allowed Great Britain to engage in subtle political and financial manipulations. The Victorian period of GS1 may be characterized appropriately as Pax Britannica.

The extent and form of adopting and imitating the organizational principles of GS1 varied greatly. The patchiness of compliance with the gold standard in time and substance amply supports this assertion. It is difficult even to put a date on the commencement of the gold standard era. In retrospect, 1821 may be considered the crucial year, but some have argued for 1867-8, when the Paris Conference took place. The latter reflected French ambitions to create a monetary union, which, through rules of precious metal coinage, would have provided an alternative to the gold standard. The negative reaction to this politicized effort inadvertently reinforced the international drive toward the politically neutral gold standard. In contemporary textbooks and literature, 1870 or 1880 is the "year." However, some particularly strict economic historians suggest 1900, by which time several major countries (including Japan and Russia) went on gold and the United States (on and off gold until that year and not completely abandoning silver) made the gold standard the law of the land.

Adherence to the gold standard was far from uniform. According to Arthur I. Bloomfield,[4] from 1880 to 1914, England and Germany adhered to the "full" gold standard; France, Belgium, and Switzerland were on a so-called "limping" gold standard (meaning some relaxation in the extent and constancy of redemption of money or commercial papers into gold); Russia, Japan, Austria-Hungary,

---

4.   *Bloomfield, 1959.*

the Netherlands, Canada, South Africa, Australia, and New Zealand were on the gold-exchange standard (meaning that the bulk, if not all, of their monetary reserves were in foreign exchange redeemable for gold); India, the Philippines, and some other Asian and Latin American countries used a more watered down version of the gold-exchange standard. Countries such as Italy, Mexico, and Bulgaria dropped out of the gold standard and then dropped back in again. Italy was mostly on the gold exchange standard, although for some periods, particularly between 1883 and 1891, it was on a stricter form of the gold standard. Several countries never adopted "gold" in any of its known modalities. Spain and several Latin American countries used paper money; China and some Central American countries stuck to silver.

Some countries had central banks; others did not. The United States lived through GS1 without one. (The Federal Reserve System became operational in 1914.) Having a central bank bolstered the national government's credibility of exchanging paper currency for precious metal and influenced its capacity to bend "the rules of the game" in pursuit of some limited form of national monetary policy.

Despite versatile applications, fluctuations in adherence to the ground rules, willful manipulations by governments and banks, and vastly different national experiences, one may still safely say that the metal-based financial and monetary regimes constituted an enduring framework for international economic relations. There was a system under which exchange rates among national currencies held stable (particularly during the closing decades of GS1), effectively linking national price levels and markets through the universal, nondiscriminatory recognition of commodity value and wealth. This system had the following characteristics: (a) national governments in the countries that formed the center of the system remained credible in their pledges to exchange paper currency for precious metal at a stipulated price; (b) the advantages offered by the inflow of capital and participation in world trade motivated compliance with GS1 principles outside the *vanguard*; (c) it was unfit for countercyclical monetary and/or fiscal policies according to the way we have come to understand these concepts since the instauration of GS2; (d) it had a restricted ability to increase the global money supply (required for the expansion of output and trade); and (e) cooperation among national governments, including central banks, if any, remained limited.[5]

---

5.   For a comprehensive assessment of the gold standard from both theoretical and historical standpoints, see the introduction by Barry Eichengreen and Marc Flandreau to the collection of essays and studies on the gold standard in *Eichengreen and Flandreau, 1997.*

Adaptations of GS1 organizing principles and mechanisms ranged from close resemblances to the British prototype to institutions that were relatively primitive and virtually outside of the system. However, by all accounts, there were enough common characteristics in national institutions and a sufficient coherence in international economic and trade relations to recognize the existence of a *global system*, a stasis in the world's socioeconomic evolution, a relatively stable dynamic regime. Growing average per capita incomes and widening, mutually beneficial international trade and other forms of economic contacts provided the shared interest for the world's most powerful countries in the system's continued existence. Dazzling technological breakthroughs, the growing mass transportation across and between continents, and the pulsating commercial and cultural life in New York, London, Paris, Berlin, Vienna, and St. Petersburg were among the many persuasive symbols of limitless progress, bolstering respect for the world order in good times and grudging acceptance in bad ones.

Nation-building and globalization characterized GS1. Turbulent and often bloody roads led to the creation of two major European nation states: Italy (1861) and Germany (1871). In both cases, a nucleus (Piedmont in emerging Italy and Prussia in emerging Germany) led territorial integration, using among other methods, trade liberalization *vis-à-vis* other territorial units as integrational catalyst. We may apply the modern concept of regional integration to the creation of Italy and Germany. This concept refers to a series of ever tighter agreements among the participants, leading from free trade (i.e., a free trade agreement) through common customs (i.e., customs union), to monetary and economic unification, and eventually to speaking with a single voice in matters of international commerce, foreign policy, and military affairs. In addition to nation-building, there were (now long-gone) international agreements such as the Latin Monetary Union, which included France, Belgium, Greece, Italy, and Switzerland. These were early signs of the regional integration so profusely attempted in the current era. (See under GS2.)

Globalization means increased international interconnectedness and decrease in the ability of a nation to get along without the rest of the world. In a strict and limited numerical sense, it occurs when cross-border activities such as trade, investment, and transportation increase in significance. Growth in the "global trade-to-output" ratio illustrates the process. It relates world exports (or imports, since the two are identical) to world output. Its growth during a given period signifies that the planet's population increased the exchange of commodities across national frontiers faster than within national frontiers. A rough estimate shows that the global trade-to-output ratio of 10-11 percent in the early 19th century grew to 15 percent by 1913.[6] The significance of growth in the ratio is even greater since, early in the 19th century, two great European economic powers, Germany and Italy, were still just a congeries of independent countries. Their domestic trade was international before unification, intranational afterwards (thus reducing global exports or imports in the numerator of the quotient). Besides augmentation in the "global trade-to-output" ratio, many other developments, such as the increasing flows of capital (mainly from Europe to the rest of the world), intercontinental telegraph, and improved quality and rising quantity of international transportation of people and commodities pointed to strengthening connectedness. Compared to their level following the outbreak of World War I, tariffs remained relatively low. The ease with which individuals could conduct international business during GS1, free from government interference, still makes some economists nostalgic as they wax eloquent about a level of globalization never to be seen again. (Contemporary, "GS2 globalization" is not quite comparable to its GS1 predecessor. See more on this subject below.)

World population and output increased during GS1. Since output growth outpaced population growth, per capita income increased. Socioeconomic equalization also progressed, particularly in the *vanguard*. Voting rights were extended. In Great Britain, the "working class" got the vote in two steps, 1867 and 1884; and by the last third of the 19th century, property, race, and religious restrictions had been abolished for males in the United States. Feminism as an emancipatory social and cultural movement found its place in the general consciousness. Unions grew stronger in the industrialized countries and some of their demands for increased government responsibility in matters of welfare were met. Public expenditures per capita increased in the *vanguard* throughout the 19th century and social security-type payments (e.g., health, unemployment insurance, and pensions) appeared on a modest scale. The great transformation succeeded.[7] *Cultural evolution* advanced. All three of its indices pointed upward. However, even as GS1 expanded across the world, and evolved and perfected itself, the undercurrents for its demise were already gathering momentum.

---

6. Author's estimate, based on data provided by *Rostow, 1978*.
7. Max Weber (1864-1920) reported that, based on a survey he conducted in Germany, workers preferred to be proletarians rather than serfs on some Junker's estate.

◆   ◆   ◆

GS1 was losing its ability to accommodate *cultural evolution*. Sooner or later, gold had to become a drag on economic growth. Expansion in the goods produced and services performed had (and still has) an agile dynamic of its own. Expansion in the supply of a precious metal (*ab ovo* rare) could not possibly keep up with and mimic this time evolution. Gold discoveries, like those in the United States (1847 and 1866), in Australia (1851), in South Africa (1885), and in Canada (1897), and advances in gold mining productivity, such as extraction by cyanide introduced in 1887, could not answer the growing demand for money and gave *random* shocks to the world's financial sector. Governments "stretched" and protected their gold supplies, for example, through the increasing use of gold as a monetary reserve and less as money in circulation, and by violating the "rules of the game;" that is, by not pursuing "cheap money" policy when gold supplies increased, nor "dear money" policy when they decreased. The clock was ticking on the ability of governments to expand the money supply needed for economic growth without losing the credibility of banks to hand out gold coins for "local purchasing power."

National governments could not engage in monetary or fiscal policies on the scale that would have countered economy-wide downward trends. Increasing the money in circulation or engaging in deficit spending would have endangered their gold reserves because both of these employment-promoting channels of state intervention tend to raise prices and depreciate the national currency, making foreign purchase of domestic gold a profitable enterprise. When two currencies are tied to gold at a fixed parity, the one that has appreciated is worth more in terms of gold in the country whose currency depreciated, creating opportunity for *arbitrage.*

At the same time, intervention into the business cycle, helping the economy get over slumps quickly and putting on the brakes when it overheats, would have been increasingly appropriate. At the outset of GS1, when Jean Baptiste Say formulated his famous "law of the markets," economies may have been expected to recover on their own. There is no reason to doubt Say's powers of observation and the perspicacity of his induction. When demand fell, prices and wages also fell, until unsold supplies became both attractive and affordable. "Supply created its own demand" and the economy moved toward full employment. However, as economies increased, became more complex, and developed more interdependent, capital intensive sectors, chances for quick, unaided recoveries disappeared.

To guarantee full employment, the desired levels of aggregate capital invest-ment and household savings must match. Not only did both variables (aggregate savings and aggregate investment) grow in size, thereby increasing the stakes for a potential mismatch between their critical subcategories, but they also became less predictable. Higher per capita income gave a measure of volatility to the level and structure of expenditures, provoking, in turn, even larger responses in capital for-mation (investment). The bigger and more complex an economy, the more it is inclined to swing up and down in the absence of conscious government policy to counteract movement away from stable growth in either direction. Even a steady increase in consumer spending is apt to generate signals for upstream industries, leading to a euphoric overestimation of the demand for productive capacity. The resultant increase in investment, added to the steady increase of consumption, means an acceleration of the national output. Once consumer expenditures slow down or decline, investment decelerates, thereby shrinking national output, caus-ing widespread lay-offs, and leaving productive capacities idle. Under these cir-cumstances, waiting for "natural," *laissez faire* style, "Sayian" recovery becomes increasingly wasteful for both labor and capital.

The economic history of 19th century capitalism proved this logic correct. The depression of 1873-1886, without a convincing recovery until 1896, began to undermine firm belief in *laissez faire*'s theoretically expected automatism to heal itself. (The Great Depression of the 1930s finished it off.) Even worse for the lon-gevity of GS1 was the growing public demand for stabilization and welfare mea-sures. This request could not be answered on a satisfactory scale because it would have required extensive macroeconomic powers to conduct fiscal and monetary policies, which was impossible under the metal money system.

By today's standards, the economic situation of the working class was appall-ing. Starvation and illiteracy were widespread. Hopelessness drove millions of Europeans to emigrate to America and to Great Britain's "white colonies" (Can-ada, Australia, and New Zealand). The conditions in the European core of GS1 cannot be ascribed simply to the lower average per capita income of the epoch. One cannot say that the level of living reflected a lower average productivity rela-tive to later periods; personal misfortunes and unsuccessful adaptations to *sur-rounding socioeconomic milieus*, blaming, in essence, the individual. The lack of legal and institutional frameworks for collective bargaining had to have an effect on the distribution of income between capital and labor.

GS1's primal *laissez faire* came with insurmountable obstacles to progress in socioeconomic equality. The organization of labor and the social safety net demand upward flexibility and downward inflexibility in wages and prices and public power to ensure economic expansion. However, retaining the profit motive presupposes the ability of business to recoup wage increases and higher taxes paid to finance public programs. Any loss in unit profit, owing to higher wages and taxes, allows businesses to keep running only if they will be more than compensated for by an increased volume of sales, thus raising their revenues. But GS1 institutions could not ensure an increase in the volume of sales, that is, economic expansion. Theoretically, balanced budgets could have been used to redistribute income; however, deficit spending was needed for countercyclical policies.

As GS1 aged, reality got away from it. Downward wage and price rigidities began to spread in contradiction to its institutional order and organizational principles. The growing political power of industrial workers prevented wages, hence also prices, from declining. This spontaneous intrusion of a future system (i.e., GS2) only underscored GS1's helpless obsolescence. It diminished chances for a *Sayian*, unaided upturn (which hinges on downward wage/price flexibility) as chances for downturns going deeper increased, not only because the economies became bigger and more complex, but also as a result of spreading wage/price inflexibility.

The lack of *multilateral* organization was the hallmark of GS1. The system did not include institutions for cooperation and coordination of economic policies among national governments. However, as trade and cross-border capital movements gained in importance and as business became increasingly prone to self-generated waves in output levels, the absence of global institutional arrangements became a growing hindrance to economic development. Tensions grew among and within nations, and the world drifted toward a period of structural instability and frenetic self-search.

◆   ◆   ◆

Germany's industrial might developed at a dizzying pace during the second half of the 19th century. The difference in the speed of economic growth between Germany and the colonial powers of Europe provides an immediate rationale for the actual scenario that led to the decomposition of GS1.

The Hohenzollern establishment profoundly disliked Pax Britannica and looked at the West European colonial powers and Russia (a Eurasian colonial power) with increasing envy and suspicion. As combustion engines spread in the early years of the 20th century, British-American control of the oil-rich Middle East became a particular irritant for German industrialists. The Kaiser's diplomacy and commercial policy extended German influence in Eastern Europe and overseas and rubbed against the interests of the Atlantic world. Berlin was convinced that France, a nation that suffered a humiliating defeat at the hands of Prussia in 1870, engaged in a conscious, militarily-backed effort to constrain Germany's international economic and political potential. The Kaiser and his entourage suspected that the French ruling elite was looking for an opportunity to break up Germany, which did not become a *bona fide* nation state until 1871. They feared that the countries allied with France shared these aspirations. In general, European states with overseas territorial possessions were concerned that Germany's ultimate geopolitical goal was a redistribution of those possessions, by force, if necessary. A sympathetic resonance to Germany's anticolonialist rhetoric within and without Europe only added to their ire. By the end of the 19th century, the European alliances that approximated the "line-up" in the First World War were already in place; however, hostilities were kept at bay by the shared concern for the conditions of stability that allowed the expansion of international economic relations.

In the spirit of untamed *laissez faire,* West European nations and Russia were engaged in a relentless competition among themselves to extend their respective spheres of influence. Toward the end of the 19th century, the "scramble for Africa" was, in every respect, as cruel as earlier campaigns of colonization. The rising industrial empire of Japan joined the fray of maximizing territorial control beyond national borders. It invaded China and annexed Korea, but not without being diplomatically challenged by Western powers that regarded Asia as their own territory to be divided up into spheres of influence among themselves. The United States expanded its control over Latin America and in the Pacific region. Anger against foreign domination and aspirations for independence emerged in Eastern Europe, Asia (particularly in China and India), North Africa, and other parts of the world.

Tensions were also building up within nations. Western Europe seemed to have all the advantages in preempting working class discontent. Not only were states in the region ahead in economic development, but they also had access to the manpower, raw materials, and markets of their overseas possessions. They were in a position to raise living standards at home in the metropolitan centers of Europe at the expense of the colonies. Yet this balancing act was only partially successful. The better educated and socially more advanced West European working class demanded more than was made available to it both in terms of material goods and socioeconomic equality. Solidarity with the colonized people began to stir in West European capitals.

Inequities between developed Western/Germanophone Central Europe (Germany and Austria) and Eastern Europe/Russia found expression in the effects of economic downturns. With a much larger segment of the population living at the subsistence level in the East, industrialization ("development") had the perverse effect of causing a greater hardship during busts than previously known. Laid-off workers were abandoned to their own devices in slum-like factory districts that became hotbeds of revolutionary agitation.[8]

There were violent strikes and demonstrations across Europe. Social upheaval and anarchy haunted Russia. The Marxist strand of the socialist-communist ideology, which gradually dominated peaceful reformists within the socialist movement, advocated class warfare and revolution on an international scale. The Marxist agitator argued that the enemy of the exploited social classes was not the other nation but the international conspiracy of the *haute finance* allied with the home-grown ruling classes. When economic difficulties surfaced, the national elites in Europe blamed other countries and the socialist agitators blamed the exploiters, regardless of nationality. The global order came under threat. During the four decades preceding World War I, it was anyone's guess whether social classes or nations would jump at each others' throats. Of course, the second alternative came to pass, although not without the influence of class warfare.

In the impenetrable fog of internal and external imbalances, the national identity attached to the soil became the only solid aspect of orientation. The triumphal military processions to the heart-lifting sounds of brass and drums, magnificent religious rituals, folklore, and folk art provided assurance. National pride took on a savage complexion. Adrenalin was flowing and muscles tensed for aggression across Europe. The voices of those who feared that war on an industrial scale meant mass graves and untold numbers of maimed survivors were stifled without reprieve. The psychological preconditions of war joined the growing forces of destabilization; they were different sides of the same phenomenon. The shared interest in maintaining and expanding the international economy and Europe's modestly successful supranational institution, the so-called *Concert of Europe,*[9] gradually evaporated.

---

8.   For a thorough analysis of Central and Eastern Europe during the 19th century, see *Berend, 2003.*

9.   The Concert of Europe was a loose consultative body that emerged after the Congress of Vienna (1814-15) from the alliance of Great Britain, Austria, Prussia, and Russia against Napoleon's France. In 1818, France joined it. During the 19th century, smaller countries became members or expressed support for the Concert's main principle, namely to head off armed conflicts with diplomatic consultations.

Every nation in Europe prepared for war, but none wanted to start it. The revolt of the world against its socioeconomic order needed and received a critical nudge from nonlinear dynamics, *chaos*. Enhanced initial condition sensitivity increased the likelihood that a totally unforeseen excitation would push the continental imperiums from a collectively unpacific to a collectively belligerent conduct. The 1914 assassination of Archduke Francis Ferdinand in Sarajevo did it. It served as the *casus belli* while entitling each warring party to the belief that it acted in self-defense. (See Chapter 10 for more on nonlinear dynamics, *chaos*, and "the butterfly effect.")

In retrospect, it is obvious that the explosion had to be territorial rather than societal. Foreign countries in military alliance against "our own" were easier to identify as enemies than the domestic classes of the privileged or the elusive international conspiracy of high financiers. The national authorities also exerted considerable efforts to head off domestic unrest, let alone revolutionary outbreaks. Agitators were imprisoned and the organization of labor was repressed to the extent possible. The political establishments provided guidance to the local public in channeling their dislike beyond the national frontiers. All these forces outweighed the attraction of socialist revolutions.

Nevertheless, domestic concerns were a major catalyst in the process of pushing the world toward a generalized territorial conflict. Logically, the Wilhelmian Reich had good reason to fear that Germany's exclusion from the possession of overseas colonies would lead to such an insurmountable gap in living standards to the disfavor of its population that socialist agitation could inflame the masses. The rulers of the colonial powers had every reason to fear that if Germany took their territorial possessions, the living standard in their countries would sink to socially explosive levels. With the *Guns of August*, the world entered an epoch of wars, revolutions, and political and moral anarchy in search of the fundamental parameters of a new socioeconomic order, a new *global system*.

◆   ◆   ◆

The war severely damaged trade and economic relations. The basic principles of GS1 ideology were violated *en gros*. Governments found themselves running industries, controlling, restricting, and requisitioning, in complete violation of hands-off *laissez faire* ideals. In the aftermath, the international community, in which the United States emerged as the new hegemone, attempted to revive GS1. The gold standard was brought back in its diluted "gold exchange standard" form, allowing liquid foreign reserves to augment the stock of metal in international payments. Relative to the strict gold standard, the system allowed limited discretionary spending by national governments. In the end, it fell between GS1, which was irrevocably gone, and GS2, which could not yet be established. At the national level, public authority in matters of economic policy was insufficient. Internationally, the system could not coalesce into a global one. The world lacked "solution concepts" and nations did not recognize the utility of mutual cooperation that might entail some sacrifice.

Labor organization and the influence of trade unions increased markedly in the industrialized countries. It was better to allow workers to participate in the political process and bargain with factory owners than to anger them to the point where they would look with nostalgia at Soviet Russia, which was already reaching beyond its borders to spread the idea and practice of revolutionary socialism. In a historic blackmail, labor leaders used rhetorical flirtations with Soviet-style collectivism and the nationalization of industries to extract concessions. Social security-type payments multiplied following the Great War.

The radicalization of the labor movement reduced the possibility of nominal wage reductions. It foreshadowed massive unemployment and trouble in the streets. During the next business downturn, firms unable to survive without cutting costs had to choose between going bankrupt or stirring up the union. (Industrial societies saw plenty of both of these alternatives during the Great Depression.) Governments faced the unpalatable choice between losing gold or being completely deprived of economic policy autonomy. The commitment to exchange currency for metal lacked credibility. Stated intentions notwithstanding, tariffs could not be rolled back to prewar levels. The final curtain fell on GS1 when Great Britain (1931) and the United States (1933) were forced off the gold.[10]

The postwar situation lived on borrowed time. The Versailles-Trianon peace treaties went even beyond codifying the disequilibrium that existed before 1914. The victorious allies devastated the former axis powers, Germany and Austria-Hungary, and were oblivious to the critically enfeebled Russia.[11] As economic growth resumed without a *global system*, a condition that includes the lack of well defined national economic institutions and policies, the next low point in the

---

10. Although a few economically important countries such as France and Belgium were not out until 1936, the end of the gold standard is still dated 1933 because Anglo-American support for the institution was generally regarded as critical. Italy, a significant player on the world stage during the epoch, also abandoned the gold standard in 1933 despite Mussolini's earlier declarations that he would defend the lira's gold parity with his life.

business cycle had to be deeper and governments had to be more helpless than ever before.

The roaring 20s slipped and then crashed into the desolate socioeconomic landscape of the Great Depression (1929-1933). Among the industrialized countries, Germany and the United States suffered the most. At the deepest point of the downturn, German output sank to 50 percent of its pre-depression level; production in the United States declined by 31 percent. Unemployment in Germany peaked at approximately 40 percent; U.S. unemployment neared 25 percent.

Three major alternatives to GS1 emerged; one in the disintegrated and devastated Russian empire (international socialism), another in the Great Depression cum Peace Treaty bankrupted Germany (national socialism), and the third (*mixed economy*) in the rest of the advanced industrialized world, most significantly in the United States. The socialist and fascist movements in Europe were propositions for a new world order.[12] They both became national socioeconomic systems; the first in the USSR and the second in Germany. As much as the ideologies and programs of these new regimes differed, they both condemned the prewar global order and considered the world's *status quo* illegitimate and untenable. The Moscow-centered international socialists (the communists) envisaged a new *global system* based on hitherto unseen (Marxist-Leninist) socioeconomic institutions. The fascist vision of the new order was based on territorial conquest. The Third Reich prepared to go even beyond the Kaiser's geopolitical goal of achieving some equitable condominium over the colonies. It dreamed about making Germans the masters of Europe in a European-dominated world. While Communism and Nazism created their respective models for a new socioeconomic order in the USSR and in Nazi Germany, respectively, the American New Deal felt its way toward GS2. No segment or aspect of the U.S. economy remained untouched. Programs boosted industry, agriculture, and trade; institutional changes redefined labor-management relations; expanded the regulation of busi-

---

11.   Russia capitulated to Germany in 1917, and by the time of the peace negotiations, the Bolsheviks seized control of the country–a situation that the world at large regarded as both unlawful and temporary.

12.   Polanyi showed that violent political movements fluctuated as efforts to restore the *laissez faire* system failed or seemed to succeed. Indeed, social upheavals in Germany, Italy, Austria, Hungary, Finland, the Baltic States, Rumania, Bulgaria, and Greece during 1917-23 subsided from 1924 to 1929 when the *laissez faire* system seemed to be reinstituted (*Polanyi, 1957*, p. 242).

ness, the state's responsibility for ensuring economic growth and a minimum of public welfare. Congress passed the Social Security Act in 1935.

All three fledgling alternatives generated support and opposition. Beyond the consolidation of the Soviet Union, the communist movement spread to other parts of the world, particularly to Asia. Hard-core, aggressive military regimes in Italy (where the push to restore *laissez faire* came to the shove of maintaining "law and order" at any price), elsewhere in Europe, in Japan, and in Latin America reinforced the fascist doctrine. Great Britain, France, and other West European states moved toward domestic socioeconomic arrangements and economic policies that were conceptually closer to the American model than to the other two. Common in all three models was the increased role of the government in guiding economic activity. Opposition to each alternative came from the other two and from those who thought that the restoration of the *laissez faire/metal money* was feasible.

Prior to World War II, nations developed hard protective shells and neglected each others' interests. Governments built their international commercial and economic policies around their political and military alliances. Politics radicalized within nations. Hatred and passion were squeezing out the trust and tolerance of those who thought differently. The ideologically committed thrived on their version of historical necessity and those who remained ideologically neutral had no idea what to expect from the next day. Surrealism, a sequel to Dada that became fashionable during World War I, flourished; astrology became a part of the pop culture.

Statehood in Germany remained essentially intact after the First World War. There was no occupation by the victorious entente; no punishment for those who were blamed for the war. This circumstance begged for a political movement that would renege on the devastating financial and economic consequences of the Versailles peace treaties. Germany's capitalist, aristocratic-military elite, as well as its middle class, obviously leaned more toward racist chauvinism and folkish nationalism, built on ethnocentric dynastic patriotism and private property, than toward state-ownership-based Marxist-Leninist internationalism. The degenerate forces that were immediately responsible for the next war were unchecked by any international organization or by the high stakes in growing, mutually beneficial international economic relations. The bewildered world, moving away from, rather than toward, greater self-organization, had to sober itself and revise its direction if *cultural evolution* was to be continued.

As we shall argue in Chapter 10, *pure randomness*, which gains in significance during systemic transitions, might have produced different personalities, different ideologies, and hence, a scenario different from the one that history has recorded. However, the final, general outcome is understandable *post factum* if we look at the world process in the suggested framework. It had to bring a higher level of intra-and international organization than what GS1 could provide. Without such a transformation, the *force motrice* (which the *chaotic* period did not weaken in the slightest) could not have proved to be the *sufficient cause* of the huge spell of *cultural evolution* that the world has witnessed since 1945.[13] Given that individual drives remained intact, the system had to change. The only mechanism capable of accomplishing it was *macroscopic chaos*, a Darwinian contest among the pooled, reduced number of alternatives, resolving themselves through stupefying horrors and consequent moral cleansing. Symbolically, "1914-1945" was the "work" of the *Opaque Artificer*.

◆   ◆   ◆

World War II ended. As if by the wave of a magic wand, minds were cleansed of the irrational devaluation of human life. The *global transformation* was over. The *vanguard* reassembled itself as a unit; its members were suddenly capable of moving beyond country-level thinking. A "virtuous circle" of positive tendencies that encouraged *cultural evolution* was set into motion.

The United States assumed the leadership in the development and introduction of GS2. The Employment Act of 1946 established government responsibility for economic performance.[14] The Labor-Management Relations Act of 1947 (the Taft-Hartley Act) fine-tuned and balanced labor-management relations and clarified the government's role in settling disputes. These were the two most critical legislative steps in creating the *mixed economy's imprimatur*. They solidified the New Deal era's basic achievements, insights, and economic ideology. The system became legally workable around clearly enunciated ground rules. Market forces allocate productive resources while the government has major powers and responsibilities to promote economic expansion and stability. In practice, the government became endowed with fiscal and monetary authority to remove liquidity ("money") in order to slow growth when the economy overheated (the

---

13. *Force motrice*, included in the Glossary, is explained in Chapter 10.

14. To vouch for its successful implementation, the Employment Act of 1946 created the Joint Economic Committee in Congress and the Council of Economic Advisors in the executive branch. Since then, legislative and administrative measures to complete, adapt, and refine the system have never stopped.

threat of inflation appeared) and introduce liquidity to stimulate it when slow-down was indicated (the threat of unemployment was identified).

The system's international dimensions began to take shape during World War II. In 1944, the United Nations Monetary and Financial Conference at Bretton Woods (New Hampshire) outlined the organization and functions of the International Monetary Fund (IMF) and the International Bank for Reconstruction and Development (The World Bank). The United Nations, along with its several organizations and independent specialized agencies (most importantly, the IMF and The World Bank) became operational soon after the war. During the same period, the General Agreement on Tariffs and Trade (GATT) was created to re-liberate international trade.[15]

GS2 institutions encourage the expansion of economic relations (e.g., trade and investment) and the coordination and integration of economic policies among nations. They provide assistance to countries in temporary payment difficulties and to those suffering from chronic underdevelopment. The adjective "*multilateral*" expresses the globalist spirit of GS2, its comprehensive and nondiscriminatory thrust. Perhaps the "most favored nations" (MFN) clause of the GATT best captures the essence of *multilateralism*. It stipulates that any trade concession given to any foreign country must be extended to the rest of the countries with MFN status. Apart from the exceptions made to provide only temporary (but renewable) MFN status to countries under communist control, membership in the GATT assured MFN status and the doors of the organization were always open.

The instauration of the *mixed economy* in the United States and the sheer existence of a credible framework for *multilateral* cooperation created what biologists call *adaptive radiation*. The new *macroscopic* force provoked an immediate rapid expansion of *mesoscopic* (national) institutions and, of course, a behavioral shift at the *microscopic*, individual, level. The variety in national adaptations may be seen in the differences among the United States, Europe, and Japan. Governments in post-World War II Western Europe moved in and out of productive asset ownership to an extent never even contemplated in the United States. Japan created a unique government-industry compact to deal with the country's external economic relations with weighty consequences for the entire economy. In smaller countries, central bank independence from political pressures could not

---

15.   GATT took the place of a so-called International Organization of Trade (ITO), which would have represented a much more ambitious and comprehensive approach to *multilateral* economic organization than what GATT permitted. Evidently, the originally envisioned approach did not match the era's political realities.

reach the level seen in the United States (i.e., through the activities of the Federal Reserve System) and in other major democracies, particularly in the EU since the establishment of the European Monetary Union that created the European Central Bank.

GS2 international institutions have evolved since their inception. The goal of the original Bretton Woods system (the so-called "gold-dollar system") was to combine the advantages of the gold standard and policy independence from supplies in the precious metal. It provided for fixed exchange rates among national currencies by tying them to the dollar that was fixed in terms of gold. Thus, the currencies of the IMF member countries remained pegged to gold through its surrogate, the dollar. However, parities were not etched in stone. In case of a "fundamental disequilibrium" (e.g., a particular country needed to devalue its currency to restore its external economic equilibrium), after due demonstration of the need and formal procedures, the country was allowed to re-peg ("adjust") its currency to the dollar (hence, also to gold and to all other currencies), without any obligation to return to the original parity. U.S. gold holdings (at a record high after World War II) underwrote the system. The U.S. Treasury stood ready to exchange the dollar holdings of foreign governments (that is, "official" but not private balances) for gold or buy gold from them at that price. The United States became the *pivot* or *epicenter* of the new world order. It supplied the reserve currency for the expansion of international economic relations and guaranteed international financial stability.

The dollar proved to be overvalued during the 1960s, a situation that brought commercial gains to U.S. trading partners and financial advantages to the United States. Nevertheless, a sense of imbalance permeated international economic relations. Partner countries, expecting devaluation, demanded gold. The drain on U.S. reserves was severe. In 1971, the Nixon Administration announced that it would no longer exchange foreign holdings of dollars for gold. This move effectively ended the "Bretton Woods system," since it interrupted the "foreign-currency-dollar-gold" circuit. Governments were no longer obligated to maintain fixed parities for their currencies. The "barbarous relic" (to use the expression of Keynes) was finally dethroned even as a symbol of world order.

Since 1971, the description, "floating exchange rates," best characterizes the international monetary system. Market forces have been set free in currency markets, with occasional efforts to rein them in through cooperative agreements and coordinated government intervention. The expression "the collapse of the Bretton Woods system" favored by textbooks overstates the case. "The United States cut the umbilical cord of a gold-free thinking world" would be more appropriate.

The ease with which the international community left "Bretton Woods" behind, moved to floating exchange rates, and warded off wild, growth-harming fluctuations and liberalized cross-country capital movements proves that the basic features of the global monetary system remained intact. "Bretton Woods" was appropriate for the immediate postwar era's limited need to fine-tune economic policy. European and Japanese reconstruction provided ample space for high rates of economic growth. Fixed exchange rates, which could, on occasion, handicap nationally conceived fiscal and monetary policies to find a balance between unacceptable levels of unemployment and inflation were not called into question. When fixed exchange rates had seen their day, GS2 shifted to an alternative system well within the limits of its essential organizing principle: The amount of money in circulation in each country (hence in the world) should be proportional to the value of goods and services in the same country (in the world). The break with "Bretton Woods" was a milestone in the history of GS2 and nothing more.[16]

Membership in the United Nations increased from the founding 51 members to 191. Although opinions as to the total number of countries differ (mainly because some areas are regarded as independent nations by some but subnational units by others), one may say that the UN incorporates the overwhelming majority of the planet's population. Membership in the IMF grew from 29 to 184; in The World Bank, from 28 to 184.[17] The creation of the World Trade Organization (WTO) in 1995 was an important step in strengthening *multilateral* ties. Whereas its predecessor, the GATT, was concerned primarily with the liberalization of international trade, the WTO is in the business of regulating it. Its scope of activities resembles the originally envisaged comprehensive approach to liberalizing the international economy under the stillborn ITO. A membership of 23, at the founding of GATT, grew to 149 under WTO.

Globalization and regionalization accompanied the history of GS2. The global trade-to-output ratio increased from approximately 8 percent in 1950 to an estimated 27 percent in 2000.[18] Since 1947, (applied) average world tariff rates for manufactured goods dropped from approximately 40 percent to about 6.5 per-

---

16.   See Barry Eichengreen's essay on the subject, "The Bretton Woods System: Paradise Lost?," in *Eichengreen and Flandreau, 1997.*

17.   "Current memberships" in *multilateral* organizations reflect 2006 data.

18.   Some estimates place the ratio as low as 22-23 percent. Since 2000, trade expansion has been less vigorous than the 6 percent average annual growth during the preceding decades. World trade actually declined during 2001, but picked up slightly in 2002 and recovered since then, according to WTO press releases in early 2006.

cent before the 1995 Uruguay Round reduced it to an estimated (applied) rate of 4.4 percent.

Regionalization refers to integration agreements among a number of countries. More than 100 regional agreements with trade liberalization among the members as the minimum objective had been reported to GATT/WTO. The EU is, by far, the most successful and most advanced regional integration effort. It evolved from a "common market" to an economic and monetary union. The North American Free Trade Agreement (NAFTA), the Mercado Común del Sur (MERCOSUR), the Association of Southeast Asian Nations (ASEAN), and the Southern African Development Community (SADC) are among the most significant regional systems. Although regional integration is discriminatory against those who are not part of it (it is *plurilateral* rather than *multilateral*), a good case can be made for its positive role in global integration. The movement toward larger territorial units of self-organization may be seen in the same positive light as the creation of nation states (e.g., Italy and Germany) earlier in history. The unification of small, rivalrous territories may help the international scene become more transparent and less plagued by the debilitating multiplicity of decision-making centers. If the total length of national borders is indicative of the challenge facing global unification, then regionalization helps. It tends to reduce the length of frontiers criss-crossing the planet; or, at least, it undermines the self-importance of border posts.

Regionalism may also be considered positive from the point of view of global integration in times when *multilateralism* cannot mobilize political will. Specifically, European unification under GS2 has established the administrative and legal precedent for the unlimited federation of nation states on democratic principles. The successful introduction of the "euro" removed the aura of Utopian dreaming from a future "world currency," even if the latter is not for tomorrow. Regionalism encourages "gene flow" among national populations, a *sine qua non* in our hypothetical "one world."

Until its collapse, the Marxist socioeconomic order in the Eastern Bloc (the USSR and its European satellites) blurred the existence of a unique *global system*. Only after the failure of the Marxist regime in the Eastern Bloc was completely exposed did it become obvious that GS2 had been the unique *global system* all along. In a *macrohistoric* perspective, the positive role that European communism might have played was that of the bogey man who frightened Capital into going beyond what it was ready to cede to Labor, causing an expansion of the public sector (e.g., spending on social programs) within the "mix" of the *mixed economy*.

Since the end of the Cold War, the spectrum of success in adapting GS2 principles became clearer and more complete. Members of the Organization for Economic Cooperation and Development (OECD) form the core, the center of the system. As of 2006, the OECD had 30 members (a significant increase from 20 at its establishment in 1960). They are considered not only the most developed countries, but also the ones that show the greatest commitment to market principles and democratic statehood; living by the rule of domestic and international law. All OECD countries are also WTO members. Perhaps the next most successful adaptation may be found among the countries that are WTO members but do not belong to the OECD. Countries that are members of The World Bank and the IMF but not of the WTO stand apart as a less successful stratum of adaptors and economic performers.

Communism represented the major form of opposition to GS2 during the Cold War. It was a direct and conscious effort to thrash and replace it. Most other anti-establishment crusades, particularly in the Third World, reflected Soviet intentions and support.

The post-Cold War era was full of promise. History seemed to have come full circle; the world appeared to be in a rational steady state, poised to conquer tomorrow. (How many noted writers and academics began to talk about the "end of history" and "post history"?) However, by the late 1990s, unsolved problems turned into dilating specters. Gaps of material wealth widened among and within nations. At present, a significant and growing number of the global population lives in vile indigence and well-reasoned advice to curb ecological degradation consistently fails to reach the status of political programs. While pushed to their limits, economic growth-stimulating policies in the *vanguard* produced meager results in terms of raising real (inflation-adjusted) incomes. Inflation and the accumulation of debt seem to be endemic to GS2 and incurable without major negative developments. Such a unidirectional phenomenon by itself reveals that GS2 has been only an escape into higher order, rather than the final form of global self-organization. (Only everlasting systems could generate recurring cycles, such as government deficits and surpluses neatly canceling one another over the long run.) Many people around the world became aware that oil and natural gas supplies are finite while demand for them is growing out of bounds—a clear menace on the horizon without a desirable and practicable solution that would either leave GS2 intact or ensure continued economic growth.

When communism died, GS2 evolved. It tried to augment the weight of the private sector in the private/public "mix" and injected a major dose of *laissez faire* into international economic relations. Post-communist, anti-GS2 manifestations also assumed new faces. The most visible and dramatic form of the predominantly nonviolent and rational opposition to GS2 is the coalition between anti-globalization and ecological movements. Both censure *multilateral* agencies (mainly the IMF, The World Bank, and the WTO) and *multilateral* fora (e.g., G7 meetings, high visibility, *vanguard*-sponsored conferences). However, the current, broad opposition to GS2 also has more secretive, Fronde-like dimensions. Internationally, there is a backlash against its *multilateralism* that appears to be congenitally incapable of preventing corporate giants from playing one nation against another and of providing full protection against the abusive practices of "foreign" governments. Intranationally, the private sector is looking backward toward GS1, wanting more *laissez faire* and the substitution of self-reliance for publicly supported social programs.

Fundamentalist religious movements are also anti-GS2. International terrorism in its Muslim garb is Luddism writ large. Destroyers of machines in early 19th century England opposed industrialization as GS1 was getting established; terrorists in the early 21st century attacked selected buildings, transportation and recreational facilities to damage GS2 by inflicting human and economic losses on the *vanguard*. Evidently, irrational and unacceptable doctrines play an important role in *macrohistoric* dynamics. In contrast, orthodox Christian convictions are refreshingly clear about the unsustainable nature of current trends. The "end-time" and the expected "revelation" move from the realm of faith to rationality when one reflects upon where the stupendous growth in the quantitative aspects of *cultural evolution* in a closed space (such as our *terrestrial sphere*) could possibly lead.

Guiding and rendering secure business is the only solution GS2 understands and can deliver. And that will surely not suffice. The inevitable end of GS2 lies in the sheer physical impossibility to solve the problems of poverty and ecological degradation through indirectly led, profit-motivated economic growth. If, by some miracle, the entire underdeveloped world (the South) embarked on a path of fast economic growth, promising to catch up with the developed world (the North), the demise of GS2 would speed up.

It is a broadly held scientific opinion that the natural resources and the pollution/waste-absorbing capacity of a planet several times larger than the one we occupy would be needed to bring the average global income to the level of the industrialized countries. And there is no sign that the South (where the majority of the human population lives) wants to settle for anything less than what people in the North enjoy or that the North wants to curb its material welfare so that the rest of the planet's population could also drive to shiny malls and buy and throw away things at an ever-accelerating tempo.

Despite fantastic misunderstandings and reciprocal hatred, there is an emergent, broadly based, worldwide sentiment united by the dislike of and opposition to GS2. Those who condemn *multilateral* organizations, those who want to blow them up, those who have harsh words about the greed of untamed multinational corporations, those who oppose capitalism, those who would like to bring it back in its pre-World War I form, those who condemn the narrow-minded selfishness of "foreign countries," the corruption and immobilism in the developing world, the tight-fisted, national-interest-maximizing conduct of the richest countries; those who demand government policies that would lead the world to an "ecological steady state"–all negate GS2 and criticize the state of the average individual's mind, as if a collectively unconscious, implicit judgment about the existing global order's unsuitability sought articulation, struggling toward the surface to become conscious and explicit.

We call the *global system* that may emerge after GS2, *two-level economy/strong multilateralism* (GS3). At one level, production in specific sectors (e.g., mining, manufacture of structural materials, certain heavily polluting industries) will have to be controlled and divvied up among nations or multinational producers; and some activities, such as space exploration, will have to be financed and organized jointly. At the second level, private enterprise and free markets would flourish under thoughtfully conceived quantitative constraints. Local socioeconomic environments may harden into close-knit self-help units or *cantons*.

These arrangements would require a new set of domestic and *multilateral* agencies. GS3 *multilateralism* would represent a profound change from GS2's "weak" version. It implies the liberal-democratically valid consent of the world's population to a moral and legal authority to overrule national preferences in the interest of long-term global interests. The accomplishment of this *global transformation* is the macro-future's optimistic scenario.

METAHISTORY

Metahistory may be thought of as the most general process that accompanies *macrohistory*. It may be derived through reductive iteration, starting with a concise formulation of *macrohistory*: Self-organization during the past two centuries occurred through *global systems*. The establishment of both GS1 and GS2 provoked relentless opposition. In general, *systems* resist, bend, and adapt, stretching themselves without breaking or fundamentally changing. But with time, they become increasingly unsuited to accommodating permanently and unidirectionally evolving socioeconomic conditions. Opposition grows; its strands sort themselves out and turn against one another with increasing vehemence. Eventually, the pressure exceeds the *system*'s point of tolerance; it is disrupted without a new *system* ready to take its place.

Even more generally, as a process grows in size and complexity, a system emerges that breeds counterpressure. As the underlying process continues, the system becomes decreasingly sustainable; and correspondingly, the forces that threaten to disrupt, drastically transform or completely replace it gain in intensity. Since the aims of the anti-system alternatives are diverse, the breakdown of the entrenched world order leads to *chaos*. However, the causal force of the process (the *force motrice*) continues to exist and the *chaos* is resolved. A new system suitable for accommodating the underlying process is found.

This is, in brief, the *metahistoric* interpretation of the past two centuries' *macrohistory*; the over-arching regularity to which the age of cohesive world orders can be reduced. To demonstrate the validity of this interpretation, we need to show that *global systems* really exist (that they are identical phenomena at some level of generality); that they come and go, and, finally, that the systemic interregnum deserves to be labeled *chaotic*.

We begin the first task by verifying that the two distinct (non-coterminous) exemplars of the *global system* are sufficiently similar to be considered two of a kind. The following similarities between GS1 and GS2 may be noted:

(1) *Cathartic birth, followed by socioeconomic Big Bang.* The introduction of both systems followed violent historical events and severe human and material losses. Both instituted changes at the *macro-*, *meso-*, and *microscopic* levels at once.

(2) *Epicenters.* Both systems crystallized around nations of pivotal importance (Great Britain for GS1 and the United States for GS2). The respective system's ideology took root, became axiomatic, and was turned into institutions there first. In both cases, the socioeconomic imperatives in the rest of the world, combined with an interest in maintaining close economic and diplomatic relations with the *epicenter*, as well as with countries that successfully imitated its institutional template, unleashed an integrative synergy that bound the world into distinct socioeconomic systems.

Under both *global systems*, the *epicenters* became "virtual administrators." Everything of significance happened with their lead or approval, or in response or opposition to them. Both *epicenters* consciously catalyzed and promoted the spread of their respective national systems; both championed free trade, and both ended up with huge and growing financial imbalances. Under both systems, the national currency of the *epicenter* became the major reserve currency, instrumental in providing the liquidity required for the expansion of international commerce. Both *epicenters* took upon themselves to solve the respective system's technical problems and to adjust its subparameters as *cultural evolution* gradually transformed socioeconomic conditions. Both acquired hegemonic positions; both faced economic, political, and military challenges; and both engaged in extraordinary efforts to retain their status as the strongest military power.

(3) *Motley pattern of followership.* Under both *systems*, the spectrum of adaptations could be subdivided into *center, periphery, semiperiphery,* and *the outside.* The level of emulation of the British gold standard may serve as the basis of classification under GS1, since it rolls conformity with the *global system's* domestic and international aspects into a single criterion. The *center* (including the *epicenter*) comprised nations on full gold standard (after 1880). Countries using the "gold exchange standard" may be put in the category of *periphery.* Countries not "on gold," but with monetary systems that allowed for their participation in the world economy, constituted the *semiperiphery.* Neglected areas in pre-nation status and isolated and forgotten tribes of Africa and Oceania were on *the outside.*

Under GS2, the classification follows participation in international organizations. Here again, compliance with the *global system's* international institutions roughly coincides with conformity in the domestic application of the system's organizing principles, that is, with the extent and quality of adhering to the institutions of the *mixed economy.* Members of the OECD (the "industrialized democracies") constitute the *center.* Given that all OECD members are also members of WTO/GATT, the *periphery* is made up of countries that belong to the second, but not to the first. Given that not all IMF and/or World Bank members belong to WTO/GATT, the *semiperiphery* contains countries that belong to the IMF, or at least to The World Bank, but not to WTO/GATT. Countries that are not members of The World Bank, plus those that are not even in the United Nations, plus areas with indeterminate status, constitute *the outside.*

The contents of categories changed over time. Countries moved in and out of the gold standard during GS1, just as countries changed their location in the spectrum of adherence under GS2. Most spectacularly, some former East European communist states that were not even members of The World Bank, and therefore belonged to *the outside,* became members of the OECD, thus moving to the *center.* Some rapidly developing countries moved from the *periphery* to the *center.* China, once on the *outside,* moved to the *periphery.*

(4) *Vanguard and national elites.* The level of adaptation to the *global system* correlates with the qualitative indices of *cultural evolution*, i.e., per capita income and socioeconomic equality. Nations that belonged to the *center* in both *global systems* form the *vanguard*. These countries have seen the greatest advances in the qualitative indices of *cultural evolution*. Under both systems, the existence of national elites has been characteristic at every level of intranational socioeconomic organization. Especially in the *vanguard*, domestic elites tended to expand. GS1 added the bourgeoisie to GS0's elite by birth; GS2 expanded the ranks of the bourgeoisie by catalyzing upward socioeconomic mobility and by giving quasi-elite status to the middle class.

(5) *Capacity for adjustment and self-preservation.* The *global system* is not a static phenomenon. It has the capacity to react to changing conditions with adjustment and development within its foundational principles. For example, GS1 introduced antitrust legislation to protect *laissez faire*, refined its monetary sector as it moved from bi-to monometallic basis, and devised ways to stretch gold supplies. GS2 eradicated even its nominal dependence on gold; it strengthened the *multilateral* framework and could shift the weight of the public sector back and forth within the private/public mix.

(6) *General peace.* Many wars and smaller-scale armed conflicts were fought among and within nations during GS1 and GS2, but there was no generalized conflagration.

◆   ◆   ◆

Global systems, regulative mechanisms of planetary scope, have limited life spans. To corroborate this fact, we must produce two birth and two death certificates. We are short of one death certificate, and this, of course, opens the door for the argument that what we call GS1 was only a phase that led to the establishment of the current and final world order. The present set of institutional arrangements created after World War II will certainly undergo change (this line of argument may continue), but whatever its future evolution entails, a break as drastic as the one that separates the *mixed economy cum multilateralism* from *laissez faire capitalism* is speculation.

To establish our case, we generalize the *global system* to include GS0 and *global transformation* to include GS0—>GS1. Moreover, we shall argue that although GS2 is not dead, it is moribund. The current modality of global self-organization is at irreconcilable odds with the psychological, ideological, and institutional requirements of a world order conceived upon the recognition of material constraints to the ongoing demographic and relentlessly pursued economic expansion. Calling GS0, GS1, and GS2 *relatively steady socioeconomic conditions* and identifying principles under which "1789-1834" and "1914-1945" can be equated, one discovers the following persistent *metahistoric* rhythm of the past half millennium:

- *Relatively steady socioeconomic conditions* (GS0, genesis of capitalism in feudalistic framework; a globally prevalent form of socioeconomic organization)

- *Chaotic transition* ("1789-1834")

- *Relatively steady socioeconomic conditions* (GS1)

- *Chaotic transition* ("1914-1945")

- *Relatively steady socioeconomic conditions* (GS2)

- *Chaotic transition* (logically derived with unknown dates)

- *Relatively steady socioeconomic conditions* (hypothetical GS3)

GS0, GS1, and GS2 showed sufficient similarities to be considered three manifestations of the same phenomenon (i.e., organizational framework for *relatively steady socioeconomic conditions*), yet they are sufficiently different to regard them as distinct stages of *cultural evolution*. During GS0 (world order without a *global system*) conditions for living under *global systems* developed and matured. Whereas GS1 was indirect and passive, GS2 became direct and active in pursuing material welfare and distributive justice. The emergence of GS3 is based on a presumed adaptive transmutation of individual behavior, preempting *cultural devolution* and phyletic drift toward extinction. Regrettably, based on current trends and behavior, the threat of *cultural devolution* may be recognized only when *homo sapiens* stands in polluted water up to his chin, annihilation starring into his eyeballs. However, the successful adaptation of the species to the new environment, which its expanding imperium wrought, may entail the emergence of a new *global system*, GS3.

We now turn to introducing the reasons why *chaotic transition* is an apt characterization of both GS0—>GS1 and GS1—>GS2. Full elaboration of the material nature of *chaotic transitions* and the demonstration of their physical inevitability are among the focal points of subsequent chapters.

◆   ◆   ◆

The lack of *relatively steady socioeconomic conditions* during "1789-1834" and "1914-1945," and the transitional character of both periods are historical facts. During both periods, principles of world organization were "up for grabs" among mutually exclusive alternatives that had to be sorted out through great loss in human life and material wealth ("transition costs"). The old, aristocracy-ruled feudalistic socioeconomic relations (AF), Jacobinical egalitarianism (JE), and classical capitalism (CC) accounted for the dynamics of the first transitional period. JE entered the stage of history on January 1, 1793, proclaimed as the beginning of a new era, and was gone by the turn of the century. Nonetheless, it lived in the minds and shadowed events until CC was successfully ensconced.

With regard to the second transition, three nationally embodied alternatives emerged in the search for solving the impasse brought on by the Great Depression: The American New Deal (AD) represented reformed capitalism, the *mixed economy*; Soviet-style communism (SC) stood for "a brand new socioeconomic system through revolution;" and the Nazi regime in Germany (NR) pushed for a "dictatorial *mixed economy* in the epicenter, satellite status in the rest of Europe, and military-colonial rule in the rest of the world." Selection through violence had to occur, leaving the global society without *relatively steady socioeconomic conditions* during the interim. (Using the Arrowian voting paradox, the Appendix illustrates that a world with three mutually exclusive alternatives is indeed confused and headed toward a Darwinian showdown.)

The two transitional epochs exhibited the symptoms of *chaos* in the word's strict, mathematical/physical sense. *Cultural evolution* is the incorporation of matter from the virtually fixed number of atoms found in the *terrestrial sphere* into the human biomass and human-crafted artifices. Therefore, *cultural evolution* is a thermodynamic process, and *culture*, with its animate and inanimate components, is a complex, far-from-equilibrium dissipative entity. As research in physics evinced, such processes must go through periods of stability, interrupted by "convulsive" and "costly" (accelerated entropy-producing) interludes of disequilibrium called *bifurcations*. Accordingly, the physical equivalent of the *metahistoric* rhythm is obtained by substituting *relative steady state* for *relatively steady socioeconomic conditions* and *bifurcation* for *chaotic transition*. If a system underwent *bifurcation*, it must have experienced *chaos*, "initial condition sensitivity," meaning that innocuous and elusive conditions at the beginning of each period led to rapidly escalating, unforeseeable developments. Thus, a physical homology (not a metaphor or analogy) underlies the periods from the storming of the Bastille to the abolition of Speenhamland in 1834, "the true birthday of the modern working class" (Polanyi); and from the *Guns of August* to Bretton Woods (1944) and the passage of the Employment Act in the United States (1946).[19]

LINKAGE TO PHILOSOPHY

Hegel taught that history is a mysterious, collective learning process that marks humankind's difficult, conflict-driven progress toward complete self-realization. In this respect, *new historical materialism* is Hegelian. The dynamics of the *macrohistory* presented may certainly be expressed through the universal proposition of thesis-antithesis-synthesis, considered the fundamental mechanism of dialectic time evolutions.[20] Dialectic is implied first by confirming the existence of the *global system*, as brought to light by the "Polanyian double movement;" and, second, in the manner it transmutates.

Existence may always be thought of as the balance of opposing processes. Life comes apart unless it maintains itself by taking in energy, as if "existence" had been challenged by its opposite, "nonexistence," to engage in a ceaseless struggle to remain distinct from it. We perceive an extant order (socioeconomic, political, or cultural in its traditional meaning) as the resultant of antinomic forces; one batch of them trying to preserve it and another intent on undoing it. This metaphysical truism, with roots in Greek antiquity, is of great importance here, given the omnipresence of *relatively steady socioeconomic conditions*. In particular, the *global system* surrounds the individual; it is everywhere. Being geographically "outside" of it is too marginal and unsuccessful to provide a credible vantage point to characterize it. The *global system* sums up the essential ways people see themselves and the world. It is also inside of us; its core attributes are built into

---

19. *Bifurcation* as interpreted here in a socioeconomic-physical sense strongly resembles the theory of "punctuated equilibrium" (rapid changes instead of painstaking gradualism) in evolutionary biology. For descriptions of "punctuated equilibrium," see *Gould, 2002*.

20. The concept of dialectics predates Hegel. It can be traced back at least to Socrates (469-399 BCE). On the other hand, the thesis-antithesis-synthesis triad may postdate Hegel. Some authors attribute it to his latter-day disciples, although some maintain that it was the contribution of Johann Gottlieb Fichte (1762-1814). Nonetheless, the dialectic method summarized in the "triad" is an unquestionable characteristic of the Hegelian philosophy of history. Invoking it in the present context is germane.

the neocortex of billions. Therefore, *relatively steady socioeconomic conditions* can be distinguished only through the clash between their staying power and the tendencies that try to weaken them or wipe them out. GS0, GS1, and GS2 are recognized through their constant negation. Without this empirically derived philosophical argument, the *global system* (as the instantiation of a *relative steady state* in the unidirectional, dissipative, nonequilibrium thermodynamic process of *cultural evolution*) could not be acknowledged and understood. If we could not "see" GS2 because it remained un-negated, the *global system* of *laissez faire/metal money* could not be called GS1.

Concerning the second point–the manner of change through *chaotic transitions*–Hegelian dialectics may also be considered a *metahistory*.

Thesis: The immediate emergence of a *global system* occurs when the intentions of a social subset to transform institutions in the *epicenter* coincide with broad, global public interests. A generally appealing and circularly defendable, paradigmatically expressible ideology demonstrates the coincidence. The central pattern of new institutions, established during a relatively short period of time in the *epicenter*, spreads across the world, mandating local adaptations. The self-sustaining equilibrium creates a new global *status quo*, a new legitimacy, a new orthodoxy.

Antithesis: The system functions only partially as was expected or "advertised." It leaves some economic and social problems unsolved and it creates new ones. Tensions begin to build among nations and between social groups within each nation. The ground shifts under the system as population and economic output increase, and, as a result of growing education and income, demands for economic security and political influence gather strength. Subject to the constraints of its intrinsic axioms and articles, the system perfects itself and evolves under pressure; it adjusts in order to survive, but grumbling and intellectual criticism directed against it become ever more strident and potentially aggressive. The self-affirming consciousness of individual and national rights augments the international and domestic political significance of disappointments and recurring spells of hardship that follow from the system's advancing caducity. Among the dominant alternatives, one intends to reshuffle power and influence among nations while another wants to alter the roles of social classes, regardless of national boundaries. The antagonism as a single phenomenon directed against the *global system* is the *antithesis*

Synthesis: The *system* becomes fragile and teeters on the verge of breakdown. A significant historic event marks the beginning of its end. The world enters an era of strife among the significantly supported alternatives. Moral and political anarchy reigns in interconnected ganglia. This is unavoidable. The old order fixed in the mind must be dissolved before the new one can be fixed, leaving a period open for a conflict-ridden competitive search. The transition will not end until the axioms and articles of the next system are identified and the historical conjuncture allows for their radical implementation. The newly installed system is the new *thesis* that will represent a *synthesis* to the extent that its institutional content and concept world become a qualitatively new amalgam of the demands that clashed. *Synthesis* is resolution through higher order. It brings qualitative improvement through the application of stronger, and in some respects, simplifying organizational principles and mechanisms.

The final, reductive generalization: "Thesis-Antithesis-Synthesis accompanies self-organization in a process that renders the self-organizing systems ever larger and more complex." This Hegelian formulation brings us one step closer to seeing world history as the fluctuation of a single substance; to hearing its rhythm, as the growing lump of matter (which includes all of us) argues with itself on how to proceed.

Hegel has been characterized as an "idealist" because he ostensibly considered the end stage of the species' historic learning process to be the full recognition of the divine. His philosophy seemed inextricable from a profound belief in the Christian doctrine. But just how much of an idealist was the mighty thinker? Some argue that he dissimulated his true views to avoid conflict with the spirit of his time, and, in particular, with his employer, the Prussian State.[21] The word "spirit" in his book, "The Phenomenology of the Spirit" (*Phänomenologie des Geistes*, 1807), in which he elaborates on the dialectics of history's directionality, may be translated as the "Phenomenology of the Mind." The German noun *Geist*, used in the (original) German title, means both. History is the human mind's learning process, but by now we know empirically that the mental is also material; the brain is animated electro-chemistry. If that is what "the Beethoven of philosophy" hid from public scrutiny; if he believed that the "mind" is the brain's function space, an extension that his references to the brain do not preclude, then

---

21.   In his exegesis on the "Phenomenology of the Mind," George Lukacs (1885-1971) notes a telling incident. The German poet, Heinrich Heine (1797-1856), recognized not only for his great lyric talent, but also for being a clear-eyed observer of human nature and society, wrote: "I stood behind the Maestro, as he composed it ["it" is not defined; Lukacs thought it was the "music of Atheism," P.P.], employing, of course, meaningless and excessively ornamented symbols, so that no one could possibly decipher it–I saw sometimes, as he anxiously looked around, fearing that someone may, in the end, still understand him…" (*Hegel, 1807*, p. 467).

the *metahistory* presented here is linked to Hegel by more than the dialectics of evolving self-organization. It is then a simple reformulation of Hegelian insights, with the help of the historical rearview mirror and common scientific knowledge two centuries later. Of course, there is no credible evidence for revising Hegel's dialectical idealism into post-Marxian dialectical materialism.

Metahistoric theorizing is a moth-eaten ancestral heritage, the mind's never-fading infatuation with self-explanation. Millions of candles have burned, a lake of ink has been spilled, a warehouse of computer discs has been filled with thoughts on the subject. It would be difficult to say something about it without immediately ringing a dozen bells. Even the idea that history witnesses a progress in the evolution of the human mind through stages has a long lineage. Besides the Hegelian connection, the reader may find it in writings from Antoine Condorcet (1743-1794) and Auguste Comte (1798-1857) through Kenneth E. Boulding (1910-1993), all the way to the stream of scholarly works "on line" from the keyboards of contemporary scientists and philosophers.

Such views, including, of course, *new historical materialism*, have an *orthogenetic* dimension. In its broadest interpretation, *orthogenesis* is the common denominator among a wide array of theories that assert the significance of internal potentials and constraints in the detected direction of change. Since *new historical materialism* links the materiality of history to disequilibrium thermodynamics, its *orthogenesis* is limited to the certainty that human hereditary material under similar physical conditions that existed during the past centuries would, *per force*, drive the organization of the planet toward global scope and increasing complexity. This process leans as much on the sediments of experience accumulated over a million years and crystallized into hereditary substance as on the socioeconomic environment's "selection power."

Metahistory sees directional changes in globally valid, *relatively steady socioeconomic conditions* as a natural process. Unlike metaphysics, which, in its Aristotelian traditions, goes "beyond physics" into the realm of profound speculations and enigmatic abstractions, our *metahistory* serves as a bridge to *physis*, to nature. By doing so, *new historical materialism* views *cultural evolution* as the transformation of the mind, productive forces and productive relations, ethics, the consciousness collective, language, and individually harbored intentionality at once. Thus, it unites the seemingly independent philosophies of Hegel, Marx, Weber, Durkheim, Wittgenstein, and Brentano. By underscoring the critical importance of the formulaic and the standardized (without an objective epistemic center) in socioeconomic arrangements, the proposed theory aligns itself with the logic of *structuralism*. By exposing the unbridgeable gap between material reality (cerebral electrochemistry enveloped into a thermodynamic unfolding) and its ever shifting and always shiftable logo-centric (language-based) interpretations, it embraces the postmodern and poststructural doubt about the identifiability of fundamental truths and universal essentials through social analysis and philosophy. Nevertheless, the suggested way of looking at world history and its mechanism of change was not conceived in a postmodern state of mind.

Whereas postmodern thought celebrates *chaos* and dismisses historical directionality, *new historical materialism* unites *chaos* with *determinism* by considering *cultural evolution* a process of *deterministic chaos*. (See Chapter 10 for details.) Although the socialization of the *force motrice* created conditions that submerge the individual in certain inexorable laws of nature, *cultural evolution* itself remains an open-ended process. It may well lead to a higher form of global self-organization that fulfills the human potential incomparably better than its current modality. Whereas postmodern ideas often leaned toward pessimism, seeing a helpless, fissured world disappear in a black hole of static disharmony, the suggested theory emphasizes the possibility of dynamic harmony; phyletic resistance to permanent *chaos*, chronic disorganization, disaggregation. A shared vision of reality can make broad consensus undeferrable; it can shock the global population into developing an all-encompassing ethos and pursuing a common agenda.

From the vantage point of a few decades hence, the place of postmodernism itself may become clear. Its entry into the intellectual, artistic, and educational-political scene during the closing decades of the 20th century coincided with the near stagnation of per capita real incomes in the *vanguard*. While as a result, the middle class index (MCI) within SEEI may have remained unchanged in the North during the period, the political/legal rights index (PLRI), propelled by postmodern cultural diversity, tried, with some undeniable success, to compensate for the slack.

This lingering postmortem of postmodernism follows from considering *cultural evolution* a material process that includes everybody's mind. Neither prophetic advocates nor revolutionary detractors or, on a smaller scale of intensity, neither ideological affirmers nor academic doubters of "true" foundations can renounce their roles in its human-sized mega-happening. The "fray" is everything and every idea is in it.

4

The Materiality of Culture, Cultural Evolution, and Socioeconomic Organization

[The nested system of material organization. The *terrestrial sphere* and its components: *culture, geocapital*, and the *global environment*. The *ecological order. Point X. Culture* as structure and function of matter, as energy and information, as stock and flow. Units of socioeconomic organization as well as relations and associated behavior can also be interpreted in these terms.]

If our eyes could penetrate customary shapes and contours and we could zoom into details at will, we would see humans and their devices as intermediary and temporal constellations of miniature nested universes in constant agitation. We would then find it natural to interpret *cultural evolution* as a swelling quantity of matter that is never at rest. Since we do not possess such sensory capacity, we must fall back on our imagination to conceptualize the world as a material continuum.

The biologist, Arthur S. Iberall, and the physicist, Harry Soodak, demonstrated direct connections between matter and social organization.[1] Quarks bond to form protons and neutrons, which bond to create nuclei, which attract electrons to complete the atom. Atoms unite to build molecules, which make up organelles in cells; cells aggregate into tissues, which combine to form organs that form systems in organisms. Individuals unite into families that constitute the communities that add up to national populations, aggregating into the planetary sum of living souls. Similarly, all life-bearing structures in human service and all human-made objects are made up of the nested system of matter. *Culture*, therefore, may be considered in terms of atoms and subatomic particles. It is a part of

---

1. See Iberall and Soodak, in *Yates, 1987.*

91

the Earth's material endowment and the Earth is part of the cosmic system that binds the planets to the stars and the stars to the galaxies. We can always imagine something greater than anything, but, ultimately, infinite space frustrates this induction and the mind falls back on faith or poetry or reductive mathematical formalisms.

Scientific knowledge metamorphoses into mystery not only as one moves toward the infinitely large, but also as one moves toward the infinitely small. Heisenberg's uncertainty principle, which reached the scientific community in 1927, provided the hard proof that humans annot examine atomic particles in the same way that they can study phenomena in the realm of classical physics. The more the momentum of a particle such as an electron is identified, the less can be known about its position. The origin of this uncertainty may be tied to the measuring instruments used to examine the particles. The observer must disturb the object it wants to measure and the effect may spread instantaneously across the universe.

There is also a simple economic constraint to microcosmic inquiry with the aid of laboratory equipment. The deeper humans delve into the nature of matter, the bigger the bill. It grows until it becomes unaffordable without the promise of ever reaching a limit. At some point, the world evidently has to stop pumping resources into the project of penetrating the secrets of matter. Many physicists now contend that elementary particles themselves are made up of vibrating one-dimensional curves (strings). If these subinfinitesimal monads were empirically confirmed, there would be a new understanding about the realities of life; there would be more assured answers to the old questions, "Who are we? Where do we come from? Where are we going?" Perhaps then the Cartesian dualism (separating the mind's attributes into spiritual and physical) would finally dissolve into knowledge of a higher order. However, prevailing opinion holds that the demonstration and proof of the "string theory" through reading instruments falls into the category of economic infeasibility. It is sobering to ponder what humanity's epic struggle against ignorance has brought. Discoveries first took away its sense of centrality and consequent importance in the universe, then its certitude in knowledge was shaken, and then the hope of ever cracking the riddle of clustered subatomic particles got stalled. This is neither an ontological sob story nor an invitation to existentialist gloom. It is only a restatement of elementary scientific information with the encouraging proviso: The final word on science can never be spoken. The future of knowledge remains open and unpredictable.

Present interest in the microcosm comes from tying *cultural evolution* to changes in the mind. Everything that is mental, such as memory, thought, and behavior, is also biological, chemical, and physical. Therefore, *cultural evolution* is inseparable from the "phenomenology of the brain." The directionality, the *orthogenesis* of *cultural evolution*, the mysteries of DNA with all its implications for the process, may well be buried in infinitesimal details that elude the human organism's "3D plus time"-oriented observational apparatus and may defy its common experience-hatched "lump and mass" image of corporeality. Mindful of these limitations, we turn to the material building blocks of *culture, cultural evolution*, and socioeconomic organization. First, the immediate framework–the *terrestrial sphere.*

The distance between the Earth's center and its surface at the equator is 3,963 miles. This is the longer way. Going poleward to the surface, the distance is 3,950 miles. If we continued along this radius 6,000 miles straight up, we would reach the outer limit of the atmosphere, where the veil of gases surrounding the planet fades into interplanetary space. The radius of this sphere is 9,950 miles. Since we are not planning a trip, there seems to be no harm in rounding the number to 10,000 miles. We call the imaginary spatial figure, which has a diameter of 20,000 miles, the *terrestrial sphere.* Some stray atoms of hydrogen and other light gases escape from its area into outer space, and meteors and cosmic dust enter it. However, the weight of the mass leaving and entering is negligible compared to the total weight of mass contained in it.[2] With regard to the stock of matter available to support *cultural evolution*, the *terrestrial sphere* is a virtually closed set. For all practical purposes, its weight may be considered constant, its inventory of atoms perpetual.

The *terrestrial sphere*'s matter is a collection of atoms and molecules. It can be broken down into elements or ensembles of elements, such as metals, semimetals, and nonmetals, or minerals and nonminerals. Oxygen is the predominant element. In volume, it is followed from a great distance by potassium, sodium, and calcium. In weight, it is followed somewhat more closely by silicon, aluminum, and iron.

Our universe comprises the sun (the nuclear furnace that makes everything possible), the moon, and the *terrestrial sphere.* There is plenty of solar energy to support earthly life and improvements in its quality, but matter is not unconstrained. To analyze this issue, we distinguish among three domains in the *terrestrial sphere*: *culture, geocapital,* and *global environment.*

---

2. The mass of the Earth is estimated at 5.97 x 10 [18] tons. Since this calculation was based on the Earth's radius, the *terrestrial sphere*'s mass must be greater than this figure.

Culture is matter incorporated into humans, other life forms in human service, and produced goods. (We simplify by dealing only with the population and material output.) Atoms outside of *culture* are either in the *geocapital* or in the *global environment. Geocapital* contains matter immediately needed and ready to be used to nourish and support *cultural evolution.* The *global environment* is the residual. In general, labor, capital, and anything made of substance containing value added, including agricultural commodities, works of art, and items regarded as wealth, are in *culture.* Exploitable natural resources and owned surfaces earmarked for agriculture are in *geocapital.* Material that falls between the cracks of *geocapital,* such as mining waste and surfaces not owned (e.g., the oceans and the atmosphere), as well as natural resources only hypothetically known and/or subeconomical to access, is in the *global environment.* This threefold compartmentalization is mutually exclusive and complete. Every single atom has to belong to one of the three and all atoms must be accounted for. Consequently, the weights of *culture, geocapital,* and the *global environment* add up to the weight of atoms in the *terrestrial sphere.*

To illustrate, an oxygen atom in the human body is *culture*; in a metallic oxide to be excavated in the foreseeable future, it is *geocapital*; in the air it is *global environment.* It is likely that some oxygen atoms have seen it all. They have been in all three domains. Although science does not follow the individual careers of atoms or molecules, it knows for certain that *cultural evolution* reduced the weight and the volume of oxygen in the *global environment.*

Given a level of technology and exploitation regime, both the *geocapital* and the *global environment* may be broken down into renewable and nonrenewable resources. Land, forests, other species, and water are renewable resources; however, overuse and abuse have made some of them nonrenewing. *Cultural evolution* is fundamentally dependent on nonrenewable resources because renewable biomass alone cannot satisfy the material requirements of industry, the backbone of material well-being. Fossil fuels remain the main source of extrasomatic energy and the metal/mineral contents of the Earth are going into *culture* as industry expands. Someday, needs for energy may be satisfied entirely by renewable sources; however, civilization has a built-in dependence on nonrenewable matter. According to rough estimates, the global output is 64 percent services, 32 percent industry, and 4 percent agriculture. The drastic shrinkage of agriculture from its historical dominance to its place today is a good indication of the extent to which nonrenewable resources squeezed out renewable ones. It should also be noted that services such as trade, transportation, education, information-processing, banking, insurance, and real estate do not exist in a nonmaterial vacuum. More of any type of service demands more of some material goods, for example, airplanes, computers, wires, cables, office space, telephones, and furniture.

The *ecological order* is the macrostate of the *terrestrial sphere*, characterized at any moment by a microstate. (See the Glossary for definitions of macrostate and microstate.) It is the world "as is" *in toto*, including every person, structure, and component of flora and fauna; every piece of land, mountain, body of water, and patch of air; every bit of scientific information, whether it is kept in the brain or on computer discs, every single artistic manifestation; every manufactured product, every electron in a TV cable, and every proton in a landfill. The *ecological order* is the most comprehensive and detailed definition imagination can conjure up to visualize the status of the *terrestrial sphere*. Theoretically, any phenomenon that exists has a corresponding configuration within the "aggregate." An ecosystem has a material structure in the same way that the bacteria living on this page do or the ink that makes visible the period that follows.

The appearance of *homo sapiens* and its *cultural evolution* have reorganized matter in the *terrestrial sphere*. The growth of human population and production transformed the position of atoms from less complex, less ordained forms into more complex, more orderly systems, altering the original *ecological order* at the cost of creating more disorder than order, as we shall see in the next chapter. This alteration captures the shrinkage of the *global environment* through structural and functional changes in the planet's stock of matter. As a subconfiguration of the *ecological order*, *culture* indicates the extent to which human agency has rearranged the *terrestrial sphere*.

Cultural evolution is the increase in the number of atoms that participate in *culture* and *geocapital*; or, equivalently, the reduction in the number of "nonparticipating" atoms. Thus, *cultural evolution* tends to eliminate the *global environment* and shrink the upper limit of *geocapital* even if the latter, owing to human ingenuity, may expand. Since *cultural evolution* draws inevitably on nonrenewable material resources, it is a dissipative process and *culture* is a *dissipative system*. (See the Glossary for a definition of *dissipative systems*.)

Separate as they are by definition, the three domains of the *terrestrial sphere* intertwine and tangle. *Culture* and *geocapital* interlock when the iron atoms in a steel instrument under the miner's control engage atoms in a layer of coal. When the airplane flies, *culture* and the *global environment* make contact. In a landfill, the molecule about to be reused through recycling (*geocapital*) and the one next to it that remains (*global environment*) rub against one another.

Since there is a continuum of decreasing degree of geological certainty and economic feasibility for any particular resource, the dividing line between the *geo-*

capital and the *global environment* is a purely theoretical proposition. Nonetheless, matter incorporated into the three domains can be analyzed in many meaningful ways. For instance, a global input-output table mimics the way *culture* is sustained through interactions within its domain and with the *geocapital*. A succession of global input-output tables would show the reduction of the *global environment*. The division of earthly material into renewing and (in our time frame) nonrenewing molecular structures is important for evaluating the prospects of *cultural evolution*. Statistics on the global economic use of materials, e.g., on an annual basis, are indicative of the rate at which *culture* is drawing down the *geocapital*. Efforts made to push hypothetical and subeconomic resources toward the "confirmed and economically appropriable" status may reveal details about the evolving quantitative relationship between the *global environment* and the *geocapital*.

If *cultural evolution* strengthens the species it also limits its potential within the *terrestrial sphere*. When the potential is exhausted, *cultural evolution* runs into an invisible and impenetrable wall. Further increases in the population and economic output begin to weaken the species. We call the level of atomistic incorporation at which *cultural evolution* becomes *cultural devolution*, *Point X*. Since *Point X* cannot be determined in advance, there is no need to estimate the ratio of "culturally engaged" atoms in the *terrestrial sphere*. We know, nonetheless, that such a ratio exists and that it must increase with *cultural evolution*.

If a very strong lightbulb represented every person, and the luminosity of everything already lit (e.g., buildings, roads, cars, trains, airplanes) became strong enough to be observed from outer space at night, one could see the globe becoming shinier with *cultural evolution*. This process cannot go on indefinitely. No process whose reservoir is a finite set of material substances, that is, no unidirectional process in a closed space, can go on forever. (There is no infinite supply of matter for lightbulbs, sockets, and wires.) *Point X* represents a combination of matter in the *terrestrial sphere* that no longer permits the planet to become "brighter." When that combination is passed, the planet must "pale." Under the current *global system*, *culture* moves toward *Point X*, toward a level where it would damage itself.

◆   ◆   ◆

The laws of nature in the nuclear world differ significantly from those that operate at our normal scale of observation. You are where you are now and not at two or more places at the same time. The car you drive, although it moves, is never at two places at once. This is not so simple in the quantum world. Atoms are unruly, they vibrate and collide, form bonds and dissolve them. Inside each of them there is a psychedelic "subatomic zoo"–hundreds of interminably squirming and hustling particles that change into one another. They do not obey the concept of time and cannot be observed without upsetting their pre-observation state. When we ask the *ecological order* to freeze for a moment, so that we may acknowledge that it has a structure, the subatomic universes cannot heed our call. Therefore, the expression "structure" as a momentary position or state of matter in the *ecological order* is applicable only to dimensions that classical physics could describe or analyze.

The notion of "structure" implies "function"–interconnected matter at work. The functions of the *ecological order* refer to characteristic patterns of biological, chemical, and physical processes during a short period of time; for example, one day. By specifying a "short" period we can step outside the evolutionary perspective, as if to say "this is what matter does now," of course, in a very rudimentary, reductive, and approximate sense. The functions may be subdivided into interactions among humans and between humans and the rest of the *terrestrial sphere*. However, they also circumscribe the interplay between nonhuman life and inanimate matter and the internal dynamic within each of these "subworlds."

Thus, *culture* is a material entity that performs natural science-interpretable functions in the context of the *ecological order*. If its structure shows the level of population and economic output and the distribution of per capita income, its functions are the movements within this structure during any period short enough to consider its level stationary. Even with this restriction, *culture* is not only a particularly arranged stock of matter that does things; it is also a flow that constantly renews itself. New arrivals into earthly existence take the places of those who depart from it; human-made objects are replaced as they are used up. *Cultural evolution* means the increase and complexification of *culture*, which is the constant flow of an ensemble of ephemeral material structures.

By the equivalence of matter and energy, *culture* is a level of energy within the grand total of energy extractable from matter. *Cultural evolution* has increased the amount of organized energy within the available grand total. As Leslie Alvin White (1900-1975) observed, "The degree of organization of a system is proportional to the concentration of energy within the system."[3]

---

3.   *White, 1959*, p. 145. In the same volume, White pointed out that the beginning of modern cultural evolution, incidental to the emergence of agriculture, may be characterized by the use of nonmetabolic (extrasomatic) energy. Up to that point, human (or humanoid) economic activities ran exclusively on metabolic (somatic) energy.

Claude Elwood Shannon (1916-2001), the founder of "communication theory," showed that information is a measurable quantity. Ilya Prigogine (1917-2003) substantiated the material nature of complexification as a process accompanied by the growing quantity of information required to increase order. Based on these achievements, we may say that *culture* corresponds to an amount of information required to ensure the cohesion and operation of *culturally* engaged atoms. Information, so defined, grew with *cultural evolution*.

Individuals and objects may be translated into unique characteristics of energy and (in theory) can be thoroughly identified through data sets and programs. Thus, the structure of *culturally* incorporated matter stated in "materialeese" can be re-stated in "energeese" or "informationeese." The functioning of this structure takes place through directed streams of matter or energy or information among people, between people and objects, and among objects. As people die and objects are discarded, matter or energy or information that corresponded to them flows through different individuals and objects at the same level of population and economic output. Existence is continuous turnover, regardless of the aspect by which we explain it (matter, energy, or information).

Each component of the nested hierarchy of *socioeconomic environments* may be perceived as structured matter in action. Each level suffices to describe the *global socioeconomic environment*, which is analogue to *culture*, since it may be characterized with the three *cultural evolutionary* indices. Let us use the smallest environment, the *personal socioeconomic sphere*, as an example. The number of *spheres* is the population. Their average size correlates to average per capita income and the distribution of their relative size is indicative of socioeconomic equilibrium. If publicly owned matter (e.g., infrastructure, land, and certain capital goods) is combined with the material contents of *personal spheres*, we obtain the material contents of *culture*, the pulsating expanse of human vitality.

◆   ◆   ◆

The *personal socioeconomic sphere*, the self-projection of individuality through the control of space and the accumulation of material objects in that space, grew over time. Particularly in the *vanguard*, *spheres* also tended to move away from levels of inequity that would have endangered social peace.

A sense of equity permeating the masses may be comparable to matter occupying space homogeneously. Such a situation promotes equilibrium because matter under these circumstances is less likely to engage in spontaneous self-disruption. This simple physical fact supports the notion that human rights have meaning independent of their socio-philosophical and constitutional law context. "Natural rights," the general premise used to foster and explain socioeconomic equalization, are tied to a physical phenomenon that existed before human society appeared and now exist outside of it. Therefore, the third *cultural evolutionary* index (SEEI) may also be interpreted in terms of physics.

It is relatively straightforward to think about the global population and output as assemblages of atoms. It is also not difficult to perceive the *personal socioeconomic spheres*, the *surrounding socioeconomic milieus*, and the *local, national,* and *global socioeconomic environments* as sets of material building blocks. We are talking, after all, about people and objects in bounded areas. One can even picture the jostling for space among bundles of personally controlled particles. But what about *socioeconomic systems*? How can fixed organizational principles of socioeconomic relations be excognated in a gigantic flux of quarks and leptons?

Socioeconomic systems are stored inside individuals (somatically) and outside of them (extrasomatically). All human relations involve mental activities, which, as mentioned before, have their specific bio-chemical-physical bases in the brain. Therefore, socioeconomic relations, a subcategory of human relations, are etched into thinking matter.

Instructions to maintain and operate any collective order are in the brain as explicit symbol/referent linkages and as implicit, nonverbal understanding. This combined intelligence informs behavior, the connective action among individuals. Its materialness must be in neuronal structure and functioning, not as a deviation from the evolved, general and specialized mechanisms of learning and memorizing, but as their concrete, history-dependent application.

Cultural evolution brought new words (symbols) with new meanings (referents) into use; it caused old referents to be expressed with new symbols, and old symbols acquired new referents. "The General Agreement on Tariffs and Trade" is an example of a symbol/referent pair that did not exist until the establishment of GS2 (new symbol/new referent). The old referent, "purchasing power," went through a series of "new" symbols: "gold," "bank note," "paper currency," "plastic," and most recently, with the apparition of cyber-money, a specific signal on the computer screen (new symbol/old referent). Describing how hard one works in the office by saying "I slave," means something totally different now than it would have in the past (old symbol/new referent). The "transvaluation" (Nietzsche) of meaning is a never-ending, continuous process. However, as the old world order loses legitimacy and the new one gains and diffuses its own, the existence of *global systems* reveals relative resting places and limits in this process, punctuated by the wholesale abandonment and adoption of symbol/referent clusters.[4]

The physical marks that stand for symbol/referent relations and for the implicit comprehension of the socioeconomic environment are the joint and interdependent products of society and the individual. Both endure as long as the system to which they correspond lasts, endowing behavior with system-specific characteristics and giving it an element of constancy and predictability. No social order can exist without the implied traction in interpersonal relations. This is a remarkable and important phenomenon, given the kaleidoscopic and easily mutable ("dynamic") nature of behavior.

In general, behavior is equilibrium between the organism's biology and the environment. *Randomness* in the transmission of hereditary material and in the reproduced material's relationship to its external world is subjected to selective evaluation by the environment. Of course, this Darwinian formula applies to the socioeconomic behavior/socioeconomic environment nexus, a subcategory of the broadest relationship between individual behavior and the environment. In the interplay between the genes and their external surroundings, socioeconomic behavior settles into relative constancy for the life span of a specific socioeconomic system. The system's duration coincides with the legitimacy of its supra-individual, extrasomatically stored legal-institutional framework. For instance, the gold standard was in effect as long as legislation stipulated the exchange of fiat money for the metal. It ceased when the legislation became null and void. Such changes must leave their marks in the brain.

Extrasomatic storage devices, such as law books, RAMs, and ROMs help remember and depersonalize information required to maintain and operate human-made socioeconomic systems. Extrasomatic devices serve a critical function, but their dependence on the living mind is total. Individuals must remember where they are and how to use them, and they must struggle over their contents. There is an inextricable symbiosis between somatically and extrasomatically stored information. Without extrasomatic storage there would be no complex social organization. Without the human memory and directed will, the extrasomatically kept information would be meaningless.

The *global system* is in the brains and in inanimate matter. As a preview of further elaboration, certain symbol/referent linkages retain a measure of homogene-

---

4.   Much of 20th century philosophy revolved around the role of language in human self-organization. Symbol/referent (or signifier/signified) relations became central to the debate among the exponents of structural linguistics, structural anthropology, and poststructuralism/postmodernism. More on this subject in Chapter 6.

ity in individuals. This homogeneity defies linguistic, cultural, and individual variations and it is preserved temporally during the lifetime of the *global system*. This may be seen by comparing GS1-and GS2-typical symbol/referent relations. (In a longer retrospective and in a more general context, the ancient/medieval/ modern contrasts demonstrate the "epochal stickiness" of institutionally and culturally specified symbol/referent pairs.)

Extrasomatically, the *global system* is in law books and in other pertinent storage devices that contain, in essence, instructions for maintaining and operating the system at the global, national, and sub-national levels. Textbooks and cultural products ensure that the *system*'s institutional values are spread wide synchronically and perpetuated diachronically.

Each *global system* has its characteristic techno-economic space, best characterized by the *system*'s technology, the distinguishing features of its capital goods. This aspect of the world order contains the largest share of extrasomatic information storage. (See more on the techno-economic space in Chapter 7.) We can see that some information pertaining to a given *global system* is maintained only somatically, some by a combination of somatic and extrasomatic means, and some only extrasomatically.

Given individual storage of symbol/referent links, and a linguistically unexpressed understanding and consciousness of the environment, skills and technical expertise are deployed to maintain and operate the *global system*. At the *macroscopic* level, such skills and expertise are in the neuronal networks of those who operate *multilateral* organizations. At the *mesoscopic* level, information required to maintain and manage national socioeconomic institutions that correspond to the *global system* are in the cerebra of government officials. The skills and technical expertise required to administer subnational units are also related to the *global system* since they are derived from *macroscopically* determined national systems.

At the *microscopic* level, the perception of the world may be reduced to the shifting image of the self-centered environment, the *surrounding socioeconomic milieu* with the *personal socioeconomic sphere* at its core. *Milieus* and *spheres* and their relationships vary greatly; nevertheless, they feature characteristics that are specific to the prevalent *global system*. The underlying uniformity and complementarity imply relatively stable neuronal pathways and electrochemical functioning at some level of detail. Certain enduring fixtures participate in evaluating and treating the stream of information that reaches the cerebral apparatus.

Two earlier points bear repetition. It is not the biologically evolved, panhuman system of the brain that changes, but the application of its transgenerationally passed on mixture of all-purpose and specialized mechanisms. However, a different application implies material differences. Further, the rationally derived similarities (isomorphisms) and complementarities (heteromorphisms) in the traces that accompany a *global system*, from its *initus* to its *terminus*, are composed of quantum netherworlds in which time is reversible, substance becomes a cloud of probabilities, and one particle may just decide to become another one. This reality, which is drastically different from, and remains unconnected to, anything we can directly examine, is involved in the exercise of human relations. It may play some role in it, but little is known about how and to what extent.

The world surrounding the individual lives in the individual. The brain contains the image of external conditions and the information to deal with them. No wonder it is difficult to discern when people speak about the world order and when the world order speaks through them. Difficult, but not impossible, once we embrace *macrohistory* and observe that a *global system*-specific vocabulary develops around its core of precise symbol/referent relations, that is, those contained in its foundational legislation, its *imprimatur*.

Human relations, and the socioeconomic relations within them, are material in nature. Further, all interpersonal communications can also be considered physical phenomena. They have always involved light, sound, touch, and smell; and since the second half of the 19th century, with the development of telegraph, telephone, radio, TV, and computer-based communications, they have made increasing use of electromagnetism. Other forms of interpersonal contacts, such as telepathy, may exist. If so, one day, when parapsychology sheds its eccentric, off-the-beaten-path science status, they may be explained by the brain's quantum intricacies.

Cultural evolution is incorporation of matter or energy or information into an existing, self-renewing structure of matter or energy or information. Socioeconomic relations may be regarded as crucial organizational characteristics in these processes. They are material phenomena because they are grounded in brains and in physical objects outside the human body, and because their realization occurs through emitting and receiving physically interpretable signals. Embracing the idea that socioeconomic relations are a constituent element of, rather than independent from, the evolution of human self-organization as a process of complexifying matter (or energy, or quantity of information required to describe its actual microstate) is indispensable. This conceptualization connects *homo sapiens* (idealized and exaggerated by social sciences) with the absolute lack of concern the laws of thermodynamics show toward our world. The combination leads to a new vantage point from which humanly interpreted logical necessities may be observed in the landscape of nature's inexorabilities.

5

Culture and Cultural Evolution in the Context of Thermodynamics

[The laws of thermodynamics apply to *culture* and *cultural evolution*. The *second law* is controversial in analyzing the physical conditions of human expansion. Its interpretations are based on the inevitability of waste when using matter/energy, on the tendency of molecular structures to deteriorate, and on the accompanying phenomenon of losing information about the environment in the process. Matter as the narrow constraint to *cultural evolution* is viewed according to the three interpretations of the *second law*. The lump-sum or fixed stock theory of low-entropy material endowment. The endogenous relationship between the aggregate state of matter and technology. Understanding the evolutionary significance of the *second law* is not an espousal of philosophical pessimism.]

Culture may be regarded as a thermodynamic system.[1] But what kind? According to the interaction with its surrounding exterior, there are three possibilities. A system is *isolated* if it does not exchange energy or matter with its exterior; it is *closed* if it exchanges energy but not matter; and it is *open* if both energy and matter are exchanged (*Kondepudi and Prigogine, 1998*). By virtue of its total count of atoms, as well as their weight, the *terrestrial sphere* may be regarded as a closed thermodynamic system. Whatever happens to matter in this sphere through natural developments such as volcanic eruptions or as a result of man's existence and activities, it remains within this sphere. The planet does not receive economically meaningful shipments of matter from the rest of the universe. This

---

1. Since *culture* has a system (e.g., GS2) we prefer to characterize it as an entity. Nonetheless, the concept is still applicable in the same way that the human organism may be called a system, even when it has its "central nervous system."

103

is probably a good thing, considering the football-field-size asteroids that roam the celestial realms. As a thermodynamic system, the *terrestrial sphere* is *closed* but not *isolated.* The sun radiates energy to the Earth. Most of what reaches the planet's hard surface is sent back into outer space. Thus, the *terrestrial sphere* exchanges energy with its exterior, but not matter.

Culture strives to preserve itself by increasing its size and, as a consequence, the complexity of its self-organization. Because it is a subset of the *terrestrial sphere*, it can engage in this enterprise as if it were an open system, but only until its growth meets binding physical constraints. Then Mother Nature, the symbol of benevolence and just rigor in contemporary patois, transmogrifies into an angry and unpredictable beast. At this point, a stunned world reluctantly learns that the openness of space for *cultural evolution* in the *terrestrial sphere* was an illusion.

Cultural evolution is subject to the laws of thermodynamics.[2] The *first law* (the Conservation Law) is that energy in a system and its surroundings, isolated together from the rest of the universe, remains constant. Considering the hot sun and the cold Earth together to be an isolated system, the total energy (capacity to perform work) within it is fixed. It can change form, as the system and its surroundings interact, but it can neither increase nor decrease; "energy can neither be created nor destroyed."

The *second law* has many formulations. Any movement (work) entails some waste of energy; hence, no *perpetuum mobile* can be constructed; entropy (bound energy; that is, energy unavailable to do work) measures the degree of disorder in a thermally isolated system; entropy in such a system tends irreversibly (though "probabilistically" or "stochastically") to grow toward its maximum. For all practical purposes, entropy changes in one direction. Since it trends upward, even if it may occasionally stagnate, Arthur Stanley Eddington (1882-1944) characterized it as "the arrow of time." Maximum entropy signifies equilibrium, a dissipated state, in which spontaneous developments are extremely unlikely.

The *third law* states that entropy at absolute zero temperature (minus 273.15 degrees Celsius) no longer increases. If absolute zero temperature prevailed in the universe it would be in a steady state. Thus, both permanently absolute zero temperature and maximum disorder represent equilibrium.

By virtue of the equivalence between matter and energy, these laws are equally valid for matter.[3] The relevance of the *first law* for *cultural evolution* is unambiguous. The weight of materials taken from the *terrestrial sphere* by the growing pop-

---

2.   Nicolas Léonard Sadi Carnot (1796-1832) and Rudolf Julius Emanuel Clausius (1822-1888) are regarded as the founders of modern thermodynamics.

ulation plus output must equal the weight of materials released into it. No atom from a dead body (not even if it is cremated) or that of a decaying electric toaster will ever leave the *terrestrial sphere*'s gravitational field. (At least as long as the current cosmic order prevails.) The molecules of the harvested sunflower will be built into other structures such as manufactured fiber, oil, soap, nectar, or fodder. But whatever the form of the molecules' further use, the organized substance that once was a sunflower will end up in a landfill as pollution, or as raw material for reuse. If we think of everything man-made (e.g., buildings, capital equipment, consumer products) as if it has already been written off (i.e., ready to be discarded), then the amount of waste output in a period (generated through resource exploitation, production, and consumption) equals the resource input in terms of number, composition, and weight of atoms. The world's economic and commercial activities may be reduced to the simple definition of organized molecular structures creating, maintaining, operating, discarding, and reusing other organized molecular structures. The time that elapses between when the shiny new automobile rolls off the assembly line and when it becomes a useless piece of junk is the grace of nature which allows the first happy and the last unhappy owner to use it through the nonsimultaneity of the two conditions. This grace is extended to living structures as well. Life and economic activity is nothing more than recycling material, leaving its magnitude unchanged.

The *first law* states that *cultural evolution* has a limit in the *terrestrial sphere*. The *second law* says that, as *cultural evolution* approaches its terrestrial limit, the latter is moving toward it, but not as a welcoming committee. The *third law* asserts that life is compatible only with a physical universe in which the restrictions of the *first* and *second laws* apply.

Most economists consider the *second law* a pessimistic banality, a recurring gadfly that keeps auditioning for a larger role; fortunately, it is easy to dismiss because it is too general to have any predictive power. We argue below that ignoring this aspect of reality prevents the establishment of meaningful links between the macro past and the macro future; and that, consequently, this omission leads to a limited and inherently unsatisfactory assessment of the human prospect.

---

3. Strictly speaking, Albert Einstein (1879-1955) established the equivalence between energy and mass. However, since, in our interpretation, matter always has mass, we use the word "matter" in the context of equivalence with a slash; i.e., energy/matter or matter/energy. When the two concepts are used together in an economic sense, an "and" is put between them; e.g., "the prices of matter and energy."

Interpretations of the *Second Law*

Energy and matter cannot be used with 100 percent efficiency. This is the "inevitable waste" interpretation. Entropy refers to the level of disorderliness, or lack of structure in matter, a condition that tends to increase. This may be called the "configurational/probability" interpretation. Finally, in a closed material system, disorder creates uncertainty for the human observer. This is the "informational" extension of the preceding interpretation.

The *second law* gives patent offices around the world the unshakable confidence to reject off hand all "inventions" of perpetual motion machines.[4] The lack of such mechanisms indicates that the loss in the transformation of energy into work is inevitable. For example, the bulk of chemical energy in gasoline is lost when it propels the automobile; or some of the heat energy is necessarily wasted as it is transformed into mechanical energy. This approach to the *second law* may be called the *inevitable waste* interpretation.

Ludwig Boltzmann (1844-1906) and Willard J. Gibbs (1839-1903) showed that the level of entropy depends positively, although at a diminishing rate, on the number of states an observed system may assume without changing its outward appearance. The larger the number of possible microstates, the larger its entropy. Evidently, the less ordered a system is, the more states its composing particles can assume because they are less "obligated" to conform to a specific mode of organization. Pouring hot water on top of cold water illustrates this principle. The separation between the two layers represents a certain level of order that limits the number of ways in which the molecules may be arranged. However, thermal agitation in the molecules and atoms inevitably mixes up the two layers. The water in the receptacle gradually becomes lukewarm, then cold. The dividing line representing the order has vanished; the number of ways in which the molecules can be arranged has increased. And the process is irreversible. Entropy has grown without a realistic *chance* of diminishing. *Random* movements of the molecules could, in principle, reconstruct the order of hot water on the top and cold water at the bottom, even make the hot layer hotter and the cold one colder, but physicists do not encourage us to wait for this to happen. (*Ruelle, 1991* elaborates on entropy in simple terms.)

In energy carriers and in matter, the level of entropy moves in the opposite direction from orderliness, structure, and availability to perform work. Low entropy means strong orderliness, coherent structure, and "free energy" in the

---

4.   *Fermi, 1936* is a classical source of explanation.

sense of "energy ready to be used;" i.e., extractable. High entropy means loss of orderliness (i.e., growth in *randomness*), less coherent structure, and an increase in "bound energy," i.e., in "energy no longer available for use." Maximum entropy means the *random* distribution of atoms. If maximum entropy prevailed in the universe, there would be a total absence not only of life, but also of any object created or developed. (Your reading this book is ample assurance that we are far from it.) The *configurational* approach, studied in statistical mechanics, quantifies entropy as the product of average entropy per particle and the number of particles in a system. It is closely related to stating the level of entropy in terms of probabilities.

Experience convinced physicists that "disorderly" macrostates (i.e., with many possible equivalently valid microstates) are more likely to occur than orderly ones. Irregular motions in particles caused by matter's perennial internal noise (at temperatures well above absolute zero) will see to that. As entropy grows, the likelihood of various states occurring tends to equalize. At maximum entropy, all states are equally likely to occur and disorderliness is complete.[5]

The concept of entropy has been expanded into the domain of information. Order means high information content. A specific material structure, as in a living organism or in *culture*, can be thought of as the quantity of information required to arrive at it from a lesser degree of order. Entropy and information may be considered equal opposites.[6] This positivist approach allows the conversion of the units of entropy into units of information ("bits") and makes it possible to state unequivocally that, in a given system, the sum of entropy and information about it (at the *macroscopic* level) is always zero.

Many prestigious mathematicians and physicists have been intrigued by the liaison between information and physical entropy. In the end, Claude Elwood Shannon (1916-2001) was credited for creating a new science, the so-called

---

5.   The *configurational/probability interpretation* is based on two famous Boltzmann functions; the one that adorns his grave, "$S = k \ln W$" and his "H-function." In the first one, S is the measure of entropy, and k is a constant multiplied by the natural logarithm of the number of possible microstates the particles constituting the system could assume. The "H-function" has the form $H = -\Sigma f_i \ln f_i$, where f_i represents the relative frequency of the microstate "i." The "H-function" has a direct probabilistic interpretation, $H(p) = -\Sigma p_i \ln p_i$. Here, in accordance with empirical observations, the frequencies become probabilities. No undergraduate physics textbook is conceivable without these equations. For an entertaining and sparingly technical rendition, see *Cropper, 2001*.

6.   See, for example, *Loewenstein, 1999*.

"information theory." The apparent similarities, and, of course, the shared name "entropy," which link physical disorder (expressed through the *probability inter-pretation* of the *second law*) and informational incertitude became the source of much controversy. However, no one disputes the fact that the larger the physical entropy in a system, that is, the more unruly the particles become, the more information is needed to describe its microstate; to give a dependable character-ization of its actual, detailed internal conditions.

Information entropy indicates the amount of information per signal. Shannon's epoch-making equation is used to estimate a communication channel's capacity to transmit messages efficiently.[7] The frequency of symbols is expressed in proba-bilities. The more often a signal occurs, the shorter its code should be (in "bits") to lower the cost of transmission. Certain risks can be taken to minimize costs by decreasing the amount of data transmitted, similar to personalized license plates where the "vitl mssge" suffices. In general, information theory provides the math-ematical guidelines on how and to what extent data can be compressed and reduced to minimize the cost of communication without taking an undue risk of not being understood.

◆   ◆   ◆

The way we are going to apply this concept is far from the calculable, orderly world of cables, optical fiber strands, and bandwidths. In the present application, the "signal system" itself may vary and more information reduces the meaning of the message.

---

7.   Shannon's famous equation, the "entropy of probability distribution" is $H(p) = -\Sigma \, p_i \ln p_i$. It is identical in concept and appearance to Boltzmann's "H-function." In infor-mation theory, the most likely signal has the highest probability. Therefore, to maxi-mize the transmission of messages at minimum cost, the most frequently transmitted signal should have the shortest possible code. The less likely the signal, the lower the probability of its occurrence, the longer the code. The genius in the approach is that the length of the signal happens to be equal to the natural logarithm of the probability of its occurrence. And, because of the quantitative relationship between numbers less than one (as probabilities always are), the larger the number, the smaller the value of its natural logarithm. When there is total certainty, a single message has a probability of one; therefore, its code is zero ($\ln 1 = 0$); and since all other messages have a prob-ability of zero, $H(p) = 0$. The equation reaches its maximum (in absolute value) when all messages are equally likely, an unacceptable case in electronic communications.

To illustrate this approach, consider a paradisiacal island in the Pacific Ocean with plants, animals, mountains, a river, and a lake. The main business of the island's expanding population is excavating, refining, cleansing, and packaging a chemical. Concern for the environment is growing. Conditions are specified to help determine whether the ecosystem's overall state is "natural," "good," "fair," "poor," or "unacceptable," according to implications for the health of the current population and for further expansion.

Like any ecosystem, the island generates a virtually infinite number of physical, chemical, and biotic phenomena. It "broadcasts" an overwhelming number of messages. The human analyst must conceive a signal system that will be selective as to what to measure, and when, where, and how to do it. The established signal system comprises indicative variables, such as qualitative and quantitative attributes of certain animal species and microbes, soil characteristics, and the level of concentration of a number of chemicals in inland waters. It is complemented by "protocols" that specify the frequency (e.g., once a month) and modalities of sampling, the taking of photographs, and other activities. A computer program summarizes the results, compares them to the standards of each possible state, and reports the ecosystem's overall condition in capital letters that vibrate in the middle of the screen. In essence, the ecosystem becomes the sender of coded messages about its overall condition, which the human analyst decodes. The whole exercise is subject to a budget constraint.

Currently, the ecosystem is considered in "good" condition and is expected to remain so in the foreseeable future. As long as the indicative variables of the signal system remain within their narrow quantitative range, there is no uncertainty; the *information entropy* is zero. However, this is no longer the case when uncertainty develops and variables turn *random*, that is, when the actual condition of the environment becomes a *random variable*.[8]

Reasonable efforts are exerted to maintain the island's environment in "good" condition. However, as the population rises and the economy grows, disturbing

---

8. Variables are *random* if they come with strings of probabilities attached. You toss a "fair" coin three times and calculate the probabilities that you get tails three times; twice, once, or not even once. Since the probability of seeing "tails" is ½ (the same as seeing "heads"), the respective figures will be 1/8, 3/8, 3/8, and 1/8. Let the number of tails be "r." We call "r" a *random variable* because a probability (P) is attached to each of its possible values. P(r) varies between 0 and 1, and the sum of all possibilities–denoting each one separately as "i"–equals one; i.e., $\Sigma P(r_i) = 1$. In the quoted example "i" goes from 1 to 4 (because there were four possibilities). The probabilities add up to one because it is 100 percent certain that one of the cases must occur.

new phenomena appear. Toxic algae are identified near the seashore, some "heavy metals" (elements from the group that includes mercury, chromium, cadmium, arsenic, and lead) are found in the lake, and never before seen deformities are discovered in frogs limping in and out of it. Belief in the signal system's reliability, coupled with the habitual way of decoding the messages obtained through it, begins to decay. Enter *information entropy*.

According to scientific consensus, there is now an 80-percent *chance* that the island's ecology will remain "good" (variable status 1) during the next 20 years. However, expert opinion attaches probabilities of 14 percent that it will slip to "fair" (variable status 2); 5 percent that it will turn "poor" (variable status 3); and 1 percent that it will become "unacceptable" (variable status 4). Costs are associated with each status.[9] For variable status 1, they represent the value of resources needed to maintain "good" conditions. For other statuses, they show the cost of returning them to the "good" level. Costs are expressed in "units." The worse the situation, the less likely it is to occur; however, more units would be needed to correct it. The following tabulation summarizes the possibilities:

Var Stat 1:	0.80 x 1 unit = 0.80
Var Stat 2:	0.14 x 2 units = 0.28
Var Stat 3:	0.05 x 3 units = 0.15
Var Stat 4:	0.01 x 5 units = 0.05
	Average = 1.28

The units weighted with the probabilities (1.28) yield *information entropy*. Given that Var Stat 1 corresponds to the chosen action, the measure combines the uncertainty of reading the "source" correctly with the costs of reading it incorrectly, i.e., not doing what would be required.[10]

The authorities continue to monitor the island's ecology and they regularly compare their findings with their 20-year assessment. (After one year, the 20-year period moves on the calendar; i.e., it is not reduced to 19.) As the ecological order

---

9.   Calculating them through cost/benefit analysis is a job for economists. They would probably need projections for interest rates, price and wage levels, an idea of the work actually to be done, and the expected annual flow of benefits from the island's preserved or restored ecology. From these data, they could tell if the contemplated investment is economically worth doing; that is, if it brings in more than the next best alternative use of capital. If it brings in less, calculations would show the extent of economic sacrifice required from the community.

further decomposes, the ecosystem will increase its *information entropy*, the average units per variable status. Revisions of the 20-year forecast will shift probabilities toward previously less likely conditions. The number of variable statuses, as well as the units required to bring the situation back to "good," will increase. All these changes would tend to augment *information entropy*. Compared to the original "probability distribution," *randomness* is on the rise. As far as probabilities are concerned, the index number reaches its maximum when all variable statuses become equally likely; that is, when there is total ignorance about which of the conditions will materialize. Regarding costs, there is no upper limit. The burden of clean-up will continue to rise. Moreover, since progression in physical entropy is expressed through "surprises," the signal system will have to be expanded and surveys and sampling will have to be conducted more frequently. The increasing expenses of monitoring are added to the rising costs of clean-up. The total will eventually become prohibitively high. For all practical purposes, paradise is lost.

Of course, the island's ecosystem represents the *terrestrial sphere*'s *ecological order*. The major difference is that the world population cannot abandon the planet by taking the next flight out. Using up ("drawing down") the planet's *ecological order* coincides with a diminished ability to read its state and with increasing economic costs to minimize the rate of its deterioration. The larger the organized subsystem (*culture*), the more underhanded nature becomes in enforcing the *second law*, the more it resorts to *chaos*.

The human observer's ability to interpret the *ecological order*'s transmissions coherently may be expressed by the following general expression, called "ecological information entropy" (EIE):

$$EIE = \Sigma \, p_i \, C_i$$

where p_i is the probability attached to variable status "i" and C_i stands for the consequences. The summation occurs over all possible variable statuses. This formulation is more general than the one used in the island example because the probability carried by the *random variable* may not stand for the consensus of experts (it may reflect public disposition or official policy) and the consequences may combine economic costs with other quantified losses in human welfare.

---

10. This approach is not identical to Shannon's H(p) function, but it monotonously translates the numerical trend found in it. The "units" are obviously not equal to the natural logarithms of associated probabilities. However, they increase just as the absolute number of natural logarithms of decreasing probabilities does. Hence, the approach provides an ordinal measure of *information entropy* proper.

These extensions and generalizations are needed if we want to apply the concept of *information entropy* to current ecological problems such as global warming.

◆   ◆   ◆

Macrostates close to equilibrium become next to impossible to assess in detail, but relatively easy to describe in general terms. A puff of cigar smoke in a closed room disperses as its order declines and its entropy increases. As the molecules spread out to occupy the space equitably, their spontaneity diminishes and they become both less interesting and less complicated to characterize globally. But *culture* is not a puff of smoke. Forcing the parallel, it is a puff that miraculously expands. And the human observer, who must always deploy coarse measures to assess microstates, falls behind in its ability to descry when and how the unstoppable tendency to create entropy will attack the expanding, "upstart" subsystem in order to pull it apart.

Looking at the problem not as an adversary relationship between *homo sapiens* and nature, but as one the world has with itself, the reallocation of resources from facilitating ever larger populations and economies to environmental monitoring and protection is not far from the explicit recognition that the inflating human complex in closed quarters has deceptively invisible, nonetheless insurmountable, limits.

The process of surveying the planet's ecological conditions is not as well developed as in the "island" example. Compared to the organization deployed and the resources spent on collecting and reporting economic data, the global ecosystem is a neglected field. There is no unanimously accepted scale for judging its condition. However, the day may be approaching when one generation will communicate its long-term assessment of the planet's ecosystem to the next. It is possible that such forward communication will try to balance ignorance and incertitude by associating lower probabilities of specific negative developments with higher costs required to deal with them. Fairness in transgenerational behavior would demand best efforts to minimize the progression of the "global ecological *information entropy* index."[11]

In terms of current issues, augmentation in *information entropy* may be detected in the growing debate about the increasing risks the environment poses to human life and welfare. The "growing debate" represents the decreasing probability with which the world (if it were a sole rational thinker) could be sure about the status of the *ecological order*. "Increasing risks" imply the rising costs of potential misjudgment. How much higher and stronger should post-Katrina levies be built in New Orleans, given that some credible scientific opinion claims that global warming tends to increase the frequency and strength of hurricanes? The split opinion about the effects of global warming stands for diminished certitude (pushing the probability distribution toward equal values). The consequences ("costs") of misjudging the material requirements (in either direction) are on the rise. These perceptions signal the increase of *information entropy*, the singularized numerical indicator of declining certitude.

◆   ◆   ◆

Whereas increase in "absolute entropy" is relative to its maximum, unchanging level, increase in "relative entropy" is measured against a reference state or benchmark; e.g., entropy of a specific system in a given period relative to its level in the preceding period. The *second law* says that when entropy grows it does so in both respects. Given a complex and expanding entity in a closed environment (e.g., *culture* in the *terrestrial sphere*), it is easier to recognize the relative build-up. Turning coal to ashes is visible, but how such acts move the configuration of matter in the living space toward more entropy relative to its maximum is hard to comprehend.

As long as *culture* expands, entropy must also grow in an absolute sense. The configuration of matter (and the likelihood of its change) in the *terrestrial sphere* does not imply a meaningful split of matter into the human system and the rest. The condition of cosmic matter/energy (along with its tendency to move toward lesser order) is a macroscopic attribute that does not take the boundary between *culture* and the rest of the *terrestrial sphere* into account.

Absolute entropy is easy to block out. There is no sign that mankind and its artifices are making the universe increasingly homogenous. The build-up evolves along a complicated path from the human time perspective, and therefore, it

---

11. On the global scale, it would be incomparably more difficult to attach values to the resources deemed necessary to safeguard the environment. The worse the planet's ecological condition becomes, the less the economic concept of opportunity cost makes sense. When the opportunity cost sinks to "zero," there is no sensible alternative for the use of a given bundle of resources. Under such conditions, cost/benefit calculations could no longer assume a properly functioning market system with positive interest rates, reflecting "time preference" ("the investor's impatience to consume"). For a description of the theoretical problems surrounding environmental investment and the related issue of transgenerational equity, see *Pearce and Turner, 1990*.

remains a qualitative generalization without any apparent relevance to "real life" problems. This is a very tricky situation, similar to the well-known horror movie device. The heroine tries to lock out the monster but the monster is already in the house. She misread the signs and locked him in, instead of out. Entropy accumulates all around us. One result is the growing information blackout about our ecological conditions, experienced through the breakdown of unanimity in reading the messages emitted by the environment.

The "loss," the "configurational/probability," and the "information-based" interpretations follow the same "arrow of time." Molecules compressed in energy carriers (e.g., coal) will perform some useless (wasteful) motions from the standpoint of heat generation; they will disperse, losing their orderliness in the process, and will blur information about where the molecules are and what they are "up to." In addition, when the system is closed, as in the *terrestrial sphere*, the growing elusiveness of its microstate (that is, our lessening ability to characterize the detailed conditions of the physical environment through selected, coarse criteria) will also mean a diminishing capability to assess threats to the planet's human order.

THE GROWING DECREPITUDE OF MATTER

Most economists shrug off entropy along these lines: "The *second law* applies to energy. Entropy build-up would limit the human economy only if we lived in a closed system. This is not our problem. Planet Earth is open. Since mechanical work comes from heat and heat comes from the sun, you might as well stop worrying; our source of energy is practically unlimited: That bright Sol will shine upon this fair Orb long enough to consider it eternity. There are plenty of other, more immediate concerns; come back to the here and now." Indeed, if you are a young economics professional, scanning the horizon for a specialization that is appreciated, you might as well look elsewhere. There are no jobs in entropy. You will never see a vacancy announcement that reads: "*Entropic Associates, Inc.* seeks a dynamic, self-starter to analyze data and model the economic-growth-constraining effects of the *second law of thermodynamics*. Excellent communication skills and ability to talk convincingly to the business community in public venues are crucial."

The *second law* is indeed forgettable if one considers solar radiation "the" constraint to *cultural evolution*. The sun bathes the Earth in a rich flow of energy, some of which, a very small proportion in fact, is used. Solar energy originates in nuclear fusion. Under conditions of incredible heat and pressure, hydrogen is converted into helium. The matter lost in the process is sent into space as radiant energy. Although our celestial lantern has an estimated lifetime of five-billion-years, in a billion years it is expected to heat up, boiling away all life on the planet. Even with this caveat, we can relax. Compared to a billion years, recorded human history is a mere rounding error. (The Moon's growing distance from the Earth is an incomparably more immediate threat against human life.) But this is not the right way to look at the species' thermodynamic situation.

To begin with, the fact that the theoretical equivalence between energy and matter means that the *second law* also applies to matter is often overlooked. Just as heat cannot be converted into work at 100 percent efficiency, matter cannot be converted into matter without loss. Matter-specific entropy in the *terrestrial sphere* cannot decrease. Further, the fact that matter and energy are not mutually convertible, their theoretical equivalence notwithstanding, is almost completely ignored. Matter is used to generate energy, but the transformation of energy into matter is not among the technologies available for economic exploitation. We cannot manufacture oil from heat, coal from electricity. The production of the biomass through photosynthesis also draws from the Earth's fixed supply of matter. Solar energy does not become substance; it only facilitates the synthesis of what is already here. This practical asymmetry makes matter into the "narrow *exergic* constraint," where *exergy* is defined as the opposite to entropy. When *exergy* is at its highest level, entropy is at its lowest. This device helps make us think of entropy as a constraint, a specific quantity that diminishes through use.

Change in a system's entropy (dS) has two variables: the entropy it produces to build and maintain itself ($d_i S$) and the entropy it expels into its surroundings ($d_e S$).[12] Entropy in closed systems tends to be positive and increase, i.e., $dS \geq 0$, since $d_e S = 0$ and $d_i S \geq 0$. However, if a system is open, it can grow and maintain itself by producing what seems like negative entropy ($d_i S < 0$), provided compliance with the *second law* is maintained through building up entropy in the system's surroundings. That is, an open system creates orderliness inside of itself at the expense of at least that much disorderliness outside of it. From the open system's limited point of view, entropy can decrease even in a closed system, but this perception is false from the entire system's point of view. Given that $dS \geq 0$ and $d_e S = 0$, $d_i S$ must be zero or positive. (It cannot be negative.)

Biological entities are open thermodynamic systems. They exchange both matter and energy with their surroundings. Humans take in low-entropy, highly

---

12. See *Prigogine, 1997*, p. 63.

organized matter (e.g., apple pie á la mode), break it down, degrade it, then expel it through the gastrointestinal tract and heat radiation. Systems under human control, such as *personal socioeconomic spheres*, individual pieces of machinery, factories, and entire industries, also act as open systems. Even nations may try to act in this way. They import low entropy (e.g., energy carriers and manufactured goods) and try to ship high entropy (waste and pollution) beyond the frontiers; knowingly when, for example, nuclear material is buried in a foreign landfill; unknowingly through degrading open-access common property (e.g., the oceans and the atmosphere). But success cannot be complete. Some of the waste and pollution will remain within the frontiers. As the limited data on "international waste trade" allow us to surmise, no nation has yet succeeded in making the rest of the world its sink hole. If, for no other reason, the damage inflicted on the "commons" haunts every human being, regardless of geographic location. General ecological degradation explains the intranational contest among individuals, areas, industries, and businesses to remain, to the extent possible, open systems.

Since all the components of *culture* are open systems, or are acting as if they were, *culture* seems to be open too. To see why this is a fallacy, let S_M be the *terrestrial sphere*'s total entropy "denominated" in matter. The world accumulates matter related entropy by degrading the substances it uses. Since *culture* does not "export" degraded matter from the *terrestrial sphere* ($d_e S_M = 0$), $d_i S_M \geq 0$ must hold. In the *terrestrial sphere*, which includes all the surroundings that individual subsystems consider "outside," the absolute value of S_M must have a tendency to grow. That is, the world accumulates disorder within its planetary confines.

The *terrestrial sphere* as a material constraint may be analyzed by looking separately at the *global environment*, the *ecological order*, and *certitude of information*. These approaches correspond to the *inevitable waste*, the *configurational/probability*, and *information-based* interpretations of entropy. Each of the three constraints should be imagined as a symbolic lump sum because physicists can, in principle, calculate the absolute level of entropy for any system. Although the methodology is different, according to which of the three approaches is highlighted, the existence of an absolute value is conceivable under each.[13] Since the level of entropy indicates how useless matter is, its exact opposite (its level of

13.   Theory is specific on the conditions that would set the value of equations measuring the absolute level of entropy to zero or infinity under each of the three approaches. Therefore, imagining concrete values between the two quantified extremes makes sense for any system, no matter how large and complicated it may be. The absolute level of entropy is expressed in "joules per kelvin." *Information-based* entropy (in communication theory proper) is in "bits per signal."

exergy) gauges its utility. If the absolute level, calculated through the mathematical formalisms under the *inevitable waste* and *configurational* approaches, ranges from zero to infinity, its *exergy*, implying "free energy" and usefulness, will range from infinity to zero. The same conceptualization is valid for *information-based* entropy. Accordingly, total certitude will appear as infinity and total incertitude as zero.

About 12,000 years ago, matter in the *terrestrial sphere* was in a specific condition. Numerically, its suggested measures had to be somewhere between infinity and zero. We arbitrarily set the level of each of the three indicators at 100 for the year 10,000 BCE. The *global environment, ecological order*, and *certitude of information* about the *terrestrial sphere* were all 100. These "one hundreds" symbolize the Earth's native state at the birth of *cultural evolution*. It is subject to natural depreciation, incidental to the planet's mere existence. Anything that happens (climatic changes, geological transformations, spontaneous chemical reactions, the life cycles of species and their competitive interactions) tends to reduce the original fixed stock. This is the safe and responsible supposition. *Cultural evolution* accelerated natural depreciation, which is presumed to be extremely slow, by ransacking nonrenewable resources with the vehement appetite of locusts but with less foresight.

The fixity of low-entropy supplies (*exergy*) represents a strictly human angle on the physical environment. Material conditions are always particular to species. Nature pushes all forms of life to expand beyond the limits constituted by renewable resources, to multiply and eat into the supportive habitat. Competition for low-entropy (space) prevents any manifestation of animate existence (deer, for instance) from populating the Earth. Whenever nature's balance is absent or kept at bay, the eagerness to live will lead to the reduction of the low-entropy stock contained in species-particular nonrenewable resources. Then the combination of evolved organism and ingrained social behavior (stamped thus far as "success" by natural selection) will face the changes in the physical environment caused by "self-engineered" over extension. Although the murderous struggles of biological evolution continue to augment absolute entropy, this process is part of a long, cosmic evolution. Its time scale is large enough not to interfere with the formation of new species on the material conditions left behind by some extinct ones. If the self-initiated end of "ecological release" (or some catastrophic event) reduced the native state of "one hundreds" for one type of life to the level at which it had to quit the scene, this would not prevent another one with a different metabolism and nascent supra-organismic scheme from yelling out in delight: "Wow! It's one hundred!" Every time a new landfill is created, expanding the cemetery of dead matter from the human perspective, an Edenic wealth of low entropy for bacteria is created. And many living creatures would find the decline or disappearance of *homo sapiens* a great opportunity for self-promotion.

Crude as this *entropometrics* may be, it forms an indispensable backdrop for viewing the world realistically. Each of the interpretations of the *second law* presented above provides separate insights into the human-development-constraining nature of *Mater*. (In Chapter 8, we shall introduce the concept of *ecoplasm*, which expresses the three *exergic* constraints as a single, integrated measure.)

◆   ◆   ◆

The *global environment* is the supply of primary substance. It becomes smaller as it is gradually transformed into *culture* and *geocapital*. The *geocapital* expands qualitatively when new items are added to the list of useful commodities and quantitatively when more of any item is found and when technological advances make previously uneconomical finds profitable to exploit. The *geocapital* contracts when individual items in its catalogue of contents are deleted (owing to exhaustion or abandonment) and when the stocks of the remaining items are reduced. Historically, *geocapital* has registered a net increase; additions and expansions more than offset exhaustions and reductions. This long-lasting, successful experience led to the culturally ingrained confidence in the possibility of its eternal continuation. Economic growth theory keeps "deriving" the same conclusion over and over again: Optimally maintained economic expansion can continue forever. Translated from evolutionary scales to our own, this is analogous to "Since I wake up every morning I must be immortal."

Cultural evolution requires increased volumes of matter and energy. As long as it continues, the *global environment* will lose weight (literally) to feed *culture* and *geocapital*. Matter conscripted into *geocapital* to serve the cause of *cultural evolution* is degraded in use; its entropy level increases. No matter how efficient the reuse or recycling technique may be, it cannot help but somewhat depreciate the *global environment*'s low-entropy fund.

The rate of transfer from the *global environment* into the *geocapital* has increased tremendously during the past two centuries. However, this rate must eventually decline and reach zero, indicating that the absolute level of low entropy included in *geocapital* reached its peak. ("Peak low entropy" is similar in a broad sense to "peak oil.") Beyond that point, the total mass of orderly substances under current and potential requisition can no longer increase. From that time forward, the general tendency of decline in the *global environment*'s low-entropy stock would have spilled over into the *geocapital's* decline of low-entropy supply. *Culture* has been (and probably still is) moving up on the curve that shows the total amount of low-entropy material claimed for human use over a historical time scale. The beat is still on. The hoarding of usable matter from the *global environment* continues.

It is impossible to determine where human civilization is now compared to the original *exergic* constraint of 100 and at what rate the remainder is declining. The actual number must be below 100 and it must continue declining, most likely at an accelerated tempo. Yet, we cannot determine when and under what conditions the *geocapital's* thermodynamic work potential will max out. Nor can anyone tell if this will occur exactly when the *global environment's* ability to support life is squeezed to its minimum. But it may still be beneficial to keep in mind that there is such a minimum and its violation would entail dire consequences. Humans need a certain amount of space to move freely, to breathe tolerable levels of oxygen in the growing jungle of buildings, shopping centers, and parking lots; to avoid the negative psychological and physiological consequences (well established by studies concerning the effects of population density on organisms in the animal kingdom) that result from overfilling a limited surface.

At the end of the thermodynamic tether, reused or recycled waste remains the only source of relatively low entropy. However, it too will have to shrink, since the *second law* disallows the maintenance of a given level of entropy by eternal reuse and recycling. Earth's bounty did not include a patent for perpetual motion machines. *Cultural evolution's* dissipation of terrestrial material is inevitable to the full extent one can trust this much abused word.

Three popular misconceptions stand in the way of accepting the proposed way of thinking. The first is not considering entropy build-up a process applicable to matter; the second may be called "the illusion of unlimited and eternal substitutability among materials," and the third is considering technology to be completely independent from the general condition of matter. To fuse the three into a single objection: "Entropy is energy that can no longer be used. This concept does not apply to matter; waste, for example, can always be recycled. Matter does not disappear like heat. Therefore, the level of (high) entropy in matter is not an absolute, but a relative concept. It all depends on technology. New methods of production will always allow scientists and engineers to consider used matter a spanking new resource."

To disperse the first misconception, we must refer the reader to textbooks on physics. They provide equations for calculating the level of entropy as a function of absolute temperature for matter in solid, liquid, or gaseous states. The second mistaken belief falters on the indispensable material needs of the growing energy input demanded to counteract the *second law*. In the long run, all economic activities will have to rely on reusing and recycling low quality stuff with the help of other low quality stuff. This process promises to be increasingly expensive. Although energy may be abundant, it cannot be produced without matter (e.g., solar *panels*, atomic energy *stations*, hydroelectric *dams*, wind *turbines*, geothermal heat *pumps*, garbage *incinerators*). In principle, more and more energy could be used to restore low entropy from increasingly dispersed matter to keep the *geocapital*'s low-entropy contents from declining. In practice, however, increased energy production would claim ever larger quantities of restored matter. Unless a totally new class of "ideal" technologies that preserves rather than degrades low entropy is discovered (a development that would be tantamount to divine intervention), the ability to produce at all must decline. *The narrow constraint to cultural evolution will become effective when the material requirements of increased energy production in substituting low quality (higher entropy) matter for higher quality (lower entropy) matter make the expansion of output levels uneconomical.* (The long-run tendency of decline in the global average profit comes from the relationship between *culture* and the *global environment*, rather than, as Marx argued, being a phenomenon of capitalism's limited capacity to accommodate economic expansion.)

The third misconception, faith in the inexhaustibility of broadly marketable technological solutions, is an opiate that dulls awareness of the fact that *segregate* successes in recovering low entropy, introducing new substitutes and making used material available again, face *aggregate* limits.

Substitution is not just a scientific-technological problem the economic significance of which is restricted to the immediate suppliers and buyers of specific substitutes. In every bravura of substitution and *geocapital* expansion, long-run social opportunity costs are associated with private and relatively short-term benefits. For example, in a growing number of products and production technologies, ceramics, glass, and plastics can be used profitably *in lieu* of metals. But clay, the major raw material for producing industrial ceramics, is a vital ingredient of high-quality soil; glass, although manufactured from abundantly available silica and sandstone, requires metal alloys, such as lead, barium, manganese, cesium, or certain semi-metals, or various metallic oxides, dependent upon the physical and chemical demands placed on the final product; and plastic comes mainly from oil, the same oil that will run out during this century unless the demand for it is drastically curtailed.

Daring new techniques to access raw materials also have negative side-effects or "costs." For instance, it is true that the ocean floor can be scooped and vacuumed for manganese nodules; but there is a "flip side." The process increases pollution and furthers the destruction of marine ecosystems. When research and development turn scientific information into production technology, *homo sapiens* looks like a mythical giant of creation. However, when one considers the full consequences of piling one piece of ingenuity upon the other, and using nonrenewable resources without the slightest forethought in the process, it looks more like a frolicking Bugs Bunny who doesn't notice the boulder bouncing toward him from behind.

In the final analysis, technology is the deployment of energy to alter, form, and move matter with the help of other matter already altered, formed, and moved. If the quantity of low entropy diminished below a certain critical level, the concepts of tangible usefulness and purposive action ("technological solutions") would also lose their sense. Scientists tell us that it is possible to make anything from anything through atomic-scale technologies. In principle, they could replace copper wires with carbon polymers and make gold from scraps of copper, but in practice they could not do it if they had to pick through the ofals of low-entropy substance in search of other material inputs. The point is that the growing disorder in material structures tends to push the costs of new production methods out of sight.

Here is another way to look at this problem. If there were no temperature differences in the world, humans could not make nature do anything for them; as a matter of thermodynamic certainty, we could not even exist. The *second law* applied on astronomical scales holds out the possibility that entropy means just such a normalization of temperatures in the cosmos. As entropy increases, the temperature tends both to decline and equalize; and when entropy is at its maximum, or very close to it, the possibility of unidirectional transformations is over. The arrow of time has vanished. Remembering that matter is pent up energy and that it forms a closed system in the *terrestrial sphere*, the increase of matter-denominated entropy tends toward eliminating temporary, but, from the human vantage point, vital energy gradients. At the end of this process, matter no longer possesses the sturdiness required to work with and on it. Forget about hammering a nail into the wall. The world is, of course, far from there, but it is moving in that direction. Between "can be done economically" and "cannot be done physically" there is a tipping point: "Can be done physically but not economically." *New historical materialism* does not claim to be able to forecast when this point will be reached. It argues only that recognizing the existence of a "peak" in the use of low-entropy matter (as in "peak oil") is in the long-term human interest.

Ignoring the big picture of planetary physics, current opinion is far from such recognition. It considers the level of entropy a function of technology rather than vice versa. Yet technology is circumscribed by the overall condition of available matter—a subject that requires a closer look.

On the Endogenous Relationship between the State of Matter and Technology

Between the microphysical measurability of entropy (under very special, controlled conditions) and the absolute certainty of entropic accumulation at the macro scale lies the *second law*'s secretive dynamic. Entropy can be and is defeated locally and temporarily in many ways. But its manifestations are so thoroughly intertwined with everything the organism does and everything that happens to it that its pervasive significance becomes lost in the muddled phenomenology between laboratory factoid and overall tendency. Clarity about a dictate of nature vital for the world remains virtually defenseless against facile and uninformed eco-sci-tech triumphalism.

The inclination to relate the general validity of the *first law* to isolated examples of the *second law* might be one source of self-deception. Descriptions of entropy in the economic process correctly emphasize the loss of free energy and the corresponding accumulation of bound energy in the environment (from coal to ashes, from gasoline to fumes, etc.) But stating that a specific pristine matter, once put through the production process, can no longer be used for the same purpose because part of the energy contained in it became bound or latent, *must* carry a caveat to ensure conformity with the law of conservation of energy and matter. If the caveat sounds like "given that the energy contained in the wasted matter is no longer readily available," the doctrinaire technologist will pounce upon the "not readily." Ashes today, potatoes tomorrow; discarded junk now, shiny office furniture tomorrow; it is all a question of human ingenuity, the flow of ideas becoming science, industry, and commerce.

The technology-relatedness of free energy may be another misleading vantage point. Free energy (broadly the same as low entropy) found in matter can always be related to a specific purpose. A substance found in nature, with the most favorable combination of qualities, given what is intended to be done with it, may be regarded as containing the maximum amount of free energy for a well defined process. This combination could be a high level of concentration (as in the case of metals), optimal ductileness, melting point, electrical and heat conductivity, etc. Reduction in these qualities (that is, in free energy, or equivalently, an increase in entropy) follows from use. The market-logical sequence of extracting the highest quality first, the second next, and so forth, ensures a graduated approach to depleting free energy or low entropy. Recycling also reduces quality. In this case, the loss may be equated with the amount of energy and matter needed to restore the degraded and dispersed substance to its usable, object-like integrity. ("Technology and market," as an imaginary single intellect, quantifies the quality of matter along a scale that can distinguish between "more" or "less" extractable free energy.) By knowing exactly what to do (technology) with what (material resource), society's interest always focuses on one particular aspect of universal free energy.

As the best combination of qualities (implying high level of free energy, low entropy) is exhausted, the angle of focus shifts. Technology and the market, the claim goes, will search for and find the material resource with sufficient extractable free energy to accomplish any productive task. Matter (element or chemical compound) degraded from the viewpoint of one technology is precious raw material for the next generation of technologies. Looking at the universe this way, free energy in matter is arguably eternal. Matter has an infinite number of qualities and science can always discover the one best suited for the technological task at hand. Inexhaustible qualities in matter are matched with inexhaustible human inventiveness in an eternal cycle of undiminished interplay, seeing to the eternal growth of the global economy.

The scale of the task faced by technology is yet a third source of misreading the malleability of nature to accommodate human wishes. The aggregate replacement of energy carriers and raw materials on their way to exhaustion with renewable sources, while assuring continued, private profit-driven economic growth, may not be available in this century. At the other extreme, laboratory-scale procedures applied to segregate problems are practically inexhaustible.

To show that entropy is ultimately apodictic and that the aggregate state of matter and the level of technology (appearances and exaggerated positivism notwithstanding) mutually determine one another, the process of matter losing free energy and gaining bound energy in the *terrestrial sphere* must be interpreted along a quantitative scale. Physical dispersion (indicative of growing entropy) provides the basis for such a conceptualization. The 90 "natural" elements in the periodic table are our starting point. Their distribution is the planet's material endowment; it is the *terrestrial sphere*'s "substantive endowment profile" (SEP). Cultural evolution (expanding and complexifying economic activity included) will not change it; it will only scatter its ingredients.

At the beginning of *cultural evolution*, SEP was 100; its dispersion was the initial condition, or the benchmark: SEP(100). Growing entropy means increasing dispersion, denoted as the series SEP(99), SEP(98), etc. SEP(0) is the completely homogenous dispersion of the elements, the fictitious end state, thermodynamic equilibrium: no nail, no hammer, nobody to do the hammering. The numbers in parentheses are purely symbolic. SEP(99) indicates that the dispersion of the elements is more advanced than at SEP(100), but less than at SEP(98). The declining scale wants to convey irrevocable quantitative deterioration—the decline of free energy found in the *terrestrial sphere*.

Next, let us mind-construct the human economy's "substantive use profile" (SUP). This is a rationally conceivable listing of the percentages that the weight of each of the 90 elements represents in *culture* and the *geocapital*.[14] Of course, the differences in the numbers will be enormous. Some of them will be two digits; others might show up only several places after the decimal point; others will be considered zero. Nonetheless, these "elemental" contributions will add up to 100 percent; or, equivalently, to "one," followed by the number of zeros after the decimal required to account for the smallest shares. Now let us subdivide the SUP into four columns. The first one, A, shows the distribution of materials in actual and potential use; that is, raw materials and energy carriers at productive establishments (already in *culture*) plus what is in the *geocapital*. The second column, B, indicates the composition of elements as used in technology, roughly the same as they occur in physical capital (machines, equipment, tools, instruments, factory buildings). Column C represents the "make-up" of all other (i.e., noncapital) goods ever produced (e.g., residential and government buildings, cultural establishments, infrastructures, durable and nondurable consumer goods). Column D identifies the breakdown of distinct atoms in humans and biomasses in human service. At any given moment, SUP is the weighted average of columns A through D. It will account for the use of elements in *culture* and in *geocapital*. The *global environment* is the *terrestrial sphere*'s residual component. The weighted average of its distribution and SUP (itself a weighted average) equals

---

14.   The synthetic, man-made, radioactive elements have not been forgotten. They are indirectly included in the SUP since their production must lean on the naturally occurring elements.

SEP, whatever its level of dispersion (i.e., 100, 99, 98). The *global environment* supplies free energy, matter considered to possess the best quality for well-defined uses, and that is where waste (material containing bound energy) goes. It is the source of low entropy and the sink for high entropy. Reuse or recycling means interaction between columns C and A: Atoms stream from produced goods into the raw material sector. When plants become raw materials in a different composition than previously used, interactions occur between columns D and A.

Technology is not an exogenous factor dependent only on human capital. The *second law* prevents movements in column B from reversing decline in SEP values. Believing in the independence of column B is the same as considering information a free variable that can undo entropic accumulation. It implies that going from SEP(99) to SEP(98) is due to ignorance and that, by reducing it through scientific advance, the human community could go back to SEP(100). Belief in the reversibility of SEP's parenthetical values is linked to the unconscious assumption that *perpetuum mobile* (a loophole in the *second law*) exists in the universe. The reality is that the global condition of growing dispersion will first tend to frustrate then completely prohibit particular solutions to the opportunistic acquisition of free energy from the *global environment*.

Dispersion being an absolute and irreversible fact puts the errant focus of scientific interest (always finding free energy for a purpose) itself in the proper light. Matter indeed has an infinite number of qualities, but its growing dispersion decreases the probability that any particular set of qualities can be used without increased amounts of energy and matter. Importantly, the potentially unlimited energy pent up in matter cannot pick up the tab alone. More energy means increased use of matter. *Geocapital's* pre-peak status obscures, but does not completely hide, the approach of material input scarcity. By now, metal recycling is considerable and the excavation of virgin materials must overcome increasingly unfavorable physical conditions to reach ever lower grade reserves.

The following basic characteristics of substance endowment and use profile are noteworthy:

(1) *SEP and SUP cannot be equal.* Each of the elemental compositions of humans (part of column D), raw materials used (column A), technology (column B), and man-made artifices (column C) is different from the "make-up" of the *global environment.* Textbook data clearly indicate inequalities among the five distributions, but there is no need to cite them here. Logical considerations alone suffice to make the point. For SUP to be equal to SEP, nothing less would be required than a concerted, worldwide effort to make technology and the economy preserve the Earth's elemental distribution. Since the elemental composition

of the planet's biomass deviates from SEP, decisions under social control would have to force the rest of SUP variables to conform to SEP, disregarding actual human needs, profitability, and technological possibilities. Obviously, *cultural evolution* occurs without such considerations or intentions. If a condition could be achieved and maintained only through conscious and continuous effort, and none had ever been exerted, the condition does not exist.

If, by a virtually unimaginable coincidence, SUP equaled SEP, this fortuitous happenstance could not hold. *Culture* does not return elements into the *global environment* in precisely the same amounts and compositions as it withdraws them. The increase in population, by itself, shows that the withdrawal of elements does not match their return. Also, made objects do not depreciate or decay uniformly. Their composite elements return to the *global environment* according to different schedule than they leave it.

(2) *There is no human control over the global environment's elemental composition.* The expansion of *culture* occurs through dim-sighted individual and group decisions. For a long time, no one cared about the effects of *cultural evolution* on the *global environment*. Although there is now a growing concern about resource depletion and ecological damage, and consequently, these issues are monitored, the physical evolution of the *global environment* is not subject to comprehensive social regulation or management.

(3) *Alterations in the global environment's elemental composition limit potential changes in SUP.* *Cultural evolution* must deal with its consequences. Its future is conditioned on its past. At any moment, the *global environment*'s distribution, evolving out of control, determines the weights attached to elements in SUP. The transformation of SUP cannot leave changes in the *global environment* unheeded and these changes constrain SUP's further transformations.

(4) *Not all alterations in SUP are rational or even conscious.* To a great extent, SUP changes as the result of technical and economic considerations. Scientifically founded, market-driven analysis affects the composition and sources of energy carriers and raw materials. The changes in column A and the extent to which its sources shift between the *global environment* and materials found in C may be attributed to collective decisions guided by analytical principles. Nonetheless, SUP's internal shifts are spontaneous to some extent. The expanding scale of human reproduction is the primary example. As the population grows, per capita income rises, and pollution spreads, subtle transformations in the elemental composition of the species' mass (column D) take place.

(5) *The evolution of techno-economic decisions will have to follow a forced directionality.* To account for an overall increase in the dispersion of earthly matter,

growth in the *global environment*'s bound energy must more than compensate for the segregate accumulation of free energy in *culture*. Since the *global environment* is the ultimate source of free energy, its depletion will tend to increase the self-use of matter via the rising material demand of higher energy input requirements.

The composition of material inputs and technology is in a mutually determining endogenous relationship within the overall endogenous interactions among all the columns of SUP and the global environment. Each of the five variables (A through D, and the *global environment*) reacts to the others; each makes the rest react, but under the commonly shared constraint of irreversible dispersion. Column B is entangled in a system of restless feed-back loops that includes all the columns. It is path-dependent. Its possibilities are structured and the structuring is not the result of reasoned foresight. Technology cannot escape the consequences of the growing dispersion of matter (higher entropy, more bound energy) it caused. In the end, the accumulation of entropy will force market-wide technological change (alterations in B), the most rational facet of social decision-making, to be directed toward accessing and saving matter at increasing costs.

The average contemporary physicist knows incomparably more about the nature of matter than Newton did–one of the greatest thinkers who ever lived. The explanation that "science and technology have evolved" is incomplete. The entire *cultural evolution* since GS0 was necessary in order to account for this progress–more people working and thinking; quantitative and qualitative increases in human and physical capital; higher per capita output allowing more individuals to specialize in science and technology, growth in the SEEI liberating human resources and keeping society from self-debilitation. Since the progress sketchily summarized as "knowledge of the average physicist today *minus* Newtonian knowledge" dissipated some of the Earth's free energy, we may add that the entropy generated by the intervening *cultural evolution* was its cost. The accumulation of entropy and the growth of human capital are stuck together. Thinking that human capital is independent from the general state of matter is a dream in which the universe operates differently from the ways it made human existence possible.

Being tied together, columns A and B are headed toward SEP(0): "No orderly matter, never mind technology." In a million years or in a billion? Impossible to tell. But the emergent need to substitute for nonrenewable resources on massive scales is a reminder that the depletion of extractable free energy is an irreversible and continuous process that *cultural evolution* has accelerated.

The entropy-ignoring view of technology does not see the unity of process and content. Process, representing technology, is not independent from the content (material input) because it also requires matter to make it operational. Both process and content feed off the same lump sum of free energy contained in matter. The economic feasibility of combining them shrinks on the average and in the long run. It is therefore an illusion to believe that less expensive and better molecular structures will always be available to build physical capital in order to process more expensive and lesser quality structures. With economic growth, market-wide technological applications are moving against stochastically enforced, but increasingly severe, constraints. Given a technical civilization, the types of material used to build machines and equipment are often the same as the types of materials they use. Global dependence on particular material resources will become obvious sometime in the first half of this century when the demand for oil to replace oil is fully recognized.

Faith in science and technology is as vital for human society as the belief in free will. What else, if not the never-ceasing flow of fresh ideas, scientific rigor, and undiminished intellectual will should be called upon to solve problems, big and small? Instead of questioning this obvious fact, *new historical materialism* intends to enlarge the perspective on it. It is, of course, heterodox. Using a certain amount of matter (containing free energy) and getting the same amount of matter with less free energy (less by the amount that became bound) is "diminishing returns" in the flesh. Yet contemporary economic growth theory annulled diminishing returns on capital (somatic and extrasomatic combined). It achieved this by making human capital autonomous to some extent, independent from the rest of the universe. This is pure "GS2 talk," the *global system's text* elaborating on itself.

Currently, prices[15] do not reflect the build-up of entropy, i.e., that *cultural evolution* draws from one single, comprehensive exhaustible resource. The reason, simply stated, is that economics, like Newtonian physics, does not account for the fact that *cultural evolution* (with you and me caught in it) is moving along a unidirectional and irreversible path. Prices would reflect the ongoing diminution of the lump sum of terrestrial low entropy if and only if markets did not anticipate the replenishment of even one single exhausted material with an economically affordable substitute. Conviction about the limitless efficacy of the "market and technology" duo thus became associated with the unconscious presumption that economic conditions are entirely under human control. Historical experi-

---

15. The dollar values of material inputs become more meaningful when they are compared to the values of some other resource. Economists often "deflate" absolute or nominal product prices by relating their increase to the increase in the price of labor, i.e., the wage rate.

ence has skewed minds toward a cyclical and time-independent rationality. These conscious and unconscious idealizations are false. The world is traveling along the road of an irreversible physical transformation, the most critical features of which are time dependence and symmetry-breaking. The recurrence of phenomena such as historical periods, business cycles, and artistic trends is of secondary importance in getting the gist of *cultural evolution.*

Nineteenth century political economists believed that the exhaustion of natural resources, land chief among them, would terminate demographic and economic expansion and lead mankind to a dismal steady state. According to contemporary economic opinion, 19th century thinkers held the view for the long run that we, having witnessed the power of entrepreneurship and the marvels of science and engineering during the 20th century, consider valid only for the short run. It seems, however, that the wisdom of our times also has its limits. It may just confuse "long run" with "forever."

◆   ◆   ◆

As human development moves one portion of the *terrestrial sphere* away from equilibrium (in the physicist's sense), nature's ability to oppose further movement from it also increases.[16] When molecular structures become complex and interdependent, as in *culture*, entropy gets help from *chaos* (nonlinear dynamics), which disrupts, downgrades, and sets back the expansion of orderliness. As complexity and interdependence grow, so do the opportunities for *chaotic* dynamics to interfere with the human system. The dissipation of the *ecological order*'s "one hundred" is connected to the average increase of entropy per particle. Averages are known to be deceptive, but one can only imagine the treachery of the "mean" when it and the standard deviation around it are unknown, except for the fact that they both tend to increase.

Environmental impairment is the proxy of the growing *ecological disorder* (a subject further elaborated upon in Chapter 7.) It is climatic deformations and the pollution of land, water, and air; it is new diseases in humans and animals. It is melting ice caps, growing volumes of garbage and effluent emissions; it is mutating viruses with their frightening potential to decimate the human biomass; acrimonious disputes within and among nations over who is to blame and who is to pay for the spread of "negative externalities." Decline in *ecological order* first

---

16. See, for example, E.D. Schneider and J.J. Kay, "Order from Disorder: The Thermodynamics of Complexity in Biology," in *Murphy and O'Neill, 1995.*

attacks the senses and injects a divisive element into human relations; then it endangers global welfare, and finally, the wholeness of the human organism.

The longer *homo sapiens* remains Earth-bound, the more the *terrestrial sphere* will become a riddle. As an accompanying phenomenon of growing entropy, there is a loss in the precise "knowableness" of the *ecological order*. Environmental science is confronted with an ever-increasing need to broaden its inquiries, while it is constantly handicapped by the emergence of new developments. It takes decades to confirm hypotheses about newly observed environmental phenomena. In addition, if *cultural evolution* generates even newer phenomena that require separate attention and interfere with the observation of the older ones, and, if the human ability to comprehend messages sent by the environment diminishes (i.e., as *information entropy* increases), the world will also encounter the Earth's material constraint through an unpalatable choice. Transfer resources into environmental sciences from other activities or suffer the consequences of increasing incertitude. The degradation of matter increases the number of conceivable messages about the microstate of the *terrestrial sphere*. And effects on the human body cannot be excluded from the consequences of this process.

Growing ignorance through increased entropy means that the gap between the information requirements to maintain *culture* and the ability to satisfy these requirements widens. Sciences that help protect the environment and human health face an uphill battle in sorting out the messages the material world broadcasts. The accumulation of entropy does not mean moving straight to inert matter without spontaneity. The situation is much trickier. As Ilya Prigogine observed, *chaos* in terms of certitude lost means increasing divergence between statistical descriptions and actual behavior of individual particles (e.g., their trajectories). Unknown particularities frustrate generalizations, which is the only way analysis can deal with the overwhelming number of physical building blocks. The growth of structure in a closed space means less certainty for the components of the structure.

The accumulation of scientific information, "bought" with increasing entropy in the *terrestrial sphere*, created an intriguing paradox. It provided more knowledge about ecological conditions and the ways they affect the world directly and in the short run, but it also reduced the knowability of the indirect and long-term effects that follow from their growing disorder. Weather reports became more detailed and accurate. However, all that theoretical understanding and technical aptitude is befuddled when it comes to giving a straightforward answer to questions like "Do human activities interfere with ongoing climatic changes, and, if the answer is 'yes,' what will the consequences be?" or "If global warming really exists will it delay the inevitable coming of a new Ice Age?" The emergence of these questions and the lack of unanimous answers to them are signs of growing *information entropy*.

Scientific progress confirms a basic fact learned in the micro-range of experience. Measuring disturbs the phenomenon one tries to examine; observation creates irreversible events. *Cultural evolution* reproduced the inescapable oneness of the observer and the observed on the macro-scale over a significant time period. It took the build-up of entropy to be able to delve into the physical environment, but entropy build-up altered the same physical environment humans set out to understand. Niels Bohr (1885-1962) emphatically asserted that quantum theory provides a complete theory of nature. Indeed, one should be wary of seeing man as separate from *Mater* even outside the nuclear physicist's realm.

ENVIRONMENTAL PROTECTION AND CONSERVATION

Not even the most helpful activities and most positive, disciplined attitudes can stop the decumulation of narrow *exergic* constraints. Matter-specific entropy cannot decrease. Pollution abatement either increases entropy or leaves it at the same level. Given present-age technological possibilities, abatement increases entropy. Recycling, which could contribute to both environmental protection and conservation, restores low entropy in one form (e.g., glass, newsprint) through destroying other forms of low entropy (e.g., using machines made of various metals). If viewed in its current technological and economic context, recycling also uses nonrenewable energy to run machines built of elements found in nature. *Cultural evolution* consumes matter beyond what naturally renewing resources could provide. Technological successes in "refreshing" the contents of *geocapital* will eventually encounter mounting limitations. "Backstop technologies" will not come on line smoothly because market-induced substitutions for materials on their way to exhaustion are bound to become less complete. Short of some totally unexpected, wondrous breakthrough in the human understanding of nature, technological development, which is supposed to ensure eternal and seamless substitution of one material for another, will come at increasing costs as the general level of orderliness in *geocapital*'s molecular structure moves down the curve.

If we dare to contemplate the distant future, we can see that *geocapital*'s net expansion will have to change to net contraction, *ecological order* must devolve, and *certitude* about the natural environment must diminish. There is no "if," only "when" and "how" these physically inevitable developments will reveal themselves as *cultural evolution*'s quantitative indices continue to grow. These are system-level processes whose extent and intensity are expected to be proportional to the accumulation of bound energy in the *terrestrial sphere*.

Nevertheless, environmental protection, conservation, recycling, the substitution of renewable resources for nonrenewable ones, conscious efforts not to turn renewable resources into nonrenewable ones by over-use; relying, whenever possible, on nature's regenerative processes rather than on matter-guzzling "reclamation" through technological solutions (never fully analyzed for their global effects) are crucial for the world. These attitudes and activities slow the depletion of exiguous structures. They moderate the drain on the *global environment*, the *ecological order*, and *informational certitude*. Without these efforts, *cultural evolution* would come to an end sooner and more nefariously. The radical perspective on the environment and natural resources (a good part of the ecology movement) envisages limits to demographic and economic growth. It explicitly recognizes that *closed space = constraints for expanding life and material output*.

What a difference the widespread acknowledgment of this principle would make! If the *terrestrial sphere*'s regenerative, self-cleansing processes were allowed to function (i.e., the environment's pollution absorbing capacity were not frustrated with ever higher levels and varied emissions); if renewable energy and material resources gained the decisive upper hand over nonrenewable ones globally, and, if human capital kept growing mostly without major additions to physical capital, all the cumulative manifestations in the growth of bound energy (negative from the human vantage point) could slow to an infinitesimal crawl. At relatively low and stable levels of population and material goods production, with all of the above positive conditions in place, not only would earthly life become sustainable for a very long time, but improvements in its quality would also be possible through refining products, increasing their variety and durability.

Although the *terrestrial sphere* became more of a riddle than it had been before *cultural evolution* began to accelerate about two centuries ago, the combination of scientific progress (especially through the build-up of human capital) and far-reaching conservation and environmental protection measures could *virtually* arrest the trend of losing certitude about the *ecological order*. This is the case because incertitude, expressed in the environment's lost long-term predictability, has a component under social control. Allowing environmental sinks to empty themselves: land, sea, and air to absorb the polluting and destructive by-products of *culture*, the situation would dramatically improve for the observation of long-term ecological evolution. The accumulation of *information entropy* could be made so small that *certitude about the environment* would appear stable and indefinitely enduring.

But careful! The goodness of having a smaller global population and economy has limits. The not-yet-happened and unimaginable represent the most crucial component of unidirectional, dissipative complexification. Sheer human biomass, operating a powerful, highly developed economy might be needed to weather unseen future challenges and threats. This "not too much and not too little" rationality calls for a new theory to analyze the planet's optimal use. The result is unlikely to call for the maximum possible return to the microstate of the *terrestrial sphere* that opened up the ecological niche for *homo sapiens*.

WHAT IS LIFE?

In 1944, Erwin Schroedinger, living in Ireland at the time, published some of his lectures to general audiences under the title *What Is Life?* The "petite" tome stimulated lasting interest in the link between thermodynamics and living organisms and presaged the discovery of DNA after the War.

The great physicist's answer to his own question came in two parts: it is "order from disorder" and "order from order." The first aphorism referred to the organism's ability to extract low entropy from the environment and use it to support its biological order. The second reflected the recognition that the organism's hereditary information, passed from one generation to the next, must unequivocally remain constant over evolutionary-scale periods. Of course, the organization of life was based on molecules and solar radiation. It did not have to start from maximum entropy, a total lack of consistency or absence of quality. This difference between total disorder and a significant starting order, which indicates a low probability of nature's state and hints at the Earth's exceptional status in the universe, keeps the debate alive between "Intelligent Design" and "puh-lueeze…"

Life, as Schroedinger famously said, was made possible by feeding on "negative entropy" or "sucking orderliness from the environment" at the cost of creating greater disorderliness somewhere else.[17] Living systems piggyback on the *second law of thermodynamics* without violating it. Through photosynthesis, the sunflower manufactures sugar from water and carbon dioxide. Although it contributes to overall entropy by wasting and degrading energy and matter, it also defies nature's wish to pull things apart through the incessant thermal agitation of

---

17. In this respect, Schroedinger modestly indicated that he only refined and further developed Boltzmann's thoughts.

molecules and their constituents. The sunflower will wither, its carefully and optimistically built structure will fall apart, but its "aperiodic" hereditary substance will pass to the next generation ("from order to order"), ensuring the continued existence of the genus *Helianthus*. Sunflower, microbe, or primate–all forms of life do essentially the same thing. Life is autocatalytic entropy defiance (called *force motrice* in humans).

Homo sapiens extended the creation of "from disorder to order" and "from order to order" through self-organization and technology. In fact, *cultural evolution* added "from order to greater order" to such an extent that the species is now flirting with the prospect of going "from great order to great disorder."

Since order (a certain configuration of matter or energy) can be measured by information, the story of life on Earth, as well as its man-made embellishments and the gathering danger facing *culture*, can be told in "bits."

Life is the ability to maintain a functioning system with high information content by devouring and metabolically disordering other information systems. A living creature (information system number one) feeds on another living creature (information system number two). If this happens to be a prey/predator relationship, two further information systems are involved. The giraffe's system of escaping is tested against the lion's system of running and catching, and each system is tested against the systems of its fellow runners. The lion's system (information system number one) is extended into the metabolism that knows how to degrade "information system number two" in order to maintain itself. Since, in every such act, some material structure is irrevocably consumed, the *terrestrial sphere* lost some certitude for the human observer. By definition, this loss equals the increase in entropy. It is hard to accept that some of the planet's orderliness (the knowability of its microstate) has been lost as a result. But this is how things are. Theoretically, even without *cultural evolution*, complete ecological steady state is a mirage.

From the standpoint of *culture*, life is information that describes the human metabolism, self-organization, and technology. Besides the organism's metabolism, self-organization is also an information system, which, as stated earlier, assumed the form of *global systems* in the 19th century. These systems change as their information contents gradually become ill-suited to accommodate movement in the direction toward which the typical individual is being drawn.

Technology may be perceived as interaction among information systems. In principle, the matter one wants to alter and shape, the tools one uses, and the way one uses them can all be described by data sets and programs. Whereas the metabolic part of the organism's information system evolves slowly, industrial metabolism (techniques of production) evolves quickly. It is, in fact, the most dynamic part of the phyletic feasting on the volume of information available for *cultural evolution.*

All three transformations, that is, "from disorder to order," "from order to order," and "from order to greater order," go "from less information to more information" in explaining life and *cultural evolution.* Since all three processes are tied to increases of entropy, we can say that life and *cultural evolution* exist through the ability to exchange entropy for information. But the *second law* does not allow us to break even. Only some of the entropy produced by *cultural evolution* is translated into information gained. Some entropy becomes lost *certitude* about the ecological order, adding to the already accumulated *incertitude.*

As the information system, *culture,* expands through its *evolution,* it takes in and disorders information systems embodied in natural resources. *Culture* is an extrasomatically extended living creature, a predatory cyborg, whose information system feeds on other information systems. To the extent matter becomes less orderly in the process, it contains less information. (In our interpretation, increase in *information entropy* means just that.) To use dispersed matter, the information system "technology" will have to increase, compensating for the loss of information in the raw material. Obviously, a limit can be reached when meeting such a demand encounters difficulties. The world will not "run out of gas" (free information found in matter), but its engine will start to wheeze and cough, forcing a stop and introspection about economic speed limits and the possibilities of capturing matter beyond this planet.

We cannot do more than pray that the impulse to "hit the brakes" will come through flaws discovered in self-organization or through experiencing difficulties in making technology obey the paradigm of profit-driven output growth. The other alternative is imponderable–indications that the information system we call metabolism has been damaged or has become partially incompatible with the material environment.

Is the thermodynamic view of history, which revolves around the concept of entropy, pessimistic or optimistic? It is neither. It ought to be considered neutrally realistic.

Even after Schroedinger's speculations became famous, the *second law* was still portrayed as death's immutable program and symbol, the backdrop for a mood of morbid decadence. Contemporary thought gives it a different reading. Life is undeniably a struggle to stave off movement toward higher entropy by competing with other animated creatures for lower entropy (i.e., chemical energy and a variety of materials stored in food), but without it, there would be no life. Modern astrophysics maintains that the long drawn-out process of universal thermodynamic disequilibrium moving back toward equilibrium is one of the conditions for intelligent life.[18] The *second law* is inseparable from our psychological or inner sense of time. Phenomena of inevitable demise (e.g., aging, depreciation of whatever humans fabricate) and the flow of time are united in human consciousness. Without the constant pressure to countervail the tendency toward disorder, there would be no thinking, no purpose, no civilization. And since there is no existence without obstacles to overcome, it is conditioned on progress.

Prigogine's nonlinear thermodynamics makes entropy's positive role even more explicit. Not all dissipated energy goes to waste. Part of it is recovered as information used to maintain and enhance the level of organization and orderliness in such systems. *Culture* may be considered a complex, far-from-equilibrium dissipative entity organized through the *global system*, and *cultural evolution* a nonequilibrium dissipative process that moves ever farther away from thermodynamic equilibrium. Without such entropy-producing, irreversible movement, it would be condemned to decline and extinction. Even to exist requires evolution ("progress"), but for that, far-from-equilibrium structures need to act like open thermodynamic systems. Since the *terrestrial sphere* is closed, the world will have to open it in order to evolve, that is, to survive in the very long run.

Cultural evolution, which ups the ante on simple life, dissipates information gradients on an increasingly massive scale. The speculation that this is nature's way of surreptitiously hastening the return to thermodynamic equilibrium cannot be disproved. It reminds us of the inevitable "heat death of the universe" way down the cosmic road. There every mile is a billion years, but this does not erase the dreadful suspicion: The *force motrice* may be in league with universal entropy.

Whether the build-up of entropy is an "objective," ontologically scripted phenomenon or merely a "subjective" one that mirrors the narrow human perspective is also an intriguing problem. Full and correct facts about the "real" reality (Kant's *Noumenon*) remain beyond the reach of science. The reason why the living organism does not notice that it is standing vertically to the center of a large revolving and moving object may well be that it has evolved from a one-cell creature, which, like a bacterium, may not notice if it flies on the toilet seat of an airplane or sits "quietly" in a jar of marmalade in someone's kitchen. The evolved human organism has retained the ability of its far-removed biological seed to block out "cosmic transportation" *and* other facts whose perception would be incompatible with existence. But could such evolution occur without taking into

18. See *Hawking, 1988.*

account things as they really are? The answer is "no" again. If scientific information, which is inextricably and irrevocably conditioned on biological evolution-created sensory limitations, were completely false, humans would not be around. (This is loosely the "anthropic principle," a term used in the philosophy of science.) Consequently, entropy and its accumulation must be a valid aspect of nature, even if science cannot fathom it and certainly cannot undo or reverse it by deliberate action.

Among the many puzzling questions about existence, consider the following: If life is a general phenomenon across the universe and if its maintenance requires the capture of increasing amounts of matter (low entropy), isn't our species on a collision course with other species we do not know about, some of which may already be technologically more advanced? UFOs!? In this case, doesn't sending signals toward distant stars resemble a hypothetical, pre-Columbian Indian civilization trying, with whatever means it considered appropriate, to send messages to whoever might be out there: "Lots of land here!…Shining metal galore!…We have bows and arrows!"? The potential reality of discovering extraterrestrial life hides developments that would prompt a rethinking of the world in ways we have never really contemplated and do not dare contemplate now.

Fascinating as these problems may be, their pursuit leads to a domain in which affirmation and doubt never part company, where the plausible and the implausible swerve into one another uncontrollably, where the conquest of everything by one is revealed as having nothing by someone else. We need to return to what entropy implies to the world on a *macrohistoric* time scale under given circumstances.

◆   ◆   ◆

If firmly rooted understanding can be equated with internal visualization, the concept of progressive general entropy faces the same difficulty as did the relationship between the sun and the Earth. To settle once and for all the issue of what revolves around what, the commonplace sequence of first understanding, then accepting, had to be reversed. Just as the sun seems to move in the sky in a semicircle above a flat Earth, all appearances speak against entropy eating up "nature's dowry to man" (as Georgescu-Roegen put it). But appearances are what they are. Beyond more than reasonable doubt, science is convinced that any use of matter destroys its order to some degree for the human species. Reusing a substance as if it were in its original state requires more substance and energy in some combination, degrading some substance again. This is as true for a mass that weighs one gram as it is for a chunk of stuff that weighs sextillions of grams. The progress of entropy in the aggregate is the soundless "cosmic draft" that moves in, around, through, and by us. It makes everything that exists possible now as well as impossible at some future time. The "everything" is meant literally. *Global systems* decline and vanish just as cows die and milk goes sour. Paradoxically, if this insight were shared worldwide, it would tend to expand rather than abbreviate the species' life span. Simple and logical as this proposition may sound, it is next to impossible to keep it in mind. "Mind" is, indeed, the relevant concept to invoke.

6

The Brain's Central Role in Cultural Evolution

[The concept of the mind may be reduced to materially interpreted functions of the brain. Not losing sight of biological evolution-created givens, this approach tentatively quarantines the "mind and matter enigma," allowing the identification of *macrohistory* as changes in the configuration and functioning of brain-anchored interactions. Each *global system* creates its characteristic behavior, connected with a *lexicon*, a socioeconomically induced emotional profile, an *ethic*, a *Weltanschauung*, and a *mentality*. These are physically "imprinted" in brains and endure roughly as long as the *global system* does. The materiality of the *global system* is recognized through coterminous phenotypical traits. If internally stored individual data and programs used to shape external behavior constituted a *Code*, a part of that, the *Code Core*, would be related to the *global system*. This makes *macrohistory* the intermittent transformation of the *Code Core* in *meta* terms.]

ONE BRAIN, THREE *MINDS*

Human social existence hinges upon individual repertoires of technical, organizational, and social skills, potential for self-motivation, ability to function within the limits of legal and moral principles, and willingness, on occasion, to question their appropriateness and legitimacy. These processes occur in particular mental states, while experiencing consciousness ("sense of self," "bare awareness," "knowing to know"). Do these phenomena occur in the brain or in the mind?

The human brain weighs approximately 2.75 pounds. It is a three-dimensional anatomical reality that lives in *The Cranium*. It is *in situ*. The mind is not so easy to "corner." It is difficult even to define. In unabridged dictionaries, the word has at least half a dozen overlapping meanings: element, part, or substance that reasons, thinks, feels, wills, and perceives, etc. Some dictionaries even list "brain" as a synonym for "mind."

Consider Leibniz's challenge. If there was a "thinking machine" big enough for you to enter and examine it in detail, you might see all kinds of fascinating things you never imagined (words, for instance, designating familiar objects), but you would never see "imagination" itself. You would also not see "perception," "conviction," "causality," "instinct," "principle," "world history," and "scientific progress;" or, for that matter, any of the above-cited processes and states required for social organization. "Free will" would not be visible, nor would the empty place where it should be, in case the thinking machine had none. Despite the inestimable progress in sciences since the 17th century, a deep abyss of puzzlement separates the intelligible realm from the material particles that make up the brain.

The ability to contemplate existence brought yearning for freedom and immortality. To satisfy it, a part of the being must be beyond the reach of forces affecting mass; it must be outside of space and time, and therefore, independent from the teeming, palpitating gelatinous tissue nested in the cranial cavity. The primary instinct of feeling free and the inadmissibility of ultimate demise could have given rise to the irresistible need to separate the mind, which includes the "I," from the body, the brain, the "It." The development of symbolic communication through language, the creation of an idea-world, culture, traditions, and the compartmentalization of academic pursuits rendered this separation natural and perhaps final. The separation of the body from the mind, with explicit openness or implicit subtleness, might just be a transgenerationally transmitted enabling condition of the indispensable sense of uniqueness in the individual.

It is possible that the evolution of thinking created a mental wall that blocks out what Sartre called the "absurdity of life" or, alternately, the "absurdity of death." And to enhance the realism of self-awareness independent of its physical groundings, the brain, like a good party host, vanished from the scene without saying as much as "Have a good time. Enjoy yourself." Of course, this "brain-created-the-mind" story is not the only one in town. The brain/mind relationship opposed philosophers in Greek antiquity and has remained a divisive issue to present times.

Dualism, monism, and *agnosticism* comprise the well-known trinity of approaches to this subject. *Dualists* see the brain and the mind as different entities. They are convinced that the mind is qualitatively distinct from the brain because it contains a mysterious and immaterial component that is inaccessible to human intelligence. They believe that "something" (call it the Soul) is connected to the mind. It "survives" without a living brain and science will never be able to link it to matter. (An irreverent hard-line materialist might add that, in this case, the Soul would either be energetically self-sufficient or it would have to be supported by some cosmic force.) *Dualism* makes no secret of being connected with the church door. In times within our *macrohistoric* scope, it appeared most prominently in the philosophy of Renee Descartes (1596-1650), but fascinatingly, it lurks in some prestigious, contemporary theories of physics.

Monists do not separate the mind from the brain. They regard the two as one and the same.[1] They hold that all feasible mental functions are computational algorithms; some of them are known and others are still to be discovered. *Monists* maintain that there is nothing metaphysical about the mind, although it is apparently capable of processing metaphysical thoughts and wishes. According to a strictly neuro-anatomic genealogy, *monists* may trace their intellectual ancestry to the physical materialism born (or reborn) in the *Renascence* and the *Enlightenment*. The liberal French aristocrat, Julien Offray de LaMettrie (1709-1751), and the enterprising Austrian, Franz Gall (1758-1828), were early empirical brain researchers who totally disregarded the mind. They operated under the strong belief of "no matter, never mind." Both men irritated the authorities and the public of their times and both had to flee their native soils. The Frenchman found refuge in Prussia and the Austrian ended up in France, as if the intellectual centers of continental Europe had been unable or unwilling to rid themselves of the seed that blossomed into dominance in the modern era. Today, *monists* come close to representing "prestigious science"–the one associated with Nobel Prizes and M.D.s on building directories.

Agnostics discard the possibility of ever clearing up the brain/mind connection in ways that would satisfy scientific rigor. If the mind is part of physical reality, its examination by the mind itself results in self-deceiving "objectivization." The intellect cannot possibly separate the object of inquiry from its subject; it is using what it examines as the tool of examination. Of course, if the mind is more than physical reality, then its full examination is a lost cause from the start. Immanuel Kant (1724-1804), Friedrich Nietzsche (1844-1900), William James (1842-1910), Sigmund Freud (1856-1939), Erwin Schroedinger (1887-1961), and Jacques Derrida (1930-2004) are some of the key references for the radical conviction that the mind's self-examination amounts to chasing one's tail. It is as

---

1.   "Monism" in philosophy also refers to teachings that consider all experiences manifestations of a single substance or force. Based on this broad criterion, Leibniz, Spinoza, Berkeley, and Hegel may be put in the same group.

hard to dismiss this argument as it is impossible to accept it. Faith in knowledge is a human adaptation to the physical environment; no philosophy can dilute or invalidate it. Even if truths concerning the mind's judgment about its own nature and functioning are "unrefuted errors," "dreamed knowledge," or "misreadings," the *primus mobile* to search and try to understand remains intact.

Seeing a "good person go bad" (antisocial, disorderly, criminal), but with a brain judged to be perfectly normal by medical science, the *dualist* would say "Aha!" The *monist's* diagnosis would be, "Something is the matter with the brain too, but at the current state of magnetic resonance imaging and positron emission tomography, we are not yet equipped to put a label on it." The *agnostic* would sigh "Who knows, you can never be sure." Concerning the more complex, abstract problem of "emergence" (the impossibility of foretelling the evolution of the whole based on the knowledge of the parts), calling the "mind" an emergent phenomenon has a *dualistic* flavor. The *monist* thinks it is sufficient to say that the brain has emergent qualities. This seemingly subtle distinction reveals a profound disjunction of philosophical outlook if you allow the protagonists to develop their respective points of view. The *agnostic* would consider the debate equivalent to trying to decide which one of two mirror images is real.

This threefold classification of viewpoints on the brain/mind nexus is rudimentary. Endless cultivation of the subject has surfaced variations and partial overlaps.[2] Some doctrines straddle two perspectives; some fuse all three.

Vitalism, which was championed by one of the early 20th century's most popular and influential philosophers, Henri Bergson (1859-1941), claims that there is a force (*élan vital*) that is qualitatively different from physical reality. Everything else is only a manifestation of this force. The most essential part of life is nonmaterial and defies natural sciences. *Vitalism*, thought to have become an intellectual relic, reappeared toward the end of the 20th century in the publications of Arthur Ernest Wilder-Smith (1915-1995) and Wolfgang Kuhn (1928-2001).[3] Its explicit anti-*monism* makes it straddle the fence between *dualism* and *agnosticism*, supporting both.

New Age philosophies openly embrace all three tendencies while some perfectly reputable, science-based approaches inadvertently synthesize them.[4]

2.   For a summary of the philosophical dimensions of the mind/brain problem, see *Schwartz and Begley, 2002.*

3.   See *Ditfurth, 1982.*

4.   *New Age* thinkers tend to base their arguments on brain research; however, their spiritual experiences transcend mortal understanding and ultimately confirm the supreme being, thus solving the ancient trilemma.

(Authors of the second genre may be legitimately concerned that their words may become testimonials in spiritual guidebooks and their tomes will end up next to them in bookstores.)

◆   ◆   ◆

The current context requires a technical definition of the mind. We dispense with this need by limiting the concept to aspects that arise from the brain's physical structure and functions. Thus, the *mind* is unequivocally tied to the *soma*; consequently, it excludes the immaterial. Putting the word in italics indicates that this is the sense in which it is applied. According to this definition, forming a thought requires configured matter in the brain and thinking takes place in the *mind*, the "brain's function space."

Some question the need for the concept of "mind." Usually there is no separate collective noun to designate the functions of an object. The word "wheel" implies a structure required for transmitting energy in uncountable applications. But, unlike for the wheel, structure and function for the brain and the mind evolved on connected but separate tracks. Consequently, the brain does things that language does not have a precise designation for in the mind, and certain qualities have been imputed to the mind whose physical equivalents remain unknown or are presumed to be nonexistent in the brain. The simplification of tying brain and mind together as if they were "table" and "to keep things at a higher level than the floor" cannot solve the intricacy of their relationship. Despite great scientific advances, the word "mind" remains justified by its existence.

Progress in "brain science" (the multidisciplinary field built around cognitive neuroscience) has been astonishing. Specialized centers of cognition have been identified, revealing the causes behind many neuropsychiatric and pathological phenomena. By now, most of what the individual feels, thinks, and remembers, as well as most of its mental functions, have empirically supported explanations.

An athlete runs his laps in a championship competition. He feels pain in his left leg and for a moment he thinks of quitting, of moving out of the way to avoid further injury. But then images flash through his *mind*: his preparation for this trial, examples of heroic athletic steadfastness he saw on some old black and white documentary; images of his parents, girlfriend, and coach praising him for toughing it out. In the midst of the pain and effort, he establishes that going through with it would not endanger his health or athletic career. He decides not to think about the pain and to concentrate his energy on finishing the remaining lap. He is now elated. He feels the strength of his character. His will triumphs over the obstacles and he keeps running.

There is nothing in this description that neurobiologists would consider wholly unconquered territory. They know how pain signals travel through the spinal chord to the hypothalamus; how emotional response is generated in the limbic system; how cortical activation (e.g., thinking thoughts, feeling emotions) can recall memories; how such information is communicated through neuronal pathways; they even have knowledge about where and how initiatives emerge and will is molded; and how, as a result, the sympathetic nervous system is mobilized, leading to an adrenalin surge, shutting off the gastrointestinal tract from "wasting" somatic energy; adjusting hormonal balance throughout the body, etc.

The general processes are known analytically; however, the anatomical details are missing. There is no detailed neuronal circuit diagram or map that would account for making our runner remember the determination on the face of an athlete far removed from his conscious retention. Similarly, it is not known at the microstate level what it takes to bring to *mind* one particular aspect of the socioeconomic environment. These are unknowns, but the supposition that they will eventually be identified is not so outlandish. They are, after all, phenomena known to have physical bases.

So far, we may recognize two aspects of the *mind*: one that is empirically explored and another that is a rational, direct, and nonmysterious extension of the empirically conquered domain. Although the neurobiological picture of the brain is still too spotty to bring the physical particularities of specific actions into sharp focus, we may assume that they exist and are obtainable. There must be a neuro-scientific explanation for why someone votes Blue or Red.

The relationship between the empirical and the rational in terms of *mind* research is similar to the way one considers a polygon with manageably small and unmanageably large numbers. We can easily draw and study an octagon (a closed plane bounded by eight linear segments). We would be perplexed if we had to draw a polygon with 88 sides, resign if the request was for one with 888 sides, and throw up our hands if the number increased to 8888. But we can still rationalize the existence of all these polygons. We can readily go from the initial octagon to a 16-sided polygon and we would see no logical obstacle to performing a similar procedure a finite number of times until a specialist (e.g., professional geometrician), with the help of a computer, could get to the desired number of sides. It is all a question of extending what science already knows and can do. To translate the simile into the present context, the octagon represents the empirically explored brain/mind, and the polygons with two-, three-, and four-digit numbers are the rationally conceivable extensions and development of empirical knowledge.

On a sobering note, not even the augmentation of the known with the knowable can pry open the secrecy of thinking. Its seal is irremovable; our fingers keep slipping off it. In addition to the *empirical* and *rational minds*, there is also a *mysterious mind*.

The possibility cannot be excluded that in more dimensions than we can commonly recognize or analytically discern, *minds* are "materially" interconnected through "paranormal" phenomena such as ectoplasmatic radiation or Jungian synchronicity. Some day, these phenomena may have explanations that would satisfy the standards of empirical research science. But here the rift appears to be much wider. Moving from the empirically explored "*mind* number one" to the explorable "*mind* number two," the analysis remains on a contiguous surface, but a canyon seems to bar the route to the third *mind*.

If "consciousness," the central focus of *third mind* research, can be explored only at the quantum level, then it cannot be investigated independently from the microstate of the investigator's brain. With the discovery of quantum mechanics, the nature of objective reality itself became subject to scrutiny and disagreement. What remains is to look for dependably recurring regularities in the entanglement between the examiner and the examined. Finding such regularities is, of course, important, but this is a radically different experience from looking at a Petri dish or through the lens of a microscope. It is unlikely that the third *mind's* materiality could be explored without getting into the brain's nuclear and subnuclear details. Hence, the mental image of the canyon barring the road to discovery.[5]

Scientific progress, the great deflator of human self-contentment, also helped reproduce the mystique of the brain. The many-worlds interpretation of quantum mechanics, string theory, and the nonlocal ("no-time, no-space") conceptualizations of the universe place matter in such a dubious and out-of-reach context that it approximates nonexistence. If one of these theories were proved to be mathematically true; that is, if it became generally accepted as correct, but could not be experientially confirmed (given the exponentially rising costs of looking deeper and deeper into the nature of matter), the brain would be declared a com-

---

5.   Completion of the brain's topological picture, to include atomic and subatomic anatomy, is in its early stages. Roger Penrose, an authority on the mathematical and physical aspects of neural research, claims that the development of a "new mathematics" that combines the approaches of classical and quantum physics is a precondition for penetrating the material secrets of the mind. See *Penrose, 1994, 1995.*

plicated storehouse of some gutless substance and the *mind* would become a scientifically explained virtual immateriality. No line in the sand in this *terra incognita*, no surgeon's scalpel, no hard-nosed academic rigor with its magic symbols can separate Cartesian "matter" in the *mysterious mind*. In some ways, contemporary knowledge turned matter into a metaphysical phenomenon.

"Consciousness" research starts out from the third *mind*. This is reasonable. As immensely complex as the materially-based *mind* may be, there is no proof that the living brain and consciousness ever part company. Yet the search for the substance of consciousness reaches a point where matter loses flesh and disperses into interstellar voids relative to near massless particles that may or may not be there. "My mind is nonplused," the researcher would cry out in a moment of complete fairness or involuntarily frustration, making both the agnostic and the preacher smile.

The limits to certainty about thinking may also be seen when we contemplate "free will." *Ad hominem*, neither satisfying individual life nor coherent social organization is conceivable without imputing "free will" to ourselves and to others. If so, the *mind* must have some independent power over the brain; the "I" over the "It." This might just be the brain's autonomous wriggling to promote the interest of its host. This is hard-line *monism*, a total fusion of "I" and "It." It "feels" incorrect because it is devoid of what we consider human. But observe where the slightest relaxation of orthodox materialism leads. If such studied manifestations of "free will" as "focusing attention," "willing one's will," "self-directed neuroplastic healing" have a material basis, it presumably resides in the subnuclear detail of cerebral tissue. Some force from the tiny universes will start a process that will effect larger conglomerations of matter. They will create action potentials in neurons, fire synapses, alter the state of brain cells, abandon old nerve paths, and create and strengthen new ones. But once you cross into the quantum realm, you must abandon all hope of finding anything but a strange jumble of probability clouds, and timeless, non-Newtonian, "now wave/now particle" counter-intuitive happenings. The current of thought is now flowing in the direction of Cartesian *dualism*, even if some may want to swim ashore quickly as soon as it reaches Heisenberg's Uncertainty Principle or Schroedinger's collapsed wave equation. Inasmuch as both deep matter and spirit lack conventional materiality, the mysterious third *mind* becomes the supernatural light-bathed platform upon which a higher form of intelligence may be detected. If you want to opt out of this debate because you do not feel comfortable taking sides, you can always embrace *agnosticism*, at least temporarily, until brain research fills the gaps of ignorance. In short, *monism* plus "free will" leads us toward *dualism* or *agnosticism.*

Now assume that there is no "free will;" that this designation is nothing more than an elemental intuition that biological and social exigencies turned into a humanistic truth. Then where do decisions come from? One must either relinquish individual sovereignty to a superior cosmic intelligence (good or almighty, according to one's belief), or once again plead *nolo contendere. Monism* minus "free will" rekindles receptiveness to *dualistic* or *agnostic* thinking.

To assure the reader that embracing *dualism* will also not let ambiguity rest, if we combine *dualism* with "free will," we end up in the long trampled and fallow "nowhere land" of theodicy and medieval logic-chopping about what God might be like as a person. On the other hand, no one wants *dualism* (that is, religion) without "free will." It implies moral anarchy. The thief who stole your watch would say that a certain horned apparition "made" him do it and the judge would gavel the trial to an end with an understanding nod. As Martin Heidegger (1889-1976) and the existentialists showed, "being" cannot be defined satisfactorily. The ontology that hides in the brain/mind relationship only reproduces the sphinx we call "existence."

The human intellect is lost in the philosophical labyrinth and, unlike Theseus who readily made use of the golden cord that Ariadne provided, it might just feel good where it is. If Theseus had been an open-minded and honest thinker, he would have been compelled by each of the three grand perspectives on the brain/mind relationship. It is not difficult to sympathize with this balanced view. People with *monistic* inclinations are the ones who may help us neuropharmaceutically; those who embrace *dualism* give us a sense of importance in the big, dark, curving, warping space-time continuum; they allow the one in love to say something other than "Oh my foolish neurotransmitters…" The *agnostics* help us get hold of ourselves. Just as pure conviction in Dostoevsky's characters invited doubt and confusion, the strengthening of one inclination provokes its inarticulate suspension even within the same *mind.* In the public arena, aggressive criticism from the remaining two directions prevents any of them from gaining dominance. Labels such as "misguided," "deluded," "fraudulent," and "intellectually rotten," along with polished variants of outright "stupid," fly like bullets in the "OK Coral." And there is good reason! Vulgar *monism* leads to a dehumanizing, primitive materialism; *dualism* reawakens concern for the rule of reason brought by the *Enlightenment;* and *agnosticism,* good in small doses, could become intellectual resignation, often proved to be totally wrong by scientific progress over the ages.

The cosmic psychiatrist would say to a worried mankind lying on the celestial sofa, "You do not really want to get out of this labyrinth. The idea of equating it with Las Vegas will help you by creating a new, therapeutic neuronal circuit in your prefrontal cortex. Focus on seeing three Ariadnes. One is a cocktail waitress, the other a pit mistress, and the third one, a professional entertainer. Now, why would you be in such a hurry to leave?" Together, neuropsychiatry, quantum theory, post-Einsteinian physics, and Buddhism can create a particularly satisfying symbiosis among our three susceptibilities, as can New Age philosophies. With compassion and a modicum of unsuppressed holistic inclination, one might see the "psychic unity of mankind" in these three views forming a single whole.

Let us invest our imagination in a daringly abstract allegory. A group of humans finds itself on a strange planet in an alien universe. They move in complete darkness, using a weak flashlight to scan the unbroken path. They do not have the slightest idea where they are or where they are going. An unknown world surrounds them. It is like the *Noumenon* in Kant's philosophy, an incomprehensible, concealed, and impenetrable reality. But some *phenomena*, such as being able to walk, to see as far as the beam of light allows, being able to hear and feel, tell them something useful. They register that their sensory organs are working, even if they might consistently distort the weird signals emanated by the other-galactic wilderness. The mechanical laws of movement they were familiar with retained at least some validity. The sheer fact that they think shows that their "grey matter" is functioning. Temperature and the air's oxygen content are in acceptable ranges. They begin to trust, because they must, the pragmatic validity and recurrence of observed regularities. It seems that, although their picture of the enveloping, intuited complexity may be vague and incomplete, it does not invalidate the knowledge they have obtained through cognition, experience, and disciplined speculation. From what they may possibly think about the fantastic unknown that surrounds them, we may recognize the three tendencies to deal with just such a situation. All three will have to be represented to form a complete spectrum required for the group's psychological balance. Empirical and rational thinking alone (that is, pure *monism*) would leave them in despair. They also need religious and romantic voices (*dualist* tendencies) and disparaging skepticism, which, on occasion, also reconciles the other two inclinations without taking sides (the *agnostic* viewpoint) to affirm their wholeness, to bolster the potency of their self-actualization.

Cultural evolution's brain-based materiality are *phenomena* in the *Noumenon* of existence. They are accompanied by certain structural and functional transformations of matter in the brain. But what is deep inside the transformed matter, what secrets are hidden in its intrinsic soundings, what surrounds it; what else and how everything else becomes altered, how the logically-deduced transformation relates to things near or far; comprehensible through classical physics or removed from our direct understanding; all that is put on hold. We whisper *ceteris paribus* because we are not sure that the "black box" in which we keep everything we do not know or cannot comprehend really exists; that is, if it may indeed be comparable to a box that can contain "something." Its lid can certainly pop open at any second, revealing the ignored linchpin that connects the transformation of the *mind* to *cultural evolution*.

This is admittedly a vague materiality, but it is a beginning, and an urgent one. It is high time to peer through the biological face of history with "X-ray eyes." Of course, the caveat can never be forgotten. New breakthroughs should complete or could totally alter the explanation of how and to what extent physical transformations in the structure of thinking matter and its functions may relate to the world process. At present, science leaves no doubt that such transformations must remain within the irrevocable biological constraints and potentials produced by evolution. The *empirical* and *rational minds* stand for the information-processing capability of the central nervous system that developed over bygone ages to solve sheer physical survival-oriented adaptive problems. The "old" *mind* is being put in ever new, specific situations, thus linking the physically hardened experiences of the deep and long past with the real and present challenges of the moment. The *mind* is "panhuman." Its characteristics are general and hardy because they evolved among recurring features of daily life and communal organization, and because they show fundamental similarities in widely varying environments.

The answer to the question posed at the beginning of the chapter, namely, do processes and mental states related to social existence occur in the brain or in the mind, is this: They occur in both because of the definitional reduction of the "mind" to functional manifestations of structured matter and because it is a scientifically accepted fact that any material transformation affects both a given configuration and its internal operations at some level of detail. This blanket statement provisionally neutralizes the *mysterious mind* and controls our *dualistic* and *agnostic* appetites.

BEHAVIOR

Phenotype is the equilibrium between biological heredity (the genotype) and the environment in which it finds itself. So defined, it "goes through" the organism, since the body's mass of particles is not restricted to the genes. Its most frequently noted parts, physiology, morphological attributes (e.g., height and other observable details of outward appearance), and behavioral traits, constitute an inseparable one. "Behavior" is the way the genes conduct their "external affairs." It is physical patrimony in social context.

Characterization of behavior may be restricted to a single individual or may be extended to groups of them, as well as to species; maximally even to the entire biomass, the totality of living matter. The examination may focus on a person's reactions to stress and anxiety, responses to praise and threat, or capacity to overcome trauma. This is the stuff of *individual psychology*. However, the study of similar reactions of entire groups, making comparisons by age, education, and gender, belongs to the domains of *social psychology* and *sociology*.

Since the environment has a collection of distinct socioeconomic aspects, socioeconomic behavior may be considered a separately examinable phenomenon. It is strategy and tactic. Strategy because it has central attributes developed to deal with general, longer-term patterns in social stratification (the "dominance hierarchy") and economic opportunity. Tactic in the sense that it enables operational maneuvering and short-term responses to the multitude of *ad hoc* developments and situations that may be characterized as social and economic in nature.

Socioeconomic behavior is brain activity that relies upon the genetic apparatus and information about the environment. The latter incorporates *global system*-specific parameters that had been worked into the *surrounding socioeconomic milieus* through increasingly local institutional adaptations. Environmental "inputs" that demand behavioral "outputs" evolved over time. They differ significantly from one *global system* to another, implying major shifts in the information that *minds* must process to generate socioeconomic behavior. Prediction and interpretation of the socioeconomic environment form a *global system*-typical information base in the neocortex.

External conditions constantly affect the organism's neuronal activities, hormone secretion, and the nervous system's excitability. They elicit reactions from the body and influence behavior. At some level of neurobiological detail, each organism is unique. Brain tissues differ in infinite ways from individual to individual if one goes deep enough into the organism's molecular structure. Given the uniqueness of the genotype, identical impulses elicit differences in socioeconomic behavior. This circumstance implies a practically unlimited behavioral versatility, which is a precondition for socioeconomic evolution since, similar in many respects to biological evolution, it also takes place through "selection."

General statements about what happens to the *mind* in the course of *cultural evolution* require an abstraction from the inexhaustible details that emerge from the indicated uninterrupted micro-scale interaction and individual uniqueness. The analysis must become "statistical." It must tune out the "noise" in order to listen only to robust signals. It must focus on "average" or "normal" behavior in a historical perspective–a promising enterprise. About 12,000 years ago, at the beginning of recognized cultural evolution, *homo sapiens* had the same brain size as contemporary humans, yet consider how much "average" or "normal" behavior has changed.

Ancient civilizations, including the gilded worlds of Greece and Rome, the deep fonts of Western culture and tradition, were peopled with adolescents parading in grown-up bodies. The Greeks may have taught their children choral music, the appreciation of the arts, and the power of reasoning, but human sacrifices did not taper off until the fourth century BCE. Rome may have produced superb engineers and administrators, but legionaries, saluting the emperor on the occasion of their return from a victorious campaign, stabbed a few among themselves to show how courageously their comrades fell in the field of honor. It was sufficient to mention the name of the emperor three times in a public place to be crucified or thrown to the beasts at the circus. Fathers could kill their children at birth, thus becoming plenipotentiary enforcers of natural selection. Under the legal code, the *pater familias* could also lawfully execute his children later in life or sell them as slaves. If the fire accidentally died out at the communal hearth of the Vesta Temple, the guilty priestess was buried alive (even if a mere child). The Pontifex Maximus had to restart the holy flame by rubbing together pieces of wood taken from the lucky tree (*Felix Arbor*) lest disaster strike Rome. Gladiator games, the most gruesome blood sport cultivated on a mass scale, lasted well into the fifth century CE.

Elaborate executions arranged by local rulers were a staple of public entertainment throughout pious medieval Europe. After an "introductory" partial hanging, the condemned was eviscerated–an act that he could witness with his own eyes. Drawing and quartering the unfortunate concluded the execution, which was followed by drinking, feasting, and general merriment.

Even in the 17th century, church authorities in Europe, in full compliance with the national (royal) and local judicature, tortured and executed individuals for causes that people could not explain in any other way except by attributing them to the Devil. Satan and his agents were suspected to have caused bad harvests, deaths of livestock, fires, and, in general, any adverse development that defied the locals' sense of *chance* variation. They looked for suspects among themselves. It did not take more to connect afflictions to a priest than catching him take a swig from the sacrificial wine when he thought no one was looking. Signs of mental disorder (such as epilepsy or hysteria), skin diseases thereto unseen, and nocturnal parties dedicated to youthful virility were all symptoms of the possessed. And God have mercy on those who were castigated to appease divine indignation.

Despite the thrilling, and in some respects unparalleled, achievements of pre-*Enlightenment* humanity, the way the average person reasoned may remind one of puppetry for preschoolers or the pathologically inflicted under clinical care—a thought world immersed in the "metamagical," human-sized, literal interpretations of the extraordinary. Their world of thoughts and emotions was far removed from ours.

Sigmund Freud, the founder of psychoanalysis, clearly articulated the notion that the mental life of children and abnormal adults can lead to satisfactory explanations of the ways ancient humans thought, felt, and acted. Children live with explanations and beliefs that reflect their undeveloped capacity for systematic thinking and limited information about the world. Much of what adults know and control as mundane reality seems "supernatural" to a child, the work of powers beyond comprehension and control. The result is a mental balance that brings the external and internal worlds into equilibrium with huge (though receding) blank spots on the map of understanding. The child's deviations from adult-controlled reality lead to the phantasy world on the "primal scene." Archeology and the anthropological study of hunter-gatherer civilizations that survived in isolation provided evidence of similarities between ancient man and the modern child.

Understandably, psychoanalytical research linked ancient humans and modern adults suffering from pathological mental problems. Neurosis is the link between them. Phobias, fetishes, manias, violent outbursts, and compulsive, anxiety-ridden behavior observed in mental institutions offer persuasive images of our prehistoric forefathers who had to live with explanations of the world that appear *random* and unfounded to us.

If we created a large number of replicas of "average adult" faces from 60,000 BCE to the present and ran them at a fast clip to create a "movie" effect, we would see the face of a madman (or a child's expression on an adult face) gradually becoming familiar, or "normal" to us. The pictures would pass through stages of looking very deranged, slightly deranged, disturbed, weird, strange, unsympathetic, quintessentially different, noticeably different. This happens *in tandem* as the glaring mismatch between the adult head and younger facial expression recedes, and then moves into the subtleties of modern times. Even members of the previous generation are not quite like our own. Photos of our parents as young people show that sometimes almost imperceptible difference.

The expression of the eyes provides the ground for the judgment as to how far the historical individual shown in the series progressed along the road of *cultural evolution*. Eyes are not only sensory receptors, they also emit rays of light, mirroring the world. The observant glance is behavior (part of the phenotype) in an inactive mode. The inner world looks at its external equivalent. If the human environment was barbaric, governed by rules that look alien to us, the observant scrutiny in the stares would reflect that. Biologically, they saw the same way, but what and how they saw socially, culturally, and economically were different. This is why many people find movies about long-gone eras so lacking. The gleam in the actors' eyes tells of contemporary material and moral conditions, Western consumer capitalism and the worldwide web.

Cultural evolution and world history may be considered a neuropsychiatric healing process from the point of view of some later generation living under a stable *global system*. This healing process is thrown into doubt during *chaotic transitions,* periods of unconscious search for the blueprint of the next stasis. The average behavior of trying to be adaptive, striving for middle class status, is disrupted and perverted by historically relevant, alternative socioeconomic organizations.

How did the *minds* cleanse themselves over time? At the beginning of 17th century France, it seemed that the religious, state, and yes, the academic infrastructure, would never be able to extricate itself from the search of the body for the *punctum diabolicum*. Yet, the practice of witch hunting was gone by the end of the same century.[6] How did it happen? What changed the perception of what is normal if the individual behaves like the world is and the world is as the individual behaves?

As knowledge in biology, physics, and medicine grew and became diffused, people learned to explain phenomena they did not understand. The link of causality between the deaths of livestock and strange skin diseases moved from the irrational, superstitious, and general toward the rational, scientific, and specific. Acceptance that the state of knowledge did not always suffice to explain things

---

6.   *Mandrou, 1968.*

grew gradually, in parallel. Naively imaged God and Satan no longer micro-managed daily lives; metamagical thinking diminished.

"Experimental behavior" (i.e., "behavioral mutation") at the individual level acted as scout and shock troop. Saying "This is stupid," in a crowd around the scaffold erected to save the soul of the possessed witch would have been a short-lived and ill-fated experiment at the beginning of the 17th century; but it probably would have provoked approving reactions toward the middle of the same century. Variation in behavior paves the way to progress, but the break with the past is sudden. Transformation into the qualitatively different stage occurs through a *Gleichschtaltung* of behavior, motivated by the authority of sanctioned and published rules. In this process, the *imprimatur* plays a central role. "The Hammer of Witches" (*Malleus Malificarum*), published in 1486 (the exact date differs according to source) with the blessings of the Vatican, legitimated the persecution of presumed witches across the entire Christian world. The definitive signal to the individual that behavior associated with witch hunting was no longer the standard of normalcy came through countermanding legal actions. (The death penalty by "Autodafe" was outlawed in England in 1736, in Prussia in 1754, and in Spain in 1834.) Thus, a particular behavioral mode or element is most prominent during a period that begins with official authentication and ends with official de-authentication.

Scientific and social evolution, driven by the motivating force for survival and differential socioeconomic success, brought new thinking and appropriately new behavior, changing the environment. Even if the brain did not change, the information it processed and the behavior it commanded and controlled did. This is the basis for considering *cultural evolution* a transformation of the *mind*; and, consequently, history a material process with direction. Looking backward, a sequence is implied. The world could not go from the polytheistic, sun-worshiping antiquity to "reason over faith," which came with the *Enlightenment*, without first passing through a monotheistic "faith over reason" period. Time for global organization came during the first third of the 19th century and, in retrospect, it could not have come earlier.

The influential postmodernist, Michel Foucault (1926-1984), showed that social institutions tend to "normalize" behavior, not the least through sanctioning deviations from culturally constructed standards. Although the *Enlightenment* did away with the crude methods of punishing noncompliance through torture and execution, modernity brought more subtle methods that work on the mind.[7]

---

7.   See *Foucault, 1965, 1970, 1995.*

Foucault's observations support the notion that a *global system* emanates *macroscopic* radiation, forcing behavior to converge toward institutionally dictated standards. This is indeed the case. Socioeconomic adaptation strengthens institutions by reproducing the environment associated with them, and strong institutions put adaptive tasks in a sharper relief. The ways of the multitude penetrate and capture the ways of the individual. Foucault's complaints remind us that *cultural evolution* as a healing process cannot be considered complete. A presentiment may haunt the current generation that posterity will wonder about its sense of reality and interpersonal relations as its members wonder about the lives and experiences of those who lived in the past. Foucault's bitterness and the aspersions he cast on the generally shared belief that the *Enlightenment* and modern life brought progress ("reason" and "freedom") relative to preceding stages of history, should be considered a cry of despair: "Why does the world have to be like this!?" followed by a slam of the door. It is somewhat reminiscent of the Hobbesian mixture of cynicism and pity, conveying repressed suasion with the faint hope about a better tomorrow.

Following Vilfred Pareto (1848-1923), we assert that rational behavior alone cannot explain human history. The mind, according to Pareto, always lives in a precarious balance between the rational and the irrational. Subconscious feelings and unstoppable impulses play vital roles in shaping the evolution of the individual and supra-individual schemes of cooperation. Rebelliousness is a part of social existence. To gain and reassert independence, the sense of freedom, ancestral domination, spiritual authority, social rules, and prestige must be mocked and confronted.

Socioeconomic evolution is unthinkable without "experimental behavior" that fails miserably at the beginning. In addition to the individually chosen "voluntarily experimental behavior," there is "involuntary, group experimental behavior." Some alternatives to the defunct world order (GS1) made it into statehood during the *global transformation*, coaxing out or forcing accommodative responses. What seemed normal and permanent in the species-wide self-destructive search phase turned out to be failed historical experiments, to personal disadvantage on a massive scale.

◆   ◆   ◆

Socioeconomic behavior, as part of the equilibrium between the genes and the environment, is material reality in the body; it is anatomy and physiology. Knowing what is permissible and useful, what is proscribed and counterproductive, having a comprehensive insight into the institutions, and showing propensities and biases, add up to the application of computational algorithms to internalized data about constraints and possibilities. Behavior, with all its aspects, is electrochemically maintained and operated in the neuronal circuits.

Socioeconomic environments create patterns of emotion. They affect physiology; in particular, the endocrine cycle. By influencing the way the body's DNA deals with the environment, socioeconomic conditions partake in determining the phenotype. Normal socioeconomic behavior implies ranges in the continua of physical properties in the brain within which differential adaptive success is feasible. Outside those ranges lie pathology and defiance.

Division of labor and socioeconomic differentiation require a structure of specific socioeconomic behaviors. But below this structure, an inner core of homogeneity underlies individual variety. Some basic features conditioned by the *global system* may be detected in everyone; individuals under specific circumstances react similarly to stimuli arising from social differentiation or presented by economic opportunity; and socioeconomic roles are interchangeable; e.g., the poor would tend to behave like the wealthy and vice versa if conditions were reversed early enough in their lives. Under a given *global system*, the fundamental fixed rules determining socioeconomic self-conduct are sufficiently similar to be able talk about *global system*-specific phenotypical traits. They cut across divisions of gender, race, nationality, and status to the panhuman *mind*, whose evolution through stages is the world's psycho-biography.

For most people, the connection between their behavior and the *global system* lives in the underground of consciousness. It is diffused and disguised in the commonplace routines and occurrences of daily life. A shared, standardized linguistic base makes such a predominantly unconscious, to some extent mechanical, global cooperation possible. This aspect of the world order is also the one that most readily supports the contention that the *global system* "lives" in interconnected brains.

LANGUAGE

The *mind* has a virtually unlimited capacity to establish linkages between things. Symbolic communication means that from the infinite number of possibilities to make one thing represent another, some have been selected and are widely understood. That is, from the unlimited number of possibilities at our disposal to generate sensory inputs for others (e.g., emit different sounds, make sundry gestures, move, move objects, gaze, and touch in varied ways) the receiver will "get" the intended meaning–the referent. A shared code enables the exchange of thoughts. Animals can do it too, but the capacity for deep and complex mutual understanding, unlimited by space and time, separates *homo sapiens* from the rest of the animal kingdom. This borderline is not hermetically sealed; some limited symbolic communication occurs between humans and animals, especially dogs and horses.

Symbolic thinking allows for the effective transmission of telescoped information. You and your friend come out of a theater. You ask "What do you think?" and you receive a shrug of the shoulders in answer. You decode it as "I am indifferent" or "I do not know yet, let me think about it." Although it may sound like a bagatelle, this slice of life involves astonishingly complicated mental and neurophysiologic processes. The sender of the signal summed up hours of observations, the accumulation of likes and dislikes, established a rough balance between positive and negative impressions, and found a concise way to express it with the reservation that "this opinion may be preliminary." The lack of words is the symbol and the tentativeness of opinion is the referent.[8] And you understood all that perfectly. The transmission was "effective" because there was a sufficient overlap between your respective interpretations of symbol and referent. For such coherence, two *minds* must work off a shared base of information.

Symbolic communications may be classified into three categories: (i) intermental communication, using human-body generated signals; (ii) intermental communication through other means; and (iii) intramental (within the same person) communication. The categories may overlap in time and can mutually trigger one another.[9]

In category (i), language, with its acoustic and visual (orthographic) signals, is the most important, but by far not the exclusive channel. Iconic gestures (showing what is being suggested), a handshake, a smile, applause, whistles, booing in a crowd–all of them with uncounted possible nuances–are nonlanguage symbols of the referents "approval," "disapproval, "indifference," "hatred," and "menace." This category includes all forms of interpersonal communications even if they are

---

8.   The words "symbol" and "referent" are used here instead of the "signifier" (*signans*) and "signified" (*signatum*) made fashionable first by structural linguists, most influentially by Ferdinand de Saussure (1857-1913), and later by the exponents of structuralism, poststructuralism, and postmodernism. Contemporary semiotics, the general theory of signs, uses both pairs (i.e., symbol/referent and signifier/signified).

9.   Russian psychologist, Lev Semyonovich Vygostky (1896-1934), introduced the *intermental/intramental* dichotomy.

not face-to-face; i.e., carried by electromagnetically transmitted signals (computers, TV and radio sets, loudspeakers) or by print (books, newspapers).

Category (ii), intermental communication based on means other than human-body generated signals, usually involves inanimate objects as symbols. These may be "actual" or "evocative"–a kind of "symbol of a symbol." The Eiffel Tower in Paris, for example, may be considered the "actual" symbol of France or the French. Its paperweight version on someone's desk thousands of miles away is an "evocative" symbol. If the referent (France or the French) has emotional associations; that is, you like or dislike France or the French, even an "evocative" symbol might activate them. A little boy declares a piece of wood to be an automatic rifle. When he points it at you and yells "ratatatatatata…" and you playfully grab at your chest and collapse, you signal that the symbol was sufficiently evocative of the suggested referent (and probably will be rewarded with peals of laughter and another salvo). Clothing is a constantly used object-based form of symbolic communication. One may dress, for instance, to convey belonging to higher socio-economic strata. A junior employee may wear a three-piece suit (symbol) to express importance already acquired or upward mobility in the corporate hierarchy. But dressing in ways to show indifference to anyone's judgment about one's status is also symbolic communication. In this case, the referent is not the elevated status, but a lack of interest in it.

Intramental symbols, category (iii), refer to conscious or subconscious processes in our own minds. To demonstrate the first, let us conjecture that you pass by a TV screen in a store and learn that a fraudulent stockbroker received a hefty jail sentence. Your internal response may be "Too bad." Of course, you did not mean it literally. "Too bad" was the symbol of a referent of condemning the knave under your breath. (Our bio-social past is haunting us. Betrayal by feigning sympathy to enhance the punishment may well be an ultrasilent echo of "chimpanzee politics" under some primordial foliage.) Such mental reactions do not even have to coalesce into full sentences. They might only be perceived in a pre-thinking mode.

As an example of the subconscious, intramental communication, suppose that someone describes to you a newly opened bakery and raves about how appetizing the freshly baked, still hot, crispy, crusty products look and smell. From the length of his own enthusiastic descriptions, the person gradually recognizes that he is getting hungry. And he may do so with annoyance, since he firmly resolved to avoid unscheduled meals. The mental process involved in experiencing and showing enthusiasm was the unconscious symbol of the referent, the growing appetite that a self-imposed dietary restriction tried to ignore. Of course, not all subconscious referents linked to subconscious symbols can be identified so easily and quickly.

The avowed methodology of classical Freudian psychoanalysis is to cure neurosis by diagnosing the repressed referent and bringing it into the bright light of full consciousness. The following is the summary of a successful treatment, reported from the prewar halcyon days of psychotherapy. A woman diagnosed with schizophrenia is put under hypnosis. She convulsively repeats the phrase "Cement between the bricks…Cement between the bricks." The analyst hypothesizes that this is the symbol of a repressed sexual trauma. Steering the patient's regression into her deep memory accordingly, the referent psychological scar emerges: "Coital assault by a brick-layer."

The exploration of how the civilized world fashioned individual thinking and behavior, in general, moves the problem of symbol/referent relations from the personal to the social scale. In his much quoted book, *Civilization and Its Discontents*, Freud blamed the psychological constraints put on our ancient instincts by civilized life for the general malaise of modern man. Making light of our misery, embracing substitute satisfactions such as creative work or numbing ourselves through intoxications of less noble sorts are the symbols that represent the referent, the repressed nostalgia for the elemental freedoms of a simpler life. This pessimistic theory, which came to light as Germany began its transmogrification into the Third Reich, is hardly supportable now. But it still trenchantly avers the existence of socially shared, communitywide unconscious symbols and referents.

Folklore, myths, and legends are examples of such phenomena. Attachment to them is the symbol of a community's belief in its distinguished identity and unique importance (the referent). Artistic products such as operas, dramas, and epic poems, as well as movies and historic novels, confound information with its embellishments. They make heroic tales and miraculous occurrences as real to individual consciousness as is the collectively forged, flattering self-image.

The symbol/referent nexus varies greatly in accuracy. Linguistic symbols (the shapes and sounds of letters) fix and standardize some symbol/referent links (e.g., scientific and legal concepts) while leaving others open to interpretation. Creative literature suggests analogies that evoke, magnify, elevate, bemuse, and beautify. It plays with our innate desire to discover that the vacuously simple is a coded message in a dark cloud and that the impenetrably mysterious is really simple and commonplace. Metaphors are words that signify something other than their literary meanings (e.g., "Beethoven's Seventh Symphony is the Apotheosis of Dance"); similes equate things that are dissimilar in the conventional sense (e.g., "destiny is like a distant drum beat"); allegories make concrete, existing characters or physical objects convey abstract, spiritual, or moral messages through dramatic stories. Although "symbol" is listed as one of the above literary devices (narrowly defined as using words or expressions to represent something other than what their conventional interpretation would suggest), "symbolic communication" (transmitting information, in general) encompasses the use of any conceivable method to send and absorb messages.

The recognition that symbol/referent relations have no individual meaning was a milestone in the history of philosophy. They are determined together, mutually, and reciprocally, much like the variables of a simultaneous equation system. Interactions in all the fields together, most importantly in social life, economic activity, science and technology, culture, and politics, mold and frame symbol/referent couples.[10]

An example from the humdrum of the quotidian: Your neighbor meets you in the street and announces "We bought a beautiful new table for the dinning room." The sound of the word "table" is the symbol and your *mind* will summon up a referent. After eliminating tables not fit for dining rooms (e.g., writing desks), taking into consideration the neighbor's taste and financial conditions (as far as you may know them), your *mind* will formulate an image. A picture complete with color, shape, dimensions, and proportions in your *mind* will stand in for a specific object you have never seen. One hundred percent identity is unlikely and there is practically no *chance* that another recipient of the same message would carpenter the exact same image you did. Yet, given an area in which a distinct homogeneous commercial culture reigns (e.g., North American suburbia) and a narrow enough time frame (e.g., the same decade), the referents triggered by symbols will remain in the "ballpark." The *minds* will work with a common information base: "We" implies "my wife and I" or the "household;" "bought" means "cash or credit;" "beautiful" is extrapolated from what you may have seen in the neighbor's house, along with some background information that allows you to see the world through another person's eyes (using your "theory of mind"); "new" equals "not second hand," i.e., "never before used;" "dining room table" implies specific utility and location in the house.

There are hidden socioeconomic variables. You may know whether or not the purchaser is status conscious. Depending on the case, you might imagine a differ-

---

10. The development of structural linguistics and the philosophy of logical positivism are largely responsible for this breakthrough. Ferdinand de Saussure (1857-1913) and Nikolai Sergeyevich Trubetzkoy (1890-1938) broke ground for the development of structural linguistics; the later work of Josef Johann Ludwig Wittgenstein (1889-1951) inspired logical positivism, orienting it toward the "language game."

ent shape, ornamentation, or size. The economic variable in the background is "price." If your neighbor also told you where he bought the table (e.g., at the fancy mall or in a giant discount house), you would have an idea about the size of the outlay. All that without effort–and instantaneously! Closeness in space and time makes imagery more accurate. This is particularly true in the quoted example since the referent you created, and thereby your knowledge about *personal socioeconomic spheres* in your *surrounding socioeconomic milieu*, are subject to iterated improvement through verbal or empirical verification. That is, you might ask for further details ("oak or cherry?") or you might stop by to look at the table, thereby enlarging and refining your information base about the *milieu*.

If you increase the geographic distance, the same announcement would convey less precise meaning. Someone calls you up from rural China and (through a translator, in case you needed one) tells you "We bought a beautiful new table for the dinning room." Because China is still a communist country, you might think that "we" stands for some sort of a collective. "Buying" might involve barter; that is, paying with farm products for the furniture made by another collective in a nearby village. What is "beautiful" in the Chinese countryside? Your mind rummages among impressions gathered in museums and Asian restaurants. "New?" In the poor Asian countryside, it might mean "without major scratches on the surface" or "not older than two years." The exact same message coming to a Sichuan farmer from North American suburbia might be just as unclear. Clarification of a gamut of symbol/referent associations is needed in order to understand each other at a satisfactory level–and this is possible. Socioeconomic conditions, behavior, and language are sufficiently similar to adjust quickly even to the most dissimilar and remote microcosm of symbol/referent relations. Growth in global-scale mass production and consumption tends to reduce the spatial variation of referents triggered by symbols of human-made objects. However, an increase in time between emission and reception erodes precision, even within the same locale.

Some symbol/referent relations are fixed and do not vary in precision as a result of interpersonal communications. The base of the Napierian logarithm "e" (2.71828...) or π, standing for the ratio of the circumference of a circle to its diameter (3.14159...), means the same for every mathematician in the world. Such symbols, as well as many other technical and scientific terms, have also been determined collectively, but here the collective refers to specialized scientific and engineering communities of experts rather than to a large and diverse public. The designation of objects (natural or man-made), elementary human sentiments and needs, and phenomena that are within our sensory reach, is straightforward and relatively unambiguous. They always evolve. Today, every computer user knows that "mouse" is not only a rodent and that a "virus" may harm something other than bodily health. And, of course, new ones are created: WYSIWYG is "What you see is what you get" in word-processing lingo.

For abstract concepts such as democracy, dictatorship, altruism, and selfishness, the variance in personalized interpretation becomes large and the "noise" that accrues through subsequent communications increases. It is unlikely that two individuals interpret a single, general-idea-connoting symbol in identical ways. Genetic tendencies ("biology"), life experience, education, occupation, place, and time are the most obvious sources of differentiation. The personalization of grammar, syntax, and style further destandardizes the coding and decoding of messages. Yet, there is sufficient overlap in associations involving symbol/referent pairs to express agreements and disagreements, share beliefs, and discuss conditions of the socioeconomic environment of any size. Even polar opposites along the ideological, political scale can understand each other as long as they are not separated by too much time. Time is like a growing wedge in reciprocal comprehension. In the first half of the 19th century, English lawmakers called anyone without the means to live in leisure "poor." This usage would make communication impossible between them and contemporary social scientists. Diachronic shifts in meanings would have to be synchronized forward or backward to enable exchange.

Philosophy is apart from the pragmatic world where symbol/referent pairs remain within a range of mutual comprehensibility and where ready willingness to understand each other reigns. Metaphysics, the most abstract of human endeavors, revolves around the close scrutiny of words and meanings. Distinctions between two sets of symbol/referent relations could determine two separate, logically coherent views about the nature of knowledge or existence or morality. When you try to answer questions such as "Is appearance the same as illusion?" or "Do humans derive the laws of nature or simply ascribe them to it?" differences in what each word means become dividing lines among professional generalizers of quintessence.

Heidegger laid bare the misleading character of metaphysical "truth claims." Under words like "Thing" or "Being" there are bottomless abysses and unidentified or forgotten assumptions that are important enough for the same sentence to imply different ontologies, that is, diverse explanations concerning the ultimate nature of existence. Derrida, a central figure of poststructuralist, postmodern philosophy, demonstrated the extent to which it is impossible to escape from linguistic abstractions. From the combination of these two closely related insights one may see that philosophical statements can neutralize our craving for deeper explanations only momentarily. Unresolved perplexity over existence, the meaning of life in secular terms, will resurface. Imprecise terms are being combined, signifying nothing "transcendent." Metaphysical theorizing may be the recombination of physically engraved, culturally determined concepts in the *mind*, a sort of improvisation strictly constrained by innate modes of thinking and discursive routines of self-expression. We think that we are saying something new and profound about "being," but in reality, our "grey matter" shimmies along chalk lines on the dance floor.

Verbal definitions refer to other definitions. They bump into one another through overlaps and repetitions and defer the final delivery of the promised good. But the "unsaid" haunts the impressive legerdemain. The statement, "Mind is a simple material extension of the brain, a biological computer," is full of provocative ambiguity. Examining the dictionary definition of each word used, one discovers that *dualism* and *agnosticism* are following this harsh *monistic* assertion. They will confront it with revolvers in the narrow, dark alley of a linguistic dead end. The triggers will be pulled and a sign will drop from both barrels: "Meaningless!" In the end, the distance between knowledge ("text") and reality ("context") cannot be narrowed by elucidations, no matter how elegant and engaging they may be. Truth claims have entangled implications and defer explanations. Human thinking remains ineluctably and terminally locked up in the "prison of language" (Nietzsche). The "context" remains in the "text." To paraphrase Derrida, the "text" is everything.[11]

This exposure of metaphysics helps us see how a *global system* preserves itself. Language-based thinking (the *global system*'s own *text*), tied to a schema of socio-economic conditions and a closed range of adaptive behavior keyed to it, severely handicaps the establishment of verbally expressed positions that are "exterior" or "ulterior" relative to it. The supra-*discourse* of the *global system* includes or dominates most other *discourse*s. That is why it seems so liberal and why it is so successful in adaptive, evolutionary self-modulation.

---

11. Whereas structuralism showed that a dominant text characterizes society with all its forms and manifestations of interaction, poststructuralism (or postmodernism) emphasized the multiplicity of texts. The way you see society and history depends on who you are. Whereas structuralism supports the image of a single material configuration with fixed characteristics in worldwide cerebral interdigitation, the poststructuralist/postmodern view focuses on the intangibility of matter (the *mysterious mind*) and on the secretive, *random* element-involving nature of collective transformation.

◆   ◆   ◆

The ability to communicate precisely through language ranges along several scales such as (1) the life span of the symbol/referent relations used; (2) their universality; (3) their level of enforcement; (4) the chance of verifying the messages empirically; and (5) the possibility of examining them from the "outside," that is, independently.

(1) There are short-lived and long-lived symbol/referent relations. Some meanings, such as those conveyed by fad and nonce words, and those used in popular culture and the fashion world, come and go, while those associated with historical events and enduring moral and cultural values remain in the public consciousness for many generations. The smaller the life span, the lesser the mutual comprehension with the passage of time.

(2) Some symbol/referent relations have only local significance and others are known worldwide. The universality scale correlates with the size of the space in which symbol/referent couples have meaning. The more local a relation is, the less clear it becomes as one tries to use it at increasing distances from its indigenous habitat.

Considering (1) and (2) together, the shorter the life span of a symbol/referent pair and the more local it is, the less intelligible it becomes as time passes and as its application is attempted over larger distances. Enduring and universal concepts are needed for global communications.

(3) Enforcement refers to both the maintenance of symbol/referent connections and a guarantee of their proper use. The entire hierarchy of socioeconomic systems hinges upon public responsibility to "enforce" in this double sense. Criminal and civil codes maintain property rights; national legislation specifies the responsibilities of the state in matters of economic policy and prescribes conduct for productive and social organizations. Strict definitions are required for the government to function. They are contained in laws, executive rulings, court records, and other official documents administered by government and professional organizations.

In the technical-scientific domain, which includes standards relating to computational methods, public authority steps in where the lack of compliance with strictly specified symbol/referent relations and their employment may jeopardize life and property. Court proceedings in the wake of a bridge collapse attributed to faulty calculations and noncompliance with building standards may be considered social enforcement of certain symbol/referent relations.

The level of sanctioning and the intensity, quickness, and sureness of triggered reactions are strongest for core concepts in well defined situations. Outside this space of severe enforcement, the listed attributes weaken and decline to zero. Macroeconomic policy must be conducted under well defined legal constraints, but it may be explained erroneously on television. Arithmetic errors in construction could result in criminal charges, but making them on a school test will not prompt police sirens. Whereas socioeconomic symbol/referent relations were at some point shaped by wide public participation, only academic and professional organizations are responsible for determining such relations in technical-scientific domains. Definitions of "cell," "compound," "Kepler's laws of planetary motion," and "purchasing power parity" are the products of academic and professional organizations. Noncompliance in sciences and the professions usually arises from ignorance and the consequences are private socioeconomic costs.

(4) Messages may be arranged along a scale of verifiability, that is, the opportunity to review their accuracy. The more a message relies on literally expressed concepts, the less verifiable it becomes. While testing your image of the neighbor's piece of furniture is at the beginning of the scale, a metaphysical declaration is at its end. The existence of a "thing-in-itself" (an essentialism that is unspoiled and undeformed by subjective human analysis and is therefore inaccessible by definition) cannot be verified empirically, since this would require sensory inputs other than words standing in for abstractions. Verification may occur through proxies, such as data, independent sources of information, and experience-based imagery. Movement along the descending degree of empirical verifiability means increased chance of misunderstanding and disagreement. Socioeconomic issues are in the middle of the scale. They are more verifiable than metaphysical statements but less so than laying eyes on a specific object. Of course, verifiability varies according to the level of socioeconomic exchange. Government actions generate data and reports through which they are expected to be transparent and subject to public control and scrutiny. Personal assessments of socioeconomic problems are seldom, if ever, verified. There are too many of them to warrant focused interest and retention.

(5) The possibility of analyzing meaning from the exterior and gaining an independent outside view can be determined according to (1) through (4) above. The more short-lived, local, and less enforced the symbol/referent relationships used in a message are, and the more empirically verifiable its content is, the easier it is to get "outside" of it, and, of course, *vice versa*. Metaphysical texts are the hardest to contemplate from the exterior because the terms they use are long-lived, universal, totally out of reach for testing, and are enforced by academic

authority. Independent, critical views on the socioeconomic system are possible, but they may entail costs, i.e., turn out to be manifestations of nonadaptive behavior. It all depends upon the level (e.g., local, national, global), the forum (private conversation, mass media, streets), the frequency, and the intensity of confrontation.

In general, the intelligibility of communication is the highest in exchanges about practical matters between two adults. It weakens as we move toward political discussion and the comparative analysis of socioeconomic conditions. It becomes the weakest in philosophical *discourse*. An increase in the number of participants and the distance in space separating them augment chances of miscommunication and discord.

Based on these observations, the language-based features associated with the hierarchy of socioeconomic organizations may be identified. From (1) and (2) we see that at least some symbol/referent relations must be enduring and universal; from (3) that underlying concepts require precise definition and rigorous application; from (4) that the use of key concepts must be verifiable to some extent; from (5) we can recognize self-preserving resilience: Some will be unable to analyze and criticize the socioeconomic *status quo*; others will be discouraged from doing so. Since criticism is possible, but with potential consequences, it will be made, by and large and on the average, only when the costs of remaining silent and passive exceed the costs of public dissent. From the total volume of negative valuations of the socioeconomic order we can separate those that are consciously directed against the *global system*'s immediate institutional and legal derivatives. Under GS2, these could be national government organizations in charge of social and economic policy and *multilateral* agencies. The *global system*'s capacity to resist direct challenges politically and through adaptability (i.e., moving within the range of its organizing principles) is a measure of its endurance.

To fulfill these requirements, each *global system* "invented" its own language. Foundational legislation constitutes its nucleus, the *lexicon*. It is the enduring *imprimatur* of transcendental rights and obligations, the source of legitimacy. Around it are "derived concepts" used in social and economic practice, symbol/referent relations understandably paralleling the existence of a *global system*. The next ring contains weaker but still "recognizable associations" with it. On the *lexicon*'s *penumbra* are terms about which one no longer can tell if their emergence or alteration has been caused by *global transformation*. The use of the *global system*'s language in practically unlimited *discourses* (in virtually infinite instances with applications of countless variety) creates the *global system*'s *text* and makes it evolve. (See *text* in the Glossary.)

◆   ◆   ◆

Obviously, there were no sirens at midnight on January 31, 1945 announcing the beginning of GS2 to time zone after time zone. The New Deal legislation had already prepared the ground for it in the United States, just as many elements of GS1 surfaced during GS0, particularly in Britain. Recorded history makes it clear that institutional construction precedes and some vestigial arrangements of the previous order linger after the induction of a *global system*. Rather than a precise demarcation, the starting point is only an agreed-upon milestone, the "symbol" of a new beginning. If we watched the gradual transition of blue into green, we would first have no doubt; it is blue. We would be in doubt for a while, but after being puzzled by liminal and presumed subliminal moments of transition, at one precise moment, our conviction would jell to certitude and we would exclaim: "Now it is green!" This is how "1834" and "1945" are interpreted as the respective birthdays of GS1 and GS2.

The *lexicon* contains precise symbol/referent relations provided by the organizational blueprint of the corresponding *global system*. Chapter 3 enumerated the legislative items that were key to creating the respective concept-worlds of GS1 and GS2. As soon as the new world order begins to function, the wholesale creation of additional concepts derived directly from those included in the foundational legislation follows. For example, "government economic policies," "social safety net," "collective bargaining," and *multilateralism* are GS2 creatures both as symbols and referents. Although they may be compared with symbol/referent pairs pertaining to national legislation on government and business relations basic to GS1, they are also so new and so different that their dialectical opposites suggest something fatefully negative, the lack of something essential. The opposite of collective bargaining implies trouble in the streets and threat to social peace; the opposite of the IMF implies disorganization in international financial relations. Around this ring of "derived concepts" there are "recognizable associations" logically coterminous with the *global system*.

During GS1, the expression *laissez faire* may have been considered the direct, large-scale application of its original meaning, as it had been elaborated by18[th] century Physiocrats and Adam Smith; that is, a consciously given *carte blanche* to private entrepreneurship as long as it did not conflict with criminal law. Since the birth of GS2, few would think of *laissez faire* as a viable single principle to organize national economies. It is rather the symbol of its historical connotation and a political rallying cry to protect private initiatives from public bureaucracies. The doctrinaire command "Stay out" under GS1 turned into "Do not mingle too much" under GS2. Other changes in specialized terminologies used in social sciences and political literature also mirror the permanent promotion of the state from GS1's clueless "security guard" to GS2's easygoing "resident manager."

"Gold" is the same element no. 79 in the periodic table as it always was, but it does not awaken the same thoughts and sentiments as it used to. The referent has undergone a significant transformation. Gold stood for "universal money" under GS1; hence, it was idealized as raw and permanent economic power. Its sight would demand instant respectability, suppressing moral scruples about the ways that may have led to its acquisition. Because of the central role shiny *aurum* played in making the world's first and most primitive order coalesce, illusions about it remained connected with ancient cultures–the legends of Croesus, the pirates, the Medicis. Today's *minds* react differently. Gold has new referents such as financial investment option and expensive dental work. Its old referent, "universal money," has new symbols such as travelers' checks denominated in convertible currencies or their pictures in brochures. Gold may still be associated with luxury and social distinction, but it no longer gives the same tactile, visual, aesthetic satisfaction it used to give.

Language and the "concept world" that accompany *cultural evolution* underwent vital changes after the first *global system* was born. Words and their connotations appeared and disappeared and meanings shifted. The *global transformation* (i.e., GS1—>GS2) may have influenced some of these changes significantly, but one can no longer be sure. Such symbol/referent relations are the entries on the *lexicon's penumbra*, on its open margins. Examples are "You" and "I."

Even the most basic symbols, such as "You" and "I," altered their referents over time. With rising incomes and improving socioeconomic balance, "I" as a symbol came to stand for the referent of selfhood that grew in significance. In the *vanguard,* more than anywhere else, the "persona" was born and gradually became recognized as the focus of social concern: *Ego habeo factum,* and the individual is fully aware of that when it pronounces "I" or writes it down.

The "You" evolved along a parallel track. Most people understand that respect and care accorded to the "I" is dependent upon the same accorded to "You." If "respect and care" could be metered cardinally, as some economists have done with utility, one might say that over the past 200-year period, hundreds of millions of individuals learned how to increase their take-home "respect and care" by willing to grant the same to others. This is not the *bone fide* altruism of heroes, only the reciprocal altruism of rational "utility maximizers." In this transformation of the referents attached to pronouns, the role of creating the welfare state and expanding labor rights under GS2 mingled with the general increase of deference and attention bestowed upon the individual as average per capita economic and political power grew over time.

1914-1945 may be considered an "inter-lexical" period. Symbol/referent relations tied to GS1 became infirm in 1914, but did not automatically die. Following the Great War, the world did not know anything better than the arrangements that framed and facilitated *cultural evolution* for nearly a century. Attempts to hang on to GS1 institutions retained its language, but it began to be transformed. Some of the new symbol/referent links mediated the establishment of transitional systems (i.e., in the USSR and the Third Reich) and some of them (particularly in the United States) marked progress in the search for the "system characteristics" that came to define GS2. From the point of view of the world as a whole, the multiple, simultaneous efforts to determine meanings produced confusion. The world was thinking amidst its self-destructive systemlessness; it was rethinking itself.

The establishment of the *lexicon* begins before its presence is universally recognized. Some of its remnants linger after it is gone and successful *entrainments* (designed to do away with it) come with their own tentative *lexicons* whose contents may get mixed up among themselves and with the "main" one. The (final) *lexicon* is elastic and dynamic. Otherwise it could not be applied to widely differing national conditions and cultures; it could not withstand the accelerations and decelerations of *cultural evolution*, the continuous stream of novelties and occasional shocks that accompany it.

Through the nested layers of adaptations of the *global system*, the *lexicon* becomes diffused and concealed in the practice of daily life. One may consciously connect certain symbols, such as political issues concerning government economic policies, to the notion that there is public responsibility for economic stability and social welfare. One may subconsciously connect the sight of government buildings, the neighborhood commercial bank, the national currency, and one's social security number to that same notion. Newspaper photos or TV broadcasts showing UN activities or meetings of the G-8 heads of state are symbols of international cooperation that did not have equivalents during GS1. But on the whole, the *global system's text* tends to make people forget about the historical nature and the mortality of the *global system*. Radical, effective reality clouds the underlying absolute reality of transience.

Individual vocabularies emerge from the sea of diffused and altered symbol/referent relations. No two such indirectly *lexicon*-determined personal sets are presumed to be equal in words or in neuro-anatomical markings. Since there are neither two equal genotypes nor two identical relations to the environment, there will be differences between any two persons' symbol/referent couplings. From a purely linguistic point of view, this may be seen just by considering that meanings are formed at varying stages of *cultural evolution* in different languages; that is, through somewhat independent collective processes. Even in the same stage of *cultural evolution* and within the same language (e.g., in a given country), people with different general and vocational education, speaking different dialects, and thinking in professional jargons and in group vernaculars, choose different symbols and attach different meanings to them. The individual stock of symbol/referent relations shifts with personal developments, aging, and constant transformations in the enveloping socioeconomic environments.

Of course, *lexicons* have never been assembled. But there is no need for a fully completed and bound handbook. (We know that we live by "social contracts" even if none of us remembers signing one.) Acknowledging that there are relevant differences in the inner core and in the next two layers under GS1 and GS2 should make the point clear: If the *text* has changed, then it must have had a materially conceivable initial state and a materially conceivable subsequent one.

◆   ◆   ◆

The subject of how the *mind* creates meaning is vital when analyzing the role of language in society and history. Language allows the unripe thought to emerge from the marshland of raw urges, feelings, and emotions into reciprocally comprehensible symbols. Through education and experience, individuals develop their specific "semanticity" (their own, always evolving, never closed, vocabulary of symbol/referent relations) and idiosyncratic use of grammar, syntax, and style, as well as their particular "decoding" algorithms (which may be infused with "encoding"); that is, the way messages received from others are absorbed.

Meaning evolved through gradual differentiation from prehistory's concrete and obvious sign/referent relations and super-simple grammar. *Cultural evolution* may be described as the network of welded *minds* going from the trivial clues of natural sounds (bow-wow!) and iconic signals to the mathematician's "let S be a communicative semi-group of multiplicative lattices with irreducible χ-ideal modules."

The genes and the environment play a joint, interactive role in developing the capacity to use language. The dispute may go on about whether children are born with a special "mental organ" for accelerated learning (as Noam Chomsky's widely accepted theory claims) or start their development from a clean slate, an unspecialized, general purpose high-potential brain. While the former assigns a greater role to nature, the latter emphasizes nurture. Ultimate certainty and final satisfaction will probably have to wait for hands-on, empirical brain research. In the meantime, we hang our reasoning on the undisputed premise that words are neurological facts in the memory.[12] Were it not so, the *mind* could not distinguish between table and chair, broccoli and orange, one and many, past and present, bad and good (not to mention "broccoli" and "good") upon hearing or seeing these words. These are comprehensible because the "receivers" have structured substances that are "close enough" to those of the "senders." Graphemes to the eyes and phonemes to the ears are arrangements of matter in the brain at the empirical and rational levels of the *mind*.

According to this logic, the use of different languages implies differences in the physico-chemical fixing of words. Properly written and pronounced, the word "airplane" in Chinese, Japanese, Khoisan, or Esperanto has the same meaning. In fact, these words translate into one another in dictionaries. Yet, because they sound and look different, the exact spatial configuration of molecules and atoms "in the semantic memory" must differ even in the same brain. If we could identify the concrete materiality of the word "airplane" in different languages, picturing each enlarged so that we could see it with our naked eyes while reducing in proportion the enormous relative distances among their constitutive components, we might see "airplane" as a complicated, nebulous object. Perhaps the word and its meaning are crammed into one and the same material phenomenon, a circumstance that would allow the simplest hypothesis to explain the presumed physical inseparability of symbol and referent.

---

12. Neuroscience distinguishes among three types of memory linked to higher cerebral functions: semantic, episodic, and procedural. Words and their meanings, concepts, objects, and perhaps information representing overall knowledge, are in the semantic memory. The episodic memory "remembers" personally experienced events, and the procedural memory "stores" information required to do things such as ride a bicycle. Distinction has also been made between short-and long-term memories. Short-term memory is somewhat similar to the "active file" of a computer and long-term memory resembles the "hard disc." Learning, the acquisition of information to be retained, is the "long-term potentiation of neuronal pathways." Pathways that correspond to the memorized information become stronger and easier to activate than before. The cortex and hippocampus play central roles in learning, memorizing, and abstract thinking. The physical configuration of the memory and several related problems are subject to intense research. *Wilson, 1999*, provides an easy-to-follow description of the brain for nonbiologists. For the organization of language in the brain, see *Garman, 1990*.

The diversity of languages leaves the world well within the bounds of mutual intelligibility in the sciences and in socioeconomic domains. The great overlap in the cognitive processes involved in social interactions allows the same words put into the identical contexts of language-neutral logical propositions to result in reciprocally comprehensible conclusions. The legend of Babel does not apply to builders and occupants of skyscrapers. Scientists at international conferences understand one another quite well without a shared mother tongue. Socioeconomic problems under stable *global systems* can be discussed meaningfully among individuals from any two countries, of all backgrounds and education, among businesses of all sizes, and government officials of all levels. Without some measure of mutual comprehensibility, even postmodern claims of meaninglessness in the sciences and in the analysis of history and social relations; the multiple clashes among diverse *discourses* (expressing "oppositional consciousness," according to race, gender, class, ethnic background, geographic area) would make no sense.

◆   ◆   ◆

In addition to its language component, the *global system* is accompanied by other collectively determined and individually reflected phenomena such as *ethic*, *Weltanschauung*, and *mentality*.

Individual adaptations require a personal *ethic*, a set of principles and moral precepts that act as general guideposts. The work of Max Weber (1864-1920), a classic of sociology, comes to mind immediately. Weber linked the success of capitalism to the "Protestant work ethic," the willingness to toil and exercise parsimony while retaining the capacity to enjoy material well-being without a troubled conscience. In a way, Weber defined the perfect "economic man" who wants to save and consume at the same time, allowing the market (interest rates) to solve his dilemma of whether to buy now or later. Being religious and ascetic, Weber's "Ideal Type" would see the will of God if things turned bad. He would endure any hardship and suffer in silence. He would not think of joining the union, nor would he rise up in arms to eliminate the "underpayment of Labor," as Marx suggested; or, heaven forbid, enjoy life on borrowed money. This was indeed the *ethic* for the stoic herd of humanity GS1 needed. It certainly prevailed in the *vanguard* during the 19th and early 20th centuries. But it would not work under GS2. From the combination of religion and asceticism, the GS2 prototype kept the first and dropped the second. Importantly, the GS2 arch *ethic* came into existence with the new *global system*. It was practically legislated. Deficit spending is at the heart of the *mixed economy*, GS2's domestic economic institutional and policy structure. Private persons must do as the government does to keep the economy from slowing down and sliding back toward the low points of capacity utilization experienced during the Great Depression. If private households did not contract mortgages and buy things on credit, the government would have to borrow even more against its future income.[13] In many other respects as well, the personal rules of conduct differ from GS1 to GS2.

Distinctive, shared consciousness about the world is peculiar to *global systems*. We may call it *Weltanschauung*, a German idiom meaning "view of the world," which the psychologist, Wilhelm Dilthey (1833-1911), made standard in philosophy. The *global system* also creates a certain *mentality*, pent-up energy with potential direction, suspended "intentionality." Given circumstances and stimulus, this *mentality* may explain why individual reactions in an epoch of relatively stable world order fall within an expected range across local cultures and national boundaries. As long as the *global system* exists, *ethic*, *Weltanschauung*, and *mentality* are omnipresent and sufficiently homogenous to be identified.

Since these concepts have been around for a long time and are well known in social and philosophical psychology, there is no need to demonstrate their existence. That has already been done.[14] Added here is only that distinctness in these aspects of reality is considered synchronous with the existence of a *global system*. They are epiphenomena that accompany *global system*-specific socioeconomic behavior and survive with it through the often tempest-like dynamic of *cultural evolution*.

Having identified several elements tied to the long-enduring features of external socioeconomic conditions (i.e., *lexicon*, *ethic*, *Weltanschauung* and *mentality*), we may rightly suppose that the personalized reflection of the *global system* corresponds to morphological states in the brain at some level of the material struc-

---

13. Facts simply overrode the reassuring contentions of early GS2 economics textbooks about government debt being eliminated from time to time through the accumulation of surpluses, elimination being dependent on "political will." Later editions labeled concerns about growing national debts as fallacies. With bold self-confidence, the contemporary GS2 *text* recommends seeing them as useful lubricators in an effectively functioning global capital market.

14. Emil Durkheim (1858-1917) and Marc Bloch (1886-1944) wrote extensively about shared consciousness in society. Individual "mentality" and its mutual determinism with the outside world were central in the writings of Marc Bloch. Franz Brentano (1838-1917) already defined "intentionality" behind concrete behavior, and the concept was used extensively by Edmund Husserl (1859-1938), the founder of modern philosophical phenomenology.

ture. The totality of internalized conditions, the interpretation of the socioeconomic environment, and predictions of how it might mutate and evolve are like a "database" upon which *global system*-specific behavior, the summary expression of internalized world order, runs like a "program."

GLOBAL ORDER IN THE BRAIN

A *global system* exists because it is "on the books," because we experience its institutional presence, and because we recognize the physical necessity of its existence. It is the periodic steady state (observable at the species level since the 19th century) in a one-way, dissipative thermodynamic process–*cultural evolution*. Some material arrangement and functioning in the brain must support it. Even broad organizational principles in human relations have no existence outside neuronal networks. This means that the material traces that stand for the *surrounding socioeconomic milieu* cannot possibly correspond to one hundred percent arbitrary mental states.

Long-term (seemingly permanent) operating conditions orchestrate distinct central tendencies in behavior. If socioeconomic environments differ between GS1 and GS2, so do certain basic aspects of socioeconomic behavior. Biological evolution (change in the genetic structure of the entire human population) is never at standstill. However, there have been no scientifically recognized alterations in the gene pool during the past two centuries that would explain the well documented change in socioeconomic relations. Only the drastic transformation of the socioeconomic environment can explain the evident alteration in socioeconomic behavior. *Global transformation* (GS1—>GS2) boiled down to the instauration of a new baseline in the core principles of social and economic interactions. The *mind's* algorithmic repertoire began to produce new behavioral outputs from new, individually stored inputs, that is, information about the socioeconomic environment.

Through the *surrounding socioeconomic milieus*, the *global system* also creates recurring patterns of short-and long-lived emotional experiences, including those that the organism uses to motivate itself and those that represent responses to external stimuli. Emotions awakened by socioeconomic pressures under GS1 and GS2 are sufficiently different to talk about *global system*-typical packages of physiological stress. Resignation, guilt, anxiety, hate, aggression, compassion, and indifference (the result of opposing and canceling emotional excitation and inhibition) occurred in a different composition under GS1 than they occur under

GS2. Given a presumed identity in genotype and living conditions, occupation, place, age, and other personal data, this difference could not have occurred without some changes in the secretion and circulation of hormones. The fact that GS1 featured emblematic conditions that were worse than under GS2 must correspond to physiological differences on a statistical level. This observation leaves the *mind*'s central role in socioeconomic evolution intact. Modern neurobiology identifies the brain as the undisputed center of the endocrine cycle, tied closely to individual behavior.

The phenotypical (behavioral and physiological) alterations attributable to *global transformation* are diluted and elusive, even theoretically, let alone empirically. We know that behavior and emotions are inseparable (for example, fear mediates behavior and behavior may result in experiencing fear). Hormonal changes arising for whatever reason, including such long-term trends as increasing pollution and population density, can affect personal conduct. Nevertheless, it seems plausible that the phenotypical changes in behavioral traits and physiology associated with the *global transformation* could not exist without alterations in neuronal pathways and in the endocrine cycle. Ultimately, the cerebral microstates of a large number of people in the leading countries must differ in certain fixed ways between GS1 and GS2 generations.

To repeat the main argument: Behavior reflects the way people think, feel, and make moral judgments as well as the way they look at the world and presume the world looks at them. Basic attitude, attention to a situation and its evaluation, selection of response, and determination to carry it out are functions of a physical structure. Behavior corresponds to synaptic connections—some broad patterns in neurochemical, neuroelectrical traffic. A part of this configuration reflects the compromise between the genotype and the socioeconomic aspects of the environment, and a part within this part stands for the compromise between the genotype and the global system. The cluster of repeated signals emitted by the surrounding socioeconomic milieu (subordinate to the global system) imparts knowledge about the space in which socioeconomic behavior is free to roam. Therefore, knowing that everything mental is also material, the global system must have distinct physico-chemical marks in the brain. The global system lives through its signature synaptic connections and flow of neurotransmitters.

The support of the *global system,* without most of the planet's inhabitants being conscious of it, may occur either by having similar, fixed traces, or different and variable ones that mutually complement and reinforce one another, or by a combination of the two extremes. This third alternative appears to be the most realistic. Widely shared perceptions about the *global system*-generated socioeconomic environment and similarity in behavior imply isomorphic and fixed material arrangements, whereas the great differences in status and function and the eternal fluidity of conditions suggest the implicit collaboration among hetero-morphic and variable ones.

For the sake of illustration, we can compare the *global system* to the engineer-ing principles that hold together and allow the operation of an elaborate machin-ery (the *global socioeconomic environment*). This machinery can work on its own in the dark for a while, letting the engineer play solitaire in the adjacent control room. Although parts of the machinery perform different functions and show dif-ferences in their physical appearance, "something" in the morphology of each part must reflect the unifying organizational principle that defines the whole. The common reflection of this unifying principle is interpreted in the *mind* as *global system*-characteristic, biological/chemical/physical isomorphisms and comple-mentary heteromorphisms.

The *socioeconomic behavior* and emotional profile of a Brazilian steel worker and a UN bureaucrat living in Switzerland are different and are subject to numer-ous dissimilar influences. However, the physical inscriptions accounting for these phenomena in their respective brains are identical in some ways and complemen-tary in others, given that the respective *surrounding socioeconomic milieus* are locked through a number of intervening strata. Individual activities are converted into a generic total of somatic energy that fuels and maintains the planet-wide coordination, fraught with uncertainties, limping and stumbling on the verge of *chaos* as it may seem to be at any given moment.

The *global system* is a web of entangled animate matter. In fact, it possesses five of the six general characteristics of life: (1) It is chemically complex; (2) cannot exist without living cells; (3) runs on somatic energy; (4) has a life cycle; and (5) responds to changes in the environment. The sixth characteristic, genetic repro-duction, which is required to consider something a life form, is not there. The *global system* does not reproduce itself biologically; only the ability to have *global system*s does. The rest is left to training and education, or the "normalization" of socioeconomic behavior to correspond to the world order. The *global system* is a quasi-living entity that may generate characteristics and events that its founders (the mover-shakers who pushed through its *imprimatur*) may have never sus-pected. In this sense, the *global system* is a supra-organismic factor. Its *text* allows the species to operate in a near-hypnotic mechanical mode that felicitously blocks out the mass-scale recognition of its future forms, keeping alive the allure of the "word" yet unspoken, the "jamais vu."

◆   ◆   ◆

The old system's phenotypical traits dissolved during the *global transformation*. "Good-by to All That," to use the title of Robert Grave's autobiographical masterpiece as a symbol for the irrelevance that the First World War brought to schemes of socioeconomic behavior and standard expectations under *laissez faire/ metal money*. Old environments no longer conditioned behavior the way they did before, and alternative global orders created new ones, coaxing out or forcing experimental behavior and bringing novel emotional experiences. Vestiges of the once globally shared *lexicon, ethic, Weltanschauung,* and *mentality* were combined with tentative substitutions for each in different parts of the world. If a GS1 archetype who was in the trenches of World War I and then went through the Great Depression and World War II could have been subjected to detailed brain scans and lab tests during the whole period, the diagnosis would be clear. A stable physiology of behavior and emotional profile disappeared and then reappeared. Test results following the instauration of GS2 would show the reestablishment of stability when compared to suddenly emerging, unusual, and short-lived patterns during 1914-1945. The endurance and systematic nature of brain functions mirroring socioeconomic conditions became more comparable to pre-1914 patterns than to the ones that prevailed during the *chaotic transition*.

Picture a single "representative brain" that went through GS1, the *global transformation,* and is alive now, under GS2. Its genotype is presumed invariant, but its phenotypical features evolved with changes in the *global socioeconomic environment*. A "collective individual" synthesized from statistically valid phenomena is admittedly a heroic abstraction, but it may help to see the complicated and muddy mess of intermental equilibrium dissolving and then reestablishing itself as intramental stasis. Besides, "our" abstract brain does not live entirely in a fictitious vat. Averaged out characteristics in the *minds* of genetically-related adults (e.g., great-great grandfather, great grandfather, and so on) in the *vanguard,* living at the same place, having roughly the same relative socioeconomic status, earning their livelihood as industrial workers from 1834 to the 1990s, then becoming "associates" in the service sector, come close to the "representative brain."

◆   ◆   ◆

It may be useful to think of all the physico-chemical imprints an individual uses to deal with the external world as *information*. Let us call the entire package of "data sets and programs" the *Code*. In this case, the information embedded into it about the *global system* is the *Code Core*. Individual *Codes* may vary widely but the *Code Cores* are homogeneous or heterogeneous in complementary ways. While some culturally perpetuated elements of the *Code* have shorter lives than a *global system* and some parts live through two (or maybe more) *global systems*, the *Code Core* is coterminous with it. The *Code Core*'s distinct substance may depend on configurations among huge numbers of molecules, atoms, and the tiny universes of the subatomic realms within them. Subtle arrangements and functioning of matter in brains are sufficiently similar or dissimilar but complementary to ensure the deeper, generally prevailing commonalities and congruities among *Code Cores*.

Global system-specific interactions among the *Code Cores* are defined as the *web*, which is the material basis of enduring principles used in the species' self-organized complexification. It is the *global system*'s roughly coterminal cerebral materiality. The *global system*'s *text* is the socioeconomically constructed semantic of this materiality. It connects, subsumes, or at least influences, all other *texts*. Therefore, it may be characterized as supra-"inter-textual" (i.e., various *texts* refer to it indirectly, thereby implicitly restating and reaffirming it). Since the *web* and its *text* must have rigidities to constitute an effective and enduring framework, they must experience rupture, a period of disorder in their transformation. This period appears on the world scene as a violent selection process that ends with finding fixed system coefficients for the next *macrohistoric* era's relatively steady socioeconomic regime.

If the transformation of interacting *Codes* accounts for the growth and complexification of global society, the transformation of the *web*, with its thermodynamic pattern, reflects the emergence and history of *global systems*. Thus, *cultural evolution* is tracked by two interrelated processes in the global networking of joined minds, one that changes with unceasing dynamism and one that is relatively stable, thereby giving support and structure to the first kind. The second kind is subject to intermittent overhaul. By virtue of the equivalence between matter and energy, the same duality between continuity and phase-like development may also be conceived in terms of organized energy.

The creation of a system of information or energy in the 19th century and its transformation to a higher level of complexity through dynamic self-search during the 20th century is *metahistory* beyond *macrohistory*.[15]

DIRECTIONALITY IN THE WORLD PROCESS

Culture as a material state depends on what is in the brains and what is going on among them. As mentioned above, interconnections are also physical phenomena. The traffic of sensory inputs and outputs occurs through sound waves, light, and electromagnetism. Particles move as the organism emits and registers information about other organismic activities and behavior. This whirling ensemble of subatomic specks that complexifies through self-organization must contain some stabilizing elements. If a process has direction; i.e., it is not a totally arbitrary sequence of events, then something must prevent it from discombobulating. Indeed, the relationship between the two *global systems,* or stages of *cultural evolution*, cannot be regarded as *random*, at least not *ex post*. Pulsatile self-transformation hints at an enduring, aperiodic factor. The antientropic, autocatalytic *force motrice* aggregated into the universal history-shaping causal force led the species to the first *global system* and then pushed it through the convulsions of an "interregnum" to the second one. Regardless of the human comprehension-defying spatial and temporal dimensions of this process in "the here and the now," it must have traces in the empirical/rational *mind*, where both institutions (imaged as traffic rules for socioeconomic interactions) and capacity for adaptive behavior reside.

Sculpted during the temporal immensities of biological evolution, the "panhuman" architecture of the *mind* features an ability to analyze reciprocity and to be sensitive to deviations perceived as asymmetry in "give-and-takes." When we combine this aspect of human nature with the unavoidable circumstance that supra-individual arrangements cannot evolve without departing from their sanc-

---

15. We may express the same thought in terms of mathematical economics in the following way: *Cultural evolution* is a three-dimensional, vector-valued function of time. Each *cultural evolutionary index* stands for one of the three dimensions and *culture* is the momentary state of the function. The control vector, which contains *global system* characteristics, is piecewise continuous. Given the lack of single or unified intellect to define and institute the control vector, *bifurcation* "selects" from the emerged potential control vectors, each vying for universal application. Instead of having a "social planner," the *Opaque Artificer* manages growth and complexification.

tioned norms, we must conclude that socioeconomic evolution is contingent on contumacy and conflict. The individual must have a capacity to *entrain* others and to be *entrained* by others to turn isolated discontent into potent social variables.

The willingness to confront at the cost of self-detriment arose during the distant past because the accumulation of disadvantages, minute as it might seem for the moment, could tend toward the extinction of kin. If the atavistic perceptions of what is appropriately reciprocal and symmetric are violated, extreme injustice and mistreatment are perceived; the individual, out of this ancient training of the *mind*, will engage in nonconformist behavior. Thus, the urge to throw rationalized compromise to the winds, to rebel at any cost, is not "unnatural." It has a biological basis. Antigone and Prometheus are the universal and eternal symbols of this deeper rationality lodged in the apparent irrationality of immediate action.

The species' cognitive apparatus evolved as the prehistoric hominid learned to deal with immediate, short-term problems. Contemporary human behavior extended the "immediate" and the "short-term," that is, the spatial and the temporal limits of concern. But it is not possible to foretell how the fundamental characteristics of the *mind* will fare under unforeseeable, future conditions. Past progress is not an expression of nature's care about *homo sapiens*; we can predict only things that happened before, and the thermodynamic perspective on history ensures us of never-ending streams of never-before-seen things.

Let us return to the people lost in an alien universe. They woke up in a nightmare that turned out to be reality. The group, comprising ten individuals, is determined to proceed together. Two among them have fixed ideas or tendencies about which way to go and how to behave toward one another, but they keep silent. The remaining eight come up with many suggestions as to direction and self-organization that the silent ones either accept or reject. Agreement between these two will dominate group decisions through *intercessio*, or passive guidance, by vetoing certain choices. They represent hereditary material in the allegory. No doubt they "know" something.[16]

---

16. Sociobiologists, who analyze gene-culture co-evolution, use the term "epigenetic rules" to refer to the "long leash," flexible, natural selection-like influence of genetic tendencies upon the evolution of human self-organization. The complete and long-term view, which encompasses prehistoric times, takes into consideration changes in the gene pool as a result of gene-guided selection of attributes in human-created environments. (See *Wilson, 1998* and *Lumsden and Wilson, 1985*.) We shall return to this subject in Chapter 9 to show that genes are also subject to selection pressures by the very organisms they use as their survival machines.

Indeed, DNA seems to have emergent properties. A new whole (*global system*) could not be deduced from the behavioral properties of the parts (individuals). However, given that the wholes do not have an independent existence (they do not reproduce like life-bearing structures), the emergent properties of the parts must be able to carry the potential for emergence. There is no other possible material locus for this potential than the hereditary material. The emergent properties of organisms and their supraorganismic creations lie concealed in DNA molecules; and, in this case, each brain anticipates posterity's approach to self-organization. The global society's potential for self-adjustment lies in the undeciphered, four-letter alphabet script edged into the "twisted stairwell" of the macro-molecules we all carry around.

Biological evolution determined the way humans acquire, store, and process information about the environment (including its socioeconomic aspects), but what is being acquired, stored, and processed changes. Consequently, there are materially conceivable differences between the "representative brain" of GS2 and that of GS1. To some extent, world history is the reorganization of matter in the brain. The ghost of Lamarck is smiling at us. It looks *as if* the descendent representative, the "GS2 brain," inherited some characteristics acquired by its ancestor, the "GS1 brain." Of course, the "representative brain" stands for stages of socioeconomic evolution, not for particular individuals.

Biological evolution is largely the history of how well or how badly species reacted to the vagaries of nature, e.g., changes in the climate. Natural selection from *random* variations in physical heredity has been and remains the main designer of life forms. Socioeconomic evolution is a different matter. The *randomness* inherent in genetic mutations and the profusion of individual compromises with the environment are crucial here too. But in contrast to natural selection's alien power and indifference in the physical environment, a vague perception of what is acceptable for the duration, and a clear rejection of what is not, guide the evolution of the same socioeconomic environment which, once inducted, will pass judgment over individual socioeconomic performance. With such guidance in the background (the genetic *intercessio*), the world has shown itself capable of providing national level, "group" initiatives for global level self-organization that became acceptable after a period of *chaos* associated with accelerated entropy production through violent deaths and the wholesale destruction of human-made objects.

The *orthogenesis* inherent in the thermodynamic take on world history suggests that (a) the mechanism of socioeconomic transformation reflects the law of complexification identified for far-from-equilibrium dissipative thermodynamic systems; (b) the recorded complexification may be labeled "progress" by agreement; (c) if *homo sapiens* has further evolutionary potential, it will have to go through the same process to regain a dynamic socioeconomic steady state after the recognition that the mindless expansion of population and economic activity tends to eliminate its ecological release, preparing the ground for its extinction; (d) by being predicated on higher than the prevalent moral and ethical principles, and by defining a "strategic world," the implied new *global system* (GS3) will represent progress compared to GS2; and finally, (e) given the vast spectrum of human behavioral variation and presuming the continued intactness of the *force motrice*, expressed among other things in scientific curiosity and physical venturesomeness, this qualitative improvement is likely. However, the genesis of GS3 (another episode of the world "rethinking" itself, symbolized by GS2—>GS3) may be more troublesome than GS1—>GS2 was.

Based on some of the qualitative aspects of the *Code Core*, we can appreciate the growing problems now faced by *cultural evolution*. GS2 *ethic* and *mentality* remain focused on the immediate environment. Its *Weltanschauung* does not include the world, only parts or selective aspects of it, and it is limited in its forward perspective. These characteristics are arrangements of material substances in the *web*. Transformation in it is constrained by what individual perceptions fixed as possibilities, necessities, and proscriptions in socioeconomic relations. The *Code Core* cannot be reprogrammed with rational arguments and moral suasion. It is the inert, hidden stabilizing element of the functioning global circuitry.

The *minds* are tuned to and by GS2. Spoken and written linguistic interpretations of the physical interconnection among the material traces of the *global system* form the prevalent socioeconomic *text*. Its dominance over other *texts* and over interactions among them, allows us to characterize it as supra-"inter-textual". It speaks through all of us, but its conditioning power is not as absolute as in the ontological relationship between human reality and what else may exist. Conventional thinking in social sciences is *global system*-legitimizing, mainly without the conscious awareness of practicing professionals. But there is also an independently thinking faction whose criticism is not aimed at exploring or adjusting system parameters. It remains within GS2's *discourse*, but it recognizes this *discourse* as a separate phenomenon.

Macrohistory suggests that only a new *global transformation* will be able to clear the road for a future that does not roll out the red carpet to *cultural devolution*. What gives us pause is that, if it took "1914-1945" (circa 70 million dead, many millions maimed, and the hardships of the Great Depression) to move the world from the most primitive form of socioeconomic self-organization to a more ordered one (a relatively minor qualitative adjustment), it staggers the imagination to contemplate what it might entail to go from "here" to the "world-as-self."

The intergalactic biophysicist's electroencephalogram would show *metahistory* (by attaching electrodes to the scalp of the "representative brain") as two roughly horizontal movements of the pen over a sheet of paper for GS1 and GS2, separated by irregular vertical lines during the *chaotic transition*. From the perspective of alien intelligence, the transition, or the world's rethinking of itself, was successful since not even one percent of the species' blood spilled in the process.

This departure from the customary moral judgment and individual responsibility-charged understanding of world history may be unsettling. Nonetheless, such a nonanthropocentric (hence, ideology-and politics-free) view may still be useful, particularly since the lines on the sheet of paper that show the "representative brain's" electrical activity tend toward the capricious vertical once again.

7

Absolute Limits and Warning Signals

[*Cultural evolution* "ought" to stop when its declining marginal benefits and rising marginal costs break even. The world is incapable of and unwilling to live by this rule. It will have to learn through experience, first by recognizing the costs, then by relating them to benefits. The perception of rising costs is slow. *Geocapital* depletion, environmental impairment, and the growing resource demands of the environmental sector are hard-to-read and seemingly unrelated saturation signals. Nonrenewable resource exhaustion and the overall neglect of nature are justly expected to generate shocks during this century. They will come from the depletion of *exergic* reservoirs and the clash between this physical process and the *global system*. Hopefully, a new *global transformation/chaotic transition* will lead to GS3. The limit to *cultural evolution* may be formulated in extreme combinations of global population and output. Search for these combinations began decades ago.]

The physical limit to *cultural evolution* is reached when the decumulation of *exergic* constraints becomes critical. If that point is ever reached, *cultural evolution* would stall like an airplane that tried to climb too fast; it would yaw and lose altitude. Population and output would embark on a mutually enforced downward path. Devolution could begin with an economic crisis, ostensibly as the result of disruptive segregate or generally disabling aggregate increases in the cost of production. The world would see in despair the insufficiency of its arsenal of technological solutions and economic policies to halt the process. Nations would engage in violent struggles for resources; looting, vandalism, and civic strife would spread like the plague from community to community. Mortality and morbidity would increase and birth rates would fall.

Regardless of how it began and by what sequence of events it gathered momentum, a protracted contraction in population/output levels would push the quantitative and qualitative indicators of *cultural evolution* below their pre-crisis high marks. Confused brutishness would contort humanity's optimistic face into a frightened and frightening grimace. We defined *Point Xs* as combinations of population and output where such reversals would occur.

No one argues with the proposition that *cultural evolution* should be mastered and redirected long before it gets even near its outermost frontiers. Unfortunately, these frontiers are unmarked and cannot be recognized to the extent that would trigger effective countermeasures until massive damage has already occurred and chances for even larger scale, imminent damages are high. The weight of *culture* is no guide to approximating the distance from *Point Xs*. At a given weight, one population/output combination may signal that an acceptable level of human presence in the *terrestrial sphere* has been surpassed; however, other combinations may not.

Perhaps global cost/benefit analysis would help. *Cultural evolution* is, after all, both a social and a physical phenomenon. Correspondingly, its limit may be perceived in terms of consequences for human welfare. This limit must be where additional benefits (*global marginal benefits of cultural evolution*) reach a balance with additional costs (*global marginal costs of cultural evolution*). Marginal benefits from *cultural evolution* may justly be expected to decline, while its marginal costs would tend to rise. Theoretically, *cultural evolution* is good for the world as long as its marginal benefits exceed its marginal costs; *ergo*, it should stop where the two values become equal. The difficulty with this theoretically unassailable truism is that it cannot be put into practice. The "benefits" (or utility derived) from having a larger population and output can be calculated in so many ways that they are quantitatively meaningless. The utility of an additional individual is different for a family, a nation, a region, and the planet; the utility of additional output cannot be fairly determined, given the huge differences in living standards across the world. A 10-percent increase in the GDP means much less for the inhabitants of Switzerland than for people living in impoverished sub-Sahara.

If the decline of marginal benefits is a qualitative symbol without a quantitative referent, the rising marginal costs are murky at best. They will reveal themselves as the consequences of drawing down the narrow *exergic* constraints. But the signals generated by this process may be weak despite an acceleration in human activities; or they may intensify erratically in periods of consciously moderated activities. On the whole, there is no telling by how much *cultural evolution*'s marginal benefits would decline and its marginal costs rise as the result of adding, for example, another 100 million new organisms to the human biomass and increasing the global output (the Gross World Output) by a further one trillion dollars. Even if an authoritative international team of experts under UN mandate could overcome the problems posed by the task, policy measures that would follow could not be introduced. The planet's inhabitants do not form a sufficiently close-knit polity and do not share a common enough perspective to conclude binding agreements and engage in concerted programs with far-reaching implications for national and individual conduct.

The world will have to fall back on a staged recognition of where the "limits to growth" are; first the costs, then the benefits. The smoker's progression provides an analogy. The cigarette tastes good (benefits derived from lighting up), but dangers to bodily health loom on the distant horizon (costs). Unable to establish an internal, quantitative relationship between the two, the smoker continues to smoke until, 20 years later, he is diagnosed with emphysema. Now he says "It's not worth it" and quits. There is an implicit quantitative assessment behind this simple declaration. The magnitude of benefits is placed below the costs. Sadly, by this time, marginal benefits are ordinally smaller than the marginal costs, indicating that the habit should have been kicked earlier. If the recognition of *cultural evolution*'s limits must follow a similar sequence, then hope for finding the equimarginal cost/benefit conditions would have to shift to an early perception of rising costs.

It is worthwhile to point out the difference between perceiving the costs of *cultural evolution* and decline in *cultural evolutionary indices*. Whereas indicators of *cultural evolution* or *devolution* represent external data, the perception of costs associated with these phenomena is the collective internal reaction to these costs by the global network of cerebral cortices. It is all in the *minds*. Importantly, costs may be recognized when *cultural devolution* is minor; they may be ignored when it is major. The ultimate bad news would be an unchanged insistence on economic and population growth even if it could not be resumed. It would be equally tragic if global level self-organization became unhinged. Either of the two would signal a failure of the species to adapt. The aggression and irrationality that accompany *chaotic transition* would not lead to new *relatively steady socioeconomic conditions*. It is disturbing that our cost-indicative signals of overusing the planet are weak and imprecise.

You call this an alarm system?

The system has three components: *geocapital depletion, environmental impairment*, and *growing resource diversion for environmental protection*.

Geocapital depletion: A siren that shrieks too late, then causes a brawl at the fire station

The *geocapital* is layered into constraints of descending profitability associated with their extraction and use. Extraction of energy carriers and raw materials proceeds from the highest-grade, easiest accessible, lowest-cost finds toward the lower-grade, less easily accessible and higher-cost ones. (Environmental economists call the distinct steps along this techno-economic descent "mineralogical thresholds.") Given identical conditions of accessibility, lower-entropy resources (well-structured, more concentrated, best-suited matter for a well-defined purpose) are preferred to higher entropy ones. The profit criterion ensures that, other things being equal, the activities of exploring and readying energy carriers and raw materials will also use the lowest available entropy substances first. With the passage of time, "science and technology" recasts the implied preferences and priority lists; more generally, it re-fashions the ways in which nature's support of *cultural evolution* is being seen, but, in the end, it cannot transcend the aggregate loss of free energy contained in matter. The emergence of shortages in profitably extractable free-energy-containing substances is a physical inevitability.

The best-case scenario is that the first major shortage, inadequately mitigated by "market and technology," already suffices to awaken and unite the international community; to make it undertake corrective measures. The best case seems unlikely. The possibility of dealing with net *geocapital* exhaustion directly and quickly is outside GS2 parameters; it is not congruent with the extant microstate of the *web*.

But first a *morceau* of "Econ 101." Prices are determined by supply and demand conditions that indicate the scarcity of particular goods. Economists often express the value of a resource in "real" terms. The division of the nominal price of the resource in question by the nominal price of labor rids the analysis of "money." It leads to a "real" figure showing the amount of resource that corresponds to one unit of labor. It is clear that when a resource becomes scarce (everything else presumed to be unchanged), its real price should go up. Appearances notwithstanding, this is no redundant wizardry. We are always aware of real prices by unconsciously "relativizing" nominal ones. If we receive a higher electricity bill, for instance, we automatically compare the increased (nominal) figure to our income (another nominal dollar figure), although few would bother to calculate the decline in the number of kilowatt hours one hour of labor can buy.

If all material resources became scarce, the weighted average of their real prices would indicate an upward trend and they would become scarce relative to labor. Until the beginning of the 21st century, studies performed on several key raw materials and energy carriers (as well as on "land") did not indicate a dramatic increase in their real prices. Moreover, material resources came to represent a small percentage of the GDP in the *vanguard*.

Particularly supportive of the nonentropic view of the world is the fact that increases in the relative prices of energy carriers and raw materials did not disable economic expansion in the past. Witness the vigorous growth of the U.S. economy following the oil price shocks of the 1970s. Increases in the relative prices of exhaustible resources can be overwhelmed as long as the global economy can siphon out increasing quantities of low entropy from the *global environment*. Under this assumption, a jump in the relative price of any given resource prompts structural and monetary adjustments, allowing growth to continue. The combined economy of the *vanguard*, which dominates economic statistics and the analysis of global economic conditions, reacts to nominal increases in raw material and energy prices by shifting toward services and conservation, and by inflating other prices, including, of course, the price of labor, i.e., wages. Conventional, *global system*-conditioned analysis overlooks the fact that, parallel with the shift to the "post-industrial" service economy in the developed countries during the last third of the 20th century, developing countries increased their industrial output and their exports of manufacturing goods to the developed world. If the global economy consisted of an industrial shop and a front office, the boasting of senior officials in the *vanguard* about the great progress made in economizing with matter and energy since the 1970s would be similar to citing what went on in the office and forgetting about the shop. According to the prevalent *text*, the scarcer a resource becomes, the less of it the world will demand. Considering free energy extractable from matter to be "the resource," the human population has been doing the exact opposite of what economic lore suggests is the case.

When past data showing man's subjugation of nature are extrapolated, projections will reveal nothing new. The next 50 years will be like the past 50 years. Neoclassical economics and its radical, GS1-nostalgic extensions do not engage in a meaningful dialogue with the future. Orthodox academe assures the world that *geocapital* depletion is an illusion. If there were such a thing in the very distant future, the market mechanism would both signal it and remedy its particular manifestations.

In contrast to this confident optimism, most environmentalists and geologists express concern about the nonrenewable resource issue.[1] Looking directly at actual reserves and their rates of exploitation, they prepare the minds for an inevitable *rendezvous* with material constraints. Indeed, if the number of passenger cars grew from thousands in 1900 to over 600 million by 2000, and if that number is expected to double by 2030, and if even then, billions and billions were craving automobile ownership, shouldn't the world be concerned, given that its oil supplies are limited and its air is already polluted? And this is only one consumer durable. And who doesn't want everything else that the average *personal socioeconomic sphere* in the *vanguard* (about 20 percent of the planet's total number of *spheres*) already contains? Raising the global level of living to the one that prevails in the developed world would completely undermine the "ecological release" *homo sapiens* has been enjoying, splashing around in it as if it were a never-ending bubble bath. While it is unlikely that the world could reach *vanguardian* living standards before finding out that its economy is bankrupt and physically unable to satisfy its huge and varied appetites, the current socioeconomic mechanism and ideology is pushing it in that direction under the standard economic banner of "rational choice." From a convinced ecologist's perspective, if one calls the allocation of resources that favors a surrealistic carbon-dioxide hell with masses of humanity staggering around abandoned vehicles and closed gas stations "rational," then one might as well consider throwing in what it takes to deal with the planet's growing drinking water problem "irrational."

If economic data show that "raw materials" make up only two percent of the output value, the opposing view considers this a 50-fold dependence on limited substance and cautions against believing that natural resources come from other human beings, e.g., "The House of Saud" or the "marketplace." Indeed, what people "dig up" from the Earth seems to be less important than what they do

---

1. Environmental ideologies may be broken down into *technocentric* and *ecocentric*. Most radical among the first is the "Extreme Cornucopian" view: Maximize output and exploit resources! Not to worry, there is infinite substitutability. The market will take care of everything. The decentralized exchange economy is invulnerable to nature. "Deep Ecology" represents the most ecocentric position. It advocates preservation, minimum resource take, and bioethics. In this spectrum of convictions, mainstream economics is affine to "Extreme Cornucopianism." For a summary of environmental ideologies, see *Pearce and Turner, 1990.*

with it, i.e., add value to it in the process of production and distribution. But statistics that demonstrate the insignificance of exploration and mining in the GDP are silent about an important distinction. Adding value to matter is an internal human affair; the irreversible diminishing of exhaustible resources in the *terrestrial sphere* refers to the relationship between the species and its natural environment.

Geocapital exhaustion is an *á priori* unreliable signal of the excessive penetration of human life and activity into the *terrestrial sphere* because neither of the two diagonally opposed rationalities can be discounted. Economic analysis finds it difficult and unnatural not to rely on GS2's good historical record; not to follow the *global system*'s powerful inspiration to devise and perpetuate economic idealizations (including algebraic formalisms and comprehensive mathematical models) that cannot see beyond circular movements, cyclical recurrences, eternal returns, and convergence toward infinitely-lasting steady state growth rates of output, physical capital, and consumption. Consequently, a significant body of respected current opinion discourages concern over nonrenewable natural resources. This institutional reasoning helps ensure that GS2 endures as long as it can accommodate *cultural evolution* and not one minute less. Without this elementary rule, the world simply would not "know" when to "move on." Should it introduce controls on demographic and economic expansion now? Should it have done so in the early 1970s when the Club of Rome began to ring the alarm bell? Should it take action when 170 eminent scholars, including nine Nobel laureates, sign a petition addressed to the United Nations? When these numbers are 200 and 19, respectively? At the species' scale, arbitrary and conflicting norms permeate rationally argued forethought. If the international community had clamped down on economic expansion in the early 1970s (as was suggested by some brilliant scientists at the time), the world would have been deprived of many great material achievements that only free markets in a dynamic environment with expanding purchasing power (economic growth) could have provided. Of course, it is clear from our previous elaboration that such a turnaround was not a real alternative. The *representative brain*, symbolizing the *web* and the reigning *global system*, remains intransigent and infrangible during its *macrohistoric* life span, even after it has passed its golden age. It cannot be expected to reprogram itself abruptly and peacefully as an intelligent person would under the combined weight of evidence and logical argument. A world without common consciousness may be more comparable to a growing tree that has no sense of its limitations. Its molecules and atoms act as if the soil's free energy contents were inexhaustible, allowing its branches to brush against the sky "in the long run."

Comprehension of the finality of *geocapital* lies beyond the prevalent *global system*'s "radical" presence. And persistent reality is always right even if ideas about it are increasingly wrong. What almost everybody thinks is considered true and rational. Conventional, growth-oriented economics proves to be correct time and time again, until one day the prism through which the future is past-like breaks into smithereens. At that point, the validity of cyclical patterns in the economy gives way to the experience, and, in a justifiably optimistic vein, to the recognition that there is also a unilateral, one-way movement that underlies the world's progression, even during its *relative steady states*.

The divided truth between "what is" and "what will have to be" mirrors the unpredictability in the evolution of *geocapital*'s fortunes. That there is such a constraint as *geocapital* to global economic growth, or *cultural evolution* in a broader perspective, will have to be deduced from disruptive episodes generated through a seemingly unrelated process of reaching peaks in the use of various nonrenewable resources in different parts of the world.

Temporarily alleviating shortages by transferring scarce resources from low-productivity to high-productivity countries delays this recognition. Such transfers appear rational as a general principle, but they will not be pretty in practice. The more developed a country, the lower its threshold of economic pain and the more likely it is to deploy any means to avoid crossing it and get below it as quickly as possible. Inadequate supplies of *geocapital* activate geopolitical and geomilitary "engineering." This is not a purely "*vanguard* versus the rest of the world" schism. There are important productivity differences and power asymmetries among developing countries as well as many tensions and flashpoints that can ignite conflicts over resources. Resource-rich developing nations with glaringly low progress in the SEEI (often with low-brow governments) are prone to internal disturbances and hostile gestures. This translates into growing threats to the stability of world resource markets from the "supply side."

Shortages of key material ingredients to maintain economic welfare raise the specter of a Hobbesian free-for-all rivalry–everyone against everyone else. The first signs of net *geocapital* depletion are likely to divide rather than unite the world. They could bring a tempest of destabilizing conflicts and confusion in the *representative brain*. It might take an extended period of hardship to convince the global populace that the insufficiency of a specific resource, expressed through its stubbornly high (real) price, is not the result of monopoly power, bad public policy, conspiracy, the egoism of strong nations, or the unscrupulousness of domestic rulers, but rather, a physical fact, irremediable for the moment by the combined forces of technological know-how, market incentives, and GS2-typical government support, i.e., tax/subsidy measures.

Environmental impairment: The hard-to-hear alarm signal

Pollution is a great communicator. Its nefariousness invades the senses. But the messages nature sends through *environmental impairment* are unclear. The *terrestrial sphere* is a restless place. It is in constant transformation. The plates that form the planet's crust move, its surface shakes, volcanoes erupt, the land slides and hurricanes devastate coastal areas; erosive chemical reactions never take a break. These are changes on a mega time scale–the stuff of which geological epochs are made. According to the *second law*, these activities increase entropy in the *terrestrial sphere*.

Cultural evolution and nature's inherent tendency to destroy the order it creates became synergistically entangled. Consequently, the contribution of man to the growth of entropy in the *terrestrial sphere* cannot be precisely separated. Although by now, most scientists agree that *cultural evolution* caused more *environmental impairment, in toto,* than would have occurred without it, the interwoven effects of the natural and man-made entropic buildup diminish the assessability of *cultural evolution*'s impact on the environment. This is particularly obvious regarding climate change. Is there a global warming? Even now, when the evidence is persuasive that there is, and that man is responsible for it, one hears opinions like "How can scientists know the temperature a hundred years from now when they cannot tell us what the weather is going to be like in two days?" Or, "Global warming. Hmm. It depends on how you measure it. Some experts say there is global cooling. And then again, is climate change attributable to human activities, or has it been a geologically scheduled development, no matter how many cars we drive? No one knows for sure." The fact that fossil fuels cause air pollution is generally admitted; however, their role in global warning is still questioned.

Signals of man-made ecological deformation will have to work their way through muffling media before they are heard as alarm bells.

Inception. Environmental problems need to reach a threshold of unpleasantness and threat before they are recognized. The use of oil and coal polluted the air long before World War II, but air quality did not become a public issue until well after the war. What is tolerated as a necessary evil of civilization varies by the intensity of the unpleasantness inflicted and by the level of welfare. The more prosperous a country, the less its inhabitants seem to accept environmental degradation, the scent of garbage, the sight of pyramids of dirt.

Making the connection. It takes a lot of evidence and time before society links *environmental impairment* with its negative consequences, the hidden costs in human lives, health, and material resources. Most people refuse to consider particular problems with the food supply (avian flu, mad cow disease, fish that contain heavy metal, uncertainty about the long-term effects of genetically modified fruits and vegetables) a single phenomenon, let alone link them to increasing congestion or the projected rise in ocean levels. (Connecting these problematic phenomena even further to the buildup of imbalances in the global economy seems to be totally out of question.) Does asbestos explain the high incidence of lung cancer among people who worked with or near it decades ago; or are these *random* occurrences, cause unknown? Answering such questions as soon as they are raised and recognizing the consequences of demographic and economic expansion became even more difficult in light of growing life expectancy, a development clearly associated with *cultural evolution*. Satisfaction with one's *personal socioeconomic sphere* and *surrounding milieu* makes the individual block out and absorb incremental inflictions on the environment; advances in medical research can overwhelm the illness-causing, life-shortening effects of *cultural evolutionary* overflow.

No unity. Environmental problems are geographically dispersed; they may vanish and reappear *randomly* with varying intensity. Such variability helps sustain the illusion that *environmental impairment* is not a global process, but rather, a composite of independent events, each of which can be addressed separately.

Information entropy. As described in Chapter 5, an accompanying symptom of entropy accumulation is the loss of information about the system in which it occurs. Global warming is an example. The growing number of possibilities regarding its status, combined with the gradually spreading perception of its potential threat, reveals an increase in *information entropy*, the synthetic measure of confusion and danger. The more *cultural evolution* progresses, the more the *terrestrial sphere* becomes a riddle. In practical terms this means that environmental science is confronted with an ever-increasing need to broaden its inquiries, while being constantly handicapped by the emergence of new phenomena. The expansion of *culture* increases the *chances* that the system of information about the basic characteristics of the environment will fail.

Disproportionate faith. There is a widespread belief in the possibility that *environmental impairment* may be brought under control without renouncing worldwide demographic and economic growth. If considerable amounts of resources were deployed for environmental protection, a high degree of environmental consciousness prevailed, and economic activities shifted toward fewer polluting activities, nature would use its self-regenerating, cleansing powers: The progression of *environmental impairment* may be arrested or even turned around. Although these factors have not coalesced to date and show no encouraging signs that they will in the near future, the mere plausibility that they might do so dulls awareness of the hard fact: The build-up of entropy, conceptualized as decline in *ecological order*, brings environmental degradation stochastically. The long-run increase in world population and in energy and material throughput from nonrenewable sources is irreconcilable with ecological self-healing on a global scale.

We live in an era of rising concern and public awareness about damages inflicted on the ecology. Progress along these lines is far from negligible. Most countries, and even some large cities, have environmental protection agencies with budget-supported programs. *Multilateral* organizations actively encourage and sponsor protection measures. There are laws and incentive programs, highly visible international meetings, scientific conferences, specialized journals, and information clearinghouses dedicated to this subject. "Biodiversity," "climate change," and "greenhouse effect" have penetrated public *discourse* and politics. The rise of environmental consciousness received a quantum boost in 2006 with the release of the documentary "An Inconvenient Truth." It was the first time that a well-known and highly respected political leader, former U.S. Vice President Al Gore, talked in scientific detail about approaching ecological disasters to the worldwide public. (See *Gore, 2006.*)

But overall, the global society lacks clear understanding, let alone determination, to deal with *environmental impairment,* if the costs of action promise to impinge upon *cultural evolution.* The world lives with the implicit notion that reductions in carbon dioxide emissions would mean reduction in the growth of employment. Yet the costs of slowing and eliminating (to the extent possible) the contamination of land, air, and water have already become so large that action on a significant scale would demand the phasing down of economic expansion.

The level of environmental protection: More a sign of being alarmed than an alarm signal

The meagerness of resources spent on environmental protection shows that the world is only slightly apprehensive. And, compared with the potentially growing dangers of *ecological disorder,* the general population is dazed by conflicting thoughts and impulses. Concern, acknowledged ignorance, satisfaction with partial results reported and experienced in pollution control and abatement (especially in the *vanguard*) add up to benign neglect. The consumer economy drives through environmental conditions with global perspective remaining in the blind spot. This is on the average. At a closer look, we see differences and heated antagonisms among and within nations.

Internationally, the disagreement is particularly sharp between the *vanguard* and the rest of the world. Environmental regulations and incentives are much stronger in the former, but their example is only halfheartedly followed. Developing countries argue that industrialized nations gained their material wealth through careless treatment of the environment in the past. Why should the poor nations stop trying to increase their economic welfare now when even the efforts of the developed world fall short of what would be required to preempt further degradation? The environmental sector represents a very small percentage of the GDP in the *vanguard* and even less in the rest of the world. It is considered woefully inadequate by many authoritative experts. There are disagreements over this issue within national societies, between environmentally conscious social groups and vested economic interests.

The world resembles Bertold Brecht's *Mother Courage*, who believed that the war (Europe's "100-year war") continued because people were reluctant to add up the losses they suffered. They would rather go on fighting than face a reality that would make them look and feel dumb. Of course, dumbness has nothing to with it. The relative pittance of resources diverted from unbridled economic growth to the "environment" shows that the GS2 *mind* cannot capture the actual and potential impact of *cultural evolution.*

Nonetheless, increased spending on this account is still useful, not the least because it makes the wider public aware of the costs of growth. As each national society and the international community grapple with the "environment versus more material goods" choice, the *minds* are moving slowly (though not decisively) toward an awareness that there is an equilibrium trade-off between growth and safety, between needs and solutions. The social choice will become apparent only when the average individual recognizes that private business cannot conform to increasingly strict environmental standards and retain its habitual dynamism at the same time.

◆   ◆   ◆

The weakness of each component of the signal system and therefore, the weakness of the entire system, may be grasped by recognizing that order in the world exists through relatively stable patterns of interaction among characteristic fissures and grooves in billions of brains. The same *global system* that made *cultural evolution* possible handicaps the discovery that this process itself, as we know it, is running out of time. The resilience of the dominant *mind*-set (or *global system* or its *text*) is translated into daily practice by ignoring or explaining away anomalies and by absorbing incremental deteriorations in *cultural evolutionary* performance. It seems that what the world needs to convince itself about the reality of its situation must go beyond the ignorable and absorbable.

NATURE'S SOLEMN WARNING WILL COME DURING THIS CENTURY

Throughout history, individuals have acted as if the Earth's physical attributes were nonlimiting, nonbinding, external data. Oil might be *modern history*'s first powerful reminder that Planet Earth is no land of Cockaigne. Eventually, the real price of oil will become high enough to make more expensive production technologies profitable. Then oil will come from squeezing shale and tar sands and drilling at sites previously protected by environmental regulations, perhaps even at the North Pole. But, according to most experts, demand will soon gobble up such "replenishment" of supplies. If global real income is to continue its growth, backstop technologies will be needed not only to facilitate the exploitation of marginal reserves, but also to look for alternative sources of energy.

Coal would last for a very long time, but burning it is blamed for much of the planet's current levels of pollution. Political pressure is on for substituting the much more environmentally friendly natural gas for coal to generate electricity, but if demand turns full-face toward this variety of hydrocarbons, it will also vanish during this century. Coal can be liquefied to produce synthetic oil and gasified to obtain "natural gas," but the conversion rates are unfavorable. If this substitution process is followed, coal reserves, considered adequate for hundreds of years, would also disappear by the end of the century. Most of the world dreads nuclear power, which could deliver the global economy from the impending energy shortage. Nations will have to resort to solar radiation, water, wind, and geothermal and bio sources to satisfy the bulk of their energy needs. This will be an expensive affair.

The future gravitates toward some mix between renewable and fossil energy sources, allowing the second group to last at least as long as it will take science to turn nuclear fusion reactors, which operate without radioactive waste, into affordable technology. Fusion technology, already being counted on to play an important role in fulfilling energy needs, is still a science frontier. It is a daring expectation, but not an impossible one. On the other hand, cold fusion, dubbed the ultimate solution to the world's energy problems, is seen by many scientists as an illusory nonstarter.

One does not have to go far into the future to discover one important handicap on the horizon. If an international effort were to be made today to replace the energy obtained from oil with renewable energy sources, the dependence of such a program on oil both as an energy source and raw material for the thousands of products used in industry and daily life would make the team of experts charged with the task break into a sweat. The amount of oil needed to replace oil would reveal itself to be incredibly large. Just to bring the members of the team together would require jet fuel. We can see them sitting on airplanes looking puzzled at the plastic utensils on the plastic trays in front of them, all of which, most likely, came from refined oil. If they wanted to take medication to calm their nerves, they had better not read the labels on the (plastic) vials. Pharmaceuticals are critically dependent on refined oil products.

Whatever difficulties the transition to new sources of energy entails, they will be aggravated by the exhaustion of particular material resources. The immediacy of the problem may also be recognized when looking at the ratios of "mineable cutoff grade to average crustal abundance" for economically important minerals and metals. The separation of several minerals (e.g., mercury, tungsten, lead, chromium, tin, and silver) from low concentration finds would have to lower the cut-off rates by factors exceeding 1,000.[2] And there are further items that would require lowering by three-digit factors. The energy demands involved in going after lower and lower concentrations of ore are bound to escalate and the material requirements associated with the increased production of energy threaten to further aggravate mineral and metal shortages. (Economic rationality is more likely to shift whole industries toward the heavy use of iron and bauxite.)

The worsening environmental conditions will demand countermeasures, imposing further costs on production. Environmental consciousness might constrain the exploitation of nonrenewable natural resources from nonconventional sources, e.g., from Alaska's protected sites. The combined effects of these saturation signals will likely cause a cathartic pause in global economic expansion. Cathartic, because the majority of people living in the *vanguard* never learned the true meaning of "shortage," because per capita income levels are expected to

---

2.   *Meadows, Meadows, and Randers, 1991*, p. 85.

decline at an uneven rate (they may even grow in some places despite the overall decline); because the lack of geographic overlap between users and suppliers of energy and material resources (and disagreements about who is to blame for pollution and who should "pay" for it) are likely to poison international relations and damage the domestic tranquility of many countries.

The problems of energy, matter, and the environment, combined with increased vulnerability and an incapacity to take deliberate actions in time and on the scale required, make a fully recognized *macrohistoric* fallout in the 21st century likely.

THE ANATOMY OF *CULTURAL EVOLUTION'S* AUTOPARALYSIS

From this unpleasant scenario we can identify the problems and weaknesses the global community faces. The focus is on weaknesses, rather than on strengths. The future is not symmetrical to the past. It brings new situations that cannot be managed with approaches that fitted the past.

In attempting to describe the ways in which the depletion of *exergic* constraints is likely to be manifest as concrete problems, we single out net *geocapital* exhaustion from among the three imperfect channels of entropic phenomenology. It is better observed and more predictable than the other two. Individuals and communities never avert their watchful eyes from *geocapital*-related economic welfare. They are slower to acknowledge and more sluggish in reacting to chemical and physical phenomena that underlie environmental degradation. They may go a long way in sacrificing environmental quality for material welfare. Implicit in this choice is the assumption that no abrupt and severe environmental or (directly) human-made calamity (e.g., a major war or some mega terror act) will occur before economic crises make the world sit up with both eyes wide open, ready to abandon its Procrustean bed. *What follows is intended to show that cultural evolution drifts toward a halt (i.e., global transformation) for basic economic reasons.*

As *geocapital* ceases to be the perfect buffer between the shrinking *global environment* and the expanding *culture*, economic problems are expected to emerge. These may take the form of difficulties involved in substituting for nonrenewable resources, encountering hidden and growing resource demands in the process, and developing sensitive dependencies throughout the economy.

"Hard substitutions" are yet to come

In conventional economic analysis, substitution can move back and forth among resources, according to what their relative prices tell producers. When wages become low relative to interest rates, business firms hire more workers and hold back on capital investment. But a firm would always have the option to change the evolution of its capital-to-labor ratio in case the relationship between interest rates (the price of capital) and wages (price of labor) began to move in the opposite direction. This complete flexibility in the direction of substitution is lost in nonrenewable natural resource exploitation. Once the best quality of a mined product has been depleted and exploitation moves to the second, then the third best finds, the path backward does not exist.

As a material resource becomes scarce, its rising real price makes extraction from sources previously considered subeconomic profitable. The backstop technology "kicks in," delivering the substitute. When oil obtainable from shallow wells is used up, producers turn to shale and sand tars; when high-concentration, easily accessible metal has been used up, they begin to exploit lower-concentration finds that are more expensive to access. But not all substitutions have been created equal. We may, in fact, distinguish between soft and hard versions. The first one refers to getting the same or very similar product from a more expensive source. The two examples quoted above may be labeled "soft substitutions." They do not imply an overhaul of technology. On the other hand, replacing fossil fuels with other sources of energy or metals with "natural fiber-enforced polymers" does imply an overhaul. These are examples of "hard substitution." They obviously demand completely new production methods and entire new industries.

Soft substitutions do not impart significant effects "downstream," meaning the direction in which natural resources move through the complex system of industrial and commercial activities toward "final consumption." Oil that was produced more expensively leaves downstream technologies, such as refineries and industries that use refined products as inputs, relatively unperturbed. The substance that gets into the economy's circulatory system remains, in essence, unchanged. In short, soft substitutions have small or no knock-on or multiplier effects in terms of substitutions downstream.

Hard substitutions connote momentous differences between the original technology and its back-stop and are accompanied by qualitative changes in the substitute material's downstream applicability. Hard substitutions among raw material inputs engender hard substitutions in their use. The replacement of oil with renewable energy sources, for example, will have a major impact on the automobile industry. Switching from the production of gas cars to renewable energy-propelled vehicles would require extraordinary amounts of investment. Moreover, new fill-up and repair facilities and parts and tools would be in demand; that many hard substitutions away from the current infrastructure of automotive civilization would reverberate across the body economic. The replacement of gas cars with hybrids, constructed mainly of super-light structural materials, e.g., carbon fiber, may be considered a substitution of intermediate hardness.

The increasingly restrictive influx of low entropy into the *geocapital* determines the following *Hidden Hand*-mediated, unconscious human strategy in advancing *cultural evolution*: "no substitution," "soft substitutions," "hard and harder substitutions." This evolution parallels "no spillover demand for substitution," "spillover demand," a lot of it; a flood. It also parallels the amount of investment capital and adjustment costs needed to accomplish transitions. The world faces the prospect of growing demand for increasingly complex processes to deal with the consequences of its hedonistic gluttony for depletable resources.

Substitution will become harder not only in an economic, but also in a scientific sense. The endogenous relationship between the aggregate quality (low-entropy contents) of matter and economically feasible technological possibilities suggests that hard substitutions demand more from science than soft ones. The tasks of substituting for exhausted low-entropy matter by combining other relatively low-entropy matter will become progressively more difficult. If we believe that scientific-technological communities will overcome all the challenges presented to them, we remain on plausibly optimistic grounds. However, we stray into "Fantasyland" if we also expect that increasingly cumbersome, economy-wide problems of complex replacements will always be solved seamlessly, without delay.

Science, technology, and the economy are closely linked but do not march in lockstep. Science must nourish technology with information to be able to respond to calls from industry, and scientific progress is, to some extent, independent from the needs of industry. Great ideas are not on tap; they do not arrive in an uninterrupted flow; rather, they come in staccato-like bursts, each a surprise. Major breakthroughs, for instance, in aerodynamics, nuclear physics, cybernetics, and biotechnology, all leading to the creation of huge and vital industries, were like artistic creations that appeared when they were ready and not when someone asked for them.

The more *cultural evolution* exhausts the *global environment*'s low-entropy supplies, the more it is likely that some calls for help from industry will remain momentarily unanswered. Profitably "technologizable" ideas will not always be delivered up like room service in a hotel. At one point, even the applied science of technology is bound to come up empty-handed.

Let us point out an important difference between the hard substitutions described here and those associated with the introduction of novel products manufactured through revolutionary new technologies, as was the case with the automobile, the airplane, and the computer. These introductions were also hard substitutions, with chain reactions of demand for more hard substitutions along the vertical linkages of the production process; however, all these were (and still are) part of a dynamic, product-diversifying expansion, pulled by excess demand. Hard substitutions that beget complementary hard substitutions related to the depletion of relatively cheap materials (perhaps also to the depletion of the environment's self-cleansing, self-regenerating capacity) are pushed by supply shortfalls. These are likely to raise prices and may not always result in products that the consuming public wants. Higher production costs and sluggish demand is a growth-disabling combination.

The increasing frequency of hard substitutions connected with growing challenges thrown at science must, in due time, make *cultural evolution* bow to a simple fact. There are no infinite unidirectional processes in a closed space (*terrestrial sphere*) that contains a finite, countable number of parts (atoms). Hard substitutions to sustain permanent economic growth must falter on the *second law*. The flow of ideas cannot substitute for decrepit matter. Only nondecrepit matter that degrades in the process can.[3]

Backstop's backlog problem

Substitution of one material for another requires resources; the harder the substitution, the larger and more far-reaching, the less predictable the demand. One of the most crucial aspects of any natural resource-related hard substitution is the "own-demand." Objects made of copper will be required to replace copper with ceramics and plastics; refined oil products will be needed to replace them with products obtained from plants. Moreover, some limited demand for the substituted material may persist after its wide-scale replacement.

---

3.   Traditional, neoclassical economics draws a sharp dividing line between raw materials and capital. We unite them as both incorporating nonrenewable natural resources. Machinery and equipment, structures and means of transportation are, after all, atoms from the *terrestrial sphere*'s limited supply.

The profit motive allows us to presume the correct identification of the substitute and the technique used in its production that jointly are the least dependent upon the expensive commodity to be substituted as input. This means that, with the passage of time, matter-saving inventions will require increasing amounts of matter already in short supply. The dependence of the backstop technology upon what it intends to replace is likely to grow. As *cultural evolution* continues to depreciate earthly substance in the aggregate, growing quantities of energy to use matter already used will be required. However, this process faces physical constraints, since, according to current understanding, energy cannot be produced without matter. In the end, the world must face in general what it is about to face in particular with regard to oil; that is, it must lean more and more on what it needs to replace: free-energy contained in matter. The generalized backlog problem sets the stage for economic difficulties, but its indefinite growth poses a much more serious threat of physically harming the human prospect.

Developing a repercussion prone economy

Each nonconsumable output is also an input. The production and use of countless substances are thus linked. Pigments, solvents, fiberglass, synthetic dyes, cellulose, plastics, glues, high friction materials, coating nails, metal filaments, steel, sand, cement, and furniture finish (to name just a few) are present in the factory where electric carts used in large stores and warehouses are produced, and every single firm that produces any of the above-mentioned materials uses such carts in their own facilities. The type and quantity of intermediary inputs must increase to keep the growing stock of physical capital profitable; that is, to ensure continued economic expansion.

This expending structure sucks pristine energy contained in matter (i.e., not matter reused or recycled) from the *global environment*, which is known to contain a fixed number and quantity of elements and chemical compounds. Put differently, a qualitatively and quantitatively unchanging array of physical structures is alimenting a system that is expected to grow forever in size and complexity. (The limit posed by the *second law* to eternal economic expansion through reuse and recycling is considered obvious.) The prevailing assumption is that human ingenuity (science and technology) has no material constraints and that market forces are intrinsically capable of taking care of any structural shifts or shocks that the connection between fixed primary and expanding intermediary material inputs might entail.

The market can take care of many things in admirable (and much admired) ways, but, like any mechanism, it has limits. Stress causes strain in a structure; bigger stress, bigger strain. When the strain-accommodating elasticity limit is passed, the structure is damaged. If the economy does not get the amount and composition of materials it requires to function and grow (an occurrence guaranteed by the ongoing depletion of the lump-sum of free energy contained in terrestrial matter), it will not function and will not grow. And, because international economic integration advanced spectacularly on GS2's watch, its sensitivity and vulnerability now has global proportions.

Students of nonlinear dynamics (*chaos*) discovered that the more complex a system is and the closer it moves to full utilization, the greater is its proclivity to engage in "interesting" time evolutions. (More on *chaos* in Chapter 10.) This has been observed in the operation of electrical grids that comprise a number of coupled subsystems, but the global economy made up of national economies as subsystems also qualifies.[4] A more complex wiring of specialized activities and dependencies into a system of ever-expanding proportions enhances the global economy's inclination to turn shortages into chain reactions that could spread across economic sectors and geographic areas. Approaching full utilization is also applicable in the current context. It means bottlenecks in the flow of particular low-entropy matter (e.g., oil) from the *global environment* into the *geocapital*.[5]

As inputs and outputs differentiate and as the matrix of interindustry flows becomes ever larger and more detailed, deepening the economy's roundabout, mutually interdependent nature, and enhancing its sensitivity to cross-sectoral repercussions, the world economy also becomes increasingly prone to unexpected behavior; that is, malfunction by the known standards of economic performance and stability. In practical terms, this means that a global economic setback could have a million unanticipated, unforeseeable immediate causes. The long-term-growth-disabling trend of rising relative resource prices, which is the real culprit, could be upstaged by the economic system's diminished ability to adjust, making government policy (e.g., inflation control), "lack of political will," some "foreign"

---

4.   See *Ruelle, 1991*, Chapter 13.

5.   The expression "full utilization" is not used in the same way as in customary economic statistics, where it indicates, for example, the level of employment and productive capacity utilization, although coming close to full capacity in an economy in this sense is also conducive to *chaotic* episodes, i.e., downturns in the business cycle. During the Cold War, "planning up to capacity" unleashed unexpected, spontaneous developments that the authorities found highly damaging in communist controlled Eastern Europe.

country's actions, or a totally unexpected financial or monetary development the ostensible culprit.

Human organizational problems: GS2

In all likelihood, the great 21st century clash between *cultural evolution* and its physical constraints will occur under the prevalent socioeconomic organization. The suppression of signals, the incapacity to accomplish resource transitions in stagnant economic environments, and misplaced optimism make us aware of the approaching impasse.

Signal suppression. The relative profusion of natural resources (the currently-lived low-entropy bubble) made the economy's apparent independence from material inputs possible. As long as there is more of most substances, having less of some others may be overwhelmed by a combination of relatively easy substitutions (soft and partially carried out hard substitutions, such as plastics for certain metals and nonexhaustible energy sources for fossil fuels) and soaring additions of value through labor and entrepreneurship of all levels.

Increase in wages is a by-product of balanced economic growth. The more society produces, the more it has to buy. Thus, the increase in value added tends to reduce the real price of natural resources, making their "productive services" appear as an insignificant fraction of the total output. This perpetrates the delusion that whatever people dig up from the Earth plays a minor, subjugated role in the economy. The direct opposite is true. Natural resources surround us in their altered, manufactured forms as omnipresent extensions and complements of the human body.

With the detached obstinacy of made-up *minds*, "GS2" will never get tired of repeating that we live in a new, post-industrial service economy that is largely independent of things mined, drilled for, and excavated in unattractive places. But the reminder that the billions of souls who minister the now dominant service economy in the *vanguard* have bodies should not come as a surprise. They depend on material goods for their work and living standards. Doctors, teachers, real estate agents, stockbrokers, yoga instructors, waitresses, chauffeurs, and *major domos* (in some rarified *socioeconomic spheres*) are just as useless without props made of matter as tools are without skilled people. And the renderers of service would also like to be housed, fed, clothed, transported, and able to buy things (made of something other than space-less ether). When national statistics tell us that raw materials are below five percent of output value, the mutual dependence between the reproducible human capital and nonreproducible resources is stood on its head. The low share covers up the essential fact that, as the world economy expands, it becomes more, rather than less, dependent on the resources it ingurgitates. Over the long run, an expanding global economy requires increasing quantities of oil, coal, steel, copper and a host of other important metals and chemicals. More matter being used in continuous and ubiquitous ways is a *sine qua non* of *cultural evolution*, human society's titanic construction project.[6]

The expansion of *geocapital's* low-entropy supply from the storehouse of the *global environment* has been underwriting the pretense that *homo sapiens* lives in a thermodynamically open system. As long as the economy can grow on irrevocably depleted finite resources, the relative price of matter, which is supposed to indicate growing scarcity, will remain silent. The world's total dependence on natural resources will begin to show when even the slightest, irreversible increase in their overall, currently insignificant real price proves to be sufficient to disable growth. An increase in the average relative price of resources for reasons of enduring supply problems is nature's tax waiting to be levied. Society cannot simply vote this kind of tax out of existence, although macroeconomic policies might try to neutralize it, engaging future generations in a sort of Ponzi game, sending chain letters to the unborn.

The limits of GS2 to manage large-scale resource transitions. The combination of *mixed economy* government authority, weak *multilateralism*, and decentralized market incentives cannot accomplish forced resource transitions smoothly, that is, by preserving economic growth, social peace, and international stability. In retrospect from a distant future, GS2's weakness in managing hard substitutions with economy-wide demands for multiple, complementary industrial restructuring may be seen in the following way. During the period, prior to the recognition that global economic growth needs global oversight, the system's built-in emphasis on consumption and related capital formation provided incentives not for, but against the accumulation (stockpiling) of commodities required for the drastic transition; when the time came, the system had neither means, nor mandate, nor ideological readiness to help the process through spots of economic stagnation. In the face of any future resource supply inadequacy, GS2 will remain inactive, waiting for market forces (aided by tax incentives, subsidies, and information provided through government monitoring) to solve the problem. When a break

---

6.   The shift from manufacturing to services in many *vanguard* countries did not reduce global demand for energy carriers and raw materials. The growth of manufacturing in the rest of the world gradually picked up the slack in demand.

threatens economic expansion, the *mixed economy* would rather engage in deficit spending than in extra-economic intervention.

To handle organized transitions, the state would have to be empowered with the authority to redirect resources and would need to dispose of large funds to deal with emergencies. GS2 was not born for that. It can accommodate *cultural evolution* under ecologically relaxed conditions. Once this relaxation is gone, it becomes helpless because active resource management is outside its parameters. Hands-on state involvement in resource transition is an obvious departure from GS2. Governments are supposed to stay at arm's length from the private economy. Even in the best of times, they constantly scrutinize and criticize each others' real or imagined support of their respective producers in world markets. A single major nation in the *vanguard* attempting to manage resource-base conversion could disrupt *multilateralism*.[7]

Misplaced optimism. GS2's "cornucopian" material resource logic sees "market and technology" through blinders. Epithets such as "emerging materials," "artificial materials," and "knowledge-based, multifunctional materials," fancy and promising as they are, do not take human society out of its earthly context. They only combine what is already here in fixed numbers. Ultrathin "nano-wires," for example, are manufactured from polystyrene and gold. Polystyrene (noted for the extraordinary environmental hazards its production poses) is a special plastic that comes most likely from refined oil or natural gas; and gold is hardly known as a metal in abundant supply. The new materials have potential use in information technology, defense, medicine, biotechnology, and construction (replacing woods with combinations of woods and other materials). These are helpful developments, but they cannot alter the fact that the overuse of nonrenewable resources is a growing problem with unpredictable concrete consequences.

◆   ◆   ◆

According to current opinion held by both the majority of economists and the defenders of ecology, a gradual and smooth (i.e., economic growth maintaining and system-preserving) transition from the predominantly nonrenewable to a predominantly renewable resource-based civilization is possible. Whereas the economist trusts the bright engineer/tireless entrepreneur combination to solve

---

7.   The fate of the *Oil Depletion Protocol* will be a test of GS2's capacity to accommodate large-scale resource transition. The protocol calls for a voluntary reduction of crude oil imports. For details, see *Association for the Study of Peak Oil* on the web.

the transition through profitable commerce, the ecologist believes that changed personal habits can force business and industry to accomplish it. Such gradual smoothness is physically impossible. Reconfiguration of the resource-base must be preceded by deconfiguration in the economic structure and an admitted systems failure of global institutions. The decentralized market economy has proved to be efficient in creating new sectors of production and shifting sectors in response to social needs, but it cannot change its own role in resource allocation.

Growing own-demand of nonrenewable materials to be substituted in combination with harder and harder substitutions will tend to curtail output. Material constraints to growth and the matching need for investment capital to overcome them will appear at the same time. If capital has to be diverted to implement transition in the resource-base, less will be available to expand consumption, yet the growth of consumption is a "must" in retaining the prevalent world order. GS2 economies need constant augmentation in consumer expenditures to keep employment from declining. If supply in consumer goods is reduced while demand for them persists, inflation and/or macroeconomic inflation control will reduce demand to match lower supplies at some unsatisfactory level of productive capacity utilization without short-run recovery in sight.

The limit to the continuation of *cultural evolution* is a complex phenomenon. In its simplest interpretation, it is the economic growth-disabling incongruity between decreasing accessibility to free energy contained in matter and the imperative to grow under the current *global system*.

Based on previous considerations, the following is a plausible scenario of global economic self-crippling. Premise 1: The world realizes that the three-year moving average of the (real) price of crude oil will never again decrease. Premise 2: Raw material (real) prices, in general, begin to attract attention. For instance, the five-year moving average of all raw material (real) prices (excluding crude oil) rises for several years. Premise 3: As a result of public pressure, government help (subsidies, tax incentives, grants) and sheer business interest, a tendency of substituting renewable (solar) material resources (both as energy carriers and raw materials) for nonrenewable ones gets underway in earnest. Premise 4: The idea that economic growth is not a monologue of the market, but a dialogue between human society and nature, begins to penetrate minds. Premise 5: GS2 continues to push for maximum economic growth.

Inference: Global economic turndown is a physically unqualified absolute.

Increasing costs of production: Some producers may become unprofitable as a result of Premises 1 and 2. (Economics instructs us that an increase in the relative price of a resource reduces the output that depends on the indicated resource. If the average relative price of all material resources increased, overall output must decline.) *Resource diversion*: Even a gradual expansion of the renewable material and energy input sector could bankrupt some industries in the rest of the economy by jolting the secular tendency of input price increases. *Procrastination*: Many businesses will try to postpone capital investment associated with the transition to renewable resources if the investment promises to do nothing more than allow them to operate. Some of them will wait until they are no longer able to finance the transition. The most powerful corporations will try to get the resources they need from nonrenewable sources until they no longer can; that is, they will procrastinate with muscle. *Manipulation*: Huge transnationals in nonrenewable resource production have every reason not to hasten the transition. Logically, they will try to pace and control the process by assuming a dominant role in it, with the likely result of aggravating the shortage of nonrenewable resources needed for and after the transition. All these phenomena intermingle among themselves as well as with critical micro-and macroeconomic variables and government policies at all levels, multiplying the number of butterflies eager to flap their wings. (See the "butterfly effect" in Chapter 10.)

◆   ◆   ◆

The *global system's representative brain* cannot make the foot on the brake dominate the foot on the gas pedal. What the world may save in the use of crude oil per car, it will absorb by encouraging overall automobile production. Measures of increased efficiency in the use of energy and material resources would dampen economic activity unless the energy and material saved is deployed to expand production. The consumer must spend the money it saves on resource-economizing products, otherwise global markets and employment would shrink, spilling over into the welfare of every single nation.

The public will have to buy increasing amounts of new and different material goods, perhaps from abroad, if domestic measures of resource transition eliminate manufacturing jobs and channel even more of the local workforce into construction and the broad category of services that includes trade, finance, insurance, real estate, and government. And let us remember: A few decades of experience in a developed country does not reflect global conditions, needs, and prospects. Looking at the day after tomorrow from the perspective of the entire world, we can see no end to the rush for nonexhaustible resources. The developing world, trying to reduce the severe inadequacy of its material goods production, will eagerly absorb any fossil fuel, metal, or other raw material not demanded by the developed countries. Even the expansion of nonindustrial activities in the economically most advanced nations is contingent on the expanding global industrial base. If manufacturing jobs disappear in one place, you can be sure that the decline will be more than compensated elsewhere. Thinking that fuel efficient cars, the diversification of software services, and unplugging toasters in Paris, Los Angeles, and Tokyo can stop the world from running down its limited resources is believing in the natural blueness of painted skies. It is the *fata morgana* of programmed minds unable to recognize the essential difference between past and future. Any decisive measure of resource transition would endanger the profitable operation of the world's growing physical capital, our basic condition for economic expansion and sufficient levels of employment.

These arguments, of course, are not expected to sway standard economic opinion. "Give me a well functioning price system, allow human imagination to put daring new ideas into practical use, and you will never have to worry about resource scarcity," broadcasts GS2 through the channels of conventional economic analysis. Celebrated economic theories elaborating upon the conditions for and the speed of convergence toward steady state *ad infinitum* economic growth are *global system*-induced, unattainable mirages, remote from biological and physical realities. Both simple buoyancy and extreme sophistication derive from the *global system*'s living *text*. Like its predecessor, GS2 also pretends that it can live forever and holds the faculty of independent thinking in a quasicataleptic state.

The *text* self-assuredly repels any attempt to demonstrate the weakness of human organization in the emerging global context. Abundant reserves of hydrocarbons exist in coastal waters and under the Rocky Mountains; there is an unlimited supply of construction material lying on the beaches; and if and when the demand for solar panels increases, the stock of solar panel-producing companies will go up, facilitating large investment projects and reallocating resources to satisfy society's needs. The leaders of huge transnational corporations and managers of financial capital around the globe anticipate the long run rationally. "Their money is at stake!" Present value maximization of capital placements and price signals in futures markets, aided by virtually instantaneous communication in the information age, are the best navigators of economic progress. Every possible economic or social problem is just another investment opportunity. Reality concerning the future is what your broker-dealer says about likely rallies and pull-backs during the next two quarters. Anything else is "Big Talk." But spectacular solutions to lingering resource problems are not put through a rigorous intersectoral economic analysis that would reveal their total and detailed demands; their environmental consequences remain suspended in the public sphere. GS2's *text* makes believe that material resources come from a bottomless well. Consequently, any energy problem or material shortage is essentially an internal human affair, solvable through methods and principles that have worked so far. Concern over the incalculable pressure that an additional three billion people might exert on the *global environment* by mid-century is offset by the joy over economic growth prospects. (Some projections foresee a fivefold increase of the global economy in less than 50 years.)

To substantiate the contention that the thermodynamic clock is still ticking, that there is a comprehensive process in the background that is breathing down on our necks, we need to refresh our vantage point; to make use of what we showed about the sequential, stage-like evolution of human identity *as a* (not like a) material process of self-organized complexification. *To put it as concisely as possible, the difference between a predominantly nonrenewable resource-based (population-size driven) and a predominantly renewable resource-based (material resource-constrained) world at peace is too big not to imply two separate global systems, that is, a global transformation. However, global transformation is the same as chaotic transition, a disruption in human self-organization. We hope that the transition will be short and merciful.* Amplification follows.

◆   ◆   ◆

Each *global system* has its own techno-economic space, meaning economic opportunities to apply production techniques on a large scale. The technical know-how acquired during the first industrial revolution had to wait for GS1's instauration to be put to wide use and to create industries that came to characterize the first *global system*'s technological landscape. The knowledge required for the massive serial production of consumer goods was available before GS2, but the first tidal wave of corresponding physical capital formation had to wait for GS2 institutions to ensure the stable and continuous availability of the purchasing power required to sell what the increasing number of assembly lines would emit. GS1's techno-economic space was incompatible with mass-produced automobiles; GS2's space embraces it comfortably, as if it were its parental home. Stating that GS1 was not capable of accommodating mass production/consumption, but that GS2 is, implies qualitative differences in technology, capital goods, and in intersectoral linkages. The quantity and quality of capital assets are key characteristics of that space. To use a simple image, the heaps of machinery and equipment one sees in factories across the *vanguard* is indicative of the *global system* under which we live.

The opportunities inherent in a techno-economic space are not unlimited. That is why economic growth-and institution-preserving transition from one techno-economic space to the next cannot run its full course. The transformation of the techno-economic space is part of *global transformation*, implying an absence of stable economic organization and performance.

The transformation from the predominantly nonrenewable to a predominantly renewable resource-based global economy, that is, the transformation of the GS2-characteristic techno-economic space into the GS3-characteristic space must have a similar limit. When and how it will be encountered remains hidden among the *chaotic* conditions that characterize the transition from one *global system* to the next The projected interregnum in world order is likely to be a period when private initiatives will wait for clear signals about what products will be in long-term demand; what levels of energy and material inputs will be reliably available, and what environmental standards will be mandated. As was the case with GS1 and GS2, at the end of the expected transition, GS3's *imprimatur* should also contain guarantees of general economic, social, and political stability.

Based on historical experience, the inevitability of a new *global transformation* (*chaotic transition/bifurcation*) is expressed through the coincidental need for *macro-*, *meso-*, and *microscopic* conversions. If, at a minimum, one of the levels may conceivably remain intact, it is theoretically possible that the rest of the level(s) need only dig deeper into the *global system*'s parameter space for the world order to reinvent itself. But the profundity and completeness of the change required to put the species in a state of integrated ecological consciousness excludes this soft-landing, iterative approach. Physics overrides decentralized wishes.

There are several optimistic scenarios for overcoming the related problems of fossil fuel use and environmental degradation. We neither disparage their optimism nor contest the accuracy of their assumptions or data. Their general invalidity is assured by being in conflict with the physical process that envelopes our socioeconomic progression on a macro time scale. Gradual and smooth transition to a renewable resource-based techno-economic space cannot substitute for *global transformation/chaotic transition* because the accomplished transition implies conversion at the *macroscopic*, *mesoscopic*, and *microscopic* levels at once. The world will need a global approach to resource management and environmental control with appropriate authority and means to harmonize national preferences (*macroscopic* alteration). At the *mesoscopic* level, national governments will have to ensure steadfast and longsighted resource management and environmental control; they will have to be equipped with administrative tools to guide their economies. They will have to provide a framework for local economic initiatives (*cantons*). *Microscopically*, the individual as a consumer will have to develop a taste for (or recover the joy of) long-lasting (slowly depreciating), high-quality products. As a producer, the individual will have to become less competitive and more cooperative; it will have to develop disinterest in extraordinary wealth and personal power; i.e., the importance of the canonical scale of socioeconomic status will have to decline. (If a GS3-typical persona were alive today, it would probably look at greedy businessmen with the same understanding and empathy that contemporary adults feel when they see children play "make-believe.") As both consumers and producers, people will have to become conscious of the environment and the need to conserve material and energy resources. The business firm (the typical association of producers under GS1 and GS2) will have to reinvent itself under hard material and energy constraints. It will have to operate in a marketplace that neither encourages nor rewards ruthless competition; it will have to extend its field of view.

If certain qualitative features of capital assets are related to a *global system*, they are also related to distinct socioeconomic behavior, *lexicon*, *ethic*, *Weltanschauung*, and *mentality*. GS3's capital assets and intersectoral linkages will be marked by a break with current levels of depreciating fossil fuel sources of energy; by approaches to production that are cognizant of the *terrestrial sphere*'s limited matter, and by environmentally conscious durable products. The anticipated *global system*'s entire technological and commercial culture, embodied in qualitatively new mechanisms, is in evident conflict with every single aspect identified as coterminous with the current *global system*. Since the *Code Core* has to traverse a period of disorganization (*chaotic transition*) to be reprogrammed, the renewal of capital assets cannot be a gradual and continuous process. If it were, the entire *web* of interconnected cerebral imprints pertaining to GS2 could change in a gradual, evolutionary fashion, in contradiction to world history being a thermodynamic process of complexifying self-organization. The latter precludes smooth transition from one relative, globally valid steady state to the next. Ultimately, the current world order's fateful insufficiencies can be deduced from the physically-mandated economic disruption associated with *chaotic transition*.

◆   ◆   ◆

We proceeded from establishing a widely anticipated global disruption during the 21st century to examining its plausible details. We arrive at the thermodynamic theory of history with one more generalization; i.e., *relative steady state/ bifurcation/relative steady state*. Deduction from the physical inevitability of this sequence indicates the disruption of global order, but without a concrete scenario. Following this route, one may conclude that a new *chaotic transition* (in terms of *metahistory*) must come because decentralized fulfillment centers (individual *minds*) moving stochastically against metastable (i.e., not rigorously fixed, not precisely determinable) constraints cannot reprogram themselves simultaneously. The *web* is capable of uniform coordination, *Gleichschaltung*, only at the end of a *chaotic transition*. It is incapable of substituting *Gleichschaltung* for *chaotic transition*. If it were, than *global system*-specific *socioeconomic behavior* (in *macrohistoric* terms) could alter itself in major ways even when it was still tenable. But history has proved that *global system*-specific *socioeconomic behavior* is impervious to spontaneous attacks and untimely efforts to reprogram it. Problems that are unsolvable without conflict must emerge to signal the need to dislodge *socioeconomic behavior*, *lexicon*, *ethic*, *Weltanschauung*, and *mentality*. And the new vortex will have to bring *macroscopic*, *mesoscopic*, and *microscopic* conversions all at once, opening the door wide for GS3's technical civilization.

To eliminate the growing disparity between the *global system*'s semantically interpreted *text* and its physical context, nothing less than a profound metamorphosis of thinking will be required. Some broad agreement among billions of *minds* will have to be found which, once translated into *surrounding socioeconomic milieus*, will allow moral fullness to shed its huckster skin.[8]

THE DIFFICULT SEARCH FOR RENEWAL

Entropy grows in the *terrestrial sphere* as the quantitative aspects of *cultural evolution* (the growth of world population and output) absorb the most easily accessible material and energy resources of the *global environment*. Indirectly, through the economic experience of *geocapital* depletion, signs of *environmental impairment*, and the rising resource hunger of the environmental sector, global society will gradually realize that *cultural evolution* is near to, or is on, a barrier; that there is a planetary carrying capacity in terms of human biomass and activity, and violating it threatens *culture*. The 21st century will have to answer this momentous general question: How much evidence does the world need in order to see that it has created a new relationship with its ecological basis?

Another *global transformation* is the only alternative to the species' decline. Going beyond *Point X* without *global transformation* means movement toward extinction. *Cultural devolution* weakens *homo sapiens*, making it increasingly vulnerable not only to the threat of mass extinction (like a weakened body succumbs to a mild flu) but also to smaller changes in the climate and other circumstances of the physical environment that could, if not confronted as they emerge, accumulate to a lethal dose. But, as shown before, *global transformation* is no simple matter. The *surrounding socioeconomic milieu* and the patterns of adaptive behavior (tied to shared and complementary information across the nested hierarchy of *socioeconomic environments* and *systems*) cannot be separated abruptly and significantly. People cannot behave as if the socioeconomic context in which they live were different from the actual. This puts fundamental institutional transformation of the socioeconomic environment beyond the reach of rational measures, ingenious reforms, new policies, and charismatic leadership.

Everybody's *mind* changing at once in the same way contradicts the *second law of thermodynamics*. If billions of microstates self-organized into a physical *Gestalt* could accomplish such a synchronized feat, the process would be *deterministic* because *randomness* occurring on such a scale must be discounted. However, if a process is *deterministic*, it could be reversed in contradiction to the necessity of entropy build-up, in other words, unidirectionality in the evolution of far-from-equilibrium self-organized systems such as the worldwide *web* of individually encoded information.

---

8.   It bears repeating that *new historical materialism* sees *cultural evolution* as a far-from-equilibrium dissipative thermodynamic process *sensu stricto*, rather than a process analogue to it *sensu lato*. Without observing this difference, the theory would fall into the logical fallacy known as "begging the question" (*petitio principii*). The following would be a flawed argument: "Far-from-equilibrium dissipative thermodynamic processes must go through their known (*relative steady state/bifurcation/relative steady state*) sequence. Having established that *cultural evolution* 'is just like such a process,' it will also have to go through a similar sequence. Since we now live under *relatively steady socioeconomic conditions, chaotic transition* is the next phase in *metahistoric* terms." Note also that the arguments presented in the current text cannot help determine how long particular natural resources (e.g., crude oil) will be able to support *cultural evolution*. Nor do they prove that GS3 is an "historical inevitability."

This does not mean that a relatively quick transformation in the global socio-economic order is inconceivable. It does fall within the bounds of feasible paths of transition, but if, and only if, we relax the requirement of total synchronicity in the reprogramming of cerebral codes. Under this restriction, one cannot preclude the possibility that some historical shock provokes an emotional catharsis and engenders moral cleansing in a critical mass of *minds*, prompting clarity as to the socioeconomic institutions and associated behavior required to live in a physical environment altered by population density and signs of resource exhaustion. This critical mass may then take the moral high ground and initiative, leading the rest of the world to a new, appropriate *global system*. The openness of this route of transformation is what separates the human-organism-centered evolutionary self-organization from all other unidirectional, entropy-producing physical or biological processes we know or can imagine.

Global transformation (GS2—>GS3) is identical to an effective reaction to the threat posed to *culture*. The reaction is effective if it is based on the correct diagnosis, gets to the heart of the quantitative overflow problem, and enjoys worldwide support. Historical experience suggests that such an "effective reaction" (e.g., through the induction of GS3) cannot come before a certain pain is endured and attempts to fork it over to someone else are abandoned. How low can the pain threshold go, how successfully can "pain" be "exported," and "under what circumstances will the quest for surplus in pain trade appear as counterproductive" are specific queries derived from the general question posed to the 21st century.

GS2's end is logically sealed. But how do we know that a GS3-like *system* (as defined) must follow GS2, given that the species follows the adaptive path?

There is neither time nor expressed need for an intervening system between *mixed economy/weak multilateralism* and *two-level economy/strong multilateralism*. *Cultural evolution* is too close to its constraints to accommodate another *global transformation* that would usher in a more effective, economic growth-promoting system. Such a development also seems superfluous. No known political movement with worldwide support has as its avowed aim to replace GS2 with a domestic and international socioeconomic system that is supposedly superior in accelerating economic expansion. All suggestions to this effect are within the framework of GS2. Therefore, the main aspiration of a post-GS2 system will have to be the control of global and, hence, national economic activity levels in full consideration of the material constraints that affect the entire human population. As mentioned before, GS2 might morph into something that would still fall short of a full-fledged GS3. Whether such a tentative approach (provided that it was widespread and endured for some time) would be considered the extension of GS2 or part of the *chaotic transition* is a toss, *ex ante*. Assuming that *homo sapiens* behaves adaptively, GS3 (as defined) axiomatically follows GS2. The new *chaotic transition* must lead to GS3.

A new *global system*, with all its attributes, including the foundations of a new techno-economic space, will have to emerge. Consequently, GS3 should not be considered an alternative to GS2, or a better way to manage the transition. Attempts to do just that, if there were any, would only modify the current system, creating an intermediary arrangement, a "GS2-and-a-half." However, *ex post*, such interpolation will clearly be seen as unsuccessful in reaching the new *relative steady state*.

How do we know that the *global transformation* has begun? By definition, it begins when the current *global system* expires. Therefore, the question may be rephrased as: "When do we know that GS2 has expired?" There are two answers; one is theoretical and the other is practical.

GS2's principal goal (as promulgated in its founding documents) is to ensure economic development, an obligation that remains valid under the condition of demographic expansion. GS2 has been "designed" by the *Opaque Artificer* to further the cause of economic development (increase in per capita income and accomplish at least some improvement in socioeconomic balance), despite the growth in population. At present, there is no doubt that world population is growing. The global average of real per capita income may also be growing, but at a slow pace. There are, however, strong doubts about whether there is any progress in socioeconomic equalization. Some indications point to no growth or even decline in global socioeconomic equality in recent years. If an analysis reliably concluded that, under the current world order, the SEEI will never resume its upward trend, the *relatively steady socioeconomic conditions* are already out and the *chaotic transition* is in. Most certainly, the world will be in *chaotic transition* when the impossibility of everlasting economic growth on Earth is widely, but not totally, accepted. At one point, competing and conflicting socioeconomic organizational alternatives ("paradigms") will separate those who want some negative; zero; some positive; and unlimited positive growth. This situation predates the possibility of operating physical capital built around a unified global perspective; of having *relatively steady socioeconomic conditions* with the accompanying manifestations of an established *global system*.

In practical terms, GS2 is considered beyond help if its domestic and *multilateral* institutions need to be suspended for whatever reason, and/or alternatives to replace them pop up. The suspension of the old and entry of the new may take the form of widespread local initiatives in energy production and environmental protection. Such a phenomenon would *de facto* presage the two-level economy (GS3). *Cantonization* may begin when high gasoline prices make more people stay in their immediate environs, encouraging the development of economic neighborhoods and increasing the social and cultural importance of grassroots communities. As GS2 draws nearer to its end, one thought will most certainly be a return to GS1. Like an unconditional reflex of the body, this is expected to happen. Rolling back GS2, making it disappear to the extent possible, seems like the easiest solution. The scope and intensity of efforts directed at the elimination of the socioeconomic safety net in the *vanguard* and matching repulsion in the political sphere are indications of the *global system*'s decay. The greater the clash of wills, the more likely that we are in "it." Thus, as of this writing, *chaotic transition* may have begun by some measures, but not in its strict, institutional definition.[9]

The main concern is the length and intensity of the coming period of *macrohistoric* instability. Even after connecting the negative fallouts and potential dangers to *cultural evolution*, willingness to join forces will not necessarily be forthcoming. Could our community, country, region, or hemisphere be isolated from the problems that affect the rest of the world? It is more than likely that such subglobal escape routes through internecine manipulation, domination, and conquest will be entertained, delaying unified rationalization and the development of an appropriate strategy to redirect *cultural evolution*. But no one can tell for how long. Knowing that the evolution of human self-organization is symmetry-breaking; hence, novelty-producing, one can always find comfort in hope. Optimism means confidence that the species' life instinct will signal outposts before *culture* suffers a bad accident. Humankind should consider itself lucky if economic problems, severe as they may be, sufficed to shock its ranks into unity of thought and action.

◆   ◆   ◆

To summarize: The gap between what is and what will be needed is too wide to be bridged by stretching GS2 parameters. New attitudes toward resources and the environment, new economic goals, new technologies, new products, new relationships in and outside the workplace, new governmental authority, and new international insti-

---

9.   It is worth remembering that the two *chaotic transitions* began with *relative-steady-state*-disruptive events: The French Revolution and a World War.

tutions mean a "switch" in organizational principles and practices that affects every aspect of life. A new global transformation/chaotic transition is implied. But the search for the blueprint of a new global system and the final selection from among the alternatives can hardly be free of strife. The revesting of interests among and within nations evidently threatens vested interests. Aligning economic growth with the capacity to expand renewable resources and ensuring the thoughtful and equitable exploitation of nonrenewable resources among the planet's inhabitants would put in jeopardy private profit-dependent employment (hence income) and would fly in the face of contemporary interpretations of national interest. A wide arena is opening up for social and national power centers to exchange heavy blows in attempts to force the future. As history has taught us, these first "forcings" may not even be tied to a conscious search for the new global system. These are the details hidden in the euphemism, "switch." Their complex dynamic harbors unknowable and uncontrollable scenarios of devastation, displacement, and trauma. To a cosmic giant observing the planet, for whom time flows much faster than it does for us, the only global transformation on record ("1914-1945") might have seemed like a violent explosion. But of course, for the human observer, the future is open. Only Cassandra may know whether the "best" (a quick global transformation), the "historically conditioned expectation," or the worst (no global transformation, not even in the wake of an ecological disaster) is in the womb of time.

◆   ◆   ◆

At present, boundaries to *cultural evolution* are being set in tentative and preliminary ways, with a more or less explicit understanding that going beyond them will have tragic consequences. But this is only the beginning. To avoid decline and extinction, the world will have to become a single decision maker. It must develop the corresponding institutions and adjust individual conduct. The propositions that (i) a "transformation curve" between population and physical output will have to be identified; (ii) that once this happens there will be a search for the optimal location on it; and (iii) that this will necessitate the weighing of alternatives lead to this conclusion. But let us begin with some numbers.[10]

Point Xs may be characterized as fatal combinations of population and output. Estimates indicate that the Earth cannot possibly feed more than 15 billion people living at the same time (*Bryant, 2002*, Chapter 16). The number was derived from the concept of *Net Primary Productivity* (NPP), defined as the total amount of solar radiation convertible into biochemical energy through plant photosynthesis, less the energy needed by the plants. Since plants feed us directly or indirectly, the total number of calories that they can produce on all cultivable land (minus what they need to maintain themselves and grow) determines the Earth's potential food supply for any given period.

A world population of 15 billion is not only virtually unachievable, but it is also unsustainable. If it is ever reached, soil erosion, water pollution, and the accumulation of urban wastes would endanger human life on a massive scale, provoking conflicts, "food fights," and resource wars. The dreaded phenomena of Malthusian "positive checks" of population growth (death from wars, famine, and disease) would become reality.

Calculations also indicate that at the current state of science and technology, the level of per capita output (real income) in the developed countries (representing about one-fifth of the world population, and shrinking) cannot become the global average without cataclysmic consequences for the environment.[11] For the sake of argument, let us define the absolute upper limit of world material output (Gross World Product minus services) to be $Y trillion. With a population of L billion, this would mean $Y/L per capita material output.

Two assumptions are critical to our theory: First, in the long run and on a global scale, the increase in the service sector and in human capital cannot occur

---

10.   The recognition among economists that growth in world population and economic activity is headed toward hard obstacles found expression in significant writing and professional debate in the late 1960s and early 1970s. Advocates of the so-called "zero population growth" (ZPG) and "zero economic growth" (ZEG) presented their arguments (and sometimes policy recommendations); their critics dismissed them, and the editors of books on the "growth debate"–or moderators at economic conferences–drew wise, middle-of-the-road conclusions. The debate became practically inaudible as neoliberalism took hold of the world during the last two decades of the 20th century. Indifference and the cold shoulder from leading academic circles notwithstanding, well researched, thought-provoking books reached the wider public.

11.   The so-called "ecological footprint analysis" is one methodology that led to this conclusion. "Ecological footprint" is the land and water surface required to maintain the living standard of a given population. The concept converts material flows (resources to be used and wastes to be discarded) of a nation into the area required to sustain the level of living of its population. Calculations allow comparison between the actual national territory and the area claimed (i.e., the ecological footprint). All nations of the *vanguard* live far beyond their official, geographic confines. Each uses an area several times larger than the one enclosed within its administrative frontiers. See William E. Rees, "Revisiting Carrying Capacity: Area-Based Indicators of Sustainability," in *Population and Environment: A Journal of Interdisciplinary Studies*, vol. 17, no. 3, Jan. 1996. The article's bibliography is a guide to the concept's genealogy.

without increasing physical assets. Moreover, the colonization of space, which is vital to avoid extinction, also depends on extrasomatic material. The larger the effort, the greater the material demand. Second, there is a trade-off between global population and world material output at the full use of the Earth's carrying capacity. The L billion and the $Y trillion cannot occur simultaneously. The descendancy will be able to augment physical output only if it sees to the reduction of the population, or vice versa. If it drifts toward maximum material wealth, it will need to "push" the level of population toward its minimum; and, if it embraces the "more the merrier" philosophy to its extreme, it will barely subsist.

The most obvious argument against the possibility of the two theoretical extremes (L billion and $Y trillion) occurring simultaneously has to do with the finiteness of the Earth's surface. High levels of population demand relatively more agriculture, allowing for less industry, whereas low human occupancy demands less agriculture and allows for more industry. If the world used all the available terrestrial surface at its disposal, then more human habitat and agriculture would take land away from industry. And vice versa. The next chapter contains some further, perhaps less obvious, reasons for the trade-off between population and material output.

There are, of course, an infinite number of intermediate combinations between *Country Club Place* (very high output with very low population) and *Malthus Point* (very low output and very high population). One that is closer to the second but much less harsh is a world in which basic human needs such as food, shelter, clothing, economic infrastructure (public utilities, transportation and communication systems) and social infrastructure (education, health care, law and order) are fully met. In short, meeting these needs guarantees decent working conditions and living standards.[12]

A large population with satisfied basic needs would leave no productive capacity for goods that could improve the quality of life. Whereas this consideration would push the choice toward low occupancy and high per capita material goods output, the individual's natural drive toward reproduction and even some general human interests (e.g., resilience to diseases, the mitigation of the effects of natural catastrophes) would pull toward higher occupancy and lower per capita material wealth. Any population/material output combination should take into consider-

---

12. If standard of living is scored between 0 and 1, as in the *Human Development Index of the United Nations Development Programme*, basic human needs are well satisfied if the index is near 1. Although calculations attempt to screen out the effects of high per capita incomes on the index, levels of living near "1" can be found only in the most developed industrial democracies; i.e., in the *vanguard*.

ation the consequences of shrinking *exergic* constraints as well as the material resource needs involved in prying open the *terrestrial sphere*'s closed thermodynamic system.

Existence near a *Point X* means living near the precipice with all the risks implied by the comparison. To secure an opportunity for "sustainable development," *cultural evolution* will have to be globally managed.[13]

---

13. World population reached 6.5 billion in 2005 and annual global output (Gross World Product, valued at purchasing power parity) was estimated at $60 trillion for the year. World population is expected to crest below 10 billion by mid-century, while projections generally anticipate a 2.5-to 5.0-fold increase in annual global output during the period. Some analysts consider these levels unsustainable. They imply, in effect, that we are not far from a *Point X.*

8

The Future Mechanism of Global Decision-Making

[The world will have to make conscious choices in order to use to the fullest the planet's ability to support human life. It will have to decide between reproduction and production under constraint; it will have to determine the population and output levels that would best suit its "present" and long-term interests. The transformation curve, known from economics, offers insight into the complexity and altered reality awaiting the species.]

A multitude of theoretically feasible and safe combinations of global population and material output is possible. One of them (or a range of them), somewhere between *Malthus Point* and *Country Club Place,* will be judged superior (optimal) compared to the rest of the possibilities. To determine this point (or range), the global society will have to allocate its most general scarce resource, free energy economically extractable from matter, between the human biomass and artifices needed to sustain and enhance the quality of life. A team of international experts, leaning on the planet's entire academic infrastructure, will have to construct the *global somatic/extrasomatic transformation curve.* This concept is likely to become vital for latter-day generations. Some elaboration on it, which adheres strictly to GS2's *text* (i.e., problems and aspirations typical of its mindset), may be worthwhile.

A QUICK DETOUR THROUGH THE REALM OF ELEMENTARY ECONOMICS[1]

The transformation curve is the visual expression of the rational, analytical approach to making choices under scarcity. Its bowed-out (concave-to-the-origin) shape, shown in Figures 1 through 4, may remind anyone who took a course in economics of the "production possibility frontier" or "production opportunity curve" or "product transformation curve." Under simplifying assumptions, it is smooth and "well-behaved" –no zigzags or gaps. Each point on the curve is an ordered pair of quantities. From any point on the curve shown in Figure 1, draw a straight line parallel with the horizontal axis to the vertical axis. The distance between the origin and the intersection created (B) will designate the quantity of the product marked along the vertical axis. Drop a vertical line to the horizontal axis from the same point and the distance shown between the origin and the intersection created (A) will indicate the quantity of the product measured along the horizontal axis.

To apply the transformation curve (our choice from among the synonyms), two conditions must be present. First, information about trade-offs must be available as one moves along the curve. That is, if we want to have more of one "thing," how much of the scarce resource will be used and how much less will we have of the alternative "thing" because of this decision. Second, some unit valuation associated with the alternative uses of the resource is needed. Valuation may take the form of prices or psychic satisfaction that expresses an implicit summary of sensed relative significance. Following the sequence of increasing complexity, the punch line below will be "competitive business firm," "monopoly," "nation," "world."

To maximize the value of its output, a firm needs to decide how to allocate its manpower between two products (A and B). Basic economics will be ready with the advice: *Mark off the point on the product transformation curve where sacrificing one unit of product A to gain some amount of product B will be equal to the reciprocal of their price ratio.* (See the point marked as "Optimum" on Figure 1.) It is not difficult to discover the logic behind this seemingly arcane rule.

The aggregate value of output, the "revenue" (R), is calculated in the following way:

$$R = Q_A \cdot P_A + Q_B \cdot P_B$$

---

1.   This is a pared down introduction. It contains only ideas and definitions required for the current text. The reader interested in a more comprehensive and detailed presentation is advised to consult a textbook on economics.

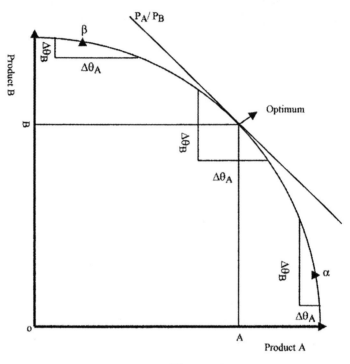

Figure 1
Transformation curve at the firm level:
Resource allocation between two products

where Q_A is the quantity produced of A, Q_B is the quantity produced of B, P_A and P_B are the prices of A and B, respectively. When the revenue is maximized, the value of production of A and B is equal. That is, when $Q_A \cdot P_A = Q_B \cdot P_B$. The equality means maximum revenue because, if the firm's management found that it could get more by increasing the output of one of the products, for example that of A, it would do so. As long as $[Q_A \cdot P_A > Q_B \cdot P_B]^2$ holds, total revenue can be further increased by producing more of A and less of B. The addition to the revenue by producing more A exceeds the loss from producing less B. As this transfer proceeds, the additional net gains become smaller and smaller, until they vanish. Equality between the two sides is established. The same logic would apply if the inequality sign happened to point in the opposite direction, meaning that total revenue could be increased by more of B and less of A. Rearranging this equality (the condition of maximum revenue), we find the rule:

$$Q_B/Q_A = P_A/P_B$$

The slope of the transformation curve is the same as the price ratio, which is actually the transformation curve's tangent at the point indicating the optimum.

A more detailed examination of firm-level equilibration will lead us closer to the calculus of choices on the social scale. Let the symbol Δ denote change, i.e., ΔR is change in revenue. This quantity will be zero at the point where the manpower is so perfectly divided that any further transfer in either direction would take away from the maximized revenue.

Every allocation of manpower has a little "wiggle room." In a firm that employs thousands, one can surely transfer a couple of workers for a few days from one product line to another without upsetting production schedules. (The idea is similar to "a blood sample will not alter your physical condition.") For instance, the management could select 10 workers and transfer them from the production of A to the production of B for a week. Let ΔQ_A denote the (relatively) tiny increase in A production and ΔQ_B the matching decrease in B production as a result of the transfer. If this process began from β (Figure 1), we will find that $P_A/P_B > \Delta Q_B/\Delta Q_A$. Or, $\Delta Q_A \cdot P_A > \Delta Q_B \cdot P_B$, which is the same. It is profitable to tilt the mix in favor of product A. Management will add A and reduce B in the mix until it arrives at the optimum solution. If it began from α, where $P_A/P_B < \Delta Q_B/\Delta Q_A$, reductions in product A and additions of product B would have led to the same solution. At that point

---

2. The sign " $>$ " means that the left-hand side value is larger than the right-hand side value.

$$0 = \Delta Q_A \cdot P_A + \Delta Q_B \cdot P_B$$

Or, equivalently,

$$-\Delta Q_B \cdot P_B = \Delta Q_A \cdot P_A$$

The negative sign on the left-hand side indicates that ΔQ_B and ΔQ_A move in opposite directions. In the present example ΔQ_A is positive because this is how much the firm gains as a result of the experimental transfer, and ΔQ_B is negative because it stands for the corresponding decrease in the production of B. If we multiply the quantity gained in A by the price of A we get a measure of "benefit." The product of the quantity lost in B and the price of B is a measure of the corresponding "cost," our short-hand for "opportunity cost."[3] Of course, the negative sign before the "cost" is only symbolic of the "loss." The equality between $\Delta Q_B \cdot P_B$ and $\Delta Q_A \cdot P_A$ means that the benefit realized by producing more of one good "broke even" with the cost of producing less of the other.

If the firm did not know the simple rule of output value maximization, it could have arrived there experimentally, through an iterative, step-by-step cost-benefit analysis, trying out trade-offs "on the margin." Rearranging the above expression again, and abandoning the symbolic negative sign, we get $[\Delta Q_B/\Delta Q_A] = [P_A/P_B]$. Economists get rid of the negative sign by giving $[-\Delta Q_B/\Delta Q_A]$ a name, such as the "marginal rate of transformation."

Iteration could have begun anywhere on the curve and could have continued to transfer manpower until the two fractions became equal. From that point on the transformation curve, a vertical line to the horizontal axis (showing the scale for the production of A as OA) and a horizontal line to the vertical axis (showing the scale for the production of B as OB) would be the same as the quantities indicated by the direct approach.

The "law of rising relative costs" explains the transformation curve's shape. Start from a point of "high product B/low product A" combination. Moving by equal increments along the horizontal axis, you may observe that the vertical segments indicating the amounts of product B sacrificed lengthen. The ratio of the increasing "product B" segments sacrificed relative to the unitary increases in

---

3. "Opportunity cost" indicates the benefit foregone by having made a particular choice. It is a resource's best, unrealized alternative use. The nostalgic feeling of having missed something when doing "this" instead of "that" is the opportunity cost of the decision associated with the actual use of time. In this instance, time is the scarce resource.

"product A" gained is the essence of the "law of rising relative costs." The well-known "law of diminishing returns" is a closely related concept. The manpower withdrawn from B will follow a schedule "most useful in A production" first (or next). As the transfer continues, fewer and fewer suitable workers will show up at the work stations involved in producing A. Returns will also diminish because we are combining increasing amounts of labor with a fixed amount of machinery. After a while, workers will be bumping into one another, contributing less and less to the revenue derivable from A.

Since the maximization of revenue produces the minimum cost (the best cost/benefit ratio) at which any revenue may be generated along the transformation curve, the firm that divides its resources according to the stipulated rule *optimizes* their use. Consequently, "revenue maximization," "output value maximization," "cost-benefit analysis," "optimization," and "finding the equilibrium" are interchangeable in the present context.

Note that in our example, the prices were independent of the firm's optimization. This is the case when market power is chopped up into so many tiny parcels among competing firms that the decision by any one of them to increase or cut back production would have no influence on prices. But what if a firm is so powerful that it "makes" rather than "takes" prices? What if it is some sort of a monopoly?

That complicates decision-making because the monopoly's move to augment its sales must be accompanied by a reduction in the price it charges (as long as the monopoly does not control a biologically indispensable good such as drinking water). The competitive firm needed to adjust only one ratio, that of the marginal quantities, because the other ratio was "fixed" by the external world. The monopoly's market-power-given opportunity to engage in a pricing strategy brings with it the challenge of having to equate two moving ratios in order to optimize the use of its resources. (Although, as many attempts to monopolize markets and the strict laws designed to counteract such efforts in well-functioning market economies prove, the added complications may be worth the extra effort.)

The archetypal example of the transformation curve applied to national societies is the "guns versus butter" dilemma (Figure 2). A country, democratic or under the thumb of a bellicose dictator, is transferring the national labor force from "butter" (civilian goods production and services) to "guns" (military equipment production and services).

When a society at full employment starts out from a very high "butter" and very low "guns" combination (e.g., point A), and keeps transferring people at a constant rate (e.g., a certain number of persons per month) to armament production and military service, it can do so only at increasing sacrifice to its civilian sector.

If labor gets paid based on the work done (and for lack of alternatives, we consider the payment an adequate measure of personal contributions to the social product), we will see an increasing ratio between what the transferred workers earned in their original occupations and what they earn as newly transferred workers in production and services related to the military effort. The numerator of the ratio shows the forgone benefit (the "opportunity cost") and the denominator shows the actual benefit to society. This fraction will increase as the transfer progresses because, from the viewpoint of any specific job at hand, the military sector will employ not only less and less efficient labor, but will also increasingly deprive the civilian sector of workers who were more useful there.

In a social balancing act, such as in the "guns versus butter" example, there are no prices, fixed or manipulable, to help make decisions. There are only implicit valuations in the minds of the citizenry. We can call these the marginal social benefit of butter (MSB_B) and the marginal social benefit of guns (MSB_G), respectively. In short, MSB_B and MSB_G replace prices in the process of "equilibration." A high MSB_G/MSB_B ratio says that society treasures victory more than comfort and luxury. Moving along the curve from the high civilian and low military goods combination toward more "guns" and less "butter" could be stated as:

$$\text{The absolute value of } [\Delta Butter/\Delta Guns] < [MSB_G/MSB_B]$$
$$\text{or}$$
$$[\Delta Butter \times MSB_B] < [\Delta Guns \times MSB_G]$$

These algebraic expressions correspond to a public sentiment that may be summarized as: "Keep on transferring the resources from butter to guns." Beyond a certain point, however, society no longer wants to continue the transfer. It is "changing its mind" about MSB_B and MSB_G. It does not want to do with less "butter." Now the inequality in the above expression changes direction, indicating that the public is against further transfers. As a matter of fact, it would like to have more "butter" and less "gun." On the way there, the transfer had to pass through a point on the transformation curve where the ratio of marginal transfers was equal (in absolute value) to the reciprocal of marginal social benefit ratios. Theoretically, that is the same optimal point on the social transformation curve that a firm uses to split its manpower between two products on a smaller scale curve. The optimal point may be called the "maximum sacrifice" beyond which a society would not wage war. It is marked as "Limit" on Figure 2.

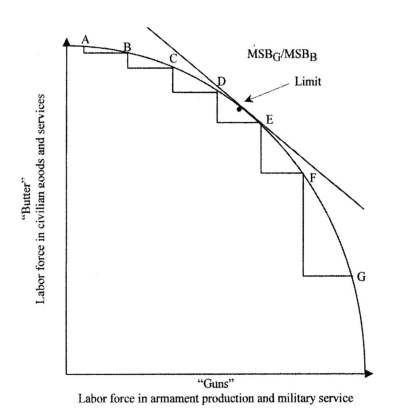

Figure 2

Transformation curve at the national level:
Allocation of labor between "Guns" and "Butter"

Although decisions that affect the allocation of resources for a democratically run country must be made without explicit valuations of the benefits and costs associated with choices, there are limits between which decisions settle down. The national society, in constant argument with itself, moves from a certain point on the curve in a given direction and stops at a certain point where further movement no longer enjoys public support.

Society's cost/benefit analysis is several degrees more complex than any monopoly's and not only because its decisions must rely on psychic rather than monetary valuations of costs and benefits (and because of a number of other obvious complicating factors). The monopoly still has a powerful external "sounding board." If its pricing policies met with public outcry, an unexpected decline in sales, or some government action, corporate management would know that it made a mistake and would have sufficient information to correct it by adjusting production plans, marketing strategies, and public relations policies. Optimizing the use of national resources through public cost-benefit analysis, i.e., gaining the maximum value from the use of resources for the community, happens in much greater isolation than decisions made even by the most powerful corporations. A society is both the decision maker and the main sounding board of its decisions.

"Main" but not exclusive. Contacts with the outside world, "the international community," still provide guidance for social choices by precedent. "See, other countries did the same thing and succeeded." Or, "See, other countries did it and failed." International agreements also limit choices. National governments in the EU, for example, cannot adopt *ad hoc* populist spending programs without consequences because the Maastricht Treaty sets limits to budget deficits. Relations among the United States, the EU, and Japan also exclude the adoption of national economic policies that would recklessly endanger international cooperation or would have a recognized negative effect on global welfare. Thus, the rest of the world is still there to give guidance and provide political arguments for self-correction. (The reader might already see one source of a qualitatively higher degree of complexity in global decision-making: There is no external sounding board.)

To date, the politically most difficult decisions involve the allocation of national resources in a democracy at peace. The division of the country's annual expenditures (GDP) between private and public goods (services subsumed to avoid repetition) is a perennial example of this.[4] The trade-off is between efficient private production, based on decentralized decisions, and the need for government to do things that private enterprise cannot do or would do badly. Government also has to ensure a minimum degree of social equity, which may be tantamount to domestic tranquility, the maintenance of property rights. Increasing the weight of public goods at the expense of private goods brings larger government and more taxation. Decreasing the second at the expense of the first means the exact opposite: smaller government and lower taxes. Decisions will generally be agonizingly slow through trial-and-error processes that may be interpreted with the help of the transformation curve. Society's goal is to maximize the use value of its resources or, equivalently, to find its equilibrium through public cost-benefit analysis.

By considering a national (annual) GDP the "scarce resource," we have extended the application of the transformation curve from physical constraints (e.g., labor force) to a constraint expressed in monetary terms. "Money" allows us to combine various types of resources, such as labor and capital, into a "compound" constraint. Such an extension increases the complexity of the optimizing process.[5]

When a nation splits its annual GDP between expenditures on private and public goods, it is deciding on the best use of the "annual dividend" on all national resources, land, labor, capital, and entrepreneurship. (GDP is at once aggregate output, income, and expenditure, as well as the return, or "dividend," on the nation's resources for a given period, e.g., one calendar year.) West European experience with the nationalization, denationalization, and partial renationalization of certain utilities in the postwar era may serve as an example of the process. After railroads were nationalized in country X, reallocating resources from private to public goods, society realized that rail service not only did not improve, but it also became more expensive. Denationalization received electoral support; railroads were privatized, reallocating resources from public to private goods. This change also did not work as expected and the government, enjoying voter support, reinjected some public participation into the system, making it into a semiprivate (or semipublic) hybrid. This search could be equated to moving on a national transformation curve that shows the division of the GDP between private and public goods (presuming the rest of the private/public division remained constant). Every step is an experimental marginal transfer of

---

4.   Private goods are those that people buy with their after-tax incomes and consume privately, such as an electronic gadget or assistance from a tax accountant. Public goods are provided by governments mostly from taxes and are consumed collectively, such as the highway system or services embodied in national defense and in the enforcement of "law and order."

5.   This does not make dealing with a single physical constraint necessarily simple. It may, in fact, be very complex, even within a firm. Its manpower may contain "heterogeneous layers," that is, employees with varying skills, qualifications, and trainability.

expenditures from one mode of application to another and comparing the ratio of transfers to the reciprocal of their associated marginal social benefit ratio.

Slow and cumbersome as this process may be, it is still being followed. For all issues facing democracies, the political system, telescoping public opinion, finds some sort of a balance, somewhere in the midsection of the transformation curve, away from the two possible extremes that most would consider outright undesirable. The elusive and changing marginal social benefits associated with movement on the imaginary transformation curve depicting the alternative uses of national resources are brought into rough equilibrium with the "marginal rate of transformation."

◆   ◆   ◆

Movement along smooth and continuous transformation curves reduces cost-benefit analysis to a wonderfully transparent mechanism. But its sweeping generalizations and simplifications threaten its practical significance. Some of the model's interrelated weaknesses and characteristics follow:

Forget about orderly transfer. Theoretically, the transfer of the scarce resource occurs in a strictly descending order of its usefulness for the expanding activity. Referring back to "guns-versus-butter," if there was a shortage of tank welders, welders working on tractors would be considered first, then welders in construction, and then nonwelders who could be trained. Of course, many other circumstances (e.g., exceptions made for humane reasons, physical distance, and *chance* developments) disable such idealizations from the outset.

Forget about perfect mobility. The transformation curve analysis considers scarce resources completely mobile between their alternative uses, assuming away difficulties, if not insurmountable obstacles, to their quick reallocation. For example, if labor happens to be the scarce resource at the national level, the model tacitly considers people willing and able to move on short notice, accept lower pay, and learn new professions almost instantaneously. No such quick and easy transformation is possible in real life.

Trying to make the model more realistic may harm its applicability. Broadening the concept of the transformation curve to represent two or more resources (and why not the totality of all available resources?) is a complexification with consequences. The more compound a constraint, the greater the opportunities for substitution within it, tending to hold at bay "the law of increasing costs," deforming the curve's characteristic concavity. If labor and capital together "is" the scarce resource, substitution in search of a minimal increase in costs, as we move along the curve, can go both ways within the (compound) resource, with the possibility of obtaining a temporary reprieve from the law of increasing costs. Although such complexification of the constraint tends to make the model more realistic, it blurs the curve's capacity to inform.

Potholes and gaps. The assumption of a smooth transformation curve, offering a continuum of economically and technically viable choices, is often unrealistic. A firm usually cannot reduce output in one product and increase output in another by such tiny steps that the transfer could be considered a continuous, unbroken activity. More likely, production possibilities represent discrete combinations (mixes) of products. Connecting these points, one obtains graphs that only vaguely resemble a concave shape. This problem is even more obvious when one considers the division of two or more resources between two products. If each resource is considered separately, one obtains as many transformation curves as there are resources. Each transformation curve shows the output combinations that may be produced with the maximum utilization of the corresponding resource. Since all the resources considered are needed to produce either of the two commodities, the only feasible combinations of the two products are those included in the area that lies under every transformation curve. Connecting the corner points (created by the intersections of individual, resource-specific transformation curves) reveals a "stylized" concave shape made up of straight or curved line segments. Under these circumstances, firms may locate optimal solutions with the help of techniques known in economics as "linear and nonlinear programming." These methods have not yet reached wide application in finding direct solutions to society-wide allocation problems. When politics is present, that is, outside the confines of profit-maximizing businesses, economic optimization techniques rarely, if ever, gain the upper hand in making final decisions.

Combinations are more likely to form a continuum when the transformation curve refers to national resources, such as expenditures between alternative uses. However, not every point on the continuum may be a stable pair. For example, in dividing the GDP between public and private expenditures (through taxation, government borrowing and spending), the political debate will focus on orders of magnitude rather than on each dollar. There are likely to be discrete mixes that represent points of equilibrium, with generous ranges around them, toward which the scarce resource-disposing community would gravitate.

Transformation curve as a moving target. Overall economic growth expands transformation curves in a "Northeasterly" direction, like the contour of one fourth of an inflating balloon. Since expansion is a continuous process, analysis can only approximate transformation curves–approximations that time renders increasingly obsolete. Further, without the ability to anticipate the changes in the proportion of resources as an economy grows or to foresee the emerging technological possibilities of substitution among resources, the continuity of expansion makes uncertainty about the detailed characteristics of transformation curves even greater.

Whose marginal social benefit? The concept of "social benefit" lends itself to divergent definitions and subjective valuations. Narrowing down the mechanism of social cost-benefit analysis to a single individual, the transformation curve suggests that adult citizens, unbeknownst to themselves, carry algebraically expressible programs in their heads to interpret political messages and formulate the reasons behind their votes and other forms of participation in public life. Not even the most conscientious and well informed individual is aware that its political opinion is the result of veiled quantitative analysis. It is also true that politically passive individuals or those who trust the system completely delegate responsibility to their governments for making decisions on their behalf. But somehow, all the imperfect, mistaken, delegated judgments are still tallied up and society will express a rudimentary sense of balance between benefits and costs regarding all the uses of all the resources at once.

Despite all its weaknesses, the transformation curve remains a cherished tradition of theoretical economics, and not only as a pedagogical ploy. Its principles may be discovered in any situation in which cost-benefit analysis is used to divide up a resource (single or compound) between two alternative uses. We can detect its underlying logic and principles in family decisions over how to split the monthly paycheck between savings and consumption; in the arguments heard around the offices and hearing rooms of local governments on how much land should be dedicated to residential and nonresidential use; in state policies concerning the division of the highway fund between new construction and maintenance, in the painstaking, iterative process of a national governance to square free trade with the protection of domestic producers; in the growing debate over balancing economic growth with environmental protection. In all these cases, the presence of cost-benefit analysis means that neither of the two alternatives should be chosen at the exclusion of the other (i.e., the benefits vary) and that the resource (single or compound) in question is not always equally useful for both alternatives (i.e., the costs in terms of benefits foregone vary).

In the end, the transformation curve is indispensable for two reasons. First, there is nothing better. If the concave-to-the-origin shape, along with its weakening simplifications, makes the conclusions reached from its application wacky, other curvatures or lines are outright misleading or totally useless. A convex-to-the-origin (caved-in) transformation curve would push the decision toward one or the other extreme (e.g., product), since equal resource transfers would yield larger and larger increases in the resource's alternative use. Evidently, such a curve would thoroughly misguide choices under scarcity. The remaining alternative, the straight line, would be the same as confessing inability to decide because the ratio of marginal transfers (the marginal rate of transformation) would coincide with the price ratio or its social equivalent, the ratio of marginal social benefits. Every combination would be equally good.

Second, empirical observations bear out the model's most general prediction. With or without the analytical chinoiserie, explicit or implicit decisions about allocating resources always tend toward a compromise, somewhere between extreme solutions. Democratic social processes manage to land decisions concerning the use of any resource somewhere in the midsegment of the transformation curve. Voters may be indifferent; their own cost/benefit analyses may remain hidden even to themselves, but only as long as the political process does not raise the specter of instituting an extreme. Attention perks up when the transfer of resources for one particular use proceeds too quickly or when it is discovered that the transfer has already gone too far. Society's lack of choosing extreme solutions in dividing up resources validates the complex process of cost/benefit analysis behind the social transformation curve because "extreme" is a quantitative measure, hiding the combination: a lot of something (let us say the "first thing") and very little of the complementary something else (let us call it the "second thing"). If the community ends up at an extreme and it has too much of the "first thing" and too little of the "second thing," it wants to move away from this combination. The average citizen's thoughts may be transcribed as

$$[\Delta \text{Amount of the first thing} \times \text{MSB}_{first}] < [\Delta \text{Amount of the second thing} \times \text{MSB}_{second}]$$

Letting some of the "first thing" go will represent a smaller cost (in terms of benefits foregone) than the benefit brought by having more of the "second thing." It is clear which political program, which candidate the voter will favor. Such analysis might just be a vague public sentiment. Political leanings may be nothing more than the nagging awareness of a high opportunity cost, the confused wish of wanting something else. If the "first thing" is the share of government in the GDP and the "second thing" is the private sector's share, the social cost/benefit analysis might be as simple as a personal opinion: "The government is too big. I support the program intended to cut taxes and lower government spending. Many who work in government offices would be more useful if they started their own business or sought employment in the private sector." When, after much public debate, false starts, and disappointments ("the political noise"), programs that enjoyed the most public support came into existence, the citizenry might feel temporarily released from the disequilibrium that burdened the community. Political hypertension subsides; people now want to talk about something other than having had too much of one thing and not enough of the other.

The process of recognizing imbalance and wanting to move toward balance implies the existence of a transformation curve in the background. It is there stylistically and imperfectly; nevertheless, it reveals the central tendency to find "goldilockean" solutions or at least reduce or avoid immoderation in public choices. Calling the result for a national society "collectively constructed equilibrium" may be a stretch. It is more like a temporary stasis, a shaky suspension of disharmony, a middle ground on which the antagonists momentarily do not wish to clash.

Decisions made under constraints by large groups (e.g., entire national populations) are tedious; they often border on the unmanageable. Unlike market prices, social valuations are somatically stored information. They are not available from published lists; they cannot be read on boards or computer screens. But the subjective nature of values attached to social choices notwithstanding, the implied marginal benefits must have a measure of rigidity and independence *vis-à-vis* actual conditions brought on by previous choices. Were it not so, the marginal benefit ratio would slavishly follow spontaneously occurring or dictatorially imposed conditions, with the result that whatever happens would "feel" optimal. Any world would be the best possible world; judgment and irritation emanating from relatively high opportunity costs would be absent.

The ability of the *mind* to distinguish between "what is" and "what ought to be" and then live by a socially-made decision, even if it diverges from one's own preference, goes beyond the requirement to have information about the current state of affairs and politically supported programs to alter them. It presupposes a nationally shared spiritual foundation that has intellectual, emotional, and legal dimensions. To make and carry out national decisions, that is, for a country to be able to deliver a coordinated strain of somatic energy, this common spiritual foundation must be manifest as individualized meaning of community and conviction about a shared destiny; that "we are in the same boat;" that there is a "we." The actual contents of this spiritual foundation depend largely on the *mesoscopic*, specific language-mediated adaptation of the prevalent *global system* (or an alternative to it during the paroxysmal times of *chaotic transition*). But the contents are also strongly influenced by the country's history, its heritage of humanistic values, and its tradition-honed ways of implanting the appreciation of unique historical experience into the individual. The legal dimension is a basic canon of law, e.g., a constitution that captures the most elementary conditions of social life and provides the abstract first principles to guide the evolving socioeconomic relations within *global system*-sanctioned institutional limits. Shared thinking, feeling, and willing submission to laws–the ingredients of the common spiritual foundation–make nations into cohesive polities.

Interaction between the rationally sensed but empirically elusive common spiritual foundation and the politically delivered choices for society's direction seems vague, perhaps even nonexistent. But this impression comes from looking too closely at the microstate of connected *minds* in a reduced time frame. In retrospective analyses on national decisions, the principle of the idealized transformation curve reappears. Actual decisions move on this curve like a ball (each decision a position) searching for its resting place.

THE TRANSFORMATION CURVE'S APPLICABILITY TO THE GLOBAL SOMATIC/EXTRASOMATIC CHOICE

Figure 3 illustrates the concept of the *global transformation curve*. The approach can help analyze the global choice between population and material output[6] only if the quantitative relationship between these two variables reflects the "law of increasing costs;" that is, if it can be illustrated by a concave-to-the-origin transformation curve, and if there is a shared sense of marginal valuation of more people versus more output at the global level. We deal with the first condition here and with the second one in the next chapter.

As said before, there is no direct and ready method to estimate the level of the three *exergic* constraints. Using up free energy in matter, for example, is no indication of the extent to which *ecological order* has diminished and *certitude about*

---

6. Material output includes all "things" made of matter. The social product, the GDP, is the final demand for material output (thus excluding intermediary inputs) plus the final demand for services. National GDPs summed and screened for double (or multiple) counting yield the Gross World Product (GWP). Global material output is GWP minus services. A rough breakdown of material output is "agriculture" and "industry." The service sector's independence from the material output is limited. Once the limit is crossed, increase in services entails increase in material output. Interdependence is also manifest when services decrease.

the environment has declined. They are presumed to be equal along some quantitative scale, since they are three manifestations of the same phenomenon.

The tragic hurricane season in the United States during 2005 was the first forceful reminder of this oneness. Top-level scientists tied the increased frequency and strength of hurricanes to global warming, implying that *cultural evolution* has already eaten deeply into the *ecological order*. Dealing with the damage will exhaust low-entropy matter because reconstruction raises the demand for material and energy. Assuming continued economic growth, i.e., no recession, the accelerated depletion of *geocapital* must entail the increased transfer of low-entropy matter from the *global environment*. The impossibility of legitimizing the knowledge that maximum-speed economic expansion, regarded as historically beneficial, may become harmful is a sign of diminishing *certitude of information* about the physical condition of the *terrestrial sphere*.

To put the thermodynamic perspective to practical use, the international community will have to overcome the difficulties involved in calculating the limits to *cultural evolution*. One solution appears to be the unification of the three *exergic* constraints into a single measure. We define *ecoplasm* as the amount of dependably usable low-entropy matter, *ecological order*, and consistent, accessible information about the environment, all at once. It will have to be approximated by taking into account the use of natural resources and the durability of environmental conditions for specific population and output combinations. (The shortcut of quantifying the original, undivided concept of free energy extractable from matter in the *terrestrial sphere* seems to be closed. Calculation of a synthetic measure must begin with the analysis of the forms through which the overall, general limit is manifest.)

A given amount of *ecoplasm* constrains growth in both somatic and extrasomatic directions and does so in conformity with the law of increasing costs. There is, of course, the negative, "nothing better out there" argument. The convex-to-the-origin shape defies the logic of scarcity, and a straight line negates the possibility of optimization. The concave-to-the-origin shape remains. However, there are also "positive ways" to grasp the validity of this assertion by looking at various trade-offs embedded in the overall somatic/extrasomatic choice, the dilemma between reproduction and production. Shifts in this choice cause changes in the use of specific resources within the overall constraint, a condition sufficient to recognize the "law of rising relative costs" and the closely related phenomenon of "diminishing returns."

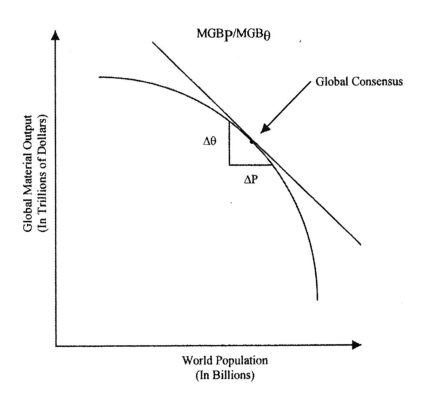

Figure 3
*Transformation curve applied to the global somatic
(people)/extrasomatic (material output) choice*

Maximizing aggregate human felicity. "Aggregate felicity" equals the felicity perceived by the average individual multiplied by the number of individuals.[7] Once a closed space is saturated, steady increase in one can be achieved only at the growing expense of the other. Therefore, the "maximum" may be found on a concave-to-the-origin transformation curve showing trade-offs between the number of people and level of per capita material well-being.

Balancing population quality and quantity to maximize strength. Substituting "phyletic strength" for "aggregate felicity" leads to the same conclusion. A very large global population, combined with a relatively small material output, would curtail progress in science, technology, and industry. Yet, without such progress, nature would "select" against the species. Given the unchangeable arrow of time and the inevitable and unpredictable depletion of *exergic constraints,* huge amounts of physical capital will be needed to control the environment, produce energy, and, ultimately, save the species by expanding its spatial presence. This line of reasoning implies high average material output per capita combinations on the transformation curve. However, survival also depends on the size of the population, on the foison of human biomass. The larger the number of people, the less diseases (caused by factors other than saturation-level population density), harmful mutations infecting the gene pool and environmental catastrophes of any source would threaten annihilation. If movement toward either extreme "increases costs," that is, damages the prospects of phyletic longevity in terms of "strength lost," intermediary solutions lead to the habitual geometric shape, offering optimal compromise.

Balancing the use of geocapital to minimize the loss of strategic options. A combination of very high population and very low material output would shift global production toward agriculture; very low population and very high output would shift it toward industry. Each extreme would endanger *homo sapiens* by narrowing strategic options in the face of nature's future challenges. The first extreme would lead to an accelerated exhaustion of soil and a drift toward lower population levels. The second extreme would run down energy and metal reserves more quickly, lowering the ceiling on global productive capacity. Moving from one extreme to the other, the danger of being forced into narrower sets of choices first decreases, then increases again. This points to the possibility of finding equilibrium on a curve that features increasing costs. Indeed, an intermediary point on a concave-to-the-origin transformation curve minimizes the loss of future population/output choices.

---

7.   This idea originates from British moral and political philosopher, William Paley (1743-1805). See *Gould, 2002,* p. 230.

Balancing the use of economic resources. Material output may be thought of as the value of a production function that contains an extrasomatic and a somatic block. With notations:

$$Q = A \text{ (extrasomatic inputs, somatic inputs)}$$

where "Q" is total material output and "A" is the function describing technology, the application of both human and physical capital. The first group of inputs includes raw material, energy, other variable material inputs, and the services of fixed capital (depreciation). Each of these components can be expressed as a flow of free energy used up in the process of production. (At present, most extrasomatic inputs come from nonrenewable resources.) The second group is labor in all its forms and levels. It is somatic energy spent in conjunction with the deployment of human capital over the full range of possible combinations, from sheer brawn to the brainstorms of a wheel-chair-bound scientist. (Since the congealment of free energy is the common factor in somatic and extrasomatic uses of *ecoplasm*, our application implies an "exergy theory of value.")

The somatic input used in producing Q is only one part of total somatic input into the economy. The rest is human energy spent to enhance the quality of life directly. Some of these efforts, such as medical care, education, and social services, are vital, and some of them are luxuries (e.g., consultation on interior decoration, hair salons for dolls). The larger the population, the larger the service sector. Going in a Northwesterly direction on the transformation curve toward more material goods and lesser population, there would have to be a transfer of services from the nonmaterial-productive to the material-productive subsector. One would first sacrifice the least desirable services to obtain the most needed goods. At one point, vital services would be lost at the cost of less needed goods. The balance point along this scale must be on a concave-to-the-origin curve. Going in a Southeasterly direction, the same logic would apply with reversed arguments.

Note also that the production of goods is tied to a certain amount of capital (at a given level of technology) and the available labor mimics changes in the population. Therefore, hidden in every choice between extrasomatic or somatic use is a capital-to-labor ratio, one of the critical concepts in the economic analysis of long term-equilibrium. (In the simplified conceptualization presented, once we select the level of labor force along the horizontal axis, capital goods, embodying "technology," become the sole variable that determines the level of physical output.)

If the world decided to move in a Northwesterly direction from a given equilibrium point to a new, higher capital/lower labor position, it would pull out labor-saving technologies from its store of accumulated scientific-technical knowledge and would begin to substitute capital for labor. Acting "economically," the first step in reducing labor and adding capital would be selected in such a way as to maximize the gain in output relative to the combined value of labor and capital inputs. The phased reduction of labor, paired with "labor-replacing" capital investment will increase output. (Automation and robotization are extreme examples of this.) The second step would result in the next best gain in output relative to the combined inputs, and so on until the policy goal is achieved or the output-augmenting potential of the capital-for-labor substituting technology is exhausted. In either case, such an "economically" conducted substitution process fits the transformation curve's shape.

If the world wanted to move in a Southeasterly direction to a lower capital and higher labor force combination, it might transfer employment from the regulated mass production sectors into the unregulated, more labor intensive activities of local services and small-scale arts and crafts. The "economical" approach mandates structural shifts in activity while minimizing the loss to world output. The sequence of growing losses in production as a result of moving toward the new target combination by phasing in employment in some chosen units once again will trace a concave curve, regardless of how many "balancing acts" had to be taken into consideration at the same time. The curve would still remain concave to the origin, reflecting some compromise among the separately considered decisions under constraint.

The future scientists of global survival strategy will have to determine a map of *ecoplasmic* layers (Figure 4). The outermost layer represents the loci of *Point X*s, the next one the loci of *Point X-1*s, and so on. We may call these *layer X, layer X-1*, etc., respectively. Layer *X-15* is the *ecoplasmic* level that allows for population/material output combinations that are uniformly 14 (model-calibrated) magnitudes more enduring and safer than next-to-lethal combinations (*Point X-1*s on *layer X-1*). In the illustration, this is the chosen layer that encloses the domain of eligible transformation curves.

The roughly concentric layers will have to be proxied. It will come down to estimating the impact of population/material output pairs upon global resources (renewable and nonrenewable) and the environment, grouping the same level of impact, period of sustainability, and risk of approaching catastrophic levels on the same (concave-to-the-origin) layer. Thresholds (jumps) in these factors would separate layers. Being below the chosen layer, marginal benefits to the species exceed marginal costs. Above it, marginal costs exceed marginal benefits.

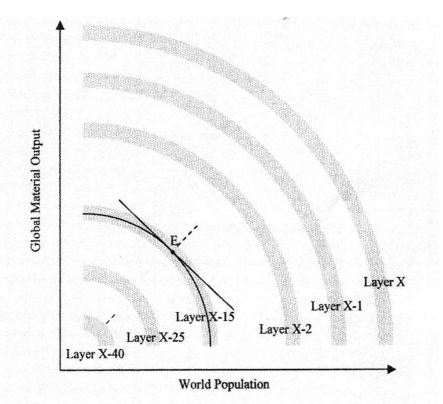

Figure 4

*A map of ecoplasmic layers with global transformation curve
in selected layer and optimal point (E) on it*

Next, the optimal transformation curve within the layer of choice will have to be found. The selected transformation curve, representing "equi-*ecoplasmic*" use, is the planet's effective carrying capacity. To minimize the consequences of presumed errors in calculations, the optimal curve would have to be placed in the midsection of the chosen layer.

The third step in finding world equilibrium is to determine the optimal position on the selected transformation curve. The value ratio, which is expected to identify it, compares the global marginal benefits of somatic and extrasomatic uses. Here, the "opportunity costs" of having more people (valued through the *marginal global benefits of population*, MGB_P) are the benefits forgone as a result of not having the material output that could have been obtained from the same amount of *ecoplasm*. Having more material output (valued with the help of the *marginal global benefits of output*, MGB_Q) means benefits forgone with the unborn who may have been supported with the amount of *ecoplasm* used for productive purposes. If the global estimate has correctly identified the optimum, the world will be in equilibrium when the following holds:

$$\Delta\text{population} \times MGB_P = \Delta\text{output} \times MGB_Q$$

This equation is similar in concept to firm-or national-level optimization discussed earlier in this chapter. It represents the canonical condition of humanity's planetary equilibrium.

It would stand to reason that a band rather than a point should be identified to avoid "knife-edge" solutions. This would allow for alternative substitutions of preferences (intramarginal trade-offs) while remaining within the bounds of identical overall desirability.

The challenges of finding the indicated optimum and accounting for its implied dynamics and consequences in reasonable detail cannot be overestimated. "They" of the far future will have to take into account that a planetary transformation curve, like Balzac's *Peau de chagrin*,[8] is expected to shrink along the time-scale characteristic of the chosen *ecoplasmic* layer. Given the same level of caution, the frontier of *cultural evolution* will contract as *exergy* is irreversibly exhausted. One of the factors that would distinguish one *ecoplasmic* layer from the rest is its period of sustainability, e.g., one generation for *layer X-1*, 30-40 generations for *layer X-15*. But these assessments will never be settled. Scientific-technological development, including estimates of *ecoplasm*, a period lived in extreme environmental consciousness and conservation, and successful exploita-

---

8.   Reference to Balzac's 1831 novel, *The Wild Ass's Skin*.

tion of extraterrestrial resources (e.g., mining the moon) may allow a generation to reduce the level of caution and initiate movement toward a higher transformation curve within the same layer or even toward a higher layer. Given that all somatic/extrasomatic combinations represent *metastable* equilibria (a collection of rigorously indefinable feasible solutions with precarious stability) but have a tendency to shrink, mankind, wanting to maximize its presence on Earth, will always be experimenting on its own skin to locate that real but elusive world equilibrium. The concept of "sustainability," frequently heard in the present *discourse* on the environment and exhaustible resources, will always have to remain relative, with unknown risks involved in the belief of having found its requisites.

The *ecoplasmic* constraint is more complex than any in the application of optimization techniques thus far. Within it, resources can be combined and recombined to play out the law of scarcity for some time. If we move, for example, from high material output/low population toward lower material output/higher population, new emphasis on education and health care could potentially prevent output from declining or might conceivably even increase it. Services would automatically expand. If, as a result, labor productivity grew, the world would experience decreasing rather than increasing costs. (Costs and productivity have a reciprocal relationship.) The creation of time capsules (like the one in which we live in the present moment) tends to shut out the ultimate reality, namely that matter is always in unidirectional movement. (Matter is, in fact, unidirectional movement.) This could make later adjustments more difficult because the law of increasing costs would eventually regain the upper hand.

Any "mobility" of significance between population and productive capacity will take generations and could easily get off the envisaged track. Goal-oriented population policies raise especially repugnant prospects. Reduction according to an optimal schedule that intends to retain "the most productive individuals," "the ones with the highest human capital" when making space for production capacity, sounds like "rid the planet of the *untermensch.*" The opposite, the process of "making space for the most productive humans" while reducing productive capacity, implies the cultivation of an *übermensch* through selective breeding or genetic engineering.

Even under the assumption of voluntary compliance, a change in population could take such a long time that the circumstances originally warranting its target level might change. Moreover, a population in the process of expansion or contraction has built-in tendencies that make projections less reliable. An increasing population "becomes younger" (on the average, of course) and this creates a momentum for further increase by raising the fertility rate above the replacement rate. When the population decreases, the opposite happens; decrease turns into deceleration. Then there is a vast space for completely spontaneous developments. Unexpected increases or decreases in fertility, mortality, and morbidity tend to counteract or exaggerate desired trends. The world would have to live with the consequences for generations. While the slowness and unpredictability of changes in the level of population will make movement to a desired "equilibrium" point on the transformation curve slow, and to some extent unpredictable, it is not difficult to identify reasons why the movement to that point could be derailed, or why the global community could be displaced from such a point once it had been reached. Two broad categories of problems are likely to upset the results of transformation calculus, even at stationary, selected allocations between somatic and extrasomatic uses.

Priority conflicts. The available material resources and population (labor force) imply a certain level of GWP (material goods output plus services). As in any other budget, the GWP will contain nondiscretionary and discretionary items. Suppose the global community has reached its targeted population/material output combination (determining a certain GWP), believing that it could stay there for a few hundred years. An unexpected rise in the demand for countering environmental decay, combined with increased costs of food and industrial energy production signals shrinkage in the transformation curve. Then what?

Evidently, the discretionary items represent the only stream of output that may be reduced without violating the equilibrium level of population and its basic requirements. Residual as it may sound by name, this category determines the availability of consumer goods. Will a future generation, fully aware that it is living on a scientifically calibrated transformation curve, give up its comfort without questioning the need for it? The public might initiate movement toward a lower lying transformation curve (reducing population and material output) within the same *ecoplasmic* layer or it might urge movement toward another layer closer to the origin. The debate might ensue over balancing "current" needs against those of even more distant future generations.

The terra-formation of the "fourth rock" and the mass transportation of people over millions of miles across the void in vehicles that may resemble autonomous human settlements, with subsidiary capability to produce food, will be very expensive and are likely to be "end-loaded." This ultimate step may be way beyond our *macrohistoric* horizon, but we can be completely sure that, given a ceiling on global productive capacity at maximum use, it will lead to the reduction in the supply of some goods as the resource demand of this multicentury undertaking overflows expectations.

The economic consequences of shifts among various uses of the material output might represent a more immediate source of difficulties. For instance, if the world economy had seven "intermediate sectors," such as agriculture, mining, energy production, manufacturing, construction, infrastructure, and services, a shift from "other goods" into "environmental protection" might require more energy than what can be released by "other goods." "Other goods" might release claims on capacity (e.g., in construction) that environmental protection does not need. What will the world decide to do if sectoral shifts create excess capacity or capacity shortage? Allow population to increase in the first case and see to its reduction in the second, with all the consequences of reshaping the critical proportion between somatic and extrasomatic inputs? In addition to such developments, contingencies that require much more or much less production may also turn up, raising the same questions.

Scientific-technological progress. Current economic theory holds that technological progress pushes out national transformation curves (in the conventional application, i.e., showing the division of productive capacity among various goods). It enables economies to stretch available resources and make them produce more than before, increasing what economists call the "total factor productivity" (the aggregate value of output divided by the aggregate value of inputs). Our theory denies the possibility that science and technology can expand a properly determined *ecoplasmic* layer without the risk involved in operating closer to *layer X*, i.e., without reducing the originally determined level of sustainability. A certain amount of free energy separates any given transformation curve from the boundary of peril. Believing that the *ecoplasmic* layer (with the selected transformation curve enclosed in it) could expand while retaining the level of safety margin implies a parallel expansion of *layer X*, in violation of the *second law*. (Scientific information cannot create free energy.) However, there is no shortage of opportunities for error. The use of *ecoplasm* may intensify, backfiring in the future. The hypothesis that a new class of technology may have reduced the shrinkage of the production possibility frontier may or may not be true.

Technological development has been a largely decentralized process. To the extent that new products and production techniques may endanger stability, limits will have to be placed on the flow of "research and development" into productive practice. The number of new products will certainly not increase at the same rate as during the mature years of classical *cultural evolution*, in the age of petroleum and ever-expanding intraindustry trade. Rather, the infusion of scientific-technical knowledge into the economy will help replace old products with new, higher quality and longer lasting ones. It is difficult to imagine today how future scientifically oriented societies will deal with these problems.

Beyond ordinary progress, which causes shifts to play out slowly over long periods, extraordinary progress and industrial and agricultural revolutions will also doubtlessly occur, redefining the optimal level of the capital-to-labor ratio and the substitutability between labor and capital. Each time this happens, the position and shape of the transformation curves will change, as if an invisible finger pushed the forward button on a slide projector and the layers showed up with altered widths and slopes. Although a "true" *ecoplasmic* constraint cannot expand, the world will never be sure if such a constraint (always indirectly determined or "proxied") is really true. The dance of layers could understandably rekindle the search for a more preferred layer and the best curve in it. It may even reopen the problem of ideal individual behavior, challenging the *global system* in place.

Barring unforeseen events, the most important, never-vanishing line of scientific research will likely aim at capturing extraterrestrial space with matter. This will be the only way to retain the pleasures and satisfaction that current generations associate with the so-called "cowboy economy" (the term some social scientists use to symbolize the limitless drive of business) in contrast to the "Dutch economy" of living behind dunes and dikes, never forgetting the imminent danger nature poses to *culture*. If things go well, the generations living on the transformation curve will be Dutch at "home" and cowboys "away from home." As "Dutch," they will have to discover the transformation curve's "laws of motion," the transitional dynamics and adjustment mechanisms involved in moving from one world equilibrium to another. They will have to learn how to recognize and avoid "traps" from which it will be difficult to break out; how to deal with emergencies that may affect several generations.

Eventually, even the protection of life on Earth will require a combination of "Dutch" and "cowboy" attitudes. Approaching asteroids will have to be diverted, perhaps by launching rockets with nuclear warheads at them. The growing distance between the Earth and the Moon (currently estimated at one-and-a-half inches per year) will increase the planet's rotational wobble, reducing its suitability for human life, beginning perhaps as early as in the next millennium. Some astrophysicists ("cowboys" at heart, no doubt) suggest protecting life on Earth by "bringing" another moon (for instance Jupiter's "Europa") into its orbit.

Actual calculations to determine World Equilibrium, *the optimal position on an optimal transformation curve inside the optimal ecoplasmic layer*, would demand an immense array of data on natural resources, technology, the economic structure, and labor. Mathematical models that allow for the simultaneous consideration of several decision dilemmas and still produce optimal solutions will be required. Economists could be of great help. Studies in general equilibrium and dynamic optimization might serve as the natural foundations for the development of formalized and comprehensive *global transformation curve* analysis.

What about "marginal global benefits?" Can anything even vaguely reminiscent of microlevel evaluations of macrolevel conditions develop? Yet without an informed and cohesive geocentric electorate, the transformation curve would be as useless for the global community as it would be for the business firm without market prices or for the citizens of a nation without their approximate sense of priorities. The ability to make intertemporal decisions that affect the species in its totality under conditions that are drastically different from current ones will have to be in the *mind* of the average future *progenitor cum producer and consummator.* The syncretistic reconciliation between levels of population and economic activity will have to be internalized.

9

Telos, Saga, and Homo Novus

[Life on the transformation curve will require global decision-making. The world will need to set goals; therefore, it must become a cohesive polity. Such development seems remote, but we may derive encouragement from what people would not accept about the future today were they fully informed and systematically polled. A scientifically founded common view of the human condition could live side-by-side with *Religion*, although not without affecting particular aspects of it. Instauration of GS3 would shed new light on the interplay between genes and the socially constructed environment; it would make the world aware of the thermodynamic rhythm of universal history.]

Even if work on the *global transformation curve* had to begin today, the international community of scientists and academics would not be at loss. The first estimates may be considered flawed and rudimentary by later judgment, but they could still be made, and during a relatively short period of time. It is all a question of organization and finance. The obstacle ahead is more psychological and political than technical. Can a socioeconomic behavior appropriate for "life on the transformation curve" develop? Could the average individual be persuaded to adhere to a fertility rate considered optimal for the species? Considering the multiple dimensions and complexity of organizing the corporate world, is there some space between enforced voluntarism and crippling conflicts, actual or menacing? Can billions of people consent to calculations that would forever affect their lives and the fortunes of their families and nations? Could this actually happen? It seems impossible, yet this is the only path that does not lead toward extinction.[1]

The world will have to become aware of itself. It will have to go from a passive to an active voice concerning its future; it will have to become an optimizing agent, a Darwinian actor, a homogeneous polity. In Freudian terminology, the

---

1. Ervin Laszlo demonstrated the inevitability of such a vital crossroad in the human story. See *Laszlo, 1994.*

species will have to graduate from its amorphous and spotty self-perception in the "Id" phase of human development to the self-conscious, reality-oriented "I" phase. Global society cannot metamorphose into a coral bush, a single organism (Robinson Crusoe stranded on a moving rock in space), or into a colony of social insects (a semi-organism with unified consciousness and billions of feelers), but it will have to get its act together. It will have to become street-wise on the Milky Way.

In individual and national development there has always been the guiding influence of a projected mirror image: successful individuals and *vanguard* nations, respectively. But a "one world" will most likely have no mirror image other than itself under different circumstances. To select its course, it will have to scan options by projecting itself into alternative futures.

The closer individuals are in their thinking, the easier it is for them to make collective decisions and to pursue common goals. A complete uniformity of thought would imply a single evolutionary decision maker. GS3 is envisaged more as the fulfillment of the minimum cohesion of human consciousness required to retain the species' long-term vitality. Needless to say, uniformed social administrators mandating compliance through the chanting of slogans (pulled from a basket of half-truths) across the globe is unacceptable. A voluntarily united and harmoniously cooperative world is the ideal. A global community that can institutionalize its conflicts and channel its particular griefs and discontents, without ever going beyond political warfare (which already implies some moral desolation and the demotion of general interest), is adequate.[2] We may identify two fundamental, strongly interdependent conditions for such a community under the hypothetical GS3: shared agenda and elevated self-identification with others.

TELOS

A fellow student in the sixth grade decided to become a physician. He checked out thick books on medicine and related subjects from the public library and, in two years, he walked and talked like an M.D. Even adults seemed to respect his understanding of medical problems and were careful not to deflate his precocity. On the way home from school one day I asked what made him decide "to become a doctor." He answered very frankly. On a hot summer day he saw a

---

2.   The world as a polity has been subject to scholarly study for decades. See *Modelski, 1972, 1987, 2003.*

beautiful young woman faint at a crowded bus stop. "Is there a doctor here?" someone shouted. There was a stir in the back and the crowd politely made way for a young gentleman, then watched in silent approbation as he quietly and confidently pulled out his stethoscope to examine the helpless angel. That was my friend's moment of decision. I guess he often replayed the scene in his mind, substituting himself for the learned man. In due time, he became a well-respected professor of medicine. The question youth counselors and personnel managers ask, "How do you see yourself ten years from now?" is quite relevant. Of course, making an early career decision does not necessarily ensure success. Temptations, impulses, other influences, and totally *random* developments could derail it.

Organizations also keep an eye on the future. From the tiny business or local government to the largest nation state and beyond, every organization has a name for the coordinated strain of individual wills, however general or vaguely conceptualized: goal, purpose, long-term strategy, mission, vision, *leitmotiv*, or simply a projected state or condition. All these terms stand for the directed flow of somatic energy, the grand total of which molds and expands the colossal atomistic configuration of phyletic self-organization.

The lack of an explicit notion of what the organization wants beyond the whirlwind of "now," with its thicket of probabilities for unexpected turns, destroys the framework necessary for effective interaction among individuals. Registering, processing, and using information (what "functioning" always is in the final analysis) require stable, time resistant points of reference. Without them, a feeling of purposefulness, direction, and collective *élan* give way to disorientation and internal conflict—the group equivalents of madness and rebelliousness. In short, no optimizing behavior is connected with present action without a *telos* (Greek for "end"). The reverse must also be true. If the organism or the organization engages in optimizing behavior, it must have a *telos*. To have one, the future must be valued; it "must loom large," as Robert Axelrod put it. We are inclined to make it loom large when we are quiet and contemplative. Even looking ahead at a distant point during a leisurely walk is reassuring.

The fact that national societies avoid extremes in the use of scarce resources proves that they are also optimizing organizations. Optimization occurs as citizens engage in implicit cost/benefit analysis in connection with their political actions. They are conscious of their collective direction. Of course, the particularities of *microscopic* adaptations and the coexistence of multiple *entrainments* make the individualized perception of a national *telos* disparate in content and intensity. For most people, it may only be a bleary awareness about how conditions could be improved. Nevertheless, the population of a modern democratic society implicitly "understands" that it "has" best future interests and wants. Being drawn in a specific direction plays the role of the general principle applied to concrete problems of allocative dilemmas.

Whether we look at an individual or an organization, the *telos* always refers to relative positions. Explicitly or implicitly, it refers to rivals. The child who aspires to become a member of a profession, the firm that wants to grow or preserve its position in the market, and the nation in quest of increased material welfare all measure themselves against comparable others: individual versus individual, firm versus firm, and nation versus nation. The *telos* is important in guiding and judging personal endeavors. It is like calcined rock in the cement that holds society together.

The modern nation state's *telos* is eternal improvement, reflecting, in essence, the wish to continue *cultural evolution*. Thus, the ultimate purpose is not an elaborated end-state, but the continuation of a process. It still is applied as an internalized "sounding board" against which individuals compare and evaluate political *entrainments* that concern society-wide decisions.

The wish to continue *cultural evolution* has never been unique to the *vanguard*. It was, and still is, the globally shared national *telos*, particularly its material wealth aspect. Every single country wants to increase its per capita income, differing only in the extent to which it has been successful. Success requires realism and a "quorum," a critical mass of public support. In retrospect, we know that communist and national socialist visions were manifestations of a transitional *macrohistoric* turbulence and failed to meet these requirements. Public support for their realization waned as their respective unrealistic natures became apparent. The present unpromising outlook for economic and social progress in many developing countries may be attributed to one of the following. They did not choose realistic paths; they did, but the policies associated with them did not enjoy or lost public support, or there is no realistic path for increasing material well-being for everybody. The first two explanations refer to relative weaknesses and disadvantageous initial conditions in the race for a higher share of world output. The third one reminds us that one of the first two must happen to some people. The Earth's physical constraints disallow the endless swelling of everybody's extrasomatic El Dorado.

◆   ◆   ◆

The world cannot measure or evaluate itself by interplanetary standards, and so far, it has not compared itself systematically to its own alternatives through forward projected images. Therefore, understandably, the *Global Telos* (*Telos*) is indeterminate. Forcing the issue somewhat, it may be identified as a future state where *cultural evolution* came to fruition. The poor became rich and the rich richer, as measured by real per capita GDP. The pursuit of this *Telos* is characterized more by compartmentalized national approaches, domestic economic and social policies, and GS2-typical "enlightened mercantilist" conduct of international economic relations, than by a united, global, *multilateral* strategy. Our *Telos* is dysfunctional. It is flawed in both means and ends. Sooner or later it will have to be abandoned.

Although the problems of changing the current limping phantom of a *Telos* into a healthy and realistic one may be formidable, the *macrohistoric* perspective is encouraging. Over the past two centuries, there has been an indisputable increase in the recognition that the success of pursuing material well-being within the confines of national borders depends on the success of similar efforts beyond the borders. International solidarity and understanding grew. This development received little recognition compared to the gushingly extolled progress in communications and transportation, "the shrinking of space and time," the exponential increase in the use of the Internet, the galloping advent of e-this and e-that. The *Code* has shown itself capable of evolving in the direction of clearly identifying a *Telos* that the world as self could not go without.

Since the human prospect depends on the long-term relationship between the species and the rest of nature, between *culture* and the *global environment*, GS3's *Telos* ought to reflect that. Without the penetration into individual consciousness that such a "big picture" indeed exists and is vitally important, there can be no tenable, explicit, and realistic *Telos;* there can be no systematic comparison of losses and gains involved in using the planet's resources because not even the dimmest notion about *marginal global benefits* associated with alternatives could develop.

Obviously, we cannot predict what *Telos* will eventually be engraved in human brains, but the following is a possibility: *Minimize the use of the (shrinking) carrying capacity and maximize preparations for multiplanetary existence while providing intervening generations with a decent standard of living and opportunity for personal fulfillment. Accumulate human capital, cultivate scientific ambitions; safeguard representative control, individual initiatives, and economic efficiency. Specifically (among the 50 major global extraterrestrial projects), terra-formation of Mars to be completed in year M; large-scale settlement activity to begin in M + k. Until M + k, the Earth's population should not exceed P billion souls and its annual material output should not exceed Q trillion in world currency units; global consensus could revise these constraints in light of new developments.*

SAGA

Just as goal orientation in the individual or in national society requires a coherent sense of self, GS3 is unthinkable without an underlying, planet-wide spiritual communality tied to a legal center (e.g., world constitution). Postwar European experience demonstrates that international integration is critically contingent upon a comprehensively binding legal source that restrains nationalistic self-centeredness equitably. The EU's difficulties in adopting a union-wide constitution also show that if the intellectual and emotional aspects of spiritual communality have not yet developed to the point at which such a constitution would be embraced, no hype about legal-technical preparations and no far-sighted government leadership could bring about popular legitimation.

We call the future globally shared way of thinking about social relations, life, and destiny the *Saga*, a word that implies a mixture of history, legend, and self-motivation. It will celebrate the past and incite romantic audacity about the future. Conceptually, it is the species-wide equivalent of the rational and emotive aspects of the common spiritual foundation that we identified in the previous chapter as characteristic of national polities.

The "ideal" *Saga* will have to be based on a scientific understanding of human society's cosmic context. It will have to recognize that thermodynamic processes frame our existence. Everything else around this unchanging Archimedean point will have to remain subject to revisions and updates as science progresses. As indicated, the *Saga* will have to fill not only intellectual, but also emotional needs in order to give meaning to life in a more cooperative and less competitive world; to sustain sacrifices and generate self-indulgent rhetorical tropes in symphonies and rhapsodies about prodigious achievements and prospects. Ideally, it will be both a doctrine of progress (since human survival requires eternal progress) and a psychic elixir. It ought to reinforce the much needed "go get it" exploratory-adventurous ideals that spur the individual to go further, to take on and transcend obstacles. It will have to be the symbol of the species' mega-perspective on existence; its life-blood, its soul.

Hopefully, this hypothetical, future ethos of phyletic self-promotion will neither be a rigidly fixed mono-ideistic writ aspiring to biblical status, nor will it turn into a vulgate. At present, only the protean, capacious, multivalent American democracy can give us an idea of the *Saga*'s place in GS3's societies. Based on this parallel, the core ideas will have to be so strong and so completely accepted that they would withstand the ambiguity required for autonomous thinking and welcome criticism and mocking in an "anything goes" free atmosphere. Indeed, where stand-up comedians are not allowed to poke fun at social values there is an "official ideology"–the wrong way to go. Unrestrained buffoonery is a required ingredient for the moral equilibrium of healthy societies.

The *Saga* will most likely refer to expressions that we would find esoteric, if not pure Orwellian "newspeak" today, but will be as familiar to "them" as capitalism, socialism, or the World Wars are to us. Perhaps it will have a flow of time structure. The following "Cliffs Notes," prepared for high-school students taking "evolutionary history" in the year 2150, illustrate the chasm between "them" and "us" that the intervening portentous events are likely to create.

We came from there (biological evolution); developed like that (cultural evolution); but after the Epoch of the Grand Catharsis, the world finally had to realize that Myopic Uncoordination would lead to ever-intensifying Endogenous Decline, Environmental Neo-Pandemics, rodent diet, anthropophagi, Life Camps, and genetic damage. Humanity crossed the crucial threshold of becoming collectively conscious. It rejected archaic divisions and internecine bloodletting; it became one nation and enabled itself to think, feel, and act as a Singular Dynasty while upholding majority rule and encouraging diversity through Equal-Status Personhood. With deep gratitude to the generations that came before us and with an unshakeable commitment to Diachronic Solidarity and scientific progress, we manage our Planetary Ecological, Social, and Economic Equilibrium and move toward the Telos to ensure our continued existence in defiance of Universal Entropy. The species' horizon is infinite. Humans intend to overcome any obstacle to secure life worthy of their culture, vitality, noble sacrifices, and the dream of fulfilling their Cosmic Destiny.

During the 1960s, Jacques Derrida, a philosopher on the short list of late 20th century's most influential thinkers, criticized the then extant East European Marxist order. (He did so also in defiance of many of his fellow intellectuals who roamed the Boulevards of Paris with copies of *l'Humanité*, France's communist daily, stuck under their arms.) "History and knowledge, *istoria* and *episteme*, have always been fixed (and not only as far as etymology or philosophy is concerned) so as to provide a subterfuge for keeping the present under control."[3] If the post-fragmented "historico-cultural" epoch that we associate with GS3 is to be considered successful from a contemporary vantage point, Derrida's generalization

---

3.   *Derrida, 1967*, p. 20.

should *not* apply to it. Manipulation and persuasion, with the help of symbolic language, will probably never cease. It will have to be right there at the inception of GS3. The search for a new global order is a continuous process, while its establishment, the creation of its *imprimatur*, is dated and localized. The *global system* spreads from a specific time and place to become universal partially through effective instigation that must contain a good dose of willful manipulation. But these actions should (according to current, democratic values) be more accurately described as noninvidious self-motivation than demagoguery–attempts to "engineer the soul of the masses" in the interest of an elite, perpetrating old or creating new inequities. We cannot envisage GS3 as effective unless it features socioeconomic stability and individual freedom, a multiplicity of voices and critiques of all stripes. As postmodern psychoanalysis demonstrated, perfect unity of thought is pathological. It signifies obsessive mania in the individual and totalitarianism in society.

By the time of GS3, the late 20th century postmodern intellectual mode may well be a distant reference. Its decline is already evident as *cultural evolution* moves closer to the new *chaotic transition*, beyond the mirage of "post-history." But its insights will remain useful and its historical instruction to accept and practice pluralism will have to be followed. Through "clear and calm cross-cultural communication" (a notion elaborated by Jürgen Habermas), the *Saga* will distill and amalgamate what may be agreed upon as the "most valid and useful" to create and preserve interpersonal valence on a global scale and to empower the collective future. Such a common vision of universal history will be indispensable. Without the "textualization" of collective memory, every second would be a new beginning, a condition that contradicts the feasibility of panhuman self-possession.

The *Saga* will have to represent everybody, speak for everybody, and allow everybody to speak. Its universalism will have to be conceived and built pluralistically. It will be unashamedly self-referential and self-reverential (*autopoétique*)–no need to unmask it through "deconstruction." And it will be "local," as postmodern philosophy advises on what may be good and real, in contrast to vested-interest-conserving, "Euro-centric" or other "essentialism"-deformed, imperially "totalizing" *meganarratives*. Its subject will not be the dispersed and unequal billions, but a nomadic gang of collective hunters that reappeared as the eternally-lived global household. If GS3 is to exist and succeed, the *Saga* will have to be transnationally, trans-socially, and transgenerationally altruistic, thus making obsolete all current political, social, and cultural *revendications*. It may well reflect the continuation of the philosophical tradition of *Pragmatism* from Charles

Sanders Peirce (1839-1914), through William James (1842-1910) and John Dewey (1859-1952), to the contemporary writings of Richard Rorty.

For a number of reasons, *Religion* cannot become the *Saga*. It has too many conflicting certainties; it excludes a large part of the population that refuses to link its thoughts and actions to mystical teachings and it does not lend itself to "falsification" in light of scientific progress. Most religiously motivated belief systems blur the human world with the rationally unembraceable void, when the purpose of the *Saga* is to reflect the best available scientific and pragmatic sense of man's place in it.

This is not to predict the triumph of *Saga* over *Religion*. The acceptance of a collective identity does not require apostasy or conversion into laicism. The emergence of global *discourse*, which would tend to make the individual-brain-anchored "micro-modeling" of the world converge, does not ban faith in the transcendental. To us, as to previous generations, no secular ideology appears capable of satisfying the deep yearning for the belief that we are in the personalized loving vigil of immutable and omniscient goodness; that something awaits each of us to erase the pain and suffering of long and tiresome individual journeys–something that prevents the "dreadful truth" (Kierkegaard) from damaging the human psyche. Surely, the safety and care individuals enjoy through family and social life, and the way the market caters to their slightest needs and whims (at least in the *vanguard*) stand in unacceptably stark contrast to being a negligible nothing in a heartless and incomprehensible universe.

From a positive, utilitarian perspective, religions, as they have evolved to accommodate *cultural evolution*, seem to have performed the vital service of preparing the individual to live by over-arching, ecumenical moral precepts (reminiscent of Freudian "superego") without feeling suffocated by them. No doubt, the ideals and passions of Abrahamic Evangelism played an important role and remain inseparable from the germination of socioeconomic equity in the *vanguard*. But needs and merits notwithstanding, childish insistence on long disproved assertions and a scientifically rooted *Saga* could not peacefully cohabit in the same *mind*. To remain plausible for those who like to think outside of handed-down systems of ideas, perceptions of an all-powerful Overseer will have to adapt again and again to new insights humans consider incontrovertible, such as the roundness of the planet (instead of the Middle Age's flat surface, showing East at the top and Eden and Jerusalem smack in the middle).

The proposed historical materialism does not disparage faith-based understanding of human progression. To see one reason, let us subdue our empirio-critical reflexes for a moment and pick up the Bible. Look at the last chapter; *The*

Revelation of St. John the Divine. It is hard not to equate *chaotic transition* with the *Great Tribulation*. We are familiar with "1789-1834" and "1914-1945," and now a new one is approaching. Bible scholars are divided as to whether the *Great Tribulation* was in the past or is in the future. According to our theory, both views are correct. The *Apocalypse* (an alternate name for the *Revelation* quoted above) was expressed in the symbolism of the first century. It could not say: "A series of grave and worsening ecological and resource problems, attributable to the poorly controlled eagerness of humans to expand their ranks and their material welfare under unexpendable terrestrial constraints, brought hardships and conflicts of never before seen proportions, pitting the world's old behavior that would lead to extinction against a not yet seen behavior that would save it." If there was any intention originating outside the human dominion of comprehension (*minds* number one and two) to pass this message to the late 20th and early 21st centuries, it had to be "handled" exactly the way it was. The message itself evolved, gradually making itself clearer until people could see both the nature of the powerful darkness loitering on the doorstep and the choice between the corrupt "Babylon the Great" and "New Jerusalem." Today we can already interpret in terms of scientific concepts and hard numbers what the "right to eat from the tree of life" implies.

It is equally intriguing to contemplate the founders of the four major faiths, the three prophets of the *Book* and Buddha, because this sectarian quartet is perfectly suited to the process of creating GS3. With *minds* skulking in pre-*Enlightenment* mist, a marble-hearted, obscenely bloodthirsty faction of Mohamed's faith is attacking the Judeo-Christian *vanguard* in open-ended global conflicts (projecting the likely "poor against rich" dimension of the coming *chaotic transition*) while a patient, collectively oriented individuality, steeped in Buddhist traditions, is waiting in the wings.

Psychoanalysis, analytical psychology, and philosophy say many fascinating things about the human need for worship and obedience, but a stable, nonspecious explanation of religion is still missing. Some doubt that it will ever exist. Matter may always have reasons that matter will not understand, but given human limitations (by now scientifically confessed) one can never preclude "miracles."

Like all mental phenomena, the *Saga* will be a material substance, an interconnected web of physico-chemical codes. It will not be an organism, but it will be much more than a fragile idea that some clever argument or physical obstacle could render null and void. Yet can any material organization last forever? The answer, "Of course not," need not be repeated until it becomes a pessimistic conviction that would undermine individual vitality. It is not possible now, nor will it be possible under GS3, to prognosticate all the selection pressures the future will bring. The cosmic strain toward thermodynamic equilibrium follows an unknowable schedule.

THE GS3 AVATAR

GS3 *socioeconomic behavior, lexicon, ethic, Weltanschauung,* and *mentality* correspond to norms and circumstances that have not yet emerged. Giving a detailed outline of these *global system* characteristics is as impossible as foretelling the evolution of interconnected microstates of matter (the worldwide *web* of *Code Cores*) into a direction it had never been before. The acknowledgment of this impossibility follows from the thermodynamic perspective on *cultural evolution.* In plain language, it is impossible to derive the advent of a world order that never existed before and for which there is no current, isolated precedent. This, however, should not prevent us from hypothetically identifying some GS3 attributes, particularly in contradistinction to those of the previous two *global systems.* The formation of the species into a "group" that takes conscious aim at the future has far-reaching implications for interpersonal relations. So do even the most general features of the envisaged world order (*two-level economy/strong multilateralism*) and the prospect of living on the *global transformation curve.*

We may begin with the most pervasive manifestation of any *global system*–the associated socioeconomic behavior. One can develop an idea about the magnitude of change from the contemporary individual to the GS3 type by focusing on two well known concepts used in evolutionary theory and sociobiology (the study of the biological foundations of behavior): "inclusive fitness" and "altruism."

Sociobiologists interpret "inclusive fitness" by fusing the individual's own reproductive success with that of its relatives.[4] In the present socioeconomic context, inclusive fitness combines what one can do for an organization or a community with the effects exerted on the ability or performance of others to serve the same organization or community.

Your inclusive fitness = benefits accrued to you directly + net benefits accrued to others

---

4.   W.D. Hamilton (1936-2000) is credited for the introduction of this concept. See *Hamilton, 1964.* The quoted work is noted for its seminal importance. Although it does not deal with human societies directly, it has weighty implications for them indirectly.

This formula may be applied to one particular behavioral manifestation or trait or to the entirety of socioeconomic behavior. Its range of effects may be restricted to an organization or community (or to parts of it) or extended to any of the nested layers of the *socioeconomic environment*. The time period for which its value is contemplated may also vary. "Net benefits accrued to others" should be thought of as a weighted average, where the weights descend in value as we move away from the workplace through the *surrounding socioeconomic milieu* and beyond. The "net" means that the "benefits" do not include "harm" caused to others. ("Net benefit" is conceptually akin to "profit," calculated by subtracting costs from revenues.)

The quantified measure of inclusive fitness (in this socioeconomic interpretation) is expected to correlate with personal income, the size of the *personal socioeconomic sphere*. In a business firm, for example, inclusive fitness extends personal fitness, which is narrowly characterized as the ability to do a particular job, with the sum of (positive) net influences the individual exerts on the rest of the employees and hence, on the "fitness" of the firm in its struggle for survival. Between two identically trained and able engineers working with the same level of intensity, the one found to be more helpful in training new employees, who cooperates more willingly, and shows greater loyalty to the organization tends to earn more. Higher income enables the earner to have more offspring or fewer offspring who are better cared for. (Both mean "reproductive success." The second is more typical of individuals living in modern, prosperous societies.) Higher income also empowers the individual to help its kin to achieve "reproductive success."

Although the definition of inclusive fitness revolves around "giving," it also implies "receiving." An individual benefits from the high inclusive fitness of the rest of the employees because it makes him or her more fit in the eyes of management, the group of individuals who ultimately determine personal income and, in most cases, one's overall socioeconomic status. Inclusive fitness implies reciprocity between enhancing others and being enhanced by them. The average person, considered a "rational maximizer," seeks to strike a balance between what it receives and what it gives in the way of mutual enhancement. The more an individual enhances the fitness of others involuntarily, through talent, physical attributes (including sheer attractiveness), and special work-related circumstances, the less it needs to make a conscious effort to reach the optimal level, the balance point between giving and receiving. Taking a judicious (if not shrewd) account of involuntarily provided services to the group, individual ambitions to enhance one's own fitness remain dominant in the inextricable melee of pursuing selfish ends and making cooperative gestures. Gains made by receiving more than giving will be prevented by equally well-playing extra-gain seekers. While giving and receiving may seem to cancel out at the personal level, they add up for the group. The total somatic energy "harvested" by a firm and in all organizations (formal groups) across a nation may hover around some average of collective additions to personal fitness, and thereby to the social product (GDP). Compared to GS1, GS2 expanded the opportunity and the incentive to raise "inclusive fitness" on the average.[5]

GS3 would radically change the "inclusive fitness game." Through moral suasion and social pressure it would render both differential reproductive and socioeconomic success obsolete. Having a stipulated number of children and limited opportunity to acquire extraordinary material wealth cannot be readily reconciled with personal ambitions to enhance one's own and someone else's fitness, measured by the summary indicator–income. To make GS3 operational, its inclusive fitness will have to be gauged by one's ability to refrain from excessive reproductive and socioeconomic success and by willingness to contribute to the living standards and general welfare of others without expanding their *socioeconomic spheres*. It will be rewarded psychologically and through the service and care of others, most directly in the *surrounding socioeconomic milieu* or in the *canton*.

GS3 puts the long debated and mysterious phenomenon of altruism on the table. In the animal kingdom, self-imposed sacrifice in order to help the kin reproduce, thereby indirectly propagating one's own, is the essence of altruism. It consists of gestures that have consequences without intentions, such as the uncontrolled, involuntarily emitted sound of alarm by the prey, warning its fellow prey (presumably out of concern for the closest kin), even if this means attracting the immediate attention of the predator in search of lunch. The reconciliation of this behavior with the overwhelming desire for the individual to survive and spread its genes provoked a long-lasting debate among biologists, a debate, which perhaps unintentionally, informed social science.

Does altruistic behavior exist because the "group" that does not have altruistic genetic traits (abbreviated into "altruistic genes") is headed toward extinction, allowing the group with "altruistic genes" to survive by default? Is it strictly an instinct of consanguinity? Or is it mere reciprocity, an implicit accord for mutual help that can be extended to others? All three explanations have been found valid, although "group selection" seems to have gone through a roller coaster ride. It

---

5. This conforms to Hamilton's conclusion. His mathematical model (applied to genetic effects) showed that "inclusive fitness" in the population tends to increase.

was accepted, then rejected, and then partially rehabilitated by the consensus of experts.

Altruism becomes a true puzzle in human life where conscious, rational thought filters intentions and impulses. Yet when the institutional props of *cultural evolution* are removed (in war or deadly danger prompted by other circumstances), the individual is capable of shifting to a behavior that is only biologically, not "game theoretically," explainable. The self-sacrifice of soldiers and firemen, the bravery of bystanders who risk life and limb to help victims of an accident have been observed so consistently that we may count on such gestures to emerge without fail in adversity. This noble side of human nature goes beyond the simplified personal conduct that fits into the crude mechanics of microeconomic rationality. There is more to humans, after all, than the "propensity to barter, truck, and exchange one thing for another" (Adam Smith).

Altruism, from simple restraint to martyrdom, may be examined through the above-shown formula on inclusive fitness. "Your inclusive fitness" can increase even if the "benefits accrued to you directly" are reduced, given that the "net benefits accrued to others" more than compensate for the decline. As a matter of simple algebra, this is true even if your benefits were negative. You caused harm to yourself in order to help others.

In the socioeconomic context, one looks with suspicion at kin-based altruism. Successful societies restrain it through "conflict of interest" laws and widely recognized ethical rules. The expansion and deepening of reciprocal altruism is the favored explanation for socioeconomic evolution, and one may say, for *cultural evolution*. It has been connected with both analytical and evolutionary game theory. Reciprocity of making and receiving favors and sacrifices, even if they are disconnected in time (although remaining within overlapping generations) and do not necessarily involve the same two persons, could result in a payoff that exceeds what the interacting individuals could have earned without "reciprocal altruism." As many important scholars and great writers have shown, cooperative interaction can develop among radically self-centered, philanthropy-belittling, short-sighted individuals as they slide into stable patterns of behavior and gradually recognize the practical benefits of seemingly idealistic mutuality.[6]

The explanation of altruism through "group selection" applies to *cultural evolution* at any level where competition is evident, most importantly among businesses and nations. The greater the reciprocal restraint among the employees of a firm, for instance, shown by a willingness to allow others to reap benefits at one's

---

6. See, for example, *Axelrod, 1984* and *Wright, 2000*.

own immediate expense, the greater the firm's competitive success, other things being equal. Success will translate into relatively higher per capita income for the employees, revealing the advantage of controlling egocentric impulses, and playing a higher-than-average-pay-off nonzero-sum game. On a broader scale, *vanguard* residents interact through a higher pay-off nonzero-sum game than people living in the rest of the world. (Developed countries not only have higher per capita incomes than the global average, but their income distribution also tends to be less uneven. A closely related assumption is that their citizens trust one another more than people in other countries.)

GS2 differs from GS1 by allowing for more elaborate nonzero-sum games ("reciprocal socioeconomic altruism") with larger pay-offs for the average player.[7] The other kind of altruism, the truly noble one, where welfare, personal wholeness, or even mere existence are on the line, has not been required by the institutional designs of GS1 and GS2. This will not be the case under GS3. To see more clearly, we must draw on another Hamiltonian idea, the one that reveals the internal calculus of altruistic gestures. The case of no altruism is captured by:

Disadvantages accrued to you directly $\geq$ Advantages accrued to others
Consequently, you will behave altruistically only when:
Disadvantages accrued to you directly $<$ Advantages accrued to others

In the first expression, advantages to others are smaller than or are equal to the disadvantages suffered by you. You will refrain from altruism. The second formula shows when you would go forward with it. The term "advantages accrued to others" has two components: the cold fact of actual benefits and the warm feelings and concerns one has toward the potential recipient(s). The first is constant and "objective" in the sense that it is socially determined; hence, every individual would understand it (more or less) the same way during a given period. The second component varies according to emotional makeup and subjective judgment,

---

7.   There are important differences between the thermodynamic perspective on world history and the theories that see socioeconomic evolution through the logic of the "n-player iterated prisoners' dilemma." *Cultural evolution* lacked the "intelligence" of subtle interdependent moves. At the microscale, the exercise of "Machiavellian virtues" propelled the advance of *cultural evolutionary indices* under both *global systems*. At the macroscale, *deterministic chaos* (see Chapter 10) led a half-conscious, nauseated humanity through the *macrohistoric* crisis of "1914-1945." The gradually increasing sophistication that leads from a noncooperative game through cooperative games to cooperation at an ever-increasing scale of human self-organization may simulate the outcome, but not the dynamics, of universal history as a material process.

although under generally valid guidelines: We rank family higher than nonfamily, a fellow citizen higher than a complete stranger, a fellow human higher than a pet. If the effects of the altruistic act are expected to diffuse beyond the closest kin, the *mind* might make an instantaneous and unconscious, speed-of-light calibration, weighing the objective advantages with their subjective coefficients. No matter how small a benefit or how little it weighs, it is the sum of the effects that ultimately matters when they are compared to the costs to self.

GS3 will demand a lowering of the threshold that constrains altruism simply because circumstances will demand incomparably more of it than they do now. Limited economic growth and much greater equality among *socioeconomic spheres* imply a voluntary forbearing of certain economic advantages on behalf of people one would never know. GS3 will require solidarity among nonoverlapping generations. Environmental and conservation measures and expansion into space will be century-long undertakings. If costs and benefits are separated by life spans, donors and recipients will evidently never exchange a smile or shake hands. In particular, the conquest of space is unthinkable without massive numbers of volunteers, heroic individuals ready for the ultimate sacrifice on the count of one. Significant restraints can occur and noble acts are conceivable only if the second equation (the pure inequality) would apply in many cases in which the first one would apply today. Disadvantages to oneself will have to be devalued, the advantages to others revalued, and the array of effects expended, indicating interest in the welfare of far away people. New beneficiaries with appropriate weights will have to enter the right-hand-side of the expression, tilting average behavior toward a greater proclivity to make altruistic transfers.

Using the nepotistic explanation of altruism, GS3 presumes a broadening of solidarity. If the human community is to resemble a permanently goal-oriented association, then individuals emphasizing their common ancestry will have to expand the circle that includes only the "near and dear." The anonymous outsider will have to become a quasi-sib. Following the logic of "reciprocity," the typical person will presume similar self-sacrifice from others. An Aristotelian *teleia philia* ("perfect friendship" engendered by insight into one another's mirror image high-mindedness) would prevail in interpersonal relations and individual behavior.

The group selection argument for the expected spread of "altruistic genes" also has its place. A sagacious global populace, considering itself to be the "group," will contemplate its juxtaposed, alternative futures with and without the spread of "altruistic genes" and will select the one that, in all likelihood, would prolong its existence. How "group selection" might work in a "one world" setting is impossible to tell, but it may play some role in the development of GS3. Let us see why.

Many economists dread the fragmentation of the international economy into three power centers, America, Europe, and Asia. Models show the loss of welfare as *multilateralism* falls victim to the power struggle among the giants. In the end everybody loses. But in a longer view, the three-way division could turn out to be a blessing. If the American continent excelled in integrating its heterogeneous population, while Europe blazed the trail in the federation of nation states, and Asia (with post-communist China) jumped to the fore in instituting a two-level economy, everybody might win. If each "group" appeared as the one "selected" for success in the eyes of the remaining two, the three-pronged "adaptive" process would deepen globalization. (Regional integration, which leads to an America, a Europe, and an Asia, also encourages gene flows among national populations. Narrow economic analysis, concerned mainly with harm to nondiscriminatory *multilateral* trade and investment, overlooks this global-integration-catalyzing aspect of "regionalism.")

Suspension of the incentive system associated with classical *cultural evolution* implies a nearly complete revolution in economic thinking. Growth theory and dynamic analysis are built on "positive" interest rates, the expansion of the stock of capital through investment, rising levels of consumption, and household preferences that may substitute consumption "intertemporally" (e.g., six years of no vacations and careful budgeting for the 12-year-old's future college education). However, if the population and the economy did not grow (we set the world's inflation adjusted interest rate to zero, which would probably happen automatically, and presume widespread altruism), the theoretical framework of choices involving the future would be lost. If people cared as much about global welfare as they did about their own families, if they were unwilling or unable to distinguish between the pleasures of consuming now or later, and if they found as much delight in the material prosperity of someone to be born a hundred years from now as in their own, contemporary economics would fall silent. When its time comes, GS3 will have to locate its economics somewhere in the vast space of human behavioral potential between (but not including) the selfish rationality of the computer-hearted *homo economicus* and ascetic sainthood. It will also have to locate a matching individual psychology that unites self-importance at level $1/P$ (where P is the global population) and willingness to view the world from the standpoint of P. Such a state is imaginable only if the flow of energy among individuals lavishly compensates for the devaluation of the self, or in more poetic terms, if everybody became committed to noble ideals.

The transition from GS2 to GS3 would represent a qualitative watershed in *cultural evolution*, a major alteration in the individual mediation of the *force motrice*; the genesis of *homo novus*. GS3 may not accomplish the entire metamorphosis into a spiritually united world, inhabited by (1/P, P) genteel types. It may be only the first *macrohistoric* phase, leaving further changes to appear in GS4, GS5, and so on.

With all this in mind, we can now make some inferences about the anticipated *global system*'s epiphenomena. A return to GS1's more stoically accepting and less intensely manipulative *ethic* (applicable to the entire socioeconomic cross section) may be anticipated. This development would confirm the widespread sentiment that today's habitual obliquity and irreverence in personal conduct, politics, and popular culture are transitory phenomena. (What the majority consistently and enduringly does not like will eventually have to go.) *Weltanschauung* will be more explicit than under GS2. People will be much more aware of the views they share about the world and more tuned into the consciousness of others. The "theory of mind" will become richer and more detailed. Willingness to self-sacrifice, generosity, and easy-going acquiescence might best characterize the envisaged *global system*'s *mentality*, the pent-up readiness to take action or react in certain ways under similar ("behavior-evoking") conditions. The *lexicon* will depend on legislation, the details of which are the secrets of the future, even if we carry in every cell of our bodies the occult inspiration to make them into ordinary routines on a latter day.

In no way should we paint GS3 in dark colors, a form of social and economic organization inimical to happiness and good times–people living in a quasi-fundamentalist, self-mortified haze, coping with the demands of survival, ready to be sacrificed for the imperatives of the *bonum commune*, watching their every step in fear of slipping off the *global transformation curve*. Changes associated with movements along the "curve" would take generations. For most of the time, "curve issues" may be absent from the forefront of preoccupations. A politico-ideologically autonomous geocentric denizen, occasionally willing and able to add its voice to the planet's *vox populi* in deciding about excess and insufficiency in the use of resources from an all-human perspective would suffice to make the envisaged corporate Earth viable and functional.

Strong multilateralism is not the rule of a Pontificus Dominus (Kim Jong Il gone global), disguised as an overworked, kindhearted UN Secretary General. It implies an institutional framework for pro-active international cooperation and coordination.[8] Even the replacement of "conspicuous consumption" with "conspicuous altruism" will not turn humans into termites. As far as consumption is concerned, there will "have to be" a shift from quantity to quality; to meaningful variety and refinements. (Economic theory has shown that increase in the variety of products and improvements in product quality are conceivable without growth in overall economic output or in population.) Local, *cantonal* activities to safe-guard and enhance living standards will probably gain in importance at the expense of the competitive cross-hauling of near perfect substitutes and the global franchise. (Good-bye expensive milky slush of stretched coffee beans; so long cheap, health-sapping mystery-meat patties from the assembly line.) Education, leisure, and joy might move to center stage. If not the end, GS3 could be the beginning of the end for poverty, economically motivated criminality, self-degra-dation through drug use, and the constant and pervasive worry about tomorrow.

Get comfortable. No one wants to see the individual turn into a faceless, gen-derless global communard living in glassy falansters, unable to tell where his or her organism ends and where its cybernetic prolongation begins. Take a deep breath and imagine life without multitasking, touch-and-go aggressiveness, all the human-made traps for reciprocal deceptions and self-deceptions. The ancient Greek ideal of people cultivating their minds and bodies, living in a global *polis* of limpid order and Apollonian measure, patience, courtesy, and harmony in human relations might just become reality, and this time around for everybody, not just for "free men." Fulfilling the dreams of so many thinkers and believers through the ages, entropy may not be the dreaded archfiend after all. This is the positive way of looking beyond the approaching *chaotic* interlude, considering the new world order a qualitatively altered state of *mind* that allows for the continua-tion of progress seen in *cultural evolution*.

Utopia? Wishful eschatology? Touchy-feely, quixotic One Worldism? No. *Homo novus* follows directly from dismissing as groundless the augury that the good fortunes of *homo sapiens* are inevitably over. Not seeing mankind turn into a

---

8.   Still, religious warnings about the rule of an "Anti-Christ" as the last stage of the vio-lent and irrational period before GS3 cannot be easily shrugged off. Both GS1 and GS2 followed in the wake of fallen dictators, Napoleon and Hitler. The end of moral catharsis on a historical scale seems to coincide with getting rid of the global trouble-maker, physically and symbolically. Past experience patterns thinking: Napoleon/ Saint Helena; Hitler/Fuehrer Bunker; Anti-Christ/? The pattern also implies rising levels of evil in the tyrants of *macrohistoric* significance. But then we know that wide anticipation of a disaster may help avoid it. Or just the opposite, the tragedy of *Oedi-pus Rex*; efforts to evade the prophecy push general behavior toward the concealed trap of events long predetermined? A global dictator that would be loved and obeyed voluntarily before feared and hated?

diffident collection of vital-sign-exhibiting fossils, begging on their knees for reprieve and forgiveness from forces they no longer try to understand, equals GS3 in the context of self-perception (*Saga*), foresight (*Telos*), and long-term optimization (*global transformation curve*). For all that, the *representative brain* will have to reprogram itself in a big way.

As Darwin eloquently noted, complexity of a higher order appears as supernatural if we are not privy to its evolutionary history. A person thawed today after being frozen for 500 years would view contemporary social organization and many human-made objects with incredulous awe. A distant goal involving similarly higher degrees of complexity and thorough changes without the ability to foresee how they could be accomplished may also prompt a frustrating sensation of insuperability now. But one step at a time for a long period can accumulate knowledge and methodology that produce unforeseeable qualitative improvements. *Stupor mundi* "today," commonplace "tomorrow." A hundred years from now, transformation curve analysis may be an intensely cultivated scientific field. In a thousand years, the idea that *homo sapiens* must change itself biologically through genetic engineering or allow itself to be shaped by different physical environments on different planets could be eagerly embraced.

◆ ◆ ◆

The following dramatization shows that a future generation might indeed just say "yes" to the path leading to GS3 because the current one would say "no" to the alternatives.

In each of the world's roughly 270 countries a grand jury is summoned. Its members are randomly selected from among people with college education, but who are unfamiliar with the full meaning of entropy, carrying capacity, and the issues of futurology in general. After unbiased experts explain these concepts to the jurors an announcement is made. Population and economic expansion have reached critical levels. The world does not yet know what to do. Three broad alternatives are under consideration before the Emergency Ecological-Economic and Social Council of the United Nations. The juries do not have to choose from among them. All they need to do is listen to the defense advocating and the prosecution attacking each alternative; then, examine the evidence, deliberate, and vote on whether or not the alternative on trial is guilty of threatening human existence and prosperity within one thousand years.

Laissez faire demographic and economic expansion. The closing argument of the defense in one of the national courtrooms may sound like "...allow free markets to do their magic, ladies and gentlemen of the jury! Instead of looking at the government for solutions, we should further restrict this overbearing parasite from sapping the creative juices of entrepreneurial energy! If the world has a problem, any problem, there is only one good solution: Cut taxes and government spending. Socialism, which gnawed into the fiber of our liberties, should bear full responsibility for the current situation. Now it sees an opportunity to throw down the gauntlet and take control under the guise of dealing with what some call a 'predicament.' Let me tell you, ladies and gentlemen, what the fully decentralized free enterprise economy, with the state off its back, would call it: A challenge with the potential of expanding capital markets to finance a new wave of cybernetically designed, super-nano-fiber-technological, environment-and conservation-conscious consumer goods; services and more services to cater better to all of our needs. This route would adapt economic expansion to its ecological constraints. It would mean rising incomes around the globe, a condition proven to curtail population growth." The prosecution will need very little time. It will state that the program in question is exactly the one that necessitated the current proceedings. It may also remind the jury that accusing socialism now or fearing the specter of its return is a bit disingenuous, given that the accused has been buried for a long enough time to consider its body fully decomposed.

Controlled Cyclicality. This alternative intends to decrease world population to a very low level through birth control. With the world economy reduced to a lesser extent than population, high living standards would make life "country club" pleasant. Birth control would then be removed, allowing demographic and economic expansion to start afresh. When a stipulated level of occupancy is approached again, another downward cycle would be instituted, and so on. The defense underscores that, for humanity, there is no place like Earth. For the moment, creating life on Mars and going outside the solar system through worm holes in self-supporting multigenerational spaceships (or what have you) is "Hollywood," computer simulations mixed with near-Earth space exploration footage. "Let us not kid ourselves" the counsel's address might conclude, "the species needs no other policy instrument than birth control: on for two hundred years then off for two hundred years. This would allow mankind to live happily, democratically, and prosperously until the sun burns out. We will have enough time to reconsider this simplest and most effective strategy if unforeseen circumstances develop or as dramatic scientific breakthroughs with practical implications warrant reconsideration."

The prosecution reminds the juries that *Controlled Cyclicality* would require more central authority than the single policy instrument of birth control would make one believe. If the joint population/output deflation is not controlled, it would give way to an unstoppable negative synergy of endogenous contraction. Decline would not approach a low usage equilibrium point smoothly. This alternative also disregards the potential threat involved in the irreversible buildup of matter-specific terrestrial entropy, a process that periodic bursts of spontaneous population/output growth would certainly aggravate.

Mini-max cum Public Choice. The recognition of the cosmic context of human existence, combined with the wish to extend it on a level that fulfills individual lives, requires that the world minimize its use of low-entropy matter and maximize its efforts to find more low-entropy matter outside planet Earth. Subject to a scientifically determined distance from dangerous levels of occupancy and activity, loci on a selected somatic/extrasomatic transformation curve will offer choices of population/material output combinations to the worldwide public. Pursuit of the indicated dual goal and the use of the transformation curve to manage global resources would require *strong multilateralism.*

The defense will cite the danger of extinction, of man finding himself in a necropolis of energetically depleted matter. It will recall the irrepressible thirst of humans to face limitless vistas as demonstrated by the rugged seafaring folks who explored the Earth and the settlers of the American frontier. The innate urge to expand, to be territorially offensive is inseparable from the inclination to defend and cultivate intensely what has been conquered. Look at the Dutch who prosper behind levees, the Japanese who turned their natural disaster-prone, resource poor archipelago into one of the great success stories of *cultural evolution.* The prosecution will mention the untold complexities involved in organizing the world in the suggested way and the scientific-technological hurdles facing the "spread out."

The votes are tallied. I think that only *Alternative Three,* implying GS3, *global transformation curve, Telos* and *Saga,* would be declared "nonguilty." Only the prospect of deliberate, comprehensive action withstands scrutiny, regardless of the current inability to guess its direction, motives, and time frames. Presuming this to be correct implies a web of material substances (opinions are physical imprints) maintained individually by billions. An undeveloped living quantum state, a gossamer of barely existing nerve paths, reflecting the accumulated results of selection pressures in the deep past, is revealing something about the way *homo sapiens* may behave once its ecological release is threatened. Not defecting on coming generations now foreshadows the possibility that the massive amount of altruism required for GS3 will evolve.

As always, the future is a receding convection of contingencies and unknowns. But this cannot destroy our deeply encoded faith in the possibility that the pre-historically acquired adaptive flexibility will secrete a self-guiding, general human interest-based intelligence bent on securing life as long as there is a chance. The creation of a *global system* under which the individual is motivated to act without reward measurable by the level of personal consumption may be among the emergent properties of DNA.

GENES AS FACILITATORS OF THERMODYNAMIC EVOLUTION

Sociobiologists call the interaction between genome and the human-created environment the "gene-culture co-evolution."[9] The socially cobbled together environment acts on genetic variance to shift the composition of genes in the direction that best corresponds to its norms while genetic composition shapes the evolution of the socioeconomic environment. To get the gist of this co-evolution, let us increase the number of marchers lost on a strange planet to 100 and the number of "silent ones," symbolizing the genes, to 20. Co-evolution means that the 80 may select a pattern of interaction (deemed useful based on their shared and remembered experience) that would make some of the 20 evaporate like camphor. Those who could not live with the new environment would vanish into the night, but would be replaced immediately.

This interplay puts genes in a less tyrannical, more cooperative light. They are not evil gnomes who use their phenotypes as mindless Mamelukes. They are trying to telegraph the "80": "We depend on your powers (stop) do not for heavens sake bungle into a scheme that would jeopardize our joint aye (stop) do not lock us onto the Strange Attractor (stop) those of us not suited to progressive new schemes will drop out (stop) nothing to it (stop) we replenish ourselves as quickly as you do (stop) never stop trying never ever (stop) *ab ovo* no-goes will be telegraphed (stop) if you ponder the extent of our resilience remember *pasteurella pestis* (stop). (They must be referring to the plague, which, beginning in the 14th century, threatened Europe with annihilation, but ran into mutating genes that resisted the bacteria. Individuals with stronger immunity multiplied, spreading

---

9.   *Wilson, 1998* gives a concise summary. For more detailed insights, consult *Lumsden and Wilson, 1985.*

the resistant genes across the population. The triumph of survival at the cost of dramatic structural shift in the genome!)

A harsh formulation of the "gene-culture co-evolution" suggested that Pleistocene biological heritage plays a determining role in mankind's future. The same forces of natural selection that developed our physical attributes also determined our behavior and behavioral potential. *Punctum.* Critics roared; academic guns rattled. Not surprisingly, many found the idea of prebarbarically determined constraints rebarbative. Human intelligence hostage to the Stone Age, perhaps disabling it from finding a scheme of socioeconomic self-organization, even if life itself was in the lot? But what if, after a self-orchestrated collective learning experience, GS3 is born? What if the genes allowed it to happen, flexibly "recomposing" themselves to survive? Was that not "in them," as a feature of their original composition, created during those sunken eons whose defining power has long receded into the far regions of forgetfulness? If altruism spreads through the gene pool because a new institutional order favors it, then where else, if not in the genes, did this ability reside?

At the species' scale, of course, it is the genome's bio-social organization (the entire force field that characterizes interaction among the replicators) that is subject to thermodynamic-style evolution. Given, however, that no pattern of interaction can develop for which the closed set of possibilities contained in the genome would not give the green light, one is led to the conclusion that any system of typical material movement that accounts for interpersonal communications and cooperation must be submerged in the time-resistant, fixed, and definitive physics of our genes.

Let us play "gene-socioeconomic co-evolution" on a checkerboard in the spirit of the *second law of thermodynamics*. We arrange 24 pieces on 64 squares. We declare one of the pieces to be the fixed point and define a concept of configuration for the rest of them (e.g., the largest number of horizontal unfilled spaces, the number of filled spaces in a quadrant). Based on the configuration selected, a decision rule will move the fixed point to an adjacent square, but never backward to a square occupied before. Every time the fixed point moves, we arrange the rest of the 23 pieces on the remaining 63 squares *randomly*. After an "evolutionary period," the fixed point traces a trajectory. It symbolizes genetic evolution. Changes in the configuration represent evolution in the socioeconomic environment. Their *randomness* suggests total freedom to invent institutions.

We erase the movement of the fixed point from the record and provide all the information a group of scientists needs to reconstitute successive configurations. We ask the group to identify *nonrandom* processes for the entire "evolutionary period." Our contention is that they will not find a single process independent from the trace left behind by the fixed point. Therefore, the life path of configurations will also be unidirectional. This conclusion does not change even if we permit the decision rules (whereby the fixed point may move) to vary within a closed set of possibilities and allow consistently followed methods other than *random* selection to place the 23 nonfixed point pieces. With these constrained relaxations, we exclude the possibility that core properties in the genes would permit any socioeconomic policy to shape their composition and include consistently pursued socioeconomic institution building. The crucial conclusion is that these institutions could not evolve independently from genetic evolution (changes in the composition of genes). Regardless of how deeply embedded materially perceived characteristics are among interrelated, materially perceived processes, their influence on the variable elements, including their own composition, as represented by the path of the fixed point, will prevail over time.

Change in the composition of the gene pool and *cultural evolution* must have been linked by reciprocal causality. If it had been otherwise, socioeconomic evolution and genetic changes would not have tracked one another in contradiction to the well supported thesis that the two processes are tied, as if by a very elastic (hence, hardly detectable) symbolic "leash."

From "gene-culture co-evolution" follows a "Catch 22" in the hypothetical GS2—>GS3 transition. Only an appropriately altered socioeconomic environment could make altruistic genes spread and only the spread of altruistic genes could create the socioeconomic environment that would reward altruism. At present, altruistic genes are not in control of typical individual socioeconomic behavior. Like its predecessor, GS2 obtains contributions to social welfare indirectly, through radically usurpative me-me-me's positive spillovers.

If altruism in its elevated (above its "selfish-gene"-dictated endurance strategic) sense is an indication of the prevalence of altruistic traits, GS2 does not seem to have increased their frequency. Few people would become inconsolably despondent and leave the dinner table upon hearing that a human being dies of starvation every four seconds. Despite tax incentives, charity donations represent a very small fraction of personal incomes in the richest countries; and "donor" governments make sure that every cent of assistance given to the "beneficiary" poor country runs through a cost-benefit analysis of national economic, political, and security interests. And so things remain, despite the accumulation of problems that are unsolvable without the voluntary sacrifice of one's own welfare on behalf of a stranger's.

Since gradual "gene-culture co-evolution" excludes the possibility of creating an altruistic *global system* without the diffusion and already important frequency of altruistic genes in the global population, and because altruism does not seem to grow by seeing others suffer, we are led back to our earlier conclusion that to contemplate a new order seriously, the world will have to be shocked out of its classical *cultural evolutionary* mode. If "1914-1945" was the concrete manifestation of a generic process (i.e., *chaotic transition*), then at the end of its GS2—>GS3 version mankind will once again look in the mirror and ask itself "Am I out of my *mind?*"

Indisputably, the fact that *cultural evolution* followed a long-term trend is no evidence that it is headed in a certain way. It is even less evidence of a reassuring future path. But if GS3 succeeded in creating the envisaged "higher" civilization, thinking about social evolution would change.

Looking at universal history from a "GS0—>GS1—>GS2—>GS3" vantage point would turn the hypothetical plausibility that global self-organization traverses sequential phases of qualitative improvements (i.e., that there is *orthogenesis* in its broad interpretation) into conscious certainty. This much rhythm would allow the world to conclude that it is involved in a great composition, helping it to explain itself *teleonomically* (rather than *teleologically* in order to avoid spiritual bias). It might formulate its self-perception through evolutionary progress by saying something like, "I am a butterfly now. I already was one when I seemed like a larva for a while, then a pupa. I bided my time, letting my glorious end state emerge as it had to." The Artificer (individual *force motrices* socialized) would no longer be opaque, although, as we shall see in the next chapter, the presence of *randomness* in *cultural evolution* disallows the conclusion that the process itself is an enchainment of preparations. The current state of *cultural evolution* (i.e., *culture*) is as much an "upshot" as it is a retrospectively discerned logical state. *Therefore, the thermodynamic interpretation of history does not suggest that cultural evolution is a determined march to regain paradise lost. It only predicts conditions under which it is likely that concern for survival would push minds toward teleonomical explanations.*

Affirmative-action collective consciousness may reshape current notions about the gene/phenotype partnership. Genes have already telegraphed us that they are not the inflexible evolutionary conspirators some made them out to be. They might even want to be engineered if that is what it takes to outlast lethal threats. *Homo sapiens* might need different limbs and internal organs if it must move from planet Earth to deep space in expectation of an eviction notice. Such a perspective could place its physical heritage in a critical light. But we are getting ahead of ourselves, trying to see through a Mount Everest-sized block of time. Old and unsolved philosophical problems haunt the reduction of a grand and enigmatic transformation into a relatively simple physical process.

10

Necessity, Chance, and Individual Freedom in Cultural Evolution

[*Necessity* and *chance* as the humanly perceivable versions of *determinism* and *indeterminism* in broader nature. Minds are inclined to blend ordinary and extraordinary *chance* occurrences with *necessity* in backward-looking analysis. *New historical materialism* offers a variety of ways to discern that, in addition to *necessity*, *chance* also played a role in recorded *cultural evolution*. Individual freedom is the sentient reflection of the *force motrice*. The species is born into the anti-entropic struggle of constructing and expanding *culture*. The reward is individually experienced "freedom from want" acquired through constrained "freedom of action." Being involved in an overriding physical process puts volitional liberty in a new light.]

America's *macrohistory*: An economic expansion unparalleled in the annals of human experience exceeded the rapid growth of the country's population. The consequent rise in the average per capita income was accompanied by measures to guarantee that income differences would not threaten social peace; that is, by progress toward legal, political, and social equality among the nation's racially and ethnically diverse inhabitants. Some philosophies claim that even such a complex process was determined from the start by an unbreakable linkage of causes. Others suggest that we have observed a mere trend that created itself minute by minute, always allowing for the possibility that it could be temporarily or terminally interrupted or obliterated. The same metaphysical dilemma haunts global *cultural evolution* at large. *New historical materialism*, which considers world events to be the pageantry of a unified material process, must take a position regarding this dilemma. Without it, the theory leaves individual lives and the joint progression of whirling particles behind billions of interconnected foreheads unconnected.

Traditions, habits, modes of thinking, and needs come into play when we look for logic in the genealogy of actualities we see around us; when we attempt to synthesize what Oswald Spengler (1880-1936) called the "world-as-history" and the "world-as-nature." Let us begin by flying over one of the most ancient battlegrounds in the history of abstract thought, the one on which the proponents and opponents of *determinism* have been engaged in hand-to-hand combat since antiquity.

Those who set out to prove that nature is ruled by an inescapable pattern of causality because every event or action is uniquely conditioned to turn out or take place exactly as it does are the *determinists*. The materialist's version of *determinism* is called *physical determinism*. *Hard physical determinists* see the history of the world as a tape, with each frame (slice of time) unchangeably linked with the rest of them.

The opposite of *determinism*, i.e., *indeterminism*, covers a wide range of theses. Any relaxation from *hard determinism* (i.e., even *soft determinism*) lands one in the broad-band coalition of those who refuse the idea that the future has already happened, i.e., that there is a "tape." Those who completely reject *determinism* and claim that *indeterminacy* is the fundamental rule of the universe represent the extreme opposite to *hard determinism*. In our era, quantum uncertainty (the common-perception-defiant, psychedelic behavior of subatomic particles) and some evidence uncovered by *chaos theory* (nonlinear science) nourish convictions of complete *indeterminacy*. One of the great accomplishments of Ilya Prigogine is his demonstration that the *indeterminism* found in the quantum world also penetrates processes that are human-sized or that occur at cosmic scales.

Hard determinists see the law of nature in inevitable causality. They profess that *chance* events are also subject to causes, but we are not able to identify them. According to this theory, the world is "one unbending fact" (William James). *Hard indeterminists* consider any process or the unfolding of any event as subject to disruption in any nanosecond. They regard explanations based on statements involving causally explained inevitability as fallacies (*ad hoc ergo propter hoc*; i.e., after it, therefore because of it) when applied *ex post* (e.g., looking backward in historical time) and self-deception when applied *ex ante* (e.g., making predictions about history's future course). The *indeterminists* think that acausality, manifest as *chance*, is intrinsic in nature. Big surprises in physical phenomena may happen any minute, but will certainly occur if we last long enough.

Hard determinists and *indeterminists* do not bargain. They mutually devour each other, seeing all concepts involved in the debate in their own light, every new discovery as proof of their own views. Both schools have their own sages, their proponents staking their claims of ancestry among the towering figures of philosophical history. (*Determinists* and *indeterminists* use Democritus and Epicurus, respectively, as classical references.)

◆   ◆   ◆

Perhaps in its longing for assurance, the human mind is inclined to connect the concepts it creates in a closed system with authoritative definiteness, returning eternally to *determinism*. Only in this way can it calm the insecurity that envelopes life and master the irritating sense of incompleteness in reasoning. But the result is bleak and unsatisfactory. It is perceived as hostile to free action and creativity, the sovereign manifestations of individual identity and associated responsibilities without which society could not exist. The need to make space for such dispositions of the conscience will engender attacks against *deterministic* theories, causing an endless conflict between two irresistible inclinations, one to solve the riddle of life and the other to get out from the straight jacket of the solution. Final victory could not be declared because pronouncements concerning the ultimate reality of being stray into the marshland of metaphysics. Not a fertile ground for tall trees.

Neither *hard determinism* nor *hard indeterminism* is harmonious with personal freedom. Antecedent events lock the individual or the collective into automaton-like behavior in the first case (suggesting fatalism and a logical basis for renouncing moral responsibility) and determination (individual or collective) comes to naught as a "plaything" in the incorrigibly perfidious hands of *randomness* in the second. A man goes to the casino and plays roulette. Ordinarily, it is unacceptable to think that both the act of going there and the way the little balls "decide" to settle into their colored and numbered spaces were already determined at the Big Bang. Nor is it acceptable that the decision to go to the casino as well as the outcome of the games played there are the products of *randomness*–the way "God's dice" happened to land, beginning with the "Brownian motion" of brain particles in our gambler's head. Individual and social needs coincide when we think that one goes to the casino out of one's free will while the outcomes of the games are "determined" by *chance*, thanks to the *randomizing* agency of the croupier's impartial gestures.

Not surprisingly, the majority of the current generation would be inclined to accept explanations that stay clear of the opposite poles of hard *determinism* and hard *indeterminism*. The influence of theories that occupy the middle ground attests to the validity of this observation. In philosophy, the *libertarians* consider human will and actions the equilibrium between causality and *chance*. Many biologists maintain that social evolution reflects the *emergent properties* of the human brain, thereby creating a balance between *determinism* and individual moral and legal responsibility. The same principle is evident in the so-called *complexity theory*: Evolution of a complex system requires that the evolving system be on the edge of *chaos*, somewhere between implacable order and hopeless disorder.

Despite the attraction of the middle ground, the recurring need to find *determinism* and renounce it, to embrace *indeterminism* and cast it off, persists. Exegetes of *hard determinism* and *indeterminism* are *not* public outcasts. *Determinism* dallies with the divine and feeds into theology. One can easily derive "God has a plan for each of us" from *hard determinism*. *Indeterminism* satisfies the psychological demand for spontaneity. Its spirit is not that far from the no-holds-barred postmodern questioning of whatever science presents to the average person as social or scientific reality. By proving the inevitability of "miracles," *indeterminism* remains competitive with *determinism* in recertifying long-held myths.

◆   ◆   ◆

The need for personally experienced and individual-specific freedom is strong enough to anesthetize even common scientific knowledge about the physical and biological facts of existence. More than a century ago, Nietzsche said that the human being is willfully "forgetful" as a means of self-defense against "the blinding light of full comprehension." The accumulation of scientific knowledge has not altered psychological reflexes all that much. People may be interested in facts that pertain to the deep reality of existence, but they quickly return to the surface and go about their business.

The *mind* shakes itself loose from knowledge that has no momentary relevance and from the philosophical debate concerning ultimate truths. The Protagorian adage, "Man is the measure of everything" prevails. By defining *freedom of the will* as individually-experienced sovereignty in directing the organism's energy, and by ignoring the theoretical possibility that every single action or gesture is predetermined or is the result of mere *randomness*, the paralyzing mental state of having two equally balanced, antagonistic views disappears. Indeed, it must;

otherwise people could hardly function the way their physical endowments predisposed them.

The coincidence of particular desires and the revealed wish of the species to strengthen itself through *cultural evolution* suggests that it is a utilitarian imperative for society to navigate its general convictions so as to avoid the Scylla of absolute causality and the Charybdis of total acausality. The conviction that the human can and will overcome obstacles is indispensable. To this extent, there is ground for *determinism*. But to allow for the free play of individuality, *indeterminism* stakes out its own ground.

The concepts of *necessity* and *chance* direct the mind toward calmer epistemic seas. *Necessity* is *determinism* and *chance* is *indeterminism* through cognitive experience. If *necessity* were paramount, *determinism* characterized universal order. If *chance* were everywhere and always, then *indeterminism*, universal disorder, reigned in nature. The bag of experience with which each of us travels the finite stretch between the two infinites (i.e., the times before birth and after death) is always a mixed one. It contains both *necessity* and *chance*.

NECESSITY IN HUMAN AFFAIRS

Necessity is the recognition of inevitability. Something happened because it had to; something will happen because it must; a specific cause under given circumstances leads unavoidably to a specific effect. Whether observed in the physical world or in individual or social life; whether in a process that is short and simple or long and complicated, *necessity* can always be explained by some causal force acting upon and transforming initial conditions. In human affairs, *necessity* may be regarded as "determination that sticks" and the applicability of this label to a specific process or outcome is generally accepted. Impartial experts would draw similar conclusions. This simplified etiology gives causality its practical meaning and role.

Abstractions, of course, are rarely as simple as they appear. "The flood damaged the building" sounds reasonably uncontroversial. The water was the causal force and material damage was the effect. Inevitability of a causal relationship, *necessity*, binds cause to effect. But this explanation may not satisfy everybody. Could the municipal government that neglected its pledge to fortify the dam be considered responsible for the damage, thereby becoming *legally* a partial cause of the effect? Does the builder bear some responsibility for the extent of the damage? The insurance company will certainly investigate such issues in order to reduce its own liability. One could also raise the question "What caused the river to rise?" and, if the answer were "Unusual amounts of rain," then "What caused that?" and so on, until we find ourselves in the middle of the old stalemate concerning *determinism*. Once the train of thought leaves human imperfections, negligence, and greed behind, and enters the realm of nature, the unflinching identification of ever more general and distant causes would turn the analysis into a plug for *determinism*. After explaining why the river rose and how the climate came about, one would have to go back to the formation of the solar system, the universe. The insurance company will not take that train. There is no legal person with a check-book waiting on the platform at the end of the line. The flood may end up being designated as "sufficient cause" for the damage. If there had been no flood, there would have been no damage. Thus, it is possible to determine causality in specific cases through agreement once the event is considered closed. Similarly, analysis aimed at establishing *necessity* in social affairs and history must also draw a line between collectively accepted, common "scientific" and deeper truths. The borderline is roughly where consensus in reasoning breaks down.

Recognition of *necessity* (i.e., inevitability) follows from identifying the initial conditions that had to be present for the named causes to produce the noted effects. In the above example in which "Flood caused the damage," the high water level summarized the initial conditions and the water's chemical properties accounted for the causes that resulted in the effect, i.e., the damage. A precondition for attributing *necessity* is that one could expect the same initial conditions and causes to be sufficient to lead to the same effect *over and over again*. When society needs decisions, the attribution of *necessity* is quick and deliberate.

The method of combining causes and initial conditions to demonstrate *necessity* can be applied to America's *cultural evolution*. The individual's determination to pursue differential socioeconomic success, the maximization of felicity through balancing growing income with growing opportunities for pleasurably spent leisure, was the causal force. Despite their appearance as totally "selfish" (personal or family or group) efforts, individual determinations turned out to be a diachronically consistent, aggregate social force that prevailed to produce a generally recognized effect. America's natural wealth, open spaces (historically favorable land-to-labor ratios), the availability of capital (historically favorable capital-to-labor ratios), and accommodating institutions were the critical initial conditions that allowed this force to succeed more effectively than in the rest of the world.

To explain the general causal force, "individual determination to pursue differential socioeconomic success," a biologist may take the relay baton from the social scientist: The force lies in human nature, the will to live and reproduce carried in the hereditary material, the genes, DNA molecules. But what motivates this double-helix enigma (wriggling in cell nuclei like a worm unable to straighten out) to go to such lengths?

The physicist might say that the coincidence of three interrelated "arrows of time" explains the development of life. Since the Big Bang (i) the universe expands; (ii) it is straining toward thermodynamic equilibrium (i.e., entropy in it irreversibly grows), and (iii) the intelligent being perceives time as "flowing" from the past, through the present, toward the future.[1] The human species registers the irreversibility of transformation in the enveloping empyreal vastness as the passage of time (i.e., time exists only in our heads). Mathematical models and laboratory experiments in modern thermodynamics demonstrated that under certain conditions (abundant and constant flow of energy, such as solar radiation, a broad and stable wavelength band of electromagnetic radiation, water, and certain chemicals) matter will organize itself locally (e.g., on the blue planet). This "contrary," anti-entropic subprocess of building ever more complex orders (far-from-equilibrium dissipative material/energy systems) is as much an imperative as the build-up of entropy is a one-way, irreversible process in the expanding universe. Disequilibrium in the cosmos appears to mandate life. "…matter in equilibrium is 'blind,' while in nonequilbrium it begins to 'see'" (*Prigogine, 1997*, p. 127). On a cosmic scale, at least, "To be or not to be" may not be the question. "To be" is a must.

The contrary tendency of matter to organize itself in the midst of universal asymmetry *may* explain the creation of a time-resistant, self-replicating information database and storage unit such as the DNA molecule. The simplicity of the elements and chemical compounds found on Earth relative to the astonishing complexity of heredity-carrying macromolecules divides scientists as to the plausibility that the latter could have been the product of "self-organization" via a "trial-and-error cum natural selection" process. To this day, the mystery of life's beginning is alive and well.

To recapitulate the common scientific opinion in the sequence of events with DNA already on the scene: Free energy (high *exergy*, meaning low entropy) available on the planet explains evolution from simple organisms to anthropic complexity. The drive of the human organism to live longer and better, to reproduce and ensure ever improving conditions for its offspring begot supra-organismic collaboration, the trend of productivity-increasing division of labor. Production outpacing population led to more complex and interdependent social organiza-

---

1. See *Hawking, 1988* on the coincidental directions of these three arrows of time.

tions and to the increased significance of the average individual (despite the growth of population) through economic opportunities and the extension of legal and political rights, the generalized process of liberalization.[2]

We call *force motrice* the human expression of the anti-entropic movement observed in matter across the universe. It is our organism-specific manifestation of a common attribute of nature, the defiance of the *second law of thermodynamics* that actually helps increase its tempo. It ought not to be considered an indestructible, never-changing constant. It exists through a permanent struggle with its opposite, the death wish, the human angle on accepting or hastening entropy's advance. The willingness to wrangle with nature declines in the elderly. Aged wisdom and craving for immortality in another life brew together until one day "The King decides to die." As release from the tiresome effort to keep the body's molecules together approaches, the individual begins to embrace the new prospect with hope. "Death is just another adventure" mused Henry Miller (1891-1980), never failing to see the *couleur de rose*, even a few days before he died.

Since the *force motrice* grows, peaks, and declines in the individual, its phyletic sum is bigger in a younger population. Gradual extinction of any species may be characterized as the mutually enforced interplay between physical circumstances and seepage of the craving for life; a collective decadence manifest in the growing wish to disengage from a ceaseless and hopeless combat.

Our driving force is obviously more than an automatic momentum to replicate. It has a complicated psychological-philosophical dimension. After recognizing in its origins our time-honored trilemma (*monism, dualism, agnosticism*), one would like to remove it from the room where the physics of social life and history are put under the magnifying glass. But that is impossible. The anthropic extension of the naked urge to survive and reproduce has immense practical implications for the world. It contains the majestically creative and warmly confederated as well as the dangerously destructive and the violently antisocial, with no impassible obstacles between the two cerebral microstates. It is the proverbial "loose canon" that can fire in ceremonial salute or into the crowd.

The human hungers to live and to know. It is driven to conquer the universe, but apathy and abrogation, despair and dejection, aggression and mass-destruction, hate and self-hate are also in its genes. In spite of all that happened during the 20th century, the race may still have an unappeased appetite for squelching

---

2.   Kenneth E. Boulding (1910-1993) is a major reference among theoreticians who put social evolution in the broader context of biological evolution and regard both types as manifestations of physical processes.

the *force motrice* in others. Murder is in the blood. The animus of Cain may have declined in the majority, but the enhanced means of annihilation has opened an infinite opportunity for the remainder. We cannot exclude the possibility that, sometime in the future, an elitist conspiracy would try to solve the Earth's population overflow and resource shortage by consigning particular ("thinged") masses to nonexistence.

If the species were the toreador and entropy the bull, there are circumstances under which the individual breaks ranks and yells "Bravo Toro!" "Bring the whole damn thing down if it doesn't go my way" has crossed many minds in the past. During the closing days of World War II, the hardest of hard-core Nazis turned against themselves and those whom they considered their own, the German people. The Soviets came close to building a "doomsday ship" which, in case they lost the war against the West, would have eliminated all life on the planet through biological agents. One may ponder what would happen if a determination to commit revolutionary suicide "Jonestown style" were augmented with "Let us take the uninformed with us." Suicide/murder made headlines in the early years of the 21st century and contemporary civilization lives with the very real threat that this form of protest may make use of ABC weaponry. The antisocial *mind* harboring a death wish for itself and others at the same time is particularly apt to flourish among those who live in abject destitution, who are surrounded by cruelty and envenomed human relations, who discount the future without regret.

Even beyond economically and politically motivated acts of extended self-destruction, *homo sapiens* has a more general, contemplated wish to flee this "vile" world. This meditated impulse has been visiting and revisiting philosophy from Socrates to Freud; we may recognize it in the anti-procreation idiocrasy of religious teachings. Lamentation about getting booted out from the Garden of Eden and sanguinity about eternal life in Heaven may certainly be interpreted as longing for the absence of the *second law*, wanting to get rid of entropy, time, life's fundamental premise. Humans love their Time but they want to kill it too. One feels the pull of Manicheism, the religion of religions, lightness and goodness in an eternal cosmic war with darkness and evil. Such comprehensive and portentous pluses and minuses in human nature, with lethal extrasomatic extensions in the background (attributes that our fellow bio-chips do not possess) make one mindful of how easy or how devastating the next *chaotic transition* could be.

These are not cheerful reflections and the only optimistic notion we can squeeze from them is that the worst is not a *necessity*. If there are two conflicting views of the world and each belongs to one of two states of brain matter that may, under conditions beyond the individuals' control, change into one other, "ambivalence" might be the best way to characterize the situation. The billions of divergent ideas about how to improve the human condition, all of which spring from the same root, testify for the sempervirent strength of the *force motrice*.

The human-specific superadd to the mainspring of reproduction has its social history, which is associated with its neural network-based natural history. This biological fact is manifest in *global system*-crossing general *ethic*, *Weltanschauung*, and *mentality*. Our tentative, hypothetical *Saga* is an expression of that—the love of life beyond oneself and one's kin.

The aggregation or socialization of individual *force motrices* created the *Opaque Artificer*, which pulled or pushed the world into GS1 and propelled it through a *chaotic* interlude into GS2. Clearly, the *Opaque Artificer* is not a force in the ordinary sense of action of one body on another. The *attractor*, a crucial concept in nonlinear sciences, including modern thermodynamics, may help make its presence more real.

The *attractor* is a relatively stable dynamic state that acts as a complex causal force. It exists in a system as the result of the properties and repeated patterns of interactions of the matter it encloses. The molecules and atoms contained are unaware that they are moving toward the *attractor*. Unawareness may persist even in a large assemblage of atoms (i.e., *culture*) composed of highly evolved organisms who read books in artificial light. The species has moved through a historically significant period of *cultural evolution* toward the state of increased quantitative and qualitative strength. The billions of individuals who lived through this period were not conscious of their involvement in this process. They were meshed through the hierarchy of *socioeconomic environments* and *systems* into a global whole that was locked on to an *attractor*. We may think of this state as the *main attractor*, capable of changing intermittently into *catastrophic attractors* so as to help locate parameters for the *global system* that would allow *culture* to resume "moving" on it.

If *cultural evolution* is a self-composed material process that reveals properties of matter that remain hidden until they are called upon as needed, these properties must exist somewhere as potential before they emerge as actual. At present, we know no other feasible "hiding place" for these emergent properties of matter linked to *cultural evolution* than DNA (of which scientists readily admit they understand only about one percent). DNA may be the "container" of the *main attractor* as well as the holder of information required to implement the *force motrice* in given environments composed of physical and socioeconomic aspects. The *Opaque Artificer*, the means to move the aggregate process of socioeconomic evolution toward its distant and indiscernible end, is thus also a materially conceivable phenomenon.[3]

A mathematician might think of the *Opaque Artificer* as the "operator" that determined the evolution of a probability distribution for the growth of *culture*. This "operator" moved the "state of the species" (characterized by a vector with three elements) over time, without the species' conscious control or awareness. In this light, the dilemma between *determinism* and *indeterminism* (the ontological extensions of *necessity* and *chance*) becomes one of whether "probability" is only the mind's way of dealing with the fact that, to it, not everything occurs at once or is part of nature's nature.

To simplify reasoning, the *force motrice* may be considered the "sufficient cause" of American, and by extension, global *cultural evolution*, because, with a great dispersion of results, the rest of the world also moved toward higher per capita income (despite the increase in global population) and greater equality among individuals during the past 200 years. The reason global *cultural evolution* lags behind its American component may be found in the inadequacy of conditions for socioeconomic progress in the rest of the world, rather than in the individual drive for differential socioeconomic success.

If we could rerun *cultural evolution* for the United States and the world on a computer screen (running time, one minute), we would recognize the trajectories. Simulating *cultural evolution* a hundred times over (identical physical and biological conditions assumed), the data points would never be scattered to such an extent that one could not recognize the trend. The possibility that *cultural evolution* during the past two centuries was a purely *random* phenomenon is flatly excluded. But saying so does not tell us whether the "reruns" would show identical or different trajectories. The first case would be argued by *hard determinists* and the second by everybody else. Equally prestigious scientific sources suggest contradictory explanations on this subject. It is evidently easier to prove the presence of *necessity* than the influence of *chance* in *cultural evolution*. The very exist-

---

3. Philosophers have been preoccupied with life's driving force at least since antiquity. The Aristotelian concept of "vital force" (the explanation behind all life forms) survived well into the 19th century, until Charles Darwin (1809-1882) and Louis Pasteur (1822-1895) successfully debunked it. One may recognize the driving force in Hegel's *Geist*, the spirit (or mind) struggling through history to reveal itself to humans; in Schopenhauer's *Will*, in Nietzsche's *Will to Power*; in Freud's *Eros*, "who" confronts *Thanatos*, and in Teilhard de Chardin's rising tide of *Noogenesis* in a live and thinking universe.

ence of the trajectory draws toward a cause-and-effect explanation. The *force motrice* left its unmistakable mark. In contrast, *chance* is not on record.[4]

CHANCE INDOMITABLE

Chance and *randomness* (the two words are used as synonyms) refer to event-producing processes whose initial conditions and/or causes the human observer either could not or would not care to determine for lack of interest or resources. Experiences with *randomness* may be classified into two categories. *Randomness of the first kind* frustrates the exactitude of projections and extrapolations, but these remain within some known framework of concepts, applied logic, and general expectations. A pair of dice is thrown and the dots show a sum of numbers. The quarterly projection of industrial output is off the range, but for a reason that does not drastically depart from the body of accumulated knowledge. The thrower of the dice did not know how they would land, but the result is no surprise; and, after the actual quarterly figure of industrial output is released, the consultant slaps his forehead: "If I had known that beforehand, I would have been right on the money. I will incorporate this hitherto overlooked factor into my forecasting model." As far as *randomness of the first kind* is concerned, the future is in the past; only insufficient knowledge of initial conditions and causes blocked the view. After the event occurs, *post factum,* everything becomes clear; the world remains as it was; unchanged and unchanging.

Randomness of the second kind brings surprises and novelties; it reveals singularities that *ex ante* analysis could not recognize. You throw a pair of dice, and after they land on the table, you find out that one of them has seven faces; the forecast is off because of a chain of unexpected bankruptcies during the period in which the forecast was made. Of course, the tricky guy who brought the seven-sided die and the people who were involved in preparing the unexpected production cutbacks were not faced with genuine novelty, *randomness of the second kind.* They only impersonated the inscrutability of nature to other individuals. To speak of *randomness of the second kind* from the general human vantage point, all "insider" knowledge must be excluded. Only those events qualify that authoritative expert

---

4.   Probably the most eloquent, simple encomium for scientific progress is that one can tie together *cultural evolution,* DNA, thermodynamics, and the beginning of the universe. Human life now may be seen as having been built by the organization of subatomic dimensions, occurring along processes that take billions of light years, but are composed of time lengths relevant in quantum physics.

or scientific opinion would consider genuine novelties to everyone on Earth. This kind of *randomness*, labeled *pure* or *extreme*, dislocates the forward-projection mechanism. Initial conditions and causes depart from what the best informed would consider normal or routine *ex ante* ignorance. We admit, after the fact, that "this was really unpredictable."

Considering world history an entropy-producing, irreversible thermodynamic process leads to the conviction that *chance* had a hand in shaping the trajectory of *cultural evolution*. But this is not so easy to prove. As attention turns from the future to the past, the perspective changes. After the fact, *necessity* is recognized behind everything and the dividing line between the two kinds of *randomness* becomes blurred. Finding cause-and-effect explanations, recognizing *necessity*, is part of evolved human psychology. Looking backward, the only difference between *randomness of the first* and *second kind* is that retrospective *necessity* seems less (perhaps much less) ordinary when established for "clear" ("universally agreed") cases of *pure chance.*

CHANCE AND NECESSITY; THE WAY WE ARE

To see how mental habits deal with *necessity* and *chance* (now split into two kinds), let us go to an automobile race. Ten cars participate. Based on the past records of the drivers and their automobiles, there is a heavy favorite. He has a 64-percent *chance* of winning and each of the rest of the contenders has a 4-percent *chance*. (The *chances* add up to 100 percent, forming the *á priori* probability distribution.) The race will get under way momentarily and one of the cars lined up in the shimmering haze of thunderous engine noise will take the trophy. The cars are off! An impending forward projected, prospective *necessity* that the seasoned, internationally renowned driver must win lingers in the stands. Of course, the race has just started; the future is open and "contingent." The famous driver is expected to win, but the contest is not over until the checkered flag comes down at the finish line. We consider three scenarios:

Scenario One. The favorite wins and is doused with champagne, as widely anticipated.

Scenario Two. The favorite collides with another car recklessly driven by an inexperienced, overly ambitious driver. A third car wins.

Scenario Three. The race begins and an earthquake shakes the area. The track crumples and the race is called off.

Scenario One is a clear case of *randomness of the first kind* and *Scenario Three* demonstrates the *second kind*. The earthquake was a genuine novelty that stepped out from the frame of reference established for the race. (It was "far" from being included in our *á priori* probability distribution.) Later, seismic experts might explain that relaxation in the strains accumulated along the nearby geological fault line caused waves through the Earth's crust. Cause and effect establish retrospective *necessity*, although knowledge, no matter how extensive it may become, can never save humans from similar anomalous, atypical occurrences in the future.[5]

What about *Scenario Two*? It is an illustration of *randomness of the first kind* because, after finding out about the accident-causing driver's state of mind, one can recognize ordinary *necessity*. *Scenario Two* is an example of the *á priori* probability distribution proving to be wrong, allowing newly acquired experience to correct it. After the race, someone may say, to the agreement of all those concerned, that "perhaps we should have taken into account the non-negligible likelihood that the difference between skill levels, combined with reckless local ambition to win, would endanger a highly skilled favorite, opening the possibility of easy victory for a third driver." An agreement among racing professionals moved the hitherto unseen ("nonexistent") into the realm of recognized possibilities.

As the race approaches its end, the psyche endorses *necessity* and demotes *chance*. *Randomness of the first kind* recedes and the *second kind*, which is generally blocked out as if it did not exist, sinks deeper into the subconscious and vanishes.

Spectators near the finish line see the outcome of the race moments before it ends. Conditions (the molecular/atomistic structures that may be described as "the determination and skill of the winning driver," "the leading car's perfect functioning," "its short distance from the finish line compared to the car following it," and "the smoothness of the road") suggest as *necessity* a final state that marks the end of the process. The race is over one second before it formally ends. Ordinary *necessity* is recognized, *chance of the first kind* becomes irrelevant in the closing second, and *chance of the second kind* is completely forgotten. This analysis can be extended backward, the relative positions of the cars in each second determining their positions in the next.

---

5.   Earthquakes are notoriously difficult to predict. But science has not given up. Satellites that capture electromagnetic radiation from places where the quakes are about to erupt hold out new hope.

Ex ante, chance dominates *necessity,* but as the process becomes shorter, *necessity* begins to gain the upper hand. *Ex post, necessity* dominates *chance* and this domination may be extended to any event, no matter how unlikely it may be. If a coin landed on its side, an occurrence for which the probability is very close to zero, someone might still come up with a generally acceptable causal explanation, turning a unique event that borders on the miraculous into *necessity.* People like to say "there is a reason for everything." After the event we smarten up. "The owl of Minerva flies at dusk," as Hegel called "Monday morning quarter-backing." By identifying the information that would have been needed to predict the totally unexpected, extraordinary event, the minds eliminate the borderline between *first* and *second kind randomness. Pure chance* is lost in the brain's electro-chemical shuffle, blurring ordinary with extraordinary *ex post necessities.* Don't knock it. Were the *mind* not this way, we would not be here. The psyche's need to "postdict" and the joy it finds in the process originate in consciousness. They come from the struggle with the *second law,* the rejection of our terminal inability to predict.

◆   ◆   ◆

If we go back into the 19th century by reading a historical novel, we rediscover the uncertainty of the present along with a habitual receptivity to encounter surprises. There is no unanimity in identifying overarching causes in the midst of effects taking shape. Could the Civil War end with a peace treaty between the Union and the Confederacy, preserving slavery in the Southern States? What particular circumstances made a family living in the mountains of Transylvania emigrate to America in the 1890s? How did the farm boy from Ohio end up loading ships in New York? Why did the young entrepreneurial talent choose a certain line of business? Why was something built in a specific place at a specific time? Why did this or that individual or corporation obtain the patent for the typewriter, the cash register, the air brake, the electric light?

During the creation of an event, or immediately following it, the answer to any of these questions would be filled with fortuity, unique stories of individual whim and will, the polymorphic hubbub of daily life. But the passage of time increases the opportunity for recognizing historical forces. The answers may converge and simplify. We know that slavery had to end one way or another because it blocked industrialization (the growth of personal incomes over the long run and the associated requirements of socioeconomic equalization); immigrants had to come to the New World because economic opportunities and social freedom beckoned; people had to move across the country as rural-to-urban migration accompanied the country's industrialization; entrepreneurial resources, coaxed out by the promise of financial rewards and status, had to find slots as commerce specialized and the number of businesses multiplied; buildings, factories, and the components of the infrastructure had to be built somewhere at some time, and scientific-technological progress that permitted the rise of productivity had to be manifest in new, patented machines, equipment, instruments, and appliances, but the automobile had to come before the airplane; the radio before the television; and the computer before the automatic pilot. In more general terms, the statistical characterization of *cultural evolution* (the trajectory) jibes with the sub-processes implied by these events; namely, population and economic activity filling up the space, and movement toward socioeconomic equity preventing the process from disruption.

Turn around the result of every single U.S. presidential election during the past 200 years and the country's socioeconomic development over the period would still have taken a course recognizably similar to the one recorded, producing conditions that resemble the actual. Can the decline and fall of the Roman Empire be explained by the interrelated causes of bad policies and decadence? To answer this question with another: "Could the best doctrine for governance and the most impeccable public morals have conserved the Empire to our days?" Italy being a prosperous member of a vast democratic confederation, the EU, rather than the dominant power on the European continent, seems to have been the logical and overwhelming orientation of *cultural evolution*. And few contemporary Italians would see it otherwise. Just ask the average citizen in Rome: "Are you better off today than your ancestors were two thousand years ago? Do you mind that your head of state is not greeted at home or abroad with "Salve mundi domine"? Your interviewee would have a good laugh, putting into perspective the ageless angst of aging hegemons.

The *force motrice* works its way through events that could and could not be predicted from past experience. From a long perspective, *cultural evolution* turns *ex ante randomness* of both kinds into *ex post necessity*. As contingencies collapse into inviolable facts, the two kinds of *randomness* fuse and then melt into summary cause-effect relations, converging toward a single reason. The disappearance of the *first kind of randomness* is reasonable; the eclipse of the *second kind* (*pure chance*) is self-deluding. To demonstrate the presence of *pure chance*, even when looking backward, we will have to appeal to the material nature of history.

THE NATURE OF HISTORY

Every human story connotes physical transformations. This is true even if the evolving flux of material constellation goes through the organizing agency of biologically autonomous human brains. These may be the most complex and fascinating things known to man, but they are still built of cells, molecules, atoms, and subatomic particles. Each of the billions of nerve cells (neurons) has a deep subatomic space, relative distances as incomprehensible as those in sidereal bodies "above." If opinions are constructs within the microstate of the brain, we can shift and slush around among a theoretically infinite number of possibilities to form them.

The volitional courses that result from individual actions expand and reduce distances among molecules and atoms and change their relations and modality of interactions every second. This consideration alone pushes assured objectivity and certitude about the state of the world through the sieve of rational comprehension like sound waves go through thin walls. It would be impossible to survey a practically infinite number of conditions. By the time we rolled up our shirtsleeves to begin, the infinite characteristics in the state of matter would have already changed in infinite and unknown ways. Unknown not only because of their sheer number, but also because physical phenomena observed on the human scale are linked to space-time-perception-defying, super-miniature nuclear universes in ways that befuddle scientific understanding.

Any analysis of the past must forego direct communication with the *Noumenon* (the untouchable microstate of the world) and rely on recognizing and connecting *phenomena*. Events and processes considered cogent are selected to explain a deeper and nontransparent actuality. The overabundance of constantly changing material conditions that lurks in *cultural evolution* as well as in the progression of the *web* (its central process) and in its surface phenomenon (world history) precludes the identification of final causes with absolute epistemic certainty.

What caused World War I? The assassination of Archduke Francis Ferdinand in Sarajevo; hegemonic competition among sword-rattling European dynasties; the Naval Arms race, the Hapsburg Ultimatum, Germany's faster economic growth than Britain's; the German ruling classes' escape from domestic anti-establishment political movements; "boredom in Europe;" South Slav nationalism, Kaiser Wilhelm's aggressive Weltpolitik; simple semantic misunderstanding: The German high command and the civilian government understood two different things by the word "mobilization." What caused the Great Depression? It was a series of short-sighted economic and monetary policies in the key countries; it was the collapse of the stock market, the vulnerability of the financial sector, protectionist trade policies, the uneven rate of development in industry and agriculture; the world economy ran out of technical innovations to be turned into mass-produced consumer goods, profit-depressing over-investment, etc.

The supple inventiveness of *homo sapiens'* (or better, *homo faber's*) ever-babbling analytical mind never fails to come up with several alternative explanations ("texts") for the same event. It tries and tries again to establish the point in time from which the orchestration of vibrating "strings" in and among the nerve cells began to produce a scene on the stage of world history. Alternative rationalizations are the verbalized expressions of material states and processes chosen from the infinite reservoir of material states and processes that correspond to each historical event. We would run out of analysts before we ran out of possibilities to explain anything completely. As long as they are clever or intriguing, new interpretations can always be added to the stock of already existing ones. As the historian, Hayden White, remarked, the more a society knows about its history, the more it can disagree. Knowing more about the past may not result in a convergence of views, although weighty developments tend to eliminate fragmentation and unite opinion.

We may call any part of history a *segment*. A limited number of people interacting in a small space during a short period of time would make a *segment* small. (A battle is a smaller *segment* than a war.) When the *mind* of the historical analyst concentrates on a *segment*, it assumes a neutral and static stance. A part of the material entity formed by interacting brains separates itself for the purpose of examining another part or the entirety of the rest of the entity. The thinking apparatus, now in an analytical, *tabula rasa* mode, creates an information base that characterizes the initial, intermediary, and final conditions. Material transformation is "coarse-grained" into symbol/referent relations, allowing the creation of a text, the description of the *segment* from beginning to end.

Finding reasons and explanations, which we equate with the identification of cause-and-effect relations and with the formulation of *necessities*, corresponds to naming the most vital streams of particles in the *segment*. These streams could always be attributed to material transformations in brains and to interactions between or among them.

Two armies face off within artillery range. Although Army A's equipment and manpower are superior, its commanding general blows it. He allows Army B to take the initiative, to outflank and surprise him. After much devastation, Army A surrenders. If we abstract away from uniforms and equipment and see human beings as lumps of atoms moving in the space of interaction particular to the *segment*, we can perceive the battle as a transformation of matter from its initial microstate to its final one. To describe the "transitional dynamic," the analysis will have to identify the crucial movements of particles, such as the streams of artillery bombardments and troop movements, and the collapse of atomistic ensembles contoured by molecules of colored textile (Army A's uniforms). The crucial movements will be the causes of the effect (defeat of Army A). They may be traced back to movements in the *minds* of the two generals, reflecting their interplay, each hypothesizing about the other's cerebral activity.

Analysis consists of separating certain material phenomena that will serve as causes to transform the initial conditions into their end state. Historical analysis is then a double separation of matter. The analyst becomes detached by assuming a neutral, passive, observant stance. This is followed by idealizing the most crucial movements of matter into causes. Using logical rules, they are reducible in number, even to a single most important one, and always traceable to material changes in human brains.[6]

The larger the *segment* (meaning more people, longer time, and larger area), the greater the opportunity to identify alternative causes for the same effect. The number of streams of particles from which to select the crucial ones becomes larger. Disagreement over causes (if not over effects) tends to increase. It is more difficult to agree about the causes and effects (*necessities*) that describe the outcome of a war than a battle. Expanding the *segment* from the French Revolution between 1789 and 1794 to European history during the 18th century increases the possibilities of plausible explanations and ways of reasoning. Some of these will uncover different aspects of the *segment*, complementing one another, some will conflict, trying to knock each other out. If and when there is a tendency to come to simple and uniformly accepted explanations, analysis reduces the number of causes. It identifies some streams of particles as crucial in the infinitely detailed process that led from an unknowable, arbitrarily declared initial microstate to a similarly unknowable arbitrary end-microstate.

---

6. In the above example, the *segment* began and ended with a (relative) standstill. The initial conditions that gave rise to the vital streams (causes) were in the *minds* of the two generals. Had we chosen as *segment* the period from the middle to the end of the battle, the causes would have been in full swing already. If we had put on our atomistic-configuration-viewing X-ray spectacles, we could have seen that the initial conditions were not only in thinking but also in happening. This qualification does not change the basic idea that vital streams of matter are part of the initial conditions.

If the outcome of the battle mentioned above had to be predicted from strictly material initial conditions, no analyst could have imaged the microstructure of matter with 100 percent accuracy through verbal "coarse-graining." They would have overlooked the details in the brains of the two generals. If they had to retrodict the initial conditions from the end state (considering its material details the initial conditions in a reverse flow of time), they would have concluded that Army B was the stronger. (Only a "backward-facing" prophet would have predicted the outcome, but even his divining powers may be equated with that certain "something" that the winner of the lottery "must have known.")

When it is imperative to establish formal cause-and-effect relations, the process of going back into the past in search of the initial conditions and selecting from among a number of possible causes is cut short by agreement. Insurance and accident investigations must conclude positively and within a given time frame. An airplane crash must be attributed to some initial conditions and causes in order to head off another one that even the only tentatively identified conditions and causes could possibly reproduce.

In legal cases or those involving issues of public safety, the conclusion of the cause-and-effect (*necessity*) is enforced institutionally or by a consensus of expert opinion. In the analysis of national or world history, acceptance of the *necessities* (identified through authoritative descriptions, juxtapositions of events, and commentaries) is not mandated, at least not in open societies. Conclusions are purely academic or motivated by politics and ideology and are subject to questioning or outright falsification. In short, the search for identifying *necessities* behind historic events may never end. The acceptance of a *Saga* under the hypothetical GS3 is comparable to reaching consensus under the duress of protecting the human world. We presume that agreement over its text will be coerced more by the recognition of threatening circumstances than by having no other variants with good claims for acceptance. The *Saga* itself (not an undisputed, foundational closure, only a collectively-agreed-upon, expediently self-referential text) will evolve in unforeseeable ways. All this leads to an indirect admission that *randomness of the second kind* has a hand in history. Below, we shall present a variety of more direct ways to see this, but first a short note on *chaos theory*.

OF *CHAOS*[7]

Nonlinear dynamics or nonlinear science, nicknamed *chaos theory*, is the mathematical approach to discovering order in physical, biological, and economic phenomena that practitioners in these fields would have considered hopeless tangles for meaningful analysis as recently as a half century ago. *Chaos*, as a science, is included in the broader field of *Dynamical Systems Theory*.

"Sensitive dependence on initial conditions" is the soul of *chaos*. Events or circumstances so tiny that they would most certainly escape explicit consideration when making predictions, are tied in undetectable ways to conditions of matter large enough to be regarded both as detectable and significant. The connection is "sensitive;" the potential for amplification is "touch-and-go." The most trivial flux in a single aspect of the submicroscopic state could escalate into major, imagination-staggering events. "The butterfly effect" (introduced by Edward Lorenz) is the favorite, eternally recurring illustration. The beautiful monarch butterfly somewhere in Mexico flutters its wings, and step-by-step, the effects of these tiny movements change the atmosphere over France and cause a nasty rain shower. Some event that we would have to attribute to *randomness of the second kind* on June 28, 1914 in Sarajevo was the fluttering of the butterfly's wings that magnified into World War I. (History notes that the assassination of the Archduke was the result of coincidental caprices of the victim and the assassin, i.e., it almost didn't happen.) The trivial managed "somehow" to become significant, and it is this "somehow" (the nonlinear dynamics) that interests the "cultivators" of *chaos*.

Usually a "system" made up of inanimate or animate matter is the focus of analysis. Its behavior is studied in periodic or in unidirectional, irreversible time evolutions. This second category is directly applicable to our theory because *cultural evolution* is unilateral and irreversible (entropy-producing) and unfolds through *global systems* that organize *culture* for *macrohistoric* periods. *Chaos* informs us that systems holding together and facilitating processes that grow in size and complexity *will have to* undergo periods of *chaotic* self-reorganization called *bifurcations*.

Technically, *bifurcation* begins when a single system parameter leaves its acceptable range and "branches" into two or more alternative solutions for the functioning of the system–an overall unstable condition. In complex systems with many parameters (such as *global systems*), a critical number of departures from the equilibrium range of parameters sets off *bifurcation*, called *global transformation* from the *macrohistoric* and *chaotic transition* from the *metahistoric* perspective. Parameters that remain within their equilibrium range, in combination

---

7.   Ervin Laszlo's publications, drawing on the discoveries of Prigogine and his associates, are particularly helpful in relating aspects of *chaos theory* to social and historical problems. See, for example, *Laszlo, 1998*.

with all the possibilities ("degrees of freedom") the complex system may posses, cannot preserve the *relative steady state*. Stability is lost, but the path has been cleared for the evolving complexity to learn, develop, try, and sort out new system coefficients in order to regain stability. *Bifurcation* generates a diversity of possible solutions for another *relative steady state*. Enduring characteristics in the "environment" (genetic dispositions critical among them) will select the most adaptive solution for survival during the next phase. This is a "generalized Darwinian process" whereby variety is reduced to a singular solution. The *web* has to go through *bifurcation* to proceed from one *relative steady state* to the next. The end of *bifurcation* signals the successful assemblage of information needed to keep the system in its new stage of relative equilibrium. Always "relative" because equilibrium in a unidirectional, irreversible process can never be considered completely stable. It remains "dynamic" under any circumstances. In our common experience this means that the present is always charged with almost untenable tensions and threats and these will always be new compared to their past versions.

If a system underwent *bifurcation*, it exhibited signs of *chaos*, the exact cause of which eludes analysis, by definition. The original trigger mechanism that was too insignificant to be noticed (e.g., brain activity in the heads of the Archduke and his assassin), let alone to be taken into explicit consideration, is forever lost. Initial condition sensitivity pulled (had to pull) the system apart to allow its adaptive transformation.

Chaotic time evolutions may be divided into completely *random* processes (*indeterministic chaos*) and those where disorder is kept under the control of a superimposed causal force, even during *bifurcation*. These time evolutions are characterized as *deterministic chaos*. We shall argue in the following pages that *cultural evolution* is *deterministic chaos*.

In general, a system is prone to "complicated time evolutions" (a synonym for *chaos*) if many points in it have periodic orbits and/or if it has a minimum of three superimposed oscillations with different wave lengths. The oscillations must be interrelated, but they must exhibit relative independence. A system consisting of coupled subsystems, again interrelated but possessing a sufficient level of autonomy to transmit changes among themselves, will also be inclined to create *chaotic* dynamics.

Chaos theory belongs primarily to the domains of mathematics and physics. It is applied to very specific problems, but has also informed philosophical *discourse* in significant ways. Inevitabilities are no longer what they used to be. *Chaos*, if its presence can be demonstrated, damages the predictability of a system's future evolution. This much is now scientific fact. Nevertheless, the generalized uncertainty inspired by the perennial presence of nonlinear dynamics remains theory. *Chaos* could not resolve the ancient dispute between *determinism* and *indeterminism* to the satisfaction of the entire scientific community. It did not dissuade the *determinist* from arguing that there are causes in *indeterministic chaos*; only some of them are quantitatively untreatable; they foil the brain's information-processing capacity. The *indeterminist* continues to disparage the *determinism* in *deterministic chaos*: "You did not wait long enough and did not consider all the dimensions in which events occur." To escape from this unsolvable problem, we defined *necessity* as a consensus-garnering, humanly observed linkage between cause and effect, and introduced *pure chance* as scientifically proven unpredictability and nonretrodictability.

Amidst history's strange and bizarre occurrences we discovered *cultural evolution* and, by identifying its cause, we have demonstrated the presence of *necessity* in this process. We recognize both the cause (the *force motrice*) and the effect (*cultural evolution*) in our own behavior and conditions, as we recognize them in the behavior and conditions of everybody else living now and in those whom time (entropy) has already digested. Thus, the *necessity* we establish flows from seeing all personal and social actions and ideas as inextricable parts of the global microstate of interdigitated *minds* straining to expand while maintaining direction. There must be physical forces, "nature," behind this direction-preserving evolution and we called their individualized, human manifestation the *force motrice*. All the alignments, oppositions, and transformations of *discourses*, current and past, are captured in this maximally inclusive, historically valid reduction. But *necessity*, so established, has never been alone in determining the iterative enhancement of the species' state. As the following five points demonstrate, *pure chance* also helped shape its course.

A. *The preponderance of physical conditions defining the world*

Cultural evolution is an anti-entropic transformation that creates more entropy than it reduces. It augments entropy as it dissipates resources. This is a "one-way street." Although particles never stop agitating, colliding, and being unruly in the growing and ever more interconnected system of matter, the *chance* that they will accidentally find their way back to the exact conditions that existed a second ago is, for all practical purposes, zero. The multitude of shuffling, excited particles is unable to switch back uniformly into their previous microstates. Going back or reproducing their *ex ante* macrostates is out of the question. (Boltzmann explained entropy's one-way directionality with the infinity of initial conditions.) Does the world know its microstate during the next second? According to Prigogine, it cannot. Macroscopic phenomena are also subject to spontaneous developments.[8]

If we were to foretell the future, a forward-projected *segment* of *cultural evolution* (e.g., the next 200 years), we would need to take into account an infinite number of initial conditions with infinite precision in this moment. Forget it. The infinite number of initial conditions is diffused in the inaccessible *Noumenon*. The analyst will take note of a finite number of trends established from past data and tie them to a rough-hewn set of (humanly communicable) facts that stand in for the unfathomable array of characteristics that would be required to define the world precisely. Subjective arbitrariness, even if completely shared by academic opinion, is inescapable when the material process we call *cultural evolution* is projected into the realm of "the not yet happened." *Ex ante* unpredictability of the future is guaranteed. From the anthropic angle, the forward projection of *cultural evolution* contains scientifically proven unpredictability; *randomness of the second kind.* For similar reasons, *cultural evolution* could not be retrodicted; world events played backward from microstates of matter would not re-create the past as recorded through historical facts. The only difference between hindcast and forecast is that the "flow of time" reveals errors in predictions more dramatically than the backward-fitting of phenomena into causal links.

Pure chance will always defy causal arguments, that is, lexically rendered *necessities.* Explanations of developments in human society become agreements "among reasonable men" as Kant put it, a view not far from Voltaire's pungent remark that history is "a fable agreed upon" or Bohr candidly admitting that what we say about nature is more important than the way it might really be. In the end, it is not possible to disprove Nietzsche's claim that there are no facts, only interpretations; and only appeals to pragmatism can calm late 20th century incredulity about the absolute value of our inescapably language-dependent truth claims.

Events that depart from past experience (genuine novelty) flow naturally from a process that combines unidirectionality with an unbounded number of physical conditions. We can easily recognize this if we stop and think for a minute. Since the future is obliged not to repeat the past indefinitely, the most significant events in world history are without precedent. The essence of the future is the "jamais vu" not the "déja vu." Of course, moving ("progressing") through the alien world in which we became conscious of being, discovering never-before-dreamed-of landscapes, does not exclude the theoretical possibility that these discoveries were

---

8.   This view is not uniformly shared among physicists.

determined in ways unknown to the *mind*. Behind the *necessity* identified in *cultural evolution*, *determinism* may rule the wilderness of existence. In this case, *cultural evolution* knows where it is going but we cannot penetrate its secret. If *determinism* is not almighty, *cultural evolution* hesitates as it unfolds. For the world it is all the same. It cannot predict its future course. Physical conditions in and around humans, never fully known, evolve toward conditions even less known. Genuine novelty on a historical scale must always pop up as either the *force motrice* or its aggregate, the *Opaque Artificer*, separated by analysis from initial conditions, acts upon the rest of them. Some of these initial conditions must remain too insignificant to be noticed by the *mind*. Sensitive dependence on their ability to secrete *post factum* causality must be present. Were it not so, the future could be predicted and the past retrodicted from strictly physical conditions.

To summarize: Genuine novelty must occur in a unidirectional process that involves a virtually infinite number of particles. Given our incapacity to survey initial conditions fully, the occurrence of the never-before-encountered is solidly implanted in every moment of our existence. Therefore, given anthropic limitations, *pure chance* must have helped shape the trajectory of *cultural evolution*. It must have influenced its core process, the evolution of the *web*, and its immediately apprehended surface phenomenon, the transformation of world life.

B. *Cultural evolution as a hybrid of deterministic and indeterministic dynamics*

The dynamic model in which time ("t") appears as an explicit variable and it does not matter whether one enters it with a positive (+ t) or negative (-t) sign, describes a *time-symmetric* process. Newton's equations, in which time is squared (i.e., t appears as t^2), describe such processes, e.g., reversible mechanical motions. We record the collision of two billiard balls on film. They approach each other, they collide and Cut! If we played the film backward for someone who did not know what we originally recorded, the person might think we were showing the billiard balls after their collision, i.e., as they move away from one another after the impact. Going forward in time makes as much sense as going backward. (By denying the relevance of time's arrow, both Schroedinger's wave mechanics, used to calculate regularities in quantum phenomena, and Einsteinian physics imply time symmetry.)

Time-symmetric processes are *reversible*. Algebraically, this follows from the model's indifference regarding the direction of time's flow, the equivalence between past and future. *Reversibility* refers to a mechanism that allows for the reversal of velocities, thereby making the process go backward into its past to the point at which it began. *Reversibility* in a physical sense also implies return to the starting point in time in an unchanged state. A *time-symmetric, reversible* process allows a system to "rendezvous" with itself unchanged. At the designated meeting place on the time line, the system imagined as going forward and coming back will be in an identical state. *Reversibility* is associated with *periodicity*. Peaks and valleys recur with unfailing regularity along a perfect wave trajectory (as on the *sine* curve); consequently, we can always arrive at any selected point from both the "past" and the "future." (A straight line dynamic equation is the trivial case of unfailing periodicity because not even peaks and valleys need to be invoked.)

Time-symmetric, reversible, and *periodic* processes that ignore *entropy* production are idealizations. *Time symmetry, reversibility, periodicity*, and *no-entropy* production are attributes of *deterministic* time evolutions. Analysis can tell in advance where a point moving along the trajectory will be at a specific time–if not exactly, then within a plus/minus range.

Time symmetry, reversibility, periodicity, no-entropy production, and *determinism* are characteristics that stick together. Any one of them implies the rest. It follows that *deterministic* descriptions of physical phenomena are modeled abstractions of reality. This is not to say that they are not important or that they necessarily contradict reality. In physics and chemistry, the assumption that matter is in equilibrium (its processes are reversible because of ideal circumstances) is of great theoretical importance. Newtonian mechanics or fundamental dynamic conceptualizations in economics also have proved to be of vital practical significance. Nevertheless, such idealizations ignore entropy, despite the knowledge that all motions, whether they are studied by the mechanical engineer or the economist, produce it.

Modern thermodynamics demonstrated the significance of (nonidealized) *indeterminate* processes in nature, characterized by being *time-asymmetric, irreversible, nonperiodic*, and *entropy-producing*. Here again, the listed features are inseparable. Discovery of *irreversibility* in a process, for example, suffices to diagnose it as *indeterminate* and therefore, exhibiting the rest of the listed qualities.

The *mind* cannot completely understand or control *indeterminate* processes. From the human observer's point of view, the curve, which mathematically corresponds to the *indeterminate* process, "does not know" where it is going. It hesitates and then decides. In *deterministic* algebraic characterizations, probability calculations can establish reliably how far off an estimate might be from its predicted future value; in *indeterminate* processes, the first use of probability is to guess what the system would choose to do next. *Determinism* produces the expected and predictable (*randomness of the first kind* when dealing with the future). *Indeterminism* generates genuine novelty; hence, it connotes unpredictability, *randomness of the second kind.*

As shown by Prigogine, far-from-equilibrium dissipative systems that complexify to avoid extinction combine *deterministic* and *indeterministic* elements. *Cultural evolution* is clearly such a process. It preserved direction (as discovered *ex post*) and produced entropy. From these two attributes alone we can recognize the hybrid. Since *determinism* is detected, we know that the process will tolerate idealizations; the discovery of regularities can provide valid information and useful insights (e.g., that the *global system* as an abstract phenomenon is manifest in its observed realizations). However, since the process is also *indeterminate*, no idealization of past data can foretell the future of *cultural evolution* in ways that would satisfy empirical rigor.

Similar to any entropy-defying animate entity, the *global system* struggles to live. It denies being a phase in *cultural evolution*, a mere segment along the unidirectional time line. Adaptive behavior in the social sciences and humanities (i.e., participation in "professional *discourses*") modulates the *text* to show, in virtually inexhaustible ways, that the *system* in place is a nondepreciating framework for everlasting cycles and cycle-less infinite continuities. The *text* tries to digest and belittle growing anomalies between *cultural evolution* and the *web* until the onset of the next *chaotic* interlude reveals its transience.

C. *Chaos through bifurcation*

Since *culture* comprises life, it is a far-from-equilibrium dissipative substance that moves farther away from thermodynamic equilibrium. As theoretical and empirical research amply demonstrated, *chaotic* transformations, called *bifurcations*, resulting in the emergence of qualitatively new, theoretically unpredictable events, accompany the evolution of such systems. Recognizing that (a) *culture* is a far-from-equilibrium dissipative entity; (b) the *global system* represents its organizational framework; and (c) a *global system* emerged (GS0—>GS1) and underwent transformation (GS1—>GS2), we can conclude that the respective connecting periods had to be *bifurcations* because far-from-equilibrium systems must move through such processes to avoid decline and extinction.

During *bifurcation* the system increases its entropy production. *Chaotic transitions* did the same. Human lives were cut short in bloody conflicts, massive amounts of property were destroyed before natural depreciation would have returned them to the *global environment*; and huge quantities of armaments, resources to destroy and to be destroyed, were produced. If we could rerun *cultural evolution* from 1500 to the present, the *chaotic transitions* (i.e., *bifurcation* applied to GS0—>GS1 and GS1—>GS2) had to occur again. And *chaotic transitions* could not accomplish the task of identifying parameters for a new global order without cataclysms (stepped-up entropy production) escalating from "1789-1834" to "1914-1945." Through *bifurcation, randomness of the second kind* influenced the selection of GS1 and GS2 parameters, hence, the trajectory of *cultural evolution.*

D. *Chaotic footprints all over the place*

There are tell-tale signs that *chaos* has been part of *cultural evolution* on a continuous basis. As indicated above, a system exhibits *chaotic* behavior if many points in it have periodic orbits. If the individual socioeconomic status is considered a point, *culture* (containing these points) has many of them. For instance, the level of personal income, the simplest measure of socioeconomic status, undergoes periodic changes. For most people, it increases, maxes out, and then declines with the progression of age. Linked together through the division of labor under *global systems*, this periodicity must cause *chaotic* phenomena.

Relatively independent oscillations have also been identified as sources of "complicated time evolutions"–an alternative expression to acknowledge the presence of nonlinear dynamics. A minimum of three quasi-independent oscillations is required to cause *chaos.* We recognize at least three types of such oscillations in *cultural evolution*: The longest was the dialectical triad (thesis, antithesis, synthesis) that accompanied GS0—>GS1 as well as GS1—>GS2; the shortest were the business cycles, while technological cycles (the appearance and disappearance of clusters of marketable scientific discoveries) were of intermediate length. The linkage of relatively independent subsystems (nations) through the growing international division of labor and globalization must have also generated pattern-breaking time evolutions.

Pure chance is present in reproduction and, consequently, in the relationship between the individual and the socioeconomic environment. From mutations (errors in copying the hereditary material) to the formation of the fertilized egg, *extreme randomness* accompanies the creation of new organisms. Not only are prenatal atomic and subatomic events far beyond what humans can predict or reconstruct, but they also take place (as far as science can know) without prior knowledge of or concern for the socioeconomic environment in which the individual will "wake up" as an adult. Thus, people themselves and their behavior are marked with *pure chance.* The coupling of billions of quasi-independent manifestations of *extreme randomness* in the world as a whole is expected to unleash chaotic dynamics–unpredictable events originating from initial-condition sensitivity.

Cultural evolution is intrinsically and quintessentially *chaos*-ridden. Such generalized *chaos* in *cultural evolution* reverses the argument from "there must be some *chaos* associated with its *deterministic* trend" to "there must be some *deterministic* force that imposes order on omnipresent *chaos*." (Of course, we know that *cultural evolution* has a memory that it cannot lose. No entity that remembers itself and whose continuation depends on its past can be totally acausal.)

Diagnosing a process as *chaotic*, or having *chaotic* components, or undergoing *chaotic* periods, is *prima facie* evidence that *cultural evolution* has been influenced by *extreme randomness*. It can be characterized as *deterministic chaos* because its underlying cause, the *force motrice*, never stopped "pushing." It never lost complete control.

E. *Insight from time series analysis*

The mixture of *deterministic* and *indeterministic* elements is a much studied phenomenon in economic time series analysis. The so-called "random walk with drift and deterministic trend" has been found to characterize many macroeconomic time series, including the historical growth of per capita income, one of the *cultural evolutionary* indices. The following general model may be helpful in illustrating the statistical structure of *cultural evolutionary indices* as "random walk with drift and deterministic trend:"

$$\Delta CE_t = a_0 + \alpha\, CE_{t-1} + a_1\, t + v$$

where ΔCE_t is change in the vector containing the three *cultural evolutionary* indices from year (t-1) to t (e.g., from 1867 to 1868); a_0, and a_1 are constants; α was tested and found to be equal to one (i.e., unit root has been found); CE_{t-1} is the vector containing the three *cultural evolutionary* indices in year (t-1); and v is the error term.

If we had a true series of *cultural evolutionary indices* (including the elusive socioeconomic equality index, SEEI), the above equation might correspond to *cultural evolution* during the past two centuries. It contains *deterministic* and *random* elements. It is "nonstationary," meaning that it has no constant mean and variance. As a result, "shocks" (events that make the time evolution different from what otherwise could be expected based on the *deterministic* nature of the curve) *do not wear off.*

Natural events (e.g., floods and earthquakes) or man-made ones (e.g., wars, the energy crises of the 1970s, and major changes in economic policy) are considered shocks. Their effects, carried by the error term v, become permanently incorporated into the time series used to characterize the data-generating process.[9] To make regression models (such as the one shown above) more reliable, the data need to be treated (mainly through "differencing") so as to leave the error term without a trend. Studies based on this approach proved to be more successful in forecasting future developments than earlier econometric models (i.e., those that were applied before the cointegration/unit root breakthrough of the 1980s). This qualitative improvement in econometric techniques also brought a fresh perspective on the augural capabilities of mathematical formalisms. Future shocks, representing *randomness of the second kind*, were proven to be unpredictable from past shocks. The previous history of the unexplainable residual does not provide a basis for determining its future evolution. With time, new, hitherto unseen functional relationships invade the error term, invalidating its limits. Banking on the continued validity of information bequeathed by the past tends increasingly to disable forecasts.

If *cultural evolution* were *deterministic*, the trajectory would be its trend and *randomness of the first kind* would play with it, making it into a stochastic, but still predictable, process. Over a two-century period, the annual error terms would sum to zero around a curve that was generated through intermittent forward projections. The thermodynamic conceptualization of *cultural evolution* tells us that this process will always produce trend-defying jolts in unforeseen and unforeseeable ways. Modern econometrics demonstrates that such jolts will have a permanent effect on the trend, even if some of them are only mere perturbations, never analyzed and soon forgotten. Even these must bear upon the trajectory of *cultural evolution*.

We said that the equation above might correspond to *cultural evolution*. The "true formula" could, in fact, be more complicated. For instance, to find ΔCE_t one might need to go back further into the past than just one year. Instead of CE_{t-1}, further differences, e.g., CE_{t-2} or CE_{t-3}, would have to be used. However, it is certain that the partially *indeterminate* nature of *cultural evolution* will always demand the inclusion of an error term, the quantitative expression of ever new manifestations of a thermodynamic progression's lack of complete predictability; shocks and perturbations that become woven into the trend. Therefore, the *pure chance* portion of what had been unforeseen becomes part of any trajectory depicting *cultural evolution* from actual data. Unforeseen impacts upon the trajectory do not cancel out. Assuming the opposite would lead us back to a *determin-

---

9.   Although the algebraic demonstration of this statement is quite simple, it is unnecessarily technical for this text. For details, see, for example, *Hamilton, 1994.*

istic trajectory, the visual expression of stationary time series in which *pure chance* melts into stable patterns in the long run. This would contradict *cultural evolution*'s entropy-generating, thermodynamic nature.

Arguments A and B showed that at no time in the past could the effects of *pure chance* upon *cultural evolution* be discounted when looking at the future of the process. Arguments C and D demonstrated that *pure chance* affected the process in the past. Argument E, dealing with the miniaturized image of *cultural evolution*, confirms both groups of observations. At no time in the past could errors anterior to the point of forecast be relied on to predict the trajectory's future, and past deviations from the trend became incorporated into the measurements of *cultural evolution*. A and B said "You can never count *pure chance* out;" C and D said "You must always count *pure chance* in," and E said "Data will show that both statements are correct."

◆　　　◆　　　◆

Necessity and *(pure) chance* jointly shaped American and global *cultural evolution*. Of course, there is no agreement on the subject of whether or not the split of influences into *necessity* and *chance of the second kind* is ontologically valid. What seem like *chaotic* elements in *deterministic chaos* might not be *chaotic* according to universal laws humans do not perceive. If we could rerun *cultural evolution*, simulating the formation of its trajectory on a computer, and saw a somewhat different path snaking up the screen every time (but at least once) we would know that the split was correct. *Indeterminacy* is not the by-product of our inherited sensory-psychological survival kit. What appears as *randomness of the second kind* is, in fact, *random*. Nature decides as it goes along. However, if we saw the same trajectory over and over again in a very large number of cases without exception, then we would accept the hypothesis of an overarching (ontological) *determinism*. What seems *random* to the *mind* was already past history when time began.

Even if the first alternative were correct, cataclysms on the scale of "1789-1834" and "1914-1945" would always reappear. The *chaotic transitions* were material phenomena indispensable for the drastic self-reprogramming of the *representative mind*. From the humanistic point of view, the loss and recovery of system-level information had to be catalyzed by moral catharsis. In a *nondeterministic* light, the *metahistoric* generalization suggests that deeply disturbing events, capable of creating a (roughly) simultaneous transformation in the socioeconomic environment and behavior, could have occurred in ways other than they actually did.

With the caveat that *necessity* and *chance* are limited to the *mind*'s discernment of *determinism* and *indeterminism*, science and common experience suggest that they jointly shape history. From a practical point of view, whether *extreme randomness* is ontologically valid or it is a mere anthropoid mirage makes no difference. The species' trek across evolutionary time has been influenced by spontaneous events that no history-honed intuition, no *hysterisis* (knowledge of the past used to say meaningful things about the reactions new conditions will prompt) could have foretold. By occurring in the global microstate of interconnected cerebral material, which may be characterized as the "collective subconscious," *cultural evolutionary* complexification has to make humanity surprise itself continuously in small ways and from time to time in big ways.[10]

INDIVIDUAL FREEDOM

The fierce neuro-electro-chemical storms, the savage bludgeoning of skulls this simple expression evoked over the ages! And in the clash between those who prove that people do not possess it and those who substantiate that they indeed do, only the *argumentum ad hominem* is a clear winner: Since, in order to live in society, individuals must be accountable for their actions, free will must be attributed to individuals.

The conviction that *freedom of action* (or *freedom to act*) exists is based on both interpersonal comparisons and introspection. The individual feels free if the election from among alternative ways of directing its somatically-generated energy, its *will*, is not more constrained than a benchmark, supplied most frequently by someone else's current level of freedom or an anterior level of its own.

Determinists claim that selecting from alternatives after careful deliberation is closer to conceding to the inevitable than to making a freely willed decision. Julius Caesar knew about the conspiracy and was warned not to go to the Senate on the Ides of March in 44 BCE. Yet, in his own universe—a material reality formed by compromise between his genetic endowments and his environment—he was compelled to go. By his own "laws of nature," heeding the advice to pro-

---

10. Research reported from different scientific fields confirms our main conclusion, namely that *deterministic chaos* best characterizes *cultural evolution*. It is of particular significance that social anthropology appears to move in the same direction. New approaches to the study of various cultures reveal the joint influence of structure (a *deterministic* component) and nonlinear dynamics in the evolution of social interactions. See *Mosko and Damon, 2005*.

tect himself would have conflicted with the image he insisted on maintaining. Napoleon Bonaparte, given his political situation, reputation, and long-term plans, did not see any alternative but to order the *Grande Armée* to cross into Russia in June 1812. You have to be *You* to know how unavoidable your decisions are, even if you are more willing than megalomaniac conquerors to expand counsel beyond "self." Self-mastery, the *determinist* may muse, is in the eye of the beholder, but not in the one that happens to look in the mirror. However, if everybody believed that only someone else experienced true autonomy, the illusion of personal freedom would have to end with the last interview.

Au contraire. Despite experiencing the gravity of circumstances and compulsions to make particular decisions, the individual has an unshakeable belief in the general sovereignty of its *will*. To name just a few sources that keep this sensation alive: We consider our thinking untrammeled and connected with a decision space, choices as to which of our thoughts should be followed with what specific action; we see others with information identical to ours react differently; we alter our preferences based on marginal changes in circumstances, sentiments, or momentary temper; we initiate action on a whim, we handle similar situations separated by space or time differently; we nearly always consider refraining from action or ceasing it a valid option; we can go back in time and say "I should have taken my umbrella" or we can go forward into the future and create visions, mental images to explore each available alternative rationally and emotionally; we can change the focus of concentration from long-term, portentous dilemmas to flavors in the ice cream parlor; we can inject play into seriously pursued goals and we can turn serious pursuits into play.

The human mind is torn between the logic of *determinism* and *indeterminism* because both make sense at some level, but neither could possibly motivate individual life. Being caught in a cobweb of *necessities* suggests fatalism, an unacceptable proposition regardless of how keen and scientifically well-founded the arguments in support of it may be. The other extreme, which claims that *chance of the second kind*, the humanly recognized form of *indeterminate* forces, guides personal actions, is equally unacceptable. Would a high-school graduate draw cards from a well shuffled deck to decide what he wants to do in life? *Ace of Hearts* means test pilot? *King of Diamonds*, professional baseball player? Even the most playful spirit would think he could do better than that. The individual rejects the notion that everything it does and everything that happens to it can always elude its *will*, that the success of its directed efforts toward a calculated end is the sole result of *chance* and has nothing to do with a *necessity* that it imposes on initial conditions and maintains until the goal is achieved. Again, pragmatic needs and common experience dismiss the ingenious arguments (invoking perhaps quantum theory and *chaos*) that omnipotent *randomness* makes the freedom of *will* illusory. Complete *determinism* and *indeterminism*, as applied to individual *freedom to act*, may even appear as profanations of human character. The first demotes *homo sapiens* to an unwitting puppet, the second to an imbecile.

Speculations do not need to embrace extremes to end up in a transcendental imbroglio. *Third mind* mysteries and eternal loops appear even if one tries to establish a balance between the roles of *determinism* and *indeterminism*. *Minds* can comprehend only causally determined events, but the unsoundable details of brain matter disallow the establishment of experientially valid connections between thought and action, motive and behavior. Deprived of solid physical localization of cause, the debate over the respective roles of *deterministic* and *indeterministic* forces in "willing the motive," "willing the will," and "willing the will to will" can go on forever among gifted theorists. Then there is the venerable subject/object confluence, consciousness examining itself with the help of the symbol/referent relations it created and by which it is recognized. Some throw in the towel. It cannot be done. It is like trying to squeeze the whole into some part of it. Language-bound thinking, a part of our evolved perception apparatus, allows us only to mutter in the impenetrable fog of existence. Others disagree and maintain that this "cop-out" debases human intelligence. The use and development of language *is* thinking. Saying that language cannot point outside of itself is the same as saying that thinking cannot move beyond thinking. Nonsense. Does thinking want to leave itself behind to become more effective? Limited as it may be, the brain has facilitated the discovery of many things, from the neutrinos that go through it to the galaxies where it would like to go, starting from zilch. We must and can rely on it to gain a complete and reliable scientific picture of our origins and destiny. Again, arguments can go back and forth like a ping-pong ball between two able players.

All this is, of course, old stuff, although interest in it never wanes. To see something new with the help of the thermodynamic theory of human self-organization, let us invoke a famous thought of Johann Gottlieb Fichte (1762-1814): Freedom is recognized negatively. It exists because it is opposed. Some of this opposition is internal; self-restraint allowing for communal existence, and some is external, coming from the rest of society and nature. Correct. Without obstacles to volitions, desires, plans, and actions we would not live in a thermodynamically conditioned universe; our ethereal bodies would move without losing energy. They would continue along trajectories in uniform motion, impersonating Newton's first law. If history were an exclusively circular process, producing nothing but periodically recurring events, the concept of free *will* would become redundant. No selection of options and strategies would be needed and all personal decisions would be "off the shelf" because no one would get in anyone's way. The personal experiences of struggle, victory, or defeat would not be known. *Freedom of action* would be expressed through the recurrence of identical behavioral manifestations. In other words, it would be useless and nil. Not to worry. The *second law* will not be repealed. *Free will* (defined here as somatic energy awaiting direction) is needed forever in the permanent struggle for existence and fulfillment.

The conviction of possessing *free will* originates from the *force motrice*, the life-creating pseudo-opposition to the accumulation of entropy as it appears in the human organism. This general precipitator of *necessity* (the autocatalytic push factor) behind *cultural evolution* itself was not born under the star of freedom. Life springs up anywhere in the universe where local conditions permit it.

We enter this world without being asked if we wanted to defy entropy, to counteract the passage of time. The *force motrice* is with us at the moment we are conceived. It drives the organism to unite its *free will* with the *free will* of others, inadvertently creating the *Opaque Artificer*, to build and expand *culture*, a process that cannot subdue nature. *Cultural evolution*, accompanied by the growth of human knowledge, must stop short of incorporating the entire crypto-physical *Noumenon*. If the *mind* had all the information to understand the universe, not only would we have defeated the entropy law (don't count on it), but also we would have eliminated the fundamental condition of existence, the "struggle," along with its inseparable associate, the consciousness of freedom in directing individual efforts.

The species participates in an all-encompassing, universal material/energy process—nature at large on the move. This participation is not voluntary, yet it is embraced. We want what nature needs; we are eager to do what we are forced to do because we have evolved so as to accomplish *cultural evolution* (part of "nature at large on the move"). In exchange for the efforts and sacrifices, *cultural evolution* has increased the combination of *freedom from want* and *freedom of action*.

The first brought relief from the harshness of the natural environment and bodily pain, from dawn-to-dusk physical labor, from the most brutal forms of social oppression, exploitation, humiliation, and neglect. And, of course, freedom from many discomforts and inconveniences has been gained through the consumer economy. Aspirin is freedom from headache; the automobile is freedom from the inability to bridge space quickly and conveniently; an evening concert is escape from the bondage of daily routine and preoccupations; gourmet food is freedom from "blah" low-entropy intake. All the improvements in the quality of life may be interpreted as gaining freedom from conditions that preceded the improvement.[11] Since the quality of life is subject to amelioration, *freedom from want* may be considered a variable that can increase or decrease, confirming its existence in separately maintained but very similar *minds*.

At the current and projected levels of global population, *freedom from want* cannot be equalized between the *vanguard* and the rest of the world. Its increase is endangered even in affluent nations as decentralized exuberance expands physical assets across the globe and uses any means to keep their operation profitable. The down-engineering of consumer durables to keep up sales and a palpable loss of quality through cost-saving measures in production are mixed with technical progress seen in genuinely new or improved products. Artificially creating wants in order to sell the means of freeing consumers from them (as well as from their money) and a lost momentum (if not an outright reversal) in equalizing the distribution of *bona fide freedom from want* are further problems in the most problem-free parts of the world. But *macrohistorically* significant conditions and trends notwithstanding, the individual still equates the quality of life with *freedom from want*. Freedom so interpreted exists because its absence (compared to its presence elsewhere), or its reduction, causes psychological discomfort, a biological phenomenon.

The balance of *freedom of action* gained and lost through *cultural evolution* has been controversial from the start. Arguments can be stacked to show a positive, negative, or zero balance. A larger and more complex *culture* brought more opportunity for careers, travel, and entertainment; it expanded the individual's decision space. But it has also imposed restrictions and forced regimentation. The Freudian mode of thinking suggests a negative balance. Civilization represses and deforms individuality; it gives rise to psychoses and discontentment. The proliferation of surveillance cameras, transparent hard discs and internet use, along with ever-new high-tech approaches to deprive the individual of privacy and anonymity make one think that some gains in *freedom from want* are paid for with losses in *freedom to act*, numbing diversity, chipping away individuality.[12] The fact that socioeconomic equalization is part of *cultural evolution* draws opinion toward a

---

11.   We knowingly combined freedom from "real" needs and those artificially created by the "kit and caboodle" fetish of advanced market civilization. The elimination of this dividing line does not alter the obvious increase in *freedom from want* through *cultural evolution*. Two hundred years ago, even in countries that are now among the *vanguard*, masses of people did not have decent food and clothing; only a privileged minority enjoyed hygienic conditions and comforts that would barely satisfy contemporary standards.

positive balance. The majority of the people living in the developing world would be happy to exchange its *freedom from want/freedom to act* package with that enjoyed by *vanguard* residents. This negative experience shows that *cultural evolution* liberated more than it enslaved mankind. The costs of *cultural evolution*, which are felt by the organism as constraints, pale when they are compared to the benefits brought by the process. On the whole, a life once "solitary, poor, nasty, brutish, and short" (Hobbes) has become increasingly solidary, rich, comfortable, pleasant, and long.

It appears, nevertheless, that an increase in *freedom from want* may be accompanied by a sense of loss in *freedom to act*, suggesting an eventual limit to classical *cultural evolution* for psychological reasons. Growing pressure on behavior may make the gains in material possessions (with dubious use value) appear to be too expensive, both in terms of *freedom of action* lost and efforts exerted to acquire them. The increasingly unsatisfactory package of freedom the average individual receives is an indication of classical *cultural evolution*'s impending autoparalysis.

Freedom from want and *freedom of action* live in symbiosis. *Will*, somatic energy in the abstract, is directed to maximize individual *freedom from want*. *Freedom of action*, as perceived by the individual, plays an important role in determining socioeconomic behavior. Since *freedom to act* is the means to acquire *freedom from want*, that is where the individual's sensitivity to restrictions is the keenest.

Through the organizing agency of the two *global systems* known thus far, history produced a curious relationship between the individual's socioeconomic existence and the species' entropy-defying autocatalysis. Focus on the first masks the presence and importance of the second. Division of labor into narrowly specialized work tasks makes one forget about the "physics" of what one is doing as a member of the species. The emphasis is on the size of one's *socioeconomic sphere*. The larger it is, the more independent its occupant may feel from wants and from other people. At present, everything extra-societal has been shoved under the rug; individuals experience the obstacles that the *force motrice* pushes them to overcome as socioeconomic constraints. It is not nature, it seems, that opposes one's volitional drives; it is other people.

The sharp distinction between "self" and "another" resulted in losing sight of the "one-on-one aspect" of the phyletic struggle with the physical environment, the efforts deployed to keep the universal strain toward thermodynamic equilib-

---

12. Freud, of course, is not the only reference for this point of view. One may also find it in the works of Jean-Jacques Rousseau (1712-1778), Margaret Mead (1901-1978), Michel Foucault (1926-1984), Claude Lévi-Strauss, and Jean Baudrillard.

rium at bay in the species' carved out domain of low entropy. Since individually experienced *freedom from want* and *freedom of action* correlate with the size of *personal socioeconomic spheres*, historically, the species' quest for self-strengthening has found expression in *personal socioeconomic spheres* jostling among themselves for expansion. The ultimate purpose of human self-propagation appears in such indirect and alienated form. This is a transitory, and hopefully introductory, segment of the human venture, explained by ecological release, the bubble of low-entropy inflow into *culture*. The essence of GS3 in terms of freedom is the creation of a new package of *freedom from want* and *freedom to act* that is equitable and satisfying, and has the potential to grow despite the constraints implied by "living on the *global transformation curve*."

Caught up in a process incomprehensibly "bigger than us" that unfolds according to a recognized physical law, we are being used in ways some people may not even want to know. A peek under the hood of *macrohistory* reveals that the apparent manifestations of personal autonomy hide the wires of a slowly moving material process that has its own generation-crossing rhythm. *Necessity* (discerned through retrospective analysis) prevailed statistically and *macroscopically*, not only over shocks of *extreme randomness*, but also over *microscopic* individuality. The following are reasons for exaggerating the role of free *will* and misconstruing its nature.[13]

Human faces of orthogenesis

Some influential people in the 1930s honestly believed that the American New Deal was a whim of Roosevelt's, that it would become discredited and repelled in the 40s and would be forgotten by the 50s. In retrospect, FDR was the central figure in creating GS2. The new *global system* would have come into existence without him (perhaps not exactly with the same detailed characteristics and timing), but having a man of his intelligence, charisma, and independence in the most influential office of the emerging world order's *pivot* was certainly expeditious in its realization.[14]

The appearance of leaders who implemented the institutions that corresponded to the *chaotic transition* was an *ex post necessity*. Historic personalities and events could have been different, as far as the human *mind* with its limited computational powers can guess, but the outcome had to be a legally fixed higher

---

13.   Besides offering many compelling observations on the admixture of *chance* and *necessity*, Ball, 2004 demonstrates the explanatory might of the physical law amidst the free-will brandishing sovereigns of human agency.

complexity in global self-organization. The underlying dynamic was simple. As the need for the next stage (GS2) intensified, the sharpening views and hardening positions multiplied the *chances* of successful *entrainments*, allowing masses of *minds* to be temporarily subjugated to the hypnotic powers of swaggering and ruthless "Caesar Men."[15] This *necessity* only used the atomistic, fragmented, discrete free *wills* to work itself through infinitely complicated details toward the *representative brain*'s subconsciously harbored stasis. In general, the stages of self-organization accompanying *cultural evolution* play out through what seems to be a free interaction among billions of independently willed ganglia.

Self-assertion rationed between reason and desire

By allowing *minds* to distinguish between profitable and self-damaging behavior, between the praiseworthy and the condemnable, socioeconomic institutions, in essence, "tell" people what they may and may not do. This is the way the collective coaxes out conformism, without which there would be no *culture*. However, if everybody always remained passively conformist, there would be no *cultural evolution* because radical changes in the socioeconomic environment are a part of it. Some will have to try to change the way the community judges individual behavior. This is the nonconformist approach to self-assertion, ignoring or bucking mimesis-generative socioeconomic force fields. It seems that individuals are free to choose between being reasonable and conforming or letting their desires take hold of them and confronting the socioeconomic *status quo*. But on the whole, and over a longer perspective, the collective manages to divide itself between the two modes of self-assertion, one that allows itself to be sculpted by the environment and one that attempts to sculpt it. The split between system-consistent obedient and system-inconsistent disobedient acts is ultimately a statistical law that submerges individually experienced sovereignty to the *Opaque Artificer*.

---

14. The current political trend aimed at rolling back the instrumentation of GS2, which originated in the New Deal, is an indication that we are nearing (or are already in) the stew of a new *chaotic transition*. It seems rather artless in light of considering a *global system* an entrenched network of neural programs, constructs of atoms operating in interlocked patterns. Trying to push the evolved microstate of the world toward its past is not unlike claiming to have discovered a *perpetuum mobile* machine.

15. Thomas Mann's visionary novella, *Mario and the Magician*, written in 1928, correctly captured the mental state of societies in the focal point of the ongoing *chaotic transition*'s final, culminating explosion.

Built-in unpredictability

World history, the intelligible reflection of a one-way change in the *terrestrial sphere*'s material organization, produces a ceaseless stream of unpredictable events. Ever new conjunctures highlight individuals and expose their conduct and the morality of their choices to public scrutiny. In the socioeconomic universe, the novelties and surprises, which keep coming practically without interruption, cannot be observed in pure form. They are always mediated by individuals with incumbent responsibilities and legal signatures. *Superis aliter visum* (heavens ordained it otherwise) in the human domain always appears as if it followed from someone's exercise of free *will*, completely or at least partially. *Ex ante* unpredictability (blind fortune), learned and accepted through experience, becomes transmuted into the belief that deliberately willed personal decisions and actions alone shape history.

A cauldron of cross-radiating wills

Trying to influence and manipulate one another is part of social existence. Individuals beam an uninterrupted flow of evaluations at each other, most often with a wish or advice for change. Corrective assessments may be issued not only to selected persons but also to groups of people, neighborhoods, villages and towns, subnational regions or entire nations, governments and institutions, corporations and professions, political parties, multinational integration schemes, international organizations, social classes, religions, and genders. Evaluative messages may label any of these stupid, egotistic, aggressive, not aggressive enough, shrewd, unreliable, narrow-minded, and dangerous. Some assessments are approving, but these are also exhortative. They urge the addressees to stay the course and ignore other sources of advice. The "broadcasts" may be informal and casual, directed to single persons (as in conversations) or they may be made on behalf of some entity and amplified by the "media," reaching wider audiences. In the universal marketplace of opinions almost everybody is a passionate salesperson, including academics who can be indefatigable in trying to convert and reform the world in order to reduce its deviation from what they consider *optime*.

Living in a permanent flow of emissions and receptions of appraisals, criticisms, advice, and menace *à priori* presumes belief in individual freedom, not only in principle and on occasion, but in daily practice and on a continuous basis. People would not emit these messages if they did not presuppose that the recipients were free to believe this today that tomorrow, and that they could change the use of their *freedom to act* accordingly. This may be a correct premise, yet, when we tune out the cross-chatter of *wills*, put the unpredictable and nontrackable individual actions behind us, and close the cover of the history book, our mind's eye can still see the upward sloping trend of *cultural evolution*. "Something" prevailed over the apparently disconnected barrage of coded messages, requiring global self-organization to transit a *chaotic* interlude in order to proceed from one *relative steady state* to the next. This pattern corresponds exactly to what science has found to be valid in the evolution of complex, far-from-equilibrium dissipative systems.

To sum up, *will* is the somatic energy generated to continue life and improve its conditions. It is the expression of the *force motrice*. The *mind* deals with constraints to the organism's *free will* by developing a sense of *freedom of action* manifest primarily in socioeconomic behavior. The perceived *freedom to act* is applied to secure *freedom from want*. Through collective effort, species-wide since the first third of the 19th century, the individual has benefited from *cultural evolution* through improvement in the quality of life, interpreted as gains in *freedom from want* ("the goods of civilization"), even if some doubts persist that restrictions on the *freedom to act* have been a largely overlooked cost behind these gains. Given that both *freedom of action* and *freedom from want* are variable and constrained (so far, opposition has been perceived as if it came mostly from the rest of society rather than from nature), the self feels its *will* to be as free as it is conscious of being alive. The two share the defiance of entropy as their common source. Nonetheless, the decentralized steering of somatic energies is caught up in a thermodynamic evolution that follows its own laws. As the human population expanded, the *force motrices* had to be socialized in larger and larger organizational units, creating a global-level pulsation that unidirectional transformations with intermittently changing frameworks cannot escape. Although the world process submerges and consumes the individual, it does, in a way, reflect the original, primal wish for more freedom. (The case of the sorcerer's apprentice.) The *Opaque Artificer* has been and still is in charge. From a multigenerational perspective, there was and still is no way out from the *macrohistoric* roller coaster which, like the Wagon of Chronos with its compass needle stuck, travels only in one direction. Despite all this, individual *will* remains crucial in *cultural evolution*, but not in the ways and to the extent the individual immersed in life's labors perceives it. *The exaggeration of one's own importance and power, and the high expectations attached to one's thoughts and actions are ingredients in the fuel that cultural evolution and its attendant socioeconomic transformations run on. The tinsel of uniqueness felt by the utilitarian mind is not a wasteful delusion. It is indispensable.*

Homo sapiens, like any other known or imaginable creature, suffers from inherent metaphysical autism. Man cannot poke his "three-dimensional" nose into the *noumenal* realm. Therefore, the human may never know if the sensation of freedom attached to its *will* is an ontological reality or only a psychological ploy used by nature to prod life on. There is no one out there in "real reality" to respond to a survey: Free will is (a) mandated, (b) encouraged, (c) permitted, (d) a sheer illusion. (Please circle the answer that best describes our situation. Use No. 2 pencil.)

Human biology is the carrier of the sovereignty of individual *will*. If this sovereignty is real, the materiality of the sense of freedom is, to some extent, independent from the environment. If it is a metaphysical hallucination, then universal forces engulf the ensemble of atomistic configurations we call the body.

If individual freedom is more than the evolvement of self-preserving intuition, then the future is indeed open and volition and intention can affect its course. Contingency is real; meliorism is what it seems; subjective faith is married to deep reason. If individual freedom is an anthropic illusion, then we are drawn into an Augustinian coincidence between a determined course and individual compulsion to follow it. Events, like self-canceling deviations, improvise themselves around an immutably sustained trend. Nature "below the radar" knows only *randomness of the first kind*. In this case, the whisperings of infinity we insist on discerning are void of ontological significance. Meliorism is the reflection of a universe misread; subjective faith and deep reason are forever divorced.

In the end, freedom (the amalgam of *freedom to act* and *freedom from want*) as perceived is what really matters. Since it is desirable, it lures; humans pursue its increase (whether this was scripted or not) and are left with one practical certainty: The larger and more concentrated the effort they deploy to achieve a goal or realize a project, and the more detailed and better quality information they possess about the conditions affecting their activities, the more they can hope for success because their control over *chance* effects will be greater and the range of uncertainty will be smaller. A world capable of thinking and rethinking itself (narratively and institutionally) as its circumstances change has an incomparably better *chance* of enduring than one that remains adrift in the paraconscious cacophony of billions of much too superficially tuned cerebral microstates. Given the awakening recognition of the bare fundamentals about man's relationship with nature, this is the beckoning finger of GS3, the long awaited new covenant beyond the dark clouds ahead—redemption of the *representative brain* from itself.

Epilogue

✦

F. Scott Fitzgerald, the Copenhagen Interpretation, and Hope Eternal

F. Scott Fitzgerald (1896-1940) said that intelligence is the ability to accept two contradictory ideas and still function. The intelligence he referred to is not a high I.Q. or some remarkable analytical or artistic talent; it is the faculty of leaving certain competing ideas, whether they are scientific propositions or articles of faith, nonconflated and unbrokered; the readiness to tolerate a conundrum without dialectical resolution or relegation of the whole problem to the waste basket.

Believing in the inexhaustibility of present moments and understanding that the moments are most certainly exhaustible are reciprocally negating notions. The individual sees the validity of both but vaporizes any possible debilitating, will-paralyzing confusion that could arise from accepting them simultaneously. One often finds balance in an emotional turmoil by not drawing conclusions. At some basic level, life itself could not exist without Fitzgeraldian Intelligence (F.I.).[1] Either-or logic handicaps transition to higher order in open-ended, adaptive reconfigurations.

One may argue that F.I. increased during the 20th century. The Copenhagen Interpretation of Quantum Mechanics, agreed upon in 1927 by some of the early legends of atomic physics, is perhaps the most obvious indication of this increase. The discovery that light could be explained either in terms of moving particles or

---

1. "Fitzgeraldian Intelligence" is not identical to "Freudian" repression in the subconscious. The contradictory ideas invoked here are on the surface of consciousness, accessible without hypnosis or a session on the psychiatrist's couch. To use an everyday example, many people feel sorry that animals are slaughtered but would not refuse a juicy piece of meat. When they shrink at the thought that those innocent bovines have been killed just to fill their stomachs, the steak dinner is curtained away, and when they cut eagerly into the tender Chateaubriand, the "animal" is absent. Indeed, the modern individual excels in balancing genteel idealism and crass materialism without the slightest sign of pathological mental deformation.

in terms of waves forced the conclusion that it was both. Physicists learned to think around the fact that some phenomena must be described by complementary theories.

The Copenhagen Interpretation dissolved the earlier reassuring assumption about a clear one-to-one correspondence between phenomenon and theory. It proved reality elusive and reduced hard scientific convictions to empirically warranted regularities. But, as ample evidence demonstrates, this development strengthened rather than weakened scientific curiosity and ambition. Witness the zeal with which physicists are trying to find the theory that would unify general relativity and quantum mechanics—the ultimate heavy lifting in speculative endeavor. Discoveries of the so-called fuzzy logic (reasoning with vague concepts) and fractals (thinking between integer dimensions) are also signs that the *mind* is groping for more complex comprehension. These advances in thinking find practical applications in engineering and software design. Paradoxically, the acceptance of ambiguity and partial truths enhances the effectiveness of control systems. A.I. (artificial intelligence) and F.I. are colleagues.

The growing ability to balance contradictory notions has not been restricted to the intellectual elite. The spread of democracy, requiring the swelling masses to weed through alternative programs presented through the reciprocal calumny of political professionals, is indicative of a general increase in the ability to live with unresolved paradoxes, to hold opinions while accepting the possibility of their incorrectness. Indeed, democracy may be regarded as the gymnasium for building F.I. muscles, although these muscles may not be challenged the same way in social-political life as they are around the dials and meters of particle accelerators and bubble chambers.

Social and political issues move rapidly across the scene. Alternative explanations and programs may be resolved through compromise or may be forgotten as new problems override old ones. In this domain, F.I. is manifest simply by making people more patient with opposing views. Individuals may hold convictions, but, by listening "with open minds," they can suspend them. When they try to see the merits of an alternative, or perhaps a completely contrary explanation or idea, they are, in effect, balancing two simultaneously held convictions without drawing conclusions and without feeling confused. Even if the increase in this ability has not immunized the world against blind indoctrination, it certainly curbed the pre-*Enlightenment* atavism of *ad hoc* subjectivity and may have facilitated release from doctrinaire fixations.

Today one can argue more easily than half a century ago that, even without Herbert Hoover (whom some blame for the Great Depression), Lenin, Stalin, and Hitler, the pre-World War I *global system* could not have transformed itself smoothly into the system that has existed since World War II. It is now readily understood that believing that Marxism had a historic mission in shaping GS2 is not the same as believing in Marxism. The postmodern turn in philosophy, historiography, art, architecture, and politics (a phenomenon of *cultural evolution*) made the individual more accepting of different perspectives without destroying its capacity to hold strong particular views and engage in political action with firm resolve.

For GS3 *socioeconomic behavior* (along with the new *global system*'s epiphenomena) to emerge, individuals will be challenged to cross a cultural evolutionary barrier as significant as going from four to two legs was in biological evolution. There too, judgment as to which one was better had to be suspended until the transition was well on its way and irreversible. Without "keeping an open mind," allowing operational circumstances to prompt standing on the two hind legs, the transition would have never occurred. Natural selection acting on individual adaptations accumulated the evidence, but successive generations of organisms still had to live in a "no-man's-land" between the conservative past approach and the incomparably more advantageous new one. An analogue situation is seen in the transition to GS3 consciousness and collective orientation, the psychological completion of the indicated decisive moment in visibly obvious biological evolution. Being able to draw on hitherto untapped potentials of F.I. will become a vital selection criterion for the species.

The individual considering itself nearly insignificant (valuing itself as 1/P), but almost infinitely significant when looking at the world (as if it were responsible for P), implies a new psychological and philosophical balance. Some of the trust vested in the egoism of others will have to yield to trust in the fairness of others. The qualitatively new relationship between personal and collective interests will require that some of this trust be blind. It presupposes that the global citizen will suspend its constant monitoring of the "domestic versus foreign," "my canton versus theirs," and "me versus them" accounts. Precise daily assessments of losses and gains on these accounts, and frequent recapping of their overall status, would effectively constrain the functioning of any social compact based on the far-reaching custody of reciprocal interests. Unrelenting accountant-like watchfulness over give-and-takes awakens dissatisfaction and leads to criticism and argument. Despite its sharpened ability and greater need to study and reason, the GS3 persona, geared toward the panoramic comprehension of human interest, will have to risk leaving some crucial socioeconomic experiences unsynthesized.

As its thinking evolves and broadens, *homo sapiens* must become aware that even *it* is only one of nature's fugitives on the run, that eventually it will be caught and integrated into the long march toward thermodynamic equilibrium. (In the long run, all species are endangered.) Therefore, the *mind* will have to do for the world then what it does for the individual now when suspending the contradiction between the bliss that seems to be eternal and the perdition that is known to be certain. To avoid mental infection and retain self-possession, this ugly *nuda veritas* will have to be made modest with a new philosophical shroud, but without the help of the fairy-tale cosmologies and naïve legends of an ever more distant childhood. The success of the human community will demand a rock solid conviction that *homo sapiens* is as immortal as are the atoms in its *culture*, that it will never run out of evolutionary time, it will never have to sign off. While the average *mind* will become scientifically better trained and intellectually more capable, it will consciously allow conclusions about reality to be suspended or postponed without bewilderment or disenchantment. "Understanding" will have to be far more complex than we can imagine today. Commitment to social, moral, and political standards will have to become more elastic. A greater psychic strength will have to be aligned with a virtually unsuspended readiness to do mental house-cleaning.

Of course, a lot of "shoulds" and "oughts" are stuck to these arguments and, as always, the supremacy of *chance* (when looking forward) thins out certainty about "winning the future." Nonetheless, hope is born and turning its realization into logical necessity is always welcome, although someone who rationalizes the inevitability of humankind's auspicious future may resemble Emile Zola's trade union agitator in *Germinal* (1885). The novel's hero got stuck while trying to weave the labor theory of value into his speech to striking miners in 19th century Normandy. He stopped mid-sentence and shrugged his shoulders in confused embarrassment. But no one booed in disappointment. The miners understood what he meant. Amidst the black dust and all the misery of their 60-hour work week, they too were aware of a faint but uninterrupted signal of a better life to come. GS2 was in them too, slowly boring its way to the surface from the fathomless shafts of the unconscious. Deep down people know things they never experienced. No wonder that the emergence of new social and economic arrangements begins with unclear and occasionally confused or exaggerated ideas. Concepts are secondary; they come after what the *entrainer* wants to express, and those that lie inchoate and dormant "somewhere" in most people will come into existence "somehow." Yes, the species does not own "the cosmic mine of free-energy-containing matter," but its members may share a dim sense of direction in this fleeting moment.

To paraphrase Kant, "The starry skies are above and the emergent wish to get there is within."

Appendix

◆

Global Transformation or Chaotic Transition Seen via the Arrowian Paradox

The Arrowian Paradox of Choice, or *Arrow's Impossibility Theorem,* refers to the mathematical demonstration of Nobel Laureate Kenneth Arrow that an irreconcilable contradiction exists between a "fair" aggregation of individual preferences and rational social choice. "Fair aggregation" is summed up by certain conditions under which individuals must be allowed to express their opinions and certain rules that must be applied in evaluating these opinions.[1]

We are at the end of GS1. World War I is approaching. The public in the mover-shaker countries (the principal national actors in the coming conflict) are divided among three alternatives. Some intend to stick to the old system (GS1); others want to overhaul its distribution of national influence, and others want to replace it with a completely new system. West European colonial empires and the United States embrace the first alternative (O). Let us call them Group A. But there are other voices in Group A. Some wish for a redistribution of influence. In particular, they want a diminution of British and French territorial dominion without changing the fundamental parameters of GS1. This is alternative O'. Revolutionaries living in the areas that belong to Group A would vote, under the idealized peacefulness of the Arrowian survey, for a totally new socioeconomic world order (N). If it were up to a fair aggregation of opinions, we might find that in Group A, O would be the number one choice, O' second, and N third.

---

1. "Fair" is the aggregation that (1) is nonrestricted (the survey of preferences among alternatives should be complete); (2) is not imposed (every community preference order must be based on unanimous individual preference orders); (3) nondictatorial (no single individual's preference order has to be followed by the rest of the community); (4) does not violate unanimity (if everybody prefers an alternative, the whole community prefers it); and (5) does not depend on irrelevant alternatives (preferences unrelated to the social choice at hand are ignored).

Those living in the Russian Empire comprise Group B. Here N would be the number one choice, followed by the wish expressed to retain the extant order (O). Those who would like to see a worldwide territorial redistribution (voting for O') would be the smallest faction, given that the Romanov Empire was a colonial power. Let Central Europe (Germany and Austria-Hungary) form Group C. Here the majority would like to see an overhaul of colonial possessions. Their number one choice would be O', followed by N (given the German speaking area's forceful socialist movement and the nationalist-rebellious undercurrents in the Hapsburg monarchy), and then by O. The following tabulation shows the hierarchy of preferences by groups, where 1 means strongly preferred, 2 indicates less preferred, and 3 signifies least preferred among the alternatives.

	O	O'	N
Group A	1	2	3
Group B	2	3	1
Group C	3	1	2

Following the usual process, let us go through preferences in pairs.[2] The choice between O and O': Group A votes for O and Group B also votes for O. Group C votes for O'. O wins 2:1. The mover-shaker world prefers O to O'. The choice between O' and N: Group A votes for O', Group B votes for N and Group C for O'. O' wins 2:1. The world prefers O' to N. Since O is preferred to O' and O' is preferred to N, the rational social choice would imply that O is preferred to N. But do not expect transitive rationality. Comparing the preferences between O and N, we find that Group A votes for O; Group B votes for N, and Group C also votes for N. The world prefers N to O? Yes and no. Its preferences are contradictory.

Some may rightfully protest that if we had counted the absolute number of votes we might have obtained a different result. Group votes led to the establishment of relative preferences. In terms of population, Group A was larger than Group B, which was larger than Group C. The last vote, which compared N and O, in particular, could be invalidated based on absolute numbers. It is likely that more people would have voted for O in the Atlantic world (Group A) than for

---

2.   The demonstration closely follows the work of professor Thayer Watkins at San Jose State University. See Thayer Watkins, at http://www2.sjsu.edu/faculty/watkins/arrow.htm, found on March 12, 2004.

"something new" in the Russian Empire (Group B) and in the future Axis powers (Group C) combined.

This is where nationally wielded military power comes into play. Under these circumstances, the threat of being crowded out or contained would trigger military build-up in the nation that wanted change but whose vision of a reformed global order was not sufficiently supported by world opinion.

By the mid-1930s, the mover-shaker group broke down into representatives of *global system* alternatives: the American New Deal (AD), Soviet communism (SC), and Nazi regime (NR). Military power stood behind each. The theoretical prevalence of popular choice overriding contradictory visions became impossible.

Let us imagine that the two dictatorships suspended their internal terror for two days and allowed a secret ballot-based electoral consultation. Citizens could vote freely. The following tabulation shows the preferences by groups.

	AD	SC	NR
America	1	2	3
Reich	2	3	1
USSR	3	1	2

The American public votes for the New Deal, but if faced with the inevitable option, it would prefer international to national socialism. Voters in the Reich, liberated to express their opinion for one day, but still reflecting the ideas of the Nazi propaganda machine, would choose NR in the largest numbers and would show the least preference for SC. Their Western traditions and experience with public works programs would make them choose AD over SC. The "Soviet people," with Stalin off their backs for the vote, remain convinced about the superiority and inevitability of socialism. They vote for SC without coercion. At that time, they would have been closer to NR than to AD in their thinking.

The choice between AD and SC: America votes for AD and the Reich votes also for AD. The "Soviet people" vote for SC. AD wins 2:1. The world prefers AD to SC. The choice between SC and NR: America votes for SC; the Reich votes for NR and the "Soviet people" vote for SC. SC wins 2:1. The world prefers SC to NR. Since AD is preferred to SC and SC is preferred to NR, the rational social choice would imply that the world prefers AD to NR. Comparing the preferences between AD and NR we find that America votes for AD; the Reich for NR, and the "Soviet people" vote also for NR. The world prefers NR to AD? Confusion again. Fairly assembled votes lead to a contradiction.

Even if we could peel away real life constraints, the international community still could not find its way out from the irrationality that descends on the world during *global transformation* or *chaotic transition* (in terms of *marcohistory* and *metahistory*, respectively). Anarchy of the minds characterizes transitional periods. Given that thermodynamic complexification mandates a resolution (i.e., a new *relative steady state* must be reached) and that forcefully assertive official ideologies, supported by state structures and military power, bar any of the alternatives from reaching global dominance peacefully, transitional periods must feature revolution, terror, and war. The always uneasy and tense relationship between fair aggregation and rational choice under majority rule turns *chaotic* and violent during such periods. The *chaotic transition* begins with convulsive deconfiguration and ends with a cataclysmic clash among alternatives to reconfigure the world order.

Of course, this is only a formalized speculation, showing the bare bones of underlying ideas about history, and not a *bona fide* logical proof. The separation between premises and conclusions is insufficient to save it from *circulatory reasoning*.

Glossary

Attractor. The relatively stable dynamic state that "pulls" a system toward itself in complex, intricate ways as if it were a causal force.

Bifurcation. The chaotic interlude that separates two provisionally stable phases in time evolutions studied in physics and mathematics. The prefix "bi" implies a branching into at least two alternative solutions from prechaotic conditions. The turbulent period during which a system capable of evolution identifies the parameters required to regain stability in a more complex form of self-organization.

Canton. The smallest territorial unit in the socioeconomic grid (and perhaps also of administrative organization) under the hypothetical future *global system*, GS3.

Cantonization. The development of *cantons* through widespread local initiatives to generate energy, protect the environment, produce food, and enhance the quality of life through arts and crafts and small-scale services. It coincides with the devolution of GS2.

Chance. An event whose initial conditions and causes the human observer could not or would not care to determine. (Same as *randomness*.)

Chaotic transition. The *metahistoric* equivalent of *bifurcation*. There were two such periods since 1500: "1789-1834" (leading to the establishment of GS1) and "1914-1945" (the transformation of GS1 into GS2). It is more general than *global transformation*, which applies only to the second period (GS1—>GS2). It is used in the text when the *metahistoric* facade of *cultural evolution* is emphasized.

Code. Internally stored individual data and programs associated with socioeconomic behavior.

Code Core. Part of the *Code* that is related to the *global system*.

Cultural evolution. Species-wide (phyletic) self-strengthening or self-propagation. Historically, it is measurable by the coincidental increase in population, in per capita income or output, and progress in moving toward social and economic equality. It may be represented as a trajectory in a three-dimensional "phase space." Physically, it means the incorporation of matter into humans, other life forms in human service, and produced goods.

Culture. The momentary state of *cultural evolution*. It may be modeled as a continuous, vector-valued function of time, where the vector has three elements, each of which is a state variable. The ensemble of atoms in the human biomass, man-made objects, and animate matter in human service. The system within this material entity has been global since the first third of the 19th century.

Determinism. The ontological ("deep philosophical") extension of *necessity* to the universe. Since everything is caused by something, all events, whether in the past or in the future, including those that seem *random* to the human observer, were determined at the beginning of time. Extended to human affairs, its claim implies that natural laws penetrate history and individual action, making the sovereignty of the *will* illusory.

Discourse. Interpersonal communication patterned by socially determined meanings (or *text*), the associated socioeconomic institutions, and set rules and routines ("discipline"). The concept, attributed to Foucault, is widely used in postmodern/poststructuralist philosophy and literary criticism.

Ecological order. The configuration of atoms in the *terrestrial sphere*. With the accumulation of entropy, the *terrestrial sphere*'s macrostate may be expressed by a growing number of equally possible microstates. This means a decrease in *ecological order* or an increase in *ecological disorder*. The actual microstate of the *terrestrial sphere* "sends" messages about the level of *ecological order*. As its level declines, the messages become less coherent, a process captured by growth in *information entropy*.

Ecoplasm. Economically extractable (free) energy from matter, *ecological order*, and *certitude about the environment* perceived as a single constraint.

Ecoplasmic layer. A concave-to-the-origin band containing feasible population/material output combinations that use the same amount of *ecoplasm*. Within it, the sustainability of any combination and the risk of accidentally reaching a lethal combination are considered invariant. It is "layer" rather than "line" to allow for the difficulties and unavoidable inaccuracies of estimation.

Effective carrying capacity. The selected *global transformation curve* within the chosen *ecoplasmic layer*.

Entrainment. Expression borrowed from biology to indicate individual political action aimed at increasing the frequency of a specific conviction of socioeconomic significance in a population. Its accumulation to global proportions has been crucial to the dynamics of *macrohistory*.

Entropy. The level of disorder or lack of structure in a system. According to the *second law of thermodynamics*, it tends to increase in closed systems. Since, for all practical purposes, the *terrestrial sphere* is closed as far as the supply of matter is concerned; and, since there is no available technology to transform energy into matter (despite their theoretical equivalence), entropy tends to increase monotonically in the *terrestrial sphere*. Growing human presence and activity have accelerated this process.

Epicenter. The most "important" country of a specific *global system*; the same as *pivot*.

Ethic. Principles and moral precepts that act as general guideposts behind *global system*-specific socioeconomic behavior.

Exergy. Level of order, intactness of structure in matter, free energy extractable from matter. The complementary opposite of entropy.

Exergic constraint. A measure of the *terrestrial sphere*'s usefulness for *homo sapiens*, viewed alternatively as economically extractable (free) energy from physical substances in the *global environment* and *geocapital* combined; as *ecological order* and as *certitude about the environment*.

Extrasomatic energy. Energy produced by human-made objects; e.g., electricity.

Far-from-equilibrium dissipative structure. A structure capable of complexification despite building up entropy that would tend to pull it apart. Such mainly life-bearing structures escape extinction by developing higher forms of self-organization. The coincidence of dissipating low-entropy resources and developing information that enables the structure to assume new, more complex forms of organization leads to the conclusion that the structure could convert entropy into information in order to evolve. Since only open thermodynamic systems are capable of the evolution ascribed to such structures, *culture* will have to incorporate extraterrestrial low-entropy matter to ensure its long-run survival.

Force motrice. The individually anchored human expression of the autocatalytic, entropy-defying push factor. It exists through the functioning of the autonomic nervous system without the conscious intervention of higher brain centers. The evolved brain combines voluntary and conscious dimensions with the involuntary will to head off extinction and is capable of analyzing this fusion. It is not an absolute constant. It can increase or decrease.

Freedom from want. The sense of liberation from physical and mental discomfort through goods and services.

Freedom of action (or **freedom to act**). The level of feeling unconstrained in directing one's *will*, gauged by the number and quality of alternatives available in the socioeconomic arena.

Freedom of will. Individually perceived sovereignty in directing one's *will*.

Geocapital. Matter immediately needed and ready to be used to feed *cultural evolution*. In terms of number or weight of atoms, *geocapital + culture + global environment = terrestrial sphere*.

Gleichschaltung. Sudden switch to uniformity in behavior. In the self-organized complexification of a dissipative entity (such as *culture*), it can occur only at the end of a *chaotic transition*, which coincides with the beginning of a new, *relatively stable socioeconomic order* marked by its *imprimatur*. The implied sweeping and comprehensive legitimation creates a new socioeconomic environment ("force field") that mandates immediate and significant uniformity in adaptive behavior.

Global socioeconomic environment. Social and economic linkages built of a hierarchy of socioeconomic environments.

Global system. The world order of socioeconomic relations; historically, GS1 and GS2. *Relative steady state* in institutional arrangements along with a host of accompanying phenomena capable of successfully coordinating *cultural evolution*. Mathematically, it is the piecewise continuous control vector of the continuous, vector-valued function of time, *culture*. The system in *culture* since the establishment of GS1. A macrophysical reality fully internalized by the individual. Its microphysical manifestations may be found in the *personal socioeconomic sphere* and in the *surrounding socioeconomic milieu*.

Global transformation. The change from one *global system* to the next, i.e., "1914-1945."

Global transformation curve. A concave-to-the-origin array of feasible population/material output combinations that use the same amount of *ecoplasm* and imply an identical length of sustainability and risk to human life and welfare.

GS0. The period from 1500 to 1789, characterized as late feudalism/emergent capitalism; the epoch during which conditions for living under *global systems* developed and finalized.

GS1. The first *global system*, called *laissez faire/metal money* that lasted from the symbolic year of "1834" until the outbreak of World War I in 1914. The period of "classical capitalism."

GS2. The second and current *global system*, called *mixed economy/weak multilateralism*, established after World War II. "Modern capitalism."

GS3. *Two-level economy/strong multilateralism*, the hypothetical *global system* following GS2. The emergence of a system that is closer to it than to GS2 is considered a *sine qua non* of long-term human survival.

Homeostasis. The capacity of organisms to keep their normal functioning intact from the effects of surrounding environments; spontaneous return to equilibrium following perturbations; macroscopic imposition on microscopic agitation. The condition of the *web* during a *global system*'s reign.

Indeterminism. The ontological ("deep philosophical") extension of *chance* to the universe. The initial conditions that prevailed at the beginning of time do not follow specific sequences, and do not tend toward any specific end state. The evolution of material configurations is subject to alterations in any nanosecond. The theory claiming that contingency is nature's true nature.

Information entropy. Amount of information (e.g., "bits") per signal. When information per signal vital to the monitoring of ecological conditions grows because of the accumulation of physical entropy in the *terrestrial sphere*, the human observer becomes less and less able to assess general and long-term environmental conditions reliably. Disagreements over environmental issues tend to grow.

Lexicon. Symbol/referent relations contained in the *imprimatur*, i.e., in a *global system*'s foundational legislation. The nucleus and primary initial source of a *global system*'s *text*.

Low-entropy matter. Physical substances containing extractable free energy from the human point of view.

Macrohistory. Flow of recorded events in the world told in terms of GS0, GS1, and GS2.

Macroscopic radiation. The force whereby *global systems* make national socioeconomic institutions align with their foundational principles and basic parameters (*mesoscopic* adaptation), ultimately resulting in *global system*-specific individual socioeconomic behavior (*microscopic* adaptation).

Macrostate. The entire system's level of entropy (disorder) as measured by the number of possible microstates that could equivalently characterize it.

Meganarrative. A broad-stroke narrative of world affairs. It is the same as "meta (or grand) narrative" in postmodern philosophy-inspired academic debate. "Mega" is used here in lieu of "meta" because the latter is applied in a different sense (see *metahistory*).

Mentality. *Global system*-characteristic patterns of individual reaction to socioeconomic stimulus; suspended "intentionality" associated with particular *global systems*.

Metahistory. A generalization of *macrohistory* into alternating stages of *relatively stable socioeconomic orders* and *chaotic transitions*. The link between actual world events, as summarized through *macrohistory*, and the disequilibrium thermodynamic process captured through the alternation of *relative steady states* and *bifurcations*.

Microstate. The actual position of every constituent atom and subatomic particle in a system. The concept is key in statistical mechanics, particularly in connection with entropy. In the current text it is used to underscore two particular points. First, *socioeconomic behavior* and its sources of information, such as data about the environment, are connected with the brain's quantum universe. Second, entropy build-up in the *terrestrial sphere* may be expressed by an increasing number of equivalently valid microstates to describe the *ecological order*.

Necessity. Broad and firm consensus regarding inevitability through cause and effect.

New historical materialism. The theory (first presented in the current volume) that regards world history as the manifestation of a thermodynamic unfolding tied to changes in interdigitated, coded cerebral matter. This conceptualization allows us to characterize *global transformation* with the expression "the world rethinks itself," and consider the reinterpretations of history and social evolution a *cultural evolution*-dictated physical necessity. The theory suggests that the recognition of the role entropy plays in human life is a vital dividing line in global evolution; that the concept of matter (therefore, the theory itself) needs to be refreshed as scientific understanding grows; and that even if the species manages to create planetary institutions to chart its course, it will never be able to foretell and completely control its future. Entropy-accumulating, unidirectional processes inevitably produce novelties and surprises.

Opaque Artificer. The symbol of the elusive historical force that resulted from the summation or socialization of individual *force motrices*.

Orthogenesis. Global self-organization along a line of retrospectively identified complexification, as seen in GS0, GS1, and GS2, and presumed in GS3. The observed path of socioeconomic evolution, considered to be the result of the *force motrice* (aggregated into the *Opaque Artificer*) acting upon biologically determined inclinations in *homo sapiens* under roughly unchanged conditions in the planet's physical environment.

Personal socioeconomic sphere. Areas and objects in individual possession or under individual control. The concept helps translate monetary wealth and other possessions into space and matter. Although the items it comprises are not located contiguously, they may be added in the abstract to form a more or less closed space, containing a specific weight and composition of matter. "Personal" and "familial" are identical. Every adult member of the kin-based household regards the entire *sphere* as his or her own. A microphysical manifestation of the *global system*'s macrophysical force field.

Pivot. The most "important" country of a specific *global system*; the same as *epicenter*.

Randomness. Same as *chance*.

Relatively stable socioeconomic conditions. Characterization that allows the combination of GS0 with the two *global systems* (GS1 and GS2) as stages in universal history.

Representative brain. Symbol of cerebrally grounded materiality in an abstract, *global system*-typical individual.

Saga. Collectively embraced universal beliefs about the world's past and future under the hypothetical GS3.

SEEI. Socioeconomic equality index, calculated by multiplying the middle class index (MCI) and the political/legal rights index (PLRI). MCI is the percentage of middle class in the total population defined in terms of mid-range income, e.g., the percentage of individuals living on an income level that excludes the bottom and top deciles. MCI = 1 would mean complete income equality, the theoretical maximum for the relative size of the middle class, making the term itself meaningless. Similarly, PLRI = 1 would signify complete equality for each (adult) individual, by statute and social acceptance.

SEP. Substantive Endowment Profile. Percentage distribution of the 90 natural elements by weight in the *terrestrial sphere*. While the distribution is considered constant, the elements disperse from an initial value (normalized to 100), as the result of *cultural evolution.*

Socioeconomic. Contraction of "social" and "economic."

Socioeconomic behavior. The individual's strategy and tactic in dealing with social stratification (dominance hierarchy) and economic opportunity. Strategy refers to general and long-term patterns. Tactic refers to operational maneuvering and short-term responses to *ad hoc* developments and situations.

Socioeconomic environment. The totality of social and economic conditions in which individual differential success is tested. Its social components are the structure of society, distribution of property, and collective mechanisms that respond to internal and external shocks or to gradual changes through the political process. Its economic aspects are macroeconomic conditions (such as aggregate income, employment, and the price level) and microeconomic conditions (those that influence producer and consumer decisions, the allocation of resources).

Socioeconomic order. Any of the following: late feudalism/emergent capitalism (GS0), classical capitalism (GS1), and modern capitalism (GS2).

Socioeconomic system. Explicitly stated principles of coordination (e.g., laws, rules, and regulations) within a *socioeconomic environment.*

Somatic energy. Human energy from the metabolic flow.

SUP. Substance Use Profile. The distribution of elements by weight in *culture* and in the *geocapital* combined. The weighted average of the elements in SUP and in the *global environment* must equal SEP. The purpose of this approach is to demonstrate that the future of technology is conditioned on its past and on interactions among other SUP variables, some of which are independent from the immediate challenges confronting technology, i.e., the practical application of scientific knowledge.

Surrounding socioeconomic milieu. The individual's immediate socioeconomic context. It includes those who determine one's level of income (typically workplace supervisors and business clients). It refers to the socioeconomic aspects of routine human interactions. *Cultural evolution* reduced distance as a criterion for inclusion, thus combining local *milieus* with distant ones through personal interactions. A microphysical manifestation of the *global system*'s macrophysical force field.

Telos. Collectively agreed-upon long-term agenda of the global society under the hypothetical GS3.

Text. Materially based (i.e., biologically, chemically, or physically perceived) linguistic interplay under given socioeconomic conditions. Its expansion and modulation within strict limits is key to understanding the socioeconomic *status quo* as *homeostasis*. The *global system*'s *text* is supra-"inter-textual" because it connects, subsumes, or at least influences, all other *texts*. GS2 talk" (particularly in politics and the social sciences) is its broadly interpreted current-day manifestation. It is formulaic insistence on the appropriateness of institutional arrangements despite the continuously changing context created by *cultural evolution*, i.e., under conditions never seen before.

Thermodynamic theory of history. Human self-organization as a material process becomes increasingly complex by going through alternate phases of *relative steady states* and *bifurcations*. These phases are revealed through *meta-*and *macro-history*. The basis of *new historical materialism*.

Vanguard. Countries that showed the best performance in terms of the qualitative indices of *cultural evolution* (per capita income and SEEI); developed countries, in general.

Web. Network of interconnected *Code Cores*.

Weltanschauung. The way the typical individual views the world under a specific *global system*.

Will. Somatic energy in the human organism used for specific purposes through conscious decisions. The neurobiological realization of the *force motrice*.

World equilibrium. The optimal population/material goods combination on the optimal *transformation curve* inside the optimal *ecoplasmic layer*.

World order. A synonym for GS0, GS1, or GS2.

Bibliography

Aitchison, J., <u>The Articulate Mammal, An Introduction to Psycholinguistics</u>, Universe Books, 1977.

Baker, M.C., <u>The Atoms of Language, The Mind's Hidden Rules of Grammar</u>, Basic Books, 2001.

Ball, P., <u>Critical Mass, How One Thing Leads to Another</u>, Farrar, Straus and Giroux, 2004.

Barkow, J.H., Cosmides, L., and Tooby, J. (eds.), <u>The Adapted Mind, Evolutionary Psychology and the Generation of Culture</u>, Oxford University Press, 1992.

Barlow, C. (ed.), <u>Evolution Extended: Biological Debates on the Meaning of Life</u>, The MIT Press, 1994.

Barnet, R.J. and Cavanagh, J., <u>Global Dreams, Imperial Corporations and the New World Order</u>, A Touchstone Book, 1994.

Barro, R.J. and Sala-I-Martin, X., <u>Economic Growth</u>, McGraw-Hill, 1995.

Berend, I.T., <u>Decades of Crisis, Central and Eastern Europe Before World War II</u>, University of California Press, 1998.

Berend, I.T., <u>History Derailed, Central and Eastern Europe in the "Long" 19th Century</u>, University of California Press, 2003.

Berlin, I., <u>Historical Inevitability</u>, Auguste Comte Memorial Trust Lecture, No.1, Geoffrey Cumerledge/Oxford University Press, 1954.

Bloomfield, A.I., <u>Monetary Policy Under the International Gold Standard: 1880-1914</u>, Federal Reserve Bank of New York, 1959.

Bryant, P.J., <u>Biodiversity and Conservation: A Hypertext Book</u>, found on Aug. 15, 2002, at http://darwin.bio.uci.edu.

Cairns-Smith, A.G., <u>Seven Clues to the Origin of Life</u>, Cambridge University Press, 1985.

Calladine, C.R. and Drew, H.R., <u>Understanding DNA, The Molecule and How It Works</u>, Academic Press, 1997.

Calvin, W.H. and Ojemann, G.A., <u>Conversations with Neil's Brain</u>, Addison-Wesley Publishing Co., 1994.

Chomsky, N., <u>Language and Mind</u>, Harcourt, Brace/Jovanovich, 1972.

Chomsky, N., <u>Reflection on Language</u>, Pantheon, 1975.

Chomsky, N., <u>Rules and Representations</u>, Columbia University Press, 1980.

Cipolla, C.M., <u>The Economic History of World Population</u>, Penguin Books, 1967.

Cole, J.C., <u>Anthropology For the Nineties</u>, The Free Press, 1988.

Conrad, C. and Kessel, M. (eds.), <u>Geschichte Schreiben in der Postmoderne</u>, Philip Reclam jun., Stuttgart (Germany), 1994.

Croce, B., <u>Historical Materialism and the Economics of Karl Marx</u>, translated by Meredith, C.M., with an introduction by Lindsay, A.D., found on Apr. 23, 2001, at http://www.socsci.mcmaster.ca.

Cropper, W.H., <u>Great Physicists</u>, Oxford University Press, 2001.

Daly, H.E., <u>Steady-State Economics</u>, Second Edition, Island Press, 1991.

Damasio, A., <u>The Feeling of What Happens</u>, Harcourt Brace & Co., 1999.

Dawkins, R., <u>The Extended Phenotype; The Gene as the Unit of Selection</u>, W.H. Freeman and Company, 1982.

Dawkins, R., <u>The Selfish Gene</u>, Oxford University Press, 1976.

Derrida, J., <u>De La Grammatologie</u>, Les Éditions de Minuit, Paris (France), 1967.

Dicken, P., <u>Global Shift</u>, third edition, The Guilford Press, 1998.

Ditfurth, H., The Origins of Life, Evolution as Creation, Harper & Row, 1982.

Eichengreen, B. and Flandreau, M. (eds.), The Gold Standard in Theory and History, Routledge, 1997.

Engels, F., The Origin of the Family, Private Property and the State, International Publishers, 1972 (first published in 1884).

Feis, H., Europe, The World's Banker, 1870-1914, Augustus M. Kelley Publishers, 1974.

Fermi, E., Thermodynamics, Dover Publications, 1936.

Foucault, M., Madness and Civilization: A History of Insanity in the Age of Reason, New American Library, 1965.

Foucault, M., The Order of Things: An Archeology of the Human Sciences, Pantheon Books, 1970.

Foucault, M., Discipline and Punish: The Birth of Prison, Vintage Books, 1995 (first published in 1975).

Frank-Kamenetskii, M. D., Unraveling DNA, the Most Important Molecule of Life, Addison-Wesley, 1997.

Freud, S., Totem and Taboo, W.W. Norton & Company, 1950 (first published in 1913).

Freud, S., Civilization and its Discontents, W.W. Norton & Company, 1961 (first published in 1930).

Fukuyama, F., The End of History and the Last Man, The Free Press, 1992.

Galtung, J. and Inayatullah, S. (eds.), Macrohistory and Macrohistorians, Perspectives on Individual, Social, and Civilizational Change, Praeger, 1997.

Gardner, H., The Mind's New Science, Basic Books, 1985.

Garman, M., Psycholinguistics, Cambridge University Press, 1990.

Georgescu-Roegen, N., The Entropy Law and the Economic Process, Harvard University Press, 1971.

Golan, A., Judge G., and Miller, D., <u>Maximum Entropy Econometrics: Robust Estimation with Limited Data</u>, John Wiley & Sons, 1996.

Goldstein, M. and Goldstein, I.F., <u>The Refrigerator and the Universe, Understanding the Laws of Energy</u>, Harvard University Press, 1993.

Gordon, R. J. and Pelkmans, J., <u>Challenges to Interdependent Economies</u>, McGraw-Hill, 1979.

Gore, A., <u>An Inconvenient Truth, The Planetary Emergence of Global Warming and What We Can Do About It</u>, Rodale and Melcher Media, 2006.

Gould, S. J., <u>The Structure of Evolutionary Theory</u>, The Belknap Press of Harvard University Press, 2002.

Habermas, J., <u>The Philosophical Discourse of Modernity: Twelve Lectures</u>, The MIT Press, 1987.

Hamilton, J.D., <u>Time Series Analysis</u>, Princeton University Press, 1994.

Hamilton, W.D., "The Genetical Evolution of Social Behavior," <u>Journal of Theoretical Biology</u>, vol. 7, 1964, pp.1-52.

Hawking, S., <u>A Brief History of Time</u>, Bantam Books, 1988.

Hegel, G.W.F., <u>Phänomenologie des Geistes</u>, Ullstein Materialien, Frankfurt/M (Germany), 1970 (first published in 1807).

Heidegger, M., <u>On Time and Being</u>, Harper and Row, 1972 (first published in 1927).

Heidegger, M., <u>An Introduction to Metaphysics</u>, Yale University Press, 1974 (first published in 1953).

Hentz, D. and Richardson, A., <u>Globalization and Regionalization</u>, found on July 25, 2000, at http://www1.vmi.edu/grants/Recipient/Hentz/Richardson.htm.

Hess, P. and Ross, C., <u>Economic Development</u>, The Dryden Press, 1997.

Hobsbawm, E.J., <u>The Pelican Economic History of Britain, Volume 3, Industry and Empire</u>, Penguin Books, 1969.

Holden, A. V. (ed.), Chaos, Princeton University Press, 1986.

Hopkins, T.K. and Wallerstein, I., World-Systems Analysis, Theory and Methodology, Sage Publications, 1982.

Hugill, P.J., World Trade Since 1431, The Johns Hopkins University Press, 1993.

Huxley, J., Heredity, East and West, Henry Schuman, 1949.

Iberall, A.S., Toward a General Science of Variable Systems, McGraw-Hill, 1972.

Jacobs, J.Q., Reflections on Prehistory, found on Apr. 21, 2001, at http://www.geocities.com.

Kenichi Ohmae (ed.), The Evolving Global Economy, A Harvard Business Review Book, 1995.

Knowles, L.C.A., Economic Development in the Nineteenth Century, George Routledge & Sons, 1936.

Kondepudi, D. and Prigogine, I., Modern Thermodynamics, From Heat Engines to Dissipative Systems, John Wiley & Sons, 1998.

Krueger, A. O. (ed.), The WTO as an International Organization, The University of Chicago Press, 1998.

Krugman, P.R. and Obstfeld, M., International Economics, fifth edition, Addison-Wesley, 2000.

Landon, J.C., World History and the Eonic Effect, Quality Books, 1999.

Laszlo, E., The Age of Bifurcation, Understanding the Changing World, Gordon and Breach, 1991.

Laszlo, E., The Choice: Evolution or Extinction?, Jeremy P. Tarcher/G.P. Putnam's Sons, 1994.

Laszlo, E., Macroshift, Navigating the Transformation to a Sustainable World, Berrett-Koehler Publishers, 2001.

LeDoux, J., The Mysterious Underpinnings of Emotional Life, Simon & Schuster, 1996.

Lenski, G. and Lenski, J., Human Societies, An Introduction to Macrosociology, McGraw-Hill, 1987.

Lévi-Strauss, C., Structural Anthropology, Basic Books, 1963.

Lévi-Strauss, C., Structural Anthropology, vol. 2, University of Chicago Press, 1976.

Lévi-Strauss, C., La Vois des Masques, Librairie Plon, Paris (France), 1979.

Loewenstein, W.R., The Touchstone of Life, Oxford University Press, 1999.

Lovelock, J., Gaia, A New Look at Earth, Oxford University Press, 1979.

Lumsden, C.J. and E.O. Wilson, "The relation between biological and cultural evolution," Journal of Social and Biological Structures, vol. 7, 1985, pp. 343-359.

Manahan, S.E., Environmental Chemistry, Sixth Edition, Lewis Publishers, 1994.

Mandrou, R., Magistrat et Sorciers en France au XVIIᵉ Siècle; Une Analyse de Psychologie Historique, Librairie Plon, Paris (France), 1968.

Marx, K., Capital, A Critique of Political Economy, The Modern Library/Random House, copyright 1906 (first published in 1867).

Marx, K. and Engels, F., Selected Works, International Publishers, 1968.

Meadows, E. H., Meadows, D.L., and Randers, J., Beyond the Limits, White River Junction, 1992.

Modelski, G., World Cities: 3000 to 2000, Faros2000, 2003.

Modelski, G., Long Cycles in World Politics, The Macmillan Press, 1987.

Modelski, G., Principles of World Politics, The Free Press, 1972.

Mosko, M.S. and Damon, F. (eds.), <u>On the Order of Chaos, Social Anthropology and the Science of Chaos</u>, Berghahn Books, 2005.

Murphy, M.P. and O'Neill, L.A.J (eds.), <u>What is Life? The Next Fifty Years</u>, Cambridge University Press, 1995.

Olson, M. and Landsberg, H.H. (eds.), <u>The No-Growth Society</u>, W.W. Norton & Company, 1973.

Pearce, D.W. and Turner, R.K., <u>Economics of Natural Resources and the Environment</u>, The Johns Hopkins University Press, 1990.

Penrose, R., <u>Shadows of the Mind</u>, Oxford University Press, 1994.

Penrose, R., "Why New Physics is Needed to Understand the Mind," in <u>What is Life? The Next Fifty Years</u>, Cambridge University Press, 1995, Murphy, M.P. and O'Neill, L.A.J. (eds).

Pinker, S., <u>The Language Instinct, How the Mind Creates Language</u>, William Morrow and Co., 1994.

Polanyi, K., <u>The Great Transformation</u>, Beacon Press, 1957 (first published in 1944).

Popper, K.R., <u>The Logic of Scientific Discovery</u>, Basic Books, 1959.

Popper, K.R., <u>The Poverty of Historicism</u>, Harper Torchbooks, 1961.

Prigogine, I., <u>The End of Certainty</u>, The Free Press, 1997.

Rostow, W.W., <u>The World Economy, History and Prospects</u>, University of Texas Press, 1978.

Ruelle, D., <u>Chance and Chaos</u>, Princeton University Press, 1991.

Schroedinger, E., <u>What is Life? Mind and Matter</u>, Cambridge University Press, 1967.

Schumacher, E.F., <u>Small is Beautiful, Economics as if People Mattered</u>, Perennial Library/Harper & Row, Publishers, 1973.

Schumpeter, J.A., <u>History of Economic Analysis</u>, Oxford University Press, 1954.

Schwartz, J.M. and Begley, S., <u>The Mind & The Brain, Neuroplasticity and the Power of Mental Force</u>, Regan Books, 2002.

Shannon, C. E. and Weaver, W., <u>The Mathematical Theory of Communication</u>, University of Illinois Press, 1975.

Smart, J. J. C., <u>Philosophy and Scientific Realism</u>, Routledge & Kegan Paul, 1963.

Steele, E.J., Lindley, R.A., and Blanden, R.V., <u>Lamarck's Signature, How Retrogenes Are Changing Darwin's Natural Selection Paradigm</u>, Helix Books/Perseus Books, 1998.

Taylor, G.R., <u>The Natural History of the Mind</u>, E.P. Dutton, 1979.

Teilhard, P. de Chardin, <u>The Future of Man</u>, Harper & Row, Publishers, 1964.

Teilhard, P. de Chardin, <u>Human Energy</u>, A Helen and Kurt Wolff Book/Harcourt Brace Jovanovich, 1969.

Truchet, F.E., "La guerre (économique) n'est pas celle que vous croyez," <u>Défense Nationale</u>, August/September 2000, Paris (France).

White, L.A., <u>The Evolution of Culture</u>, McGraw-Hill Book, 1959.

Wilson, E. O., <u>Consilience, The Unity of Knowledge</u>, Vintage Books, 1999.

Wilson, E. O., <u>Sociobiology: The New Synthesis</u>, The Belknap Press of Harvard University Press, 2000.

Wright, R., <u>Nonzero, The Logic of Human Destiny</u>, Vintage Books, 2000.

Yates, E.Y. (ed.), <u>Self-Organizing Systems, The Emergence of Order</u>, Plenum Press, 1987.

Index

978-0-595-41079-8
0-595-41079-0

Printed in the United States
66195LVS00003B/69